THE CHEYENNE WAY

Conflict and Case Law in Primitive Jurisprudence

By

K. N. LLEWELLYN

And

E. ADAMSON HOEBEL

William S. Hein & Co., Inc.
Buffalo, New York
2002

Library of Congress Cataloging-in-Publication Data

Llewellyn, Karl N. (Karl Nickerson), 1893–1962.
   The Cheyenne way : conflict and case law in primitive
jurisprudence / by K.N. Llewellyn and E. Adamson Hoebel.
      p. cm.
   Originally published: Norman : University of Oklahoma
Press, ©1941, in series: The civilization of the American
Indian series ; v. 21.
   ISBN 1-57588-717-7 (cloth : alk. paper)
   1. Cheyenne law. 2. Law, Primitive—Great Plains.
I. Hoebel, E. Adamson (Edward Adamson), 1906– . II. Title.
KF8228.C53 L59 2002
340.5'2—dc21   2002073666

This book has been digitally archived to maintain
the quality of the original work for future generations
of legal researchers by William S. Hein & Co., Inc.

This paper meets the requirements of
ANSI/NISO Z39.48-1992 (Permanence of Paper).

William S. Hein & Co., Inc.
Buffalo, New York
2002

The Civilization of the American Indian Series

THE CHEYENNE WAY

Medicine, Black Wolf, and Little Chief

THE CHEYENNE WAY

Conflict and Case Law in Primitive Jurisprudence

By

K. N. LLEWELLYN

And

E. ADAMSON HOEBEL

Norman and London
UNIVERSITY OF OKLAHOMA PRESS

ISBN: 0–8061–1855–5

The Cheyenne Way: Conflict and Case Law in Primitive Jurisprudence is Volume 21 in *The Civilization of the American Indian Series.*

10   11   12   13   14   15   16   17   18   19   20   21   22   23   24   25   26   27   28

To

Emma and Fran

Our Co-authors

PREFACE

THE Cheyenne Indians are one of the famous tribes of the Great American Plains. Divided as they were after 1833, into a northern division which centered its life in the high plains of southeastern Montana and eastern Wyoming, and a southern division which centered in western Oklahoma and eastern Colorado, they wove a web of their activities across the entire breadth of the Great Plains. They were known to the travelers of both the Oregon and Santa Fe trails. Originally inhabitants of the woodland lake country of the upper Mississippi valley, they had come at the beginning of the century past to an effective adoption of the new horse culture and buffalo-hunting economy of the Plains tribes. Theirs was a nomadic, semi-pastoral and hunting existence. With the Arapahoes and Gros Ventres the Cheyennes are the westernmost representatives of the important Algonkin group of tribes. And though the specialist recognizes some traits in the Cheyenne culture which are characteristic of their cognates of the Northeast Woodlands, in its general aspects Cheyenne culture is Plains.

The reader who, perchance, is unfamiliar with the background and details of Cheyenne life will, if he so desires, find a rich and competent presentation in George Bird Grinnell's classic, *The Cheyenne Indians*. Here, too, will be found the known history of the Cheyenne migrations. Those who wish to follow all the stirring heroics of the Cheyenne wars—first against the enemy tribes, and in later years against the tidal wave of whites—will find the complete epic thriller in Grinnell's *The Fighting Cheyennes*.

In this book we make no presumptions of doing over again what George Bird Grinnell has done so nobly for the tribe he loved. It is not our aim or function to redescribe Cheyenne society and technology. We are presenting a description and analysis of a vital phase

vii

of social life which was ethnologically *terra incognita* in the days of Grinnell. We have aimed at the development of a social science instrument for the recording and interpretation of law-ways among primitive peoples; the Cheyennes and their Way provide the subject material.

The new data for these chapters are the result of field investigations among the Northern Cheyennes on the Tongue River Reservation at Lame Deer, Montana. In the summer of 1935, both authors shared in the field work, and in 1936, Hoebel returned to an additional summer's work for completion of the materials. The theory of investigation—a case method procedure of going in the first instance after cases of trouble and how they were handled —is the result of the joint efforts of the authors, one of whom is a specialist in law, the other in anthropology. Both are students of human behavior: proponents of realistic sociology. The method has been developed for what we hope will be a series of studies of the dynamics and functioning of legal institutions. It received its preliminary testing in the investigations of the Comanches of Oklahoma done by Hoebel as a member of the ethnology field group led by Ralph Linton in 1933, and then of the Fort Hall Shoshones (Idaho) in 1934, as also in Llewellyn's continuing work on American legal institutions and his studies of legal processes in smaller modern groups. By the time we came to do the field work for this culture a fairly adequate working technique had been articulated. Where needed refinements have been discovered, they are indicated in the text.

The manner of interpretation rests in the first instance on the technique of the American case lawyer, save that each case is viewed not lopsidedly and solely as a creator or establisher of correct legal doctrine, but is viewed even more as a study of men in conflict, institutions in tension, and laymen or craftsmen at work on resolution of tension. Law-stuff, seen thus, is seen more deeply and more sharply, simply as law-stuff. It is our firm conviction that to see it thus is to see it also in its working relation to social science at large. Modern American jurisprudence can thus enrich, and be enriched by, the study of non-literate legal cultures.

PREFACE

The method is grounded in the American System of case law in which we root; especially in the modern treatment of cases at law as being not only crucial tests of the meaning of rules of law, but also as exhibits of law's processes and techniques, and of the interaction of the legal system and the legal craft-specialists with the social, economic, political, and indeed individual aspects of the society concerned. In this, the present volume not only builds on, but also supplements and cross-lights Llewellyn's series of studies on the ways of case law in the United States; i.e., the possibilities of the method for developing lines of significant comparison between superficially quite dissimilar systems of law are not hypothetical, but have already been tested.

We undertook the study of the Cheyennes because after the formlessness of Shoshone law-stuff and the violent individualism of the Comanches we wanted to study the legal processes of a people with a known sense of form and structured institutions, who were yet within the similar general economic and cultural context of the Plains. We did not expect, or even suspect, the juristic beauty which Cheyenne work was to reveal; nor that structured institutions would be caught in felt cross-tensions and in a flux which one can follow in the cases, almost with the eye. Indeed, three years of puzzlement went into the analysis of the material before order emerged; and this happened (as it does in modern case law) when the data of sixty or eighty years (*ca.* 1820–1880) were arranged not on a flat time-plane, but against the moving time-perspective of the culture and the individual life.

Attention of the reader is called to the Case-Finder at the back of the book. We hope that it will be found useful for purposes of cross reference. Case numbers which are given in the body of the text refer to the Case-Finder.

The cases in this book are presented in the language of the Cheyenne informant as it came to us through the careful interpreting of Willis Rowland, High Forehead. We have done as little editing as possible. Except for the cases which stand alone in the first chapter, the case materials are separated from the running text by French quotes   «   «   «   »   »   ».

ix

PREFACE

Our interposed comments, which appear at some essential points in the cases, have been put in brackets. As a canon of method, we have striven to keep our factual data distinct from our interpretation and evaluation of those data.

Permission to quote from George Bird Grinnell's *The Cheyenne Indians* and *The Fighting Cheyennes* has been given by the respective publishers, the Yale University Press and Charles Scribner's Sons.

Our gratitude is due the Columbia University Council for Research in the Social Sciences for their assistance in field work and in publication, and to the American Council of Learned Societies for their assistance in field work. Emma Corstvet's schooling in modern sociological field work gave us invaluable stimulation while she was with us in the field, and both she and Frances Gore Hoebel helped more than we find it easy to express, in giving meaning to the material and form to its presentation. Our Cheyenne friends will, we hope, accept this book as a record of our lasting gratitude.

K. N. Llewellyn
E. Adamson Hoebel

New York City

CONTENTS

ILLUSTRATIONS

PART I

The Study of Primitive Law

"The Indian on the prairie, before there was the White Man to put him in the guardhouse, had to have something to keep him from doing wrong."

—HIGH FOREHEAD

Chapter I

FIVE HISTORIES

CASE 1. *When Two Twists Led the Cheyennes Against the Crows.*[1]

RED Robe's two sons were killed by the Crows quite a while back; their father in his grief stood before his lodge in mourning and called out, "All of my horses are for those who take them." He threw the whole herd away, not keeping even one for himself to ride upon.

The Dog Soldiers went out to herd his horses together, because they simply were not going to see the old man afoot. "No one is going to take these horses," they said. Then they sent an old man to see Red Robe.

"Your sons died like men," this messenger reminded him. "They died the glorious death, not in bed sick. Why don't you take back some ponies?"

"No," Red Robe replied, "Maiyun [the Supernatural] wanted my sons to die in battle and it wants that I should be afoot awhile." Whatever they said, they could not budge him.

Finally, four soldier troops [the Elk, Bowstring, Dog, and Fox] decided to go talk to him. He had been a good man in the tribe and here he was destitute. When the camp moved, he was the last to come along. He had nothing to camp with, but just stayed in the open. This had gone on three or four months when the soldiers got together. They all came to Red Robe, but one or two did the talking for them all. "We are begging you to do what we ask you—we are not alone—see them all—every company among us is here. We still have your horses. Come in among the people."

Still he was unmoved by all their pleading. At last Two Twists,[2]

---

[1] Informant: Stump Horn. For analysis, see pages 162 f.
[2] An earlier Two Twists than the one who had the squabble with Last Bull.

a chief of the Bowstring Soldiers, came forward. "Say yes," he implored the old man. "Say yes, and we will promise you to go to war against the Crows wherever they may be. Say yes, and I'll get revenge for you whatever the risks. If they be in breastworks, I'll drive them out."

"I accept," the bereaved old man finally answered. "I did not want to take those horses back after giving them away. It's like taking back a thing given to a friend."

"No, it is not like that to us," the soldiers all assured him.

So Red Robe came into camp. In the days which followed after, Two Twists prepared his pipe, taking it to all the soldier societies. Everyone smoked, whole troops pledging themselves to vengeance on the Crows. When all was ready the societies moved to the raid in a body. Women and children went too, for the whole tribe was on the march. Two Twists was the leader of them all.[3]

When they had come close to the enemy, Two Twists rode about the camp accompanied by his crier, who called for the people to listen. Two Twists spoke in this vein. "Look at me now. Soon I am about to follow the two sons of Red Robe. My friends, behold me; I shall never return from this raid."

The women all came out of their lodges to gaze at him. They sang him many heartening songs of which one was this—"Only the rocks lie here and never move. The human being vapors away." That night Two Twists sang the war songs of the Bowstring Soldiers.

The people were anxious to face the enemy, but the chiefs held them in. In the meantime the Crow scouts had spotted the Cheyennes and warned their camp. That night they built a breastwork of all their tipis arranged in a semi-circle.

The next morning Two Twists was out in the camp again. "I sing

[3] This moving of the entire tribe against an enemy was a rare occurrence. According to George Bird Grinnell in *The Fighting Cheyennes* (New York, C. Scribner's Sons, 1915), 69, there were but six such movements in the nineteenth century. It is likely that the story given here was the action against the Crows which took place in 1820 as a punitive expedition for the annihilation of thirty-two Cheyenne warriors in the previous year. Grinnell (*ibid.*, 22-27) gives an account of this affair. It was the greatest of many encounters with the Crows and the second remembered move of the Medicine Arrows against a hostile tribe. No mention was made of the Arrows by the informant, but the taking of the Medicine Hat indicates that this was one of the important tribal movement occasions.

for the last time," he cried. "People, behold me! This is my last time to walk on earth."

From all around folks brought him feathers, to help him in the thing he was to do. They tied them to his war bonnet, to his horse's mane, and to its tail.

At last the fighters went toward the Crow camp. Two Twists led them, armed only with a sabre. When they were before the enemy, he ordered his followers to hold back; he had his promise to fulfill. And so they all watched as he rode out alone toward the waiting enemy.

Straight at the tipis and into the breastwork he charged, slashing off the head of a Crow warrior as he broke through. He wheeled about, charging into the thick of them again, working havoc where his sword fell. The Crows shot, but missed and missed. Then our people saw Two Twists disappear among them in hand-to-hand struggle.

Then the Cheyennes charged into the Crows killing them on all sides. Red Robe's wife charged with an ax. Wherever she found a Crow dead or wounded she split his skull to smear the blood of the enemy upon her face and arms [pantomimed by the informant with proper gusto]. Red Robe joined in by cutting the arm from a dead Crow. He carried it into the scalp dance to scare the women with. E-E-E-E—he would hit them in the back with it; they would run screaming.

Two Twists was not killed, and from his deeds he derived the greatest honor. People said he had done his work; they would never let him do so again; he need not fulfill his vow to die. Back in camp, Two Twists sent for Red Robe and his two wives and children. He himself stripped them of their mourning rags and dressed them well. Many things were given to the women, and now Red Robe took back his horses. They, too, participated in the victory joy of the camp.

Red Robe went back to his lodge and in his turn sent for a crier to get Two Twists. Red Robe was accepting felicitations from everybody. To each person who came to greet him he gave a horse. He painted the faces of all adult comers with black charcoal—the symbol of joy in the death of the enemy. Of all his horses he kept only a few for himself, and this time he was not stopped by the soldiers.

At the end, he adopted Two Twists for his son. Two Twists was not a tribal chief then, only the leader of a soldier society; later he was made a big chief, but on that one occasion he had charge of the whole tribe. He had wanted to wear the Medicine Hat in the battle, and he had told the keeper he wished to wear it, but the keeper gave no answer. It was the keeper's wife who refused him. "You are going to war never to return. I do not think it right for us to give you the Hat. You will get it bloody; you would bring us great trouble; blood on the Hat would mean blood for all the tribe."

CASE 2. *Pawnee Punished by the Bowstring Soldiers and Rehabilitated by High Backed Wolf.*[4]

Pawnee was a Southern Cheyenne when he was a very young man, but in his later years he lived up here with us. He was all the time looking out after the people's morals and counseling the boys on good behavior. I have heard him tell his story many times when I was a youth, because he was always telling it to us as a lesson. He had been an awful rascal down there in Oklahoma when he was young, stealing meat from people's racks, taking their horses for joy-rides without asking them for them, and then when he got to where he was going he would just turn the horse loose and let it wander back to its owner—if it did. He was disrespectful to people and sassed them back. Everyone thought he was a mean boy, and whatever happened in the camp he got blamed for it. This story I am going to tell happened just after that trouble Wolf Lies Down had over the borrowed horse when the soldiers made the rule that no one in the camp could take another person's horse without permission. This is what Pawnee used to tell us:

Down there [in Oklahoma] were two spotted horses well liked in their family. One day I took them and headed west. Three days passed and I found myself still safe. Now I was out of trouble's way, so I began to feel pretty good. On the fourth day, as I looked back

4 Informant: Black Wolf. For analysis, see page 129.

I saw some people coming up. "It is nothing," I thought, "just some people traveling." When they overtook me, I saw they were Bowstring Soldiers out after me.

"You have stolen those horses," they cried as they pulled me from my horse. "Now we have trailed you down." They threw me on the ground and beat me until I could not stand; they broke up my weapons and ruined my saddle; they cut my blankets, moccasins, and kit to shreds. When they had finished they took all my food and went off with the horses, leaving me alone on the prairie, sore and destitute, too weak and hurt to move.

The next day I started back, traveling as best I could all day long. I knew there was a small camp of buffalo hunters out and for them I was looking. I travelled all day. The next day I thought I would die. I had no food, only water. Late in the afternoon I camped on a creek. My feet were bleeding and I could not walk farther. I crawled slowly on my hands and knees to the brow of a high hill to find a place to die. I waited in mourning. Far to the south of me I could see the rolling country; to the west my view was blocked. My pipe and tobacco were gone. Without smoke I sat there thinking of a great many things as I watched the blood drip from my swollen feet.

As I gazed steadfastly into the south, a hunter came up the hill from behind me. When he saw me he stopped and watched me for a long time. After three days and two nights in my condition I must have been nearly deaf, for I did not hear him until he spoke from his horse right behind me. I was naked. I fell over in a fright when I heard his voice start out in the silence.

This man dismounted and hugged me. He wept, he felt so bad at seeing my plight. It was High Backed Wolf,[5] a young man, but a chief. He put his blanket about me and took me home. The camp was on the creek below, hidden just around a bend where I had not seen it. His wife gave me food and nourished me.

Then High Backed Wolf sent for the chiefs who were in the camp. Four or five came, one of whom was a soldier chief.

High Backed Wolf spoke to the soldier chief first. "This is the

[5] Later a famous chief killed in a skirmish with American troops at the Platte Bridge, July 25, 1865. Grinnell, *The Fighting Cheyennes*, 218.

first time since I have become a big [tribal] chief that I have happened upon such a poor man; now I am going to outfit him. Until he is fixed up, I shall ask no questions. Then we shall learn how he came to be naked. I am not going to ask you to give anything unless you wish to do so. I know this man," he said. "He is a great smoker. But I shall give him no smoke until he has first eaten." (In my own mind I said, "I'd rather smoke first.")

First they gave me a little soup; then some meat.

High Backed Wolf then filled the pipe. As he held it to the five directions he prayed, "This is my first good act as a chief. Help this man to tell the truth." Then he held the pipe for me to smoke; then he gave it to the next man and to the others. Now he faced me again. "Now you tell the truth. Have you been caught by enemies and stripped? Or was it something else? You saw me smoke this pipe; you have touched it with your own lips. That is to help you tell the truth. If you tell us straightly, Maiyun will help you."

I told them the whole story. I told them whose horses they were, and I told them it was the Bowstrings who had punished me.

High Backed Wolf knew I was a rascal, so he lectured to me. "You are old enough now to know what is right," he preached. "You have been to war. Now leave off this foolishness. If it had been that I had not ridden out into the hills today you would have died. No one would have known the end of you. You know how we Cheyennes try to live. You know how we hunt, how we go to war. When we take horses, we take them from enemies, not from Cheyennes. You had better join a military society. You can learn good behavior from the soldiers. Yet I ask only one thing of you. Be decent from now on! Stop stealing! Stop making fun of people! Use no more bad language in the camp! Lead a good life!

"Now I am going to help you out. That is what I am here for, because I am a chief of the people. Here are your clothes. Outside are three horses. You may take your choice!" He gave me a six-shooter. "Here is a mountain-lion skin. I used to wear this in the parades. Now I give it to you." He offered me all these things and I took them.

The others gave me beaver skins to braid in my hair, beads, and extra moccasins, and two more horses.

Then High Backed Wolf ended it. "Now I am not going to tell you to leave this camp. You may stay here as long as you wish. I shall not tell you which direction to go, west or south."

I had a sweetheart in the south, but when these people did this for me, I felt ashamed. I had all those things with which to look beautiful, but I did not dare to go back, for I knew she would have heard what the Bowstrings had done to me. I thought it wisest to go north until the thing was dead.

When the Arrows were next renewed, the Foxes put up their lodge to get more men. I went in [joined]. Still, I never got it out of my heart that it had been those Bowstrings. Whenever my Fox troop was on duty I was out looking for those men or their families to do something wrong. I always looked for a Bowstring to slip, so I could beat him well. I stayed with the Northern Cheyennes a long, long time, until the Horse Creek Treaty.[6] Though I came to be a chief of the Fox Soldiers among the Northern people, I never amounted to much with the Southern bands. Those people always remembered me as a no-good.

You boys remember that. You may run away, but your people always remember. You just obey the rules of the camp, and you'll do all right.

CASE 3. *The Tribal Ostracism and Reinstatement of Sticks Everything Under His Belt.*[7]

Once, at a time when all the Cheyenne tribe was gathered together, Sticks Everything Under His Belt went out hunting buffalo alone. "I am hunting for myself," he told the people. He was implying that the rules against individual hunting did not apply

---

[6] Horse Creek Treaty—a famous occasion when in the summer of 1851 Siouxs, Assiniboines, Gros Ventres, Crows, Shoshones, Arikaras, Arapahoes, and Cheyennes to the number of eight to twelve thousand met under the aegis of two American agents to agree to peace among themselves and toward the whites. The treaties, though not ratified by Congress, were observed for several years by the Indians. Pierre-Jean De Smet, *Western Missions and Missionaries* (New York, J. B. Kirker, 1863), 101 ff.

[7] Informant: Black Wolf. For analysis, see pages 124–26.

to him because he was declaring himself out of the tribe—a man on his own.

All the soldier chiefs and all the tribal chiefs met in a big lodge to decide what to do in this case, since such a thing had never happened before. This was the ruling they made: no one could help Sticks Everything Under His Belt in any way, no one could give him smoke, no one could talk to him. They were cutting him off from the tribe. The chiefs declared that if anyone helped him in any way that person would have to give a Sun Dance.

When the camp moved, Sticks Everything Under His Belt moved with it, but the people would not recognize him. He was left alone and it went to his heart, so he took one of his horses (he had many) and rode out to the hilltops to mourn.

His sister's husband was a chief in the camp. This brother-in-law felt sorry for him out there mourning, with no more friends. At last he took pity on his poor brother-in-law; at last he spoke to his wife, "I feel sorry for your poor brother out there and now I am going to do something for him. Cook up all those tongues we have! Prepare a good feast!"

Then he invited the chiefs to his lodge and sent for his brother-in-law to come in. This was after several years had passed, not months.

When the chiefs had assembled, the brother-in-law spoke. "Several years ago you passed a ruling that no one could help this man. Whoever should do so you said would have to give a Sun Dance. Now is the time to take pity on him. *I* am going to give a Sun Dance to bring him back in. I beg you to let him come back to the tribe, for he has suffered long enough. This Sun Dance will be a great one. I declare that every chief and all the soldiers must join in. Now I put it up to you. Shall we let my brother-in-law smoke before we eat, or after?"

The chiefs all answered in accord, "Ha-ho, ha-ho [thank you, thank you]. We are very glad you are going to bring back this man. However, let him remember that he will be bound by whatever rules the soldiers lay down for the tribe. He may not say he is outside of them. He has been out of the tribe for a long time. If he remembers these things, he may come back."

Then they asked Sticks Everything Under His Belt whether he wanted to smoke before or after they had eaten. Without hesitation he replied, "Before," because he had craved tobacco so badly that he had split his pipe stem to suck the brown gum inside of it.

The lodge was not big enough to hold all the chiefs who had come to decide this thing, so they threw open the door, and those who could not get in sat in a circle outside. Then they filled a big pipe and when it was lighted they gave it to Sticks Everything Under His Belt. It was so long since he had had tobacco that he gulped in the smoke and fell over in a faint. As he lay there the smoke came out of his anus, he was so empty. The chiefs waited silently for him to come to again and then the pipe was passed around the circle.

When all had smoked, Sticks Everything Under His Belt talked. "From now on I am going to run with the tribe. Everything the people say, I shall stay right by it. My brother-in-law has done a great thing. He is going to punish himself in the Sun Dance to bring me back. He won't do it alone, for I am going in, too."

After a while the people were getting ready for the Sun Dance. One of the soldiers began to get worried because he had an ugly growth on his body which he did not want to reveal to the people. He was a good-looking young man named Black Horse. Black Horse went to the head chiefs asking them to let him sacrifice himself alone on the hilltops as long as the Sun Dance was in progress.

"We have nothing to say to that," they told him. "Go to the pledger. This is his Sun Dance."

Black Horse went to the brother-in-law of Sticks Everything Under His Belt, who was a brother-in-law to him as well.[8] "Brother-in-law," he begged, "I want to be excused from going into the lodge. Can't you let me go into the hills to sacrifice myself as long as you are in there, to make my own bed?"

"No," he was rebuffed, "you know my rule is that all must be there."

"Well, brother-in-law, won't it be all right if I set up a pole on the

8 This means he was a classificatory brother to the pledger's wife.

hill and hang myself to it through my breasts? I shall hang there for the duration of the dance."

This brother-in-law of his answered him in these words, "Why didn't you take that up when all the chiefs were in the lodge? I have agreed with them that everyone must be in the lodge. I don't want to change the rule. I won't give you permission to go outside."

Then Black Horse replied, "You will not make the rules my way. Now *I* am going to put in a rule for everybody. Everyone in there has to swing from the pole as I do."

"No," countered the brother-in-law. "That was not mentioned in the meeting. If you want to swing from the pole, that is all right, but no one else has to unless he wishes to."

When they had the Sun Dance everyone had a good time. Black Horse was the only one on the pole, and there were so many in the lodge that there was not room enough for all to dance. Some just had to sit around inside the lodge. Though they did not dance, they starved themselves for four days. This dance took place near Sheridan, Wyoming, seven years before Custer.[9] I was only a year old at that time, but what I have said here I was told by Elk River and others. We call this place "Where The Chiefs Starved Themselves."

CASE 4. *Cries Yia Eya Banished for the Murder of Chief Eagle.*[10]

Cries Yia Eya had been gone from the camp for three years because he had killed Chief Eagle in a whiskey brawl. The chiefs had ordered him away for his murder, so we did not see anything of him for that time. Then one day he came back, leading a horse packed with bundles of old-time tobacco. He stopped outside the camp and sent a messenger in with the horse and tobacco who was to say to the chiefs for him, "I am begging to come home."

The chiefs all got together for a meeting, and the soldier societies were told to convene, for there was an important matter to be con-

[9] The Northern Cheyennes date most events from the 1860's to the nineties as so many years before or after the annihilation of the Custer command at the Indian village on the Little Big Horn, June 25, 1876.

[10] Informant: Calf Woman. For analysis, see page 139.

sidered. The tobacco was divided up and chiefs' messengers were sent out to invite the soldier chiefs to come to the lodge of the tribal council, for the big chiefs wanted to talk to them. "Here is the tobacco that that man sent in," they told the soldier chiefs. "Now we want you soldiers to decide if you think we should accept his request. If you decide that we should let him return, then it is up to you to convince his family that it is all right." (The relatives of Chief Eagle had told everybody that they would kill Cries Yia Eya on sight if they ever found him. "If we set eyes on him, he'll never make another track," they had vowed.) The soldier chiefs took the tobacco and went out to gather their troops. Each society met in its own separate lodge to talk among themselves, but the society servants kept passing back and forth between their different lodges to report on the trend of the discussion in the different companies.

At last one man said, "I think it is all right. I believe the stink has blown from him.[11] Let him return!" This view was passed around, and this is the view that won out among the soldiers. Then the father of Chief Eagle was sent for and asked whether he would accept the decision. "Soldiers," he replied, "I shall listen to you. Let him return! But if that man comes back, I want never to hear his voice raised against another person. If he does, we come together. As far as that stuff of his is concerned, I want nothing that belonged to him. Take this share you have set aside for me and give it to someone else."

Cries Yia Eya had always been a mean man, disliked by everyone, but he had been a fierce fighter against the enemies. After he came back to the camp, however, he was always good to the people.

Case 5. *When Walking Rabbit Raised a Problem.*[12]

A war party was organizing. Walking Rabbit approached the leader with a question. "Is it true that you have declared we must all go afoot? If so, I would like to be able to lead a horse to pack my moccasins and possibles." The leader gave him an answer. "There is a reason for my ruling. I want no horses, that it may be easier for

---

[11] On this supernatural physical effect of murder, see below, page 133.
[12] Informant: Black Wolf. For analysis, see page 191.

us to conceal our movements. However, you may bring one horse."
Then Walking Rabbit asked for instructions concerning the location of the first and second nights' camps, for he would start late
and overtake the party.

Walking Rabbit's sweetheart had been married only recently to
another. "My husband is not the man I thought he was," she told
her former suitor. So Walking Rabbit took her to join the war party.
[The Cheyennes have a phrase for the single man who marries a
one-time married woman—"putting on the old moccasin."] In this
way, it turned out that the "moccasin" he was packing was a big
woman.

When they saw this woman there, the warriors got excited. The
party turned into the hills and stopped. The leader opened his pipe.
The leader's pipe was always filled before they left the camp, but it
was not smoked until the enemy was seen or their tracks reported.
Now the leader spoke. "When we take a woman with us it is usually
known in the camp. Here is a man who has sneaked off with
another's wife. Now what is going to happen?" That is what they
were talking about.

The leader declared, "The only thing this man can do is return
and make a settlement with the husband. Then he may follow
us up."

One warrior was for aiding Walking Rabbit. "Why can't we let
him stay?" was his proposal. "If we take any horses, we can give
them to her husband." That was rejected.

The decision was that he had to go back. "If you had told us you
wanted her so badly, we might have waited for you to settle for her.
Then we could have taken her the right way. If you really want to
go to war with us, you will be able to overtake us. We are afoot."

Then three or four warriors spoke up, each promising Walking
Rabbit a horse to send to the husband. Everyone gave one or two
arrows to be sent as well.

In the meantime Walking Rabbit's father had fixed it up with
the aggrieved husband. Since he and his wife were incompatible,
he was willing to release her. When Walking Rabbit came in and
told his father the story of the soldiers' action, the father said, "Just

let that stand. The thing is fixed. When those fighters come back they may want to give to the girl's parents. You go back after your party." But Walking Rabbit preferred to stay at home.

When Walking Rabbit did not go out, his closest relatives raised a big tipi. When they heard of the approach of the returning war. party, everything was in readiness.

The warriors came charging in, shooting; they had taken many horses. The first coup-counters were in the van.[13] Walking Rabbit's father had a right to harangue; he was a crier. "Don't go to your homes! Don't go to your own lodges! Come here to the lodge of Walking Rabbit, your friend!"

When they were all in this lodge the old man entered and told them his story. "I had this thing all settled before my son returned. You have sent arrows and promised horses. Now I have kept this girl here pending your return. I shall send her back to her parents with presents. I have waited to see what you are going to do."

The leader replied for his followers. "Yes, we will help you. We promised to help your son. When you send her back, we'll send presents with her." The men who had promised horses went out to get them. Others gave captured horses.

Sending her back with these presents was giving wedding gifts. Her relatives got them all. They gathered up their goods to send back. The war party was called together once more; to them this stuff was given. It was a great thing for the people to talk about. It was the first and last time a woman was sent home on enemy horses the day they came in.

Such is the Cheyenne material as it comes from the informants. If one goes back over the accounts, not as stories merely, but as indicators of Cheyenne law-ways, one finds that even these five are rich no less with perplexity than with illumination.

Take some of the doubts first. Here are presented in succession a war hero in the manner of American juvenile fiction, a confirmed and utter reprobate reformed by a single punishment and noble

[13] These are the men who had won what corresponds to our military decorations, on the raid.

example, a case which reminds one of our traditional Man Without a Country, a repentant murderer restored to society, and a love-romance. Not one but is romantic in theme, color, plot, and happy ending. This may mean that the cases are wishful-legend or conscious fiction. Or else it may mean that we are faced with a singularly resourceful and effective legal and socio-legal system. Or else it may mean that these five cases are violently non-typical of the run of events. Which?

All five of the cases involve munificent giving or sacrifice. If they are fiction, this represents an ideal. But does the ideal represent an actuality? The "largesse" tradition was once so touted by family bards and begging minstrels of Western Europe as to rouse severe distrust of its actual wholesale prevalence; nor can any man take seriously the horses "shod with gold" of the Old English Ballads. These five stories are curiously shod with great giving.

But if the giving be fact, and indeed even if it be of a type which the Cheyennes considered it proper to glorify, it raises other problems. Cries Yia Eya, the murderer, brings gifts: Is he presented as bribing his way back? Is the implication that only the rich could buy reprieve? Was the horse laden with tobacco in the nature of an atonement, or composition? In the nature of a fine? In the case of Sticks Everything Under His Belt, the great giving was by a relative; and Walking Rabbit's father is reported as having made a settlement for his son's elopement with a married woman. This has the appearance of a regime of composition, in criminal cases as in civil, and also of a regime of kin responsibility. On the other hand, the giving by High Backed Wolf to Pawnee, and its follow-up of general giving, stood apart from any trace of kin responsibility and flowed to a culprit, not to an aggrieved. Then when High Backed Wolf is found basing his action on his position as a chief, one thinks back to the brother-in-law of Sticks Everything Under His Belt; one remembers that he was not only a brother-in-law, but a chief, as well, and the meaning of the affair with relation to "group responsibility" grows muddy. The pledge of Two Twists, with the support of all the soldier societies, was to risk life to avenge killing by the enemy; but he was no kin of the bereaved Red Robe.

The giving by the war party to Walking Rabbit looked indeed toward atonement, but again derived from no tie of kinship. Finally, three of the cases involve not outright gift, but involve instead a promise—followed by performance. Is this the institution known today as contract? The Sun Dance pledge might be seen as a vow rather than a promise; yet there is a return made, and the details run off as if the pledger and the chiefs had made, and were abiding by, a contractual agreement. Two Twists again might be read to be making a vow instead of a contract; yet he, too, exacted a return from the grieving father. But the war party's promises to Walking Rabbit were wholly secular; not only that, but they involved no return at all, and the promises were not undone or withdrawn when it was found that their occasion (the need for settling with the aggrieved husband) had disappeared.

What all this may mean is not yet clear. But what does grow clear is a suspicion that whatever legal "system" there may have been among the Cheyennes was hooked up closely with "private" beneficence of some kind. Does this indicate that the wealthy were in materially better case "before the law" than were the poor?

Except in regard to the Sun Dance, there is an interesting absence of religion and sorcery from the cases; in Two Twists' exploit the Medicine Hat, which might have accounted for his extraordinary escape, is even explicitly excluded from operation (which, it may be noted, would have to be reckoned a queer way to build legend, if legend it be). The law, then, if it be law, or the fiction, if it be fiction, is curiously secular in flavor for a deeply religious people. And some of the material, at least, must either be or mirror law. Walking Rabbit's case refers to the making of a precedent which was thereafter abided by, and the talk there is of a "right way" of taking a woman who was another man's wife. There is a "ruling" on Sticks Everything Under His Belt. "Soldiers" pursue and execute some sort of posse-justice on a horse "thief" caught with stolen horses. There is a murderer; there is an elaborate procedure looking to a readmission to the tribe after he had been "ordered away" by the chiefs.

The point of fact or fiction, or of atypicality, must be postponed.

The test for those lies in a greater body of material. Here it is enough to point out that whatever the answer, there is a body of assumed, or presupposed, institutions running through the cases, which have their interest independently of whether the cases represent the telling of true stories or merely romantic or "realistic" narrative. Government is assumed, with chiefs, a council, military societies, "soldiers" serving in some manner as police. A tribal hunt, under regulations, is taken for granted. Homicide within the tribe is known—and is also under some sort of sanction; killing by (or of) an enemy is seen as different. "Private" property of some kind is plainly familiar in horses, personal equipment, tobacco, food; it is dealt with by gift, promise, payment, and misdealt with by theft. War is assumed, with predatory war—even a tribal **war** expedition on the grand scale—operating under a leader and under "rules." Inside the tribe marriage is taken for granted; but so also is some manner, more or less regularized, of changing husbands. There are kin groups, mourning-destitution, perhaps kin responsibility. These cases thus move against a moderately extensive range of institutional development.

Moreover, fact or fiction, the cases begin to purvey to the reader a curious and subtle flavor on the juristic side. Chief Eagle's father is reported as putting on the readmission of Cries Yia Eya a most interesting condition: the killer was to walk softly all the days of his life. If this is fiction, it is the fiction of a shrewd teller. The judgment to exclude eloping couples from a war party, whether because the elopment was unregularized or because honeymooners are bad for war parties, is again a shrewd judgment, but even shrewder is the educational and face-saving management of the rebuff to young Walking Rabbit. High Backed Wolf handles Pawnee, if you will, in the high romantic tradition; but he handles the others who are present with a sureness and a dignity which stir envy. And if the ruling on Sticks Everything Under His Belt is fiction, the author was gifted less in romance than in the legal art and in the logical. There runs through the cases, indeed, a juristic deftness as a background. It runs to detail and process, not merely to result. Consider the procedures used for feeling out and crystalizing public opinion. *And this deftness is taken for granted.* If the main body of the material bears this out, then Cheyenne law-ways will prove worth study.

There is another point, however, over which we crave leave to pause. We have said that these cases come to us with a whole body of institutions presupposed. For it is impossible to tell a story without the use of words which carry flavor far beyond the mere behavior-sequence of events. "War," "war party," "tribe," "kin," "government," "chief," "council," "private property," "theft," "police," "gift"—each one of such words inevitably sketches out a background and fills it in with flavor, color, weight, tension. The cases are told in terms of some such conceptual structure because words offer no other way of telling them.

The best one can do is to try to make his own conceptual structure somewhat explicit, so that the reader may be warned by it. If that be done, and if that structure be taken, so far as may be, not as a something given in nature, but as a working hypothesis, then it may be possible to let any odd, sharp corners of the cases be felt and continue to be felt in whatever intellectual discomfort they may offer, until the conceptual frame reshapes itself to hold *all* the cases —each of their uncomfortable corners still sharp—in their own unique relation to one another. This we have tried to do.

But our own approach to the material requires to be set out. General theory guides inquiry. It conditions not only interpretation but recording. It conditions the very seeing of the data. It also lends to data their significance. The data react upon it, in turn, and remodel it; but that merely means that they are then presented in the frame of a more adequate conceptual framework, and so with a modified significance.

What, then, has been our general theory?

Chapter II

A THEORY OF INVESTIGATION

LAW has as one of its main purposes to make men go round in more or less clear ways; law does in fact to some extent make men go round in more or less clear ways. Law purposes to channel behavior in such manner as to prevent or avoid conflict; and law does in important degree so channel behavior. Without the purpose attribute, law is unthinkable; without the effect attribute, law cannot be said to "prevail" in a culture, to have "being" in it.

But there is more to law than intended and largely effective regulation and prevention. Law has the peculiar job of cleaning up social messes when they have been made. Law thus exists also for the event of breach of law and has a major portion of its essence in the doing of something about such a breach. By its fruits is it to be known; indeed, if it fails to bear fruit on proper occasion, its very existence is drawn into question. The nature of law, moreover, is such that if a particular type of result is understood to follow on breach, it is likely not to be long before any other result, especially any graver or more severe result, is felt as non-law, or even anti-law. This is one real sense in which law becomes self-limited by its fruiting.

What has been said lays out three roads into exploration of the law-stuff of a culture. The one road is ideological and goes to "rules" which are felt as proper for channeling and controlling behavior. Students of ethics and legal philosophers are likely to call these felt standards for proper behavior "norms." Students of modern law, accustomed to clothing such norms in words, and to meeting them chiefly in verbalized form, speak of them as "rules" for behavior. In any event, they are ideal patterns, "right ways" against which real action is to be measured.[1] The second road is descriptive; it deals with practice. It explores the patterns according to which behavior actually occurs. The third road is a search for instances of hitch, dispute, grievance, trouble; and inquiry into what the trouble was and what was done about it. Beyond this, for the third approach, there lies—if it can be discovered—the problem of motivation and result of what was done.

The three approaches are related; indeed, they flow each into the others. For it is rare in a simple group or society that the "norms" which are felt or known as the proper ones to control behavior are not made in the image of at least some of the actually prevalent behavior; and it is rare, on the other hand, that they do not to some extent become active in their turn and aid in patterning behavior further. Practices build up subtly, and they build sometimes with amazing emotional power, companioning normative drives which tend to produce continuance of the practices and to choke off deviation. It is, moreover, the felt "norms" for conduct, whether or not derived from practice, which are likely to be injected into the case of breach. Per contra, it is the case of hitch or trouble that dramatizes a "norm" or a conflict of "norms" which may have been latent. It forces conscious attention; it forces the defining of issues. It colors the issues, too, as they are shaped, with the personalities which are in conflict, and with matters of "face," and with other flavors of the culture. It forces solution, which may be creation. It forces solution in a fashion to be remembered, perhaps in clear, ringing words. It is one more experiment toward new and clearer or more rigorous patterning both of behavior and of recognized and recognizable "norm" into that peculiarly legal something one may call a "recognized imperative."

The three approaches are thus related; nor can any of them be understood without the others. To attack the matter from the other side, "norms" for conduct differ in quality and in power according

[1] It has been argued that "culture" in general is of this nature. G. P. Murdock, "The Cross-Cultural Survey," *American Sociological Review*, June 1940. The authors incline to see this as one phase of culture, beside which there sits always in interaction the actually prevailing patterned and unpatterned behavior. But Murdock's description brings out very well the ideological nature of such a set of standards, whether legal or otherwise.

as they do or do not coincide with the clearer practices of life. Practices, in turn, have variant meaning not only according to the degree, range, and sharpness of their existence, but according also to the kind and power of "norms" which sustain or oppose them. Further, "norms" and practices alike take flavor from the frequency of breach and from the nature and regularity of what is done in case of trouble. "Themis," the judgment on the case of trouble, and "custom," which is a fused, confused word suggesting at once a very general practice and a felt sense of its rightness —these play upon each other. Even as what is done in trouble-cases draws inspiration, in its nature and in its extent, from what are known as practices or felt as "norms," so also what has been done in trouble-cases shapes later living in its image. The three, then, are intimately related. The question is, which road, taken as the main road in an investigation, gives best results, surest results, and clearest results?

If one takes as his mainroad (the others being feeders) the road of felt or known "norms," he meets in some cultures with bafflement on the part of the informant. A Comanche,[2] or a Barama River Carib,[3] does not like to think that way. He finds trouble in reducing such general "norms" to expression or in stating a solution for an abstract or a hypothetical case. But if that difficulty is waived, there remain yet others. The first of these is the easy divergence between what may be called ideal and practical morals; between Sunday School and Fourth of July orations and the world of business and politics. In a culture liquid and relatively free of tension, it is possible for felt "norms" to give and flow with each unnoticed shift of living over the generations; but even there, it is rare. And if older "norms" have come to be "crystallized" and also to be out of line with current need, there may develop a disregard for them which moves through the secret and the scandalous into the dubious, on into the almost licit, and at last into the "really" right. When

[2] Ralph M. Linton, *The Study of Man* (New York, The Century Co., 1936), 228 f.; also E. Adamson Hoebel, *The Political Organization and Law-Ways of the Comanche Indians (Memoirs of the American Anthropological Association, No. 54, 1940, Supplement to American Anthropologist, Volume 42, No. 3, Part 2), 6.

[3] John Paul Gillin, "Crime and Punishment Among the Barama River Carib of British Guiana," *American Anthropologist,* Volume 36 (1934), 331-44.

one meets such discrepancy among felt "norms," it is extremely convenient to treat as "law" for the culture that "norm" *which will be recognized as proper to prevail in the pinch*—a matter to which we shall return. We make here the point only that there may be divergence between felt or known *right* (the moral, the decent, the proper) and felt or known *authority* (the line which prevails under the existing regime), and that when such divergence occurs, then in primitive cultures, as in modern, the *legal* is best seen as that which is marked by authority—which is recognized as imperative.

The matter is at once simplified and obscured by reference to modern American culture. Both with and without conflict on the same subject matter, there may be found in the United States a welter of "norms" for conduct, on different levels and of different kinds. One is familiar with tact, with good taste and etiquette, with fashion; with sportsmanship and with playing in a different manner "to win"; with morals in assorted varieties from "gangster morality" through to saintliness. These all play upon, and sometimes against, one another, and the manner of the play is different for different groups and different persons. It will be noted at once that deviations from any of these lines of standard are of two main kinds: some deviations are rebuked; others are not. Indeed, one phenomenon of law, as of institutions in general, which has received altogether too little attention save in relation to bills of rights and the due process clause, is the two *ranges of leeway* of man's conduct which are a part of any legal or social system—the range of permissible leeway, and the range of actively protected leeway. For the kind and degree of permissible variation, invention, experiment, and "play" are as important a part of any institutional scheme as the kind, degree, and direction of its canalizing or organizing of behavior.

The point at which this view of modern culture clarifies the primitive picture appears in the concept that not all devices which canalize conduct need be thought of as "law." The point at which it obscures is in suggesting that only when officials of the political state come into the reckoning does it pay to think of any canalizing device as being law-stuff. For, functionally, the vital difference remains between that deviation which is rebuked and that breach which is not. And, plainly, that functional difference finds its qualitative degrees in terms of *who* does the rebuking, and of *how* it is done. No political state is needed to make that line of inquiry significant, or to make the trouble-case a fruitful inquiry into the nature and the range of any "norm" which may be concerned in it.

Even within the field of the thoroughly canalized, there is no need that what "is done" even approach law-stuff in nature. Thus mother-in-law avoidance is "done" in Cheyenne culture; yet one mother-in-law, on one occasion, broke over to her own satisfaction, and nothing happened (CASE 34). "The world won't come to an end if I beat my son-in-law," she cried. Nor did it. That case is ambiguous because of the justification which was present, but our guess is that mother-in-law avoidance was in general "social" rather than "legal" in its nature. Certainly it appears that even "socially" the prohibition was not absolute. Similarly, much of technical practice, though it have all the flavor of "the right way," must in any culture be regarded with care to see whether departure from it upsets others enough to show in their behavior. If it does not, then however right it is felt to be, one runs into confusion in treating it as "law."

We have no desire to insist on words, so let us leave it this way: Norms, "right ways," departure from which involves somebody's doing something about it, are significantly different from norms whose disregard has no such consequence. And the feature of something's being done about it, and done with felt propriety, the feature of who does something, and of what that something is —these are sufficiently significant in what a developed society conceives of as "law" to give some hope of being worth watching accurately in a less developed one. A person can watch them effectively, however, only in cases of departure, of dispute, of trouble.[4]

As indicated, it is these same cases of trouble which offer the test for various other discriminations that warrant making. A norm can be known to be perhaps religious if it is promulgated by a priest (though a priest may promulgate a purely secular norm, too). A

[4] See Hoebel, *Political Organization . . . of the Comanche Indians*, 45-49.

norm can be known to be certainly religious if it carries explicitly a supernatural sanction; but it can be known to be exclusively religious only in terms of absence of any secular reaction to its breach. This, as Linton is fond of pointing out, is rare; he notes also that a witch doctor, for instance, has a secular prestige-stake in making sure that something "supernatural" does happen, if something supernatural has been arranged by him.[5]

Again, what has been spoken of as "neutral custom"[6] can be known as wholly neutral only if departure from it proves not to be a debit entry in a man's career and does not carry that flavor of mild misdemeanor which shows itself in gossip, covert or overt ridicule, or in provision of good taunting-material to build up the adversary's case in a dispute; in a word, if in truth nothing is done about it.

Yet again, the matter of *who* does anything about it can open up the lines of the structure of the society. Not only in modern society, when the political state does nothing, but in primitive society, where there may be no political state to do anything, any person who takes action in a trouble-case stands forth to observation. Always, he stands forth as "representing" some person or some entirety, and the lines of that representation, if they can be determined, are lines of significant organizational cleavage and structure. Indeed, the heart of what men know as "legality" in action, which follows on infraction or alleged infraction of a "norm," lies in such matters as: what social backing the person taking action in the case has or lays claim to, what pressures he can enlist or tries to enlist—these, along with the matters of what predictabilities are in the picture, what patterns or alternative patterns are at hand for his action, what the known or felt proper limits on his action are. Whether such legalities find expression simply in patterns or semi-patterns of action or ritual which are felt to be correct, or whether they come into verbal expression in the form of "rules" governing proper procedure, is not to the purpose here. The point is that in either aspect the regulation of conduct which is effected or attempted is

[5] Lecture, at joint seminar in criminology, Columbia, 1940 (unpublished).
[6] See Branislaw Malinowski, "Introduction," in Herbert Ian Hogbin, *Law and Order in Polynesia* (New York, Harcourt, Brace & Co., 1937).

not of ordinary conduct, but of conduct-after-grievance, or conduct-in-a-dispute. Such situations deal with what Vinogradoff segregated from the "general custom" as "litigious custom."[7] They are purest law-stuff. What person, or what range of persons is the proper one to proceed? What penalty, or what variety of penalties, is proper for such an offense? What tribunal, or what ritual, or what form of notice and summons, or of declaration before retaliation, is prescribed? Or what set of alternative procedures, all distinguishable from conduct in other, non-conflict, situations, is to be followed? Such regulations may be already crystallized into known traditional lore, capable as in ancient Iceland of being allegedly recited in full before the great assembly over a three-year space. Yet if there be one thing in which modern jurisprudence and Iceland's sagas would teach a common lesson, it would be in this: that even when such rules are known and clear in words, one still does not know the legal system save as he studies case after case in which the rules have come into question, or have been challenged or broken. Thus only as one makes cross-check in action on how far the known "rules" are rules which are followed, and on how they are "followed," and on what else happens, in addition to their being followed, can he be certain what his data are. A fortiori must one go to the cases of hitch or trouble when procedural and remedial matters lack ritual or verbal form.

For, to repeat, the idea of "legality" carries with it the idea not only of right, but of remedy. It includes not only the idea of prescribed right conduct, but that of prescribed penalty (or type of penalty) for wrong. Part of the process of specializing law-stuff out of the vague general matrix of what-is-and-ought-to-be-done, into some more particularized recognizability, is the specializing out also of recognizably proper persons to deal with offenders; or of recognizably proper ways of dealing with offenders and of recognizable limits on proper dealing with them.

And at whatever moment, in any culture, such matters come to take on clarity enough to be *felt*, at that moment begins an eternal

---

[7] Sir Paul Vinogradoff, *Outlines of Historical Jurisprudence* (2 volumes, London, Oxford University Press, 1920-22).

juristic struggle. It is the struggle between an institution as a structure and the life purpose of the institution. In the case of law-stuff it takes the form of a struggle between the recognized form, which limits at once arbitrariness, passion, and vision and the underlying function of justice and social wisdom, to serve which the form first came into being. Perfection of the legal, unmitigated, is also perfection of legalism. And again the test of what is there lies only in the cases of trouble, dispute, breach, disturbance; for no "norms" for lay conduct, however explicit, and few "norms" for the conduct of tribunals or officials, give much light on the juristic "way" of the society. They tell little about whether the "norm" and the official are made to serve the people, or whether the people are made to serve the official or the "norm." The techniques of *use* of any legal form or rule are, if anything, more important than the form and rule themselves. The techniques of operation of the legal personnel, and the latter's manner of handling the techniques—these commonly cut further into the nature of a society's legal system than does the "law" itself. But they must be dug out of the cases in which actual troubles have been dealt with.

There is another point in which the case of trouble or disturbance seems crucial in the evidence it offers. "Law," as we see it, purports to speak for and lay down norms for the Entirety which is in question. If in a given society one can recognize, for instance, a tribe, various associations, a governmental staff, bands, and families, he recognizes thereby a number of subgroups—smaller entities within the great Entirety. No such subgrouping can fail to have its own order, and some disruptions within this smaller order are to be expected. We are as little inclined to treat the handling of such disruptions as per se pertaining to the law *of the tribe* as we are to disregard the possibility that they may so pertain. If a mother in a primitive culture may spank her naughty child without interference or ostracism by her neighbors or the authorities, then it seems probable that under tribal law she has leeway to do so. If most mothers do, then use of the leeway seems to be tribal practice, felt socially as right practice. If unreasonable or extreme spanking results in trouble, then questions emerge concerning how far the leeway accorded by tribal law extends. But the whole focus changes if a family is viewed as a unit. There may then be found utterly and radically different bodies of "law" prevailing among these small units, and generalization concerning what happens in "the" family or in "this type of association" will have its dangers. The total picture of law-stuff in any society includes, along with the Great Law-stuff of the Whole, the sublaw-stuff or bylaw-stuff of the lesser working units. The two are not the same, but they are both important. Both are needed to complete the picture, but they cannot be presented without confusion if they are not distinguished. Accurately seeing what entirety is involved in each given instance, and how far the revealed norm ranges throughout the society studied, is greatly furthered by focusing on the cases of trouble, and especially on who it is that takes action, and with what support of opinion or active aid. Description is in turn made materially easier by distinguishing tribal or societal law-stuff from the bylaw-stuff of any smaller grouping.

All the above matters go to the value of the case of trouble as a main road into inquiry, in terms of its offering objective evidence which furthers needed discriminations, in terms of its giving sharper context to the data; in terms of its affording material which can be *known* to be more than merely what "is done" in general living, or merely what men *say* ought to be done in general living.

There are, however, two other aspects of the study of cases of trouble which warrant no less attention. The first has to do with the relation of the culture to the individual. The second has to do with the living interaction of differing aspects of the culture.

The case of trouble may have for the individual a quality of crisis. The man and his society or his subgroup appear in dramatic relation at a moment of maximum pressure, each upon the other. The study of crises is not the study of the normal and the regular; let that be granted. Nonetheless, the study of series of such crises offers a possibility of study of a culture at work on and through its people, for which no schematization of "norms" can substitute. It offers an insight into the personality factors when those factors glow in the white heat of internal, as well as of external, conflict. And, as the good case lawyer knows, it offers for a schematization of norms a set of sure foundation points, each of which has stood the test of trial.

The case of trouble, again, is the case of doubt, or is that in which discipline has failed, or is that in which unruly personality is breaking through into new paths of action or of leadership, or is that in which an ancient institution is being tried against emergent forces. It is the case of trouble which makes, breaks, twists, or flatly establishes a rule, an institution, an authority. Not all such cases do so. There are also petty rows, the routine of law-stuff which exists among primitives as well as among moderns. For all that, if there be a portion of a society's life in which tensions of the culture come to expression, in which the play of variant urges can be felt and seen, in which emergent power-patterns, ancient security-drives, religion, politics, personality, and cross-purposed views of justice tangle in the open, that portion of the life will concentrate in the case of trouble or disturbance. Not only the making of new law and the effect of old, but the hold and the thrust of all other vital aspects of the culture, shine clear in the crucible of conflict.

The trouble-cases, sought out and examined with care, are thus the safest main road into the discovery of law. Their data are most certain. Their yield is richest. They are the most revealing.

Cases are valuable, provided they are valid. What of the present cases?

They date, most of them, from about 1820 to 1880. They were reached through memory or hearsay, and through an interpreter. They are recorded in notes made as the interpreter spoke and while he was going forward with the informants. The usual ethnologist's practice was observed, of showing no emotion over any information, as to whether it was pleasing or peculiarly interesting. Stories when once started went on uninterrupted. Questioning followed stories; first, requests for more cases of the same sort; second, exploration of what looked like leads: "What did people say about it?" "Do you know of any other cases?" As a last resort, there were questions on felt "norms": "Why did he do that?" "Would it have been different if"—followed again, if it "would have been different" by inquiry for cases. In the main, one case led to another.

The interpreter was Willis Rowland (High Forehead), slow-spoken, solid, careful. His father, a white man, had lived with the tribe and married into it; he himself had served as a Cheyenne Scout under General Miles. He had interpreted much for George Bird Grinnell.[8] He was bothered for a time by the obvious interest in trouble, until he began to perceive the interest in what got done to clear trouble up. But even while bothered, he worked like a craftsman. His translation of questions took the full time our phrasing had taken; his rendering of the Cheyenne came in painstaking detail. He almost never interjected comment while interpreting, though after a day's session was over, his comment and additional instances were worth listening to. His vocabulary was apt, and his use of it careful; if a word did not satisfy, he reconsidered and corrected the rendition: "No, he don't say just that . . ." There may be interpreters more accurately careful and more coöperative; but we have never found one. Any invalidity the cases may suffer under does not rest with High Forehead.

The other informants were a number of old Cheyennes, ten more in all. Stump Horn was eighty-six when he was consulted. A careful, somewhat conventional gentleman, an observer of all decencies—among them, truth. His accounts began always with the location of the camp and where it moved during the story. Twice he caught himself on a point of doubt and went out to check with "another old man," and found himself correct. A number of times such consultation came before he spoke or before he stated inability to get the matter straight. Pauses for pondering on a detail, to bring either the answer or a failure of it, made accurate notes easy on the writing hand: "He says he is sending his heart back over the years." "He wants to let his mind go away to think on that." For

---

[8] George Bird Grinnell was a regular visitor and investigator among the Northern Cheyennes for twenty-five years beginning in 1890.

three days Stump Horn would not address us with these accounts from the old days, but held his eagle-feather fan between his face and us, and spoke to High Forehead. If noise or movement outside attracted his attention, he would lean forward to peer out the door, under the fan. There was a flat, disruptive silence, once, when a matter touching religion had been mentioned. But later, having mentioned an oath himself, he let his "heart" go away to think, dropped the fan, and felt he might better talk out the rest of the matter, "so you could get it right." If man can be accurate in the circumstances, Stump Horn was accurate.

Calf Woman, though a most valuable informant, has her value in other characteristics. Eighty-five, the wife of a chief, an enthusiastic, gossipy *raconteuse,* a shrewd and strong-willed trader on those decencies which were to her only what they threatened in action or what they could be made to yield, Calf Woman's memory was sharp for any weakness or any discomfiture of another which a long life of eager attention to such matters had yielded her. Her placing of cases was not in terms of the camp, but by what the women— naming them—had said about it. Calf Woman had the skilled teller's nose for context and for the characteristic. Detail she may have added, and may have spiced; where that has occurred, detail was spiced and added not only for realistic effect, but by one who had sure knowledge of what effect was Cheyenne-realistic. When it was possible to check the story against another informant's version, all relevant legal points of Calf Woman's stories were corroborated, save this: that whatever in a Calf Woman story turns to the glory of Calf Woman is to be regarded with more than suspicion.

Black Wolf was a generation younger. Serious, intelligent, a student of the old ways, a ponderer on old ways and on new ones, he is a leader among his people. What old men had told him, Black Wolf had listened to with the curious intentness of the boy who one day was to be known for wisdom: consider his reproduction of the autobiography of Pawnee (Case 2). His carefulness was of a piece with Stump Horn's. When he came east to Washington on tribal business, he had a letter written from the train to "Morning Star,

New York," which, somehow, failed to be delivered. In Washington, all his business was held up while he kept inquiring for Morning Star. A telegram came to Columbia Law School from the Indian Bureau: "Are you Morning Star Black Wolf of the Northern Cheyenne is here has to see Morning Star says some points need to be cleared up." Hoebel did happen to be Morning Star. The needed points were clarified. Some of them were matters of religion. "Last summer we were there. Now I am in your country. It will not hurt the people for me to say these things here."

These were the four major informants of the eleven.

Wholly apart from the accounts, such personalities lent both validity and meaning to the cases. They are in singular degree contrasting types, and typify among them the most striking legal facets of the Cheyenne culture. Stump Horn, accepting his culture and living it, in spirit as in form, shaped by it utterly, and following it and its leaders, shows a relative gentleness and tolerance toward elbowers and grabbers, unless things should get utterly out of hand. High Forehead, a heavier hand, a tougher mind, a practical soldier, whose acceptance of discipline and tradition called for a rough assay of both against horse sense, is no man to overlook either fun or gain, but one to give solid backing to solidity, in any pinch. Calf Woman, accepting her culture in good part as setting the prestige goals which stirred her interest, adds of her own greed or passion what else she might come to want. Receiving her culture above all as a set of tools to shape men and matters to her need, she breaks over any and every time she has sufficient urge and thinks it safe; but in her own way, she gives return by leadership. Had she been born a man, Calf Woman is the type which would have been the turbulent rising warrior; she would have given the vigor, the arbitrary flavor, the expansion of the law administration of the soldiers. Against this, Black Wolf typifies that combination of tolerance and firmness, of feeling for pattern and vision for problem and purpose, which was Cheyenne administration of the law in the upper age brackets, and among the younger leaders of the more sober stripe. The single troublesome type, once not too frequent, which the cases show and which is not represented among the four, is the slider and sponger; and that phase of the older culture shows up with sad promptness under reservation conditions, where the balancing pressures of responsibility for food and defense, of the prestige to be gained from effort in hunt and raid, no longer operate. Not Stump Horn, but the swarm of relatives and friends who were "camping on him," made that aspect of things live.

Distortion of the evidence due to twisting in interpretation, or to deliberate coloring, seems thus relatively slight in most matters and determinable as to its nature in most others. The one important bias which might have crept in would be that toward glorification. It is, for instance, by no means clear that the full fame of Two Twists (CASE 1), in each detail of the combat, is to be taken as history. But on the side of the law-stuff, we doubt the presence of any such tendency. The cases are cases of trouble, which is one guaranty against over-prettification. And the solutions, amazing as they prove when one ponders on the full patterns they reveal, seemed simple portions of the individual stories to the informants. They were not given as stories of achievement; their juristic beauty is beauty for eyes familiar with other cultures and the juristic problems of other civilizations. It became clear only as the ways of the living culture took slow shape around the cases themselves.

More troublesome is the matter of trustworthiness of any cases built on pure memory or tradition running back sixty years or twice that long. One can accept as probable a tendency for early memory to be vivid in the aged. One can accept as peculiarly developed among the non-literate an accuracy of memory impression undisturbed by the daily wash of headline and sensation. One is still left with two distortion and displacement factors. First, if the narrative has assumed fixed verbal form, repeatable by rote, the process of its verbalization is extremely likely to have introduced conventionalizations. The repeaters of it may have added glosses, conventionalizing and rationalizing any extraordinary feature. Whereas, on the other hand, the unfixed narrative is subject to omission, substitution, and improvised conscious or unconscious artificial coloring. The most careful historian likes his tale to be vivid, to stir interest; and youthful "memories" can turn into highly selective distortions.

Two or three instances will indicate both the difficulty and our estimate of its bearing. When Little Wolf had killed (CASE 8), the tale says that he went up to a hilltop, that he spoke: "If anyone wants to see me, I am here." It is not certain that he said just that. It does seem clear that the conventional behavior in the circumstances was for a proper man to go to some handy spot, out of immediate sight of the slain man's kin, and to wait there publicly for what might come. And the exact words appear often enough to have been very possibly a semi-ritual formulation. But whether Little Wolf said those words, or not, no man can know. The case is typical of the kind of detail in a story which may too easily have been filled in with what "just would have happened." On the other hand, there is no doubt at all about Little Wolf's ostentatious wait in a convenient spot. That, as opposed to what words may have been used, is essential to the pattern; and Little Wolf's character would have required his conformance. His behavior in any other fashion could not have been forgotten, could not have escaped comment.

Again, in Pawnee's narrative (CASE 2) there are two features introduced for pure storyteller's effect. Pawnee twice slipped in sly hits against himself, to bring a laugh, to drive home to boys that he was more than preacher: he wished he could have smoked before they fed him; he never got over his grudge against those Bowstrings. Both points are probably true; they are, however, the very type of the easy, the pardonable, the unreliable addition. The chief's speech which led to the climax is another matter. It is high art. Is it the chief's art, or is it Pawnee's: an oration "of Spartacus to the gladiators" by a novelist-historian? In either case, it was a lovely job, addressed out of the culture to a crisis-situation, moving with sure strokes into a planned effect. What tells in favor of its historicity is the straightness of the narrative of the behavior and the rightness of the behavior to the situation. The tale is of what happened, not of assumed motivation. Where it gives assigned motivations, they are an orator's assignment of his own motivations, blocking prospective adversary moves. If they are also real motiva-

SPIRIT WOMAN

tions, the revelation of the real motivations is not their function in the tale. If the matter be in this particular case open to a critic's doubt, because motivations are indeed mentioned in the account (and because certain of them are good preachment for listening boys as well as for the chiefs who, in the story, are the listeners), the point runs, nevertheless, without such challenge throughout the bulk of the material. The accounts move in terms of *behavior,* rarely in terms of reasons therefor. Now behavior-sequences, when reported just as such, either turn up an internal unity with significant turning points—points of pattern and crisis on which not only dramatic interest hinges, but the whole meaning of the tale as well —or else they become loose and empty anecdote. Drama does not have to be added to a case of trouble; it is given in the situation. The situation, moreover, devoid of its significance, is hard to recall. To recall it at all is to recall the pregnant lines of that significance, the lines and points of pattern and of crisis which made it worth noting when it happened and worth remembering at all. It is such points that we have taken as the valid ones in these stories, as the "sharp corners" that need puzzling over, as the essential or critical aspects of a crux of tension or of conflict. The possibly ornamental bits have not been neglected, but an attempt has been made to weight them in a different way. They give evidence of the flavor which the situation might have had in the culture, in the view of some narrator down the line. They reveal, perhaps, the flavor this situation did have in history. In a word, the conflict behavior and the behavior of conflict-resolution have been taken as the material for this study.

The cases themselves are of two strikingly divergent types, and each of the two types reaches its own problems not only of validity, but of significance. The one is the case of personal experience or observation, the other the case of a tribal figure of note.

As to validity, the personal experience case rests on first-hand knowledge and gives closer access to matters of background, detail, motivation. It has, on the other hand, the possible twists of personal interest, of selective observation, of selective memory. Where exaggeration in any direction may have crept in, there is no ordinary wherewithal for cross-check by another informant. In our belief, the less profound social importance of the individual case helps accuracy here, since there is less urge to idealize. And we believe that the simpler, face-to-face culture which permitted wider observation of what occurred at the time helps such cases into trustworthiness. Certainly among old folk of our own culture one finds early experiences reported with all indication of a far higher degree of accuracy when they concern a face-to-face group than when they concern more highly developed groupings, of whose work the narrator saw, and took in, only part.

The case centering about the tribal figure, on the other hand, has frequently passed through report before it has reached the informant. The tribal figure is the person whose doings made up a good portion of the general talk when the tribe came together. We have assumed that such talk, with participants on hand to be listened to and questioned, settled down into common report of the camp, the substance and color of which became truly common in terms of the felt significance of the incident. We have assumed that it is from such a common reservoir that these stories flow. One notes again in the trouble-cases the relative absence of that urge toward idealization with which tales of war glory are affected. But most of the older cases of this type have passed through one more mind and memory. They have come from the father, who lived through the common report, to the son or other "youngster," from whom we heard it. Fortunately, one type of test exists, of the kind and degree of loss or distortion on the way, for some stories came in two or several versions which can be checked against each other. Such versions prove to differ, regularly, somewhat in richness of incident, and somewhat in artistic flavor. They do not differ in the significant detail of conflict and of its resolution. It is legitimate to see such plural-versioned cases as a sampling on which the general accuracy of single versions has been checked.

In sum, on the matter of validity, the evidence is accurate and solid enough to warrant not only attention, but careful study. It is full enough not only to raise problems, but to admit of what seems sound solution for most of them. There are gaps, there are ambiguities, there are borderlands of dubious reliability. The number of available, personally trustworthy, informed repositories of material is limited. Yet sustained inquiry into the cases of trouble reported to us has elicited so much that not only fits with and into, but interprets, discriminates, and sharpens the vast investigations of Grinnell, that the cases are given guaranty-in-use of being in significant measure both trustworthy and meaningful. They show, secondly, an internal coherence among themselves too strong to be the fruit of accident. And it is a coherence which was gained neither by smoothing down nor by leaving out. Finally, and on the side of the way things legal move, the cases both fit into and illuminate what we learn from other cultures. On the basis of this threefold testing out in use we hold it to be clear that as between the distortion possibilities which rest in the nature of the data, and their possibilities of accuracy, the latter have maintained the definite dominance.

Apart from questions of validity, the two different types of case which have been mentioned have differing significance to the theory of investigation. The case of the tribal figure is typical only in the sense in which the legal difficulties of a president of the Stock Exchange or of a major New York bank, or those of Chicago's number one gangster or of a pillar of the Tammany machine might be conceived as "typical" today. Such cases can no more be generalized into pictures of the life of the common man than can the life of the feudal great hall, the conflict of knights in tournament, or the prestige battles of the potlatch lords among the Indians of our Northwest Coast. Significant, hugely significant, such cases may be —not only of incident in a major career, but as indicative of clash between emergent powers and an older order, or as revealing the degree to which power and personal force may work to blur or color legal right. They can be significant, too, as being the "great" remembered and crucial cases, as the cases of John Hampden, John Wilkes, Dred Scott, or Al Capone may have significance beyond the case of Richard Roe. Yet the thinness of present knowledge, say, of ancient Iceland, rests precisely upon the terrific pressure of the saga machinery to squeeze away so much as even chance mention of a petty man. It is a thinness which is partially cured only by the facts that power was mobile, that one meets little men in the process of its movement, and that the greatest were not so great as to be too much unlike the little.

Thus the personal experience cases from the Cheyennes provide a treble counterweight to distortion by the cases of the great figure. They show something of standards of right and patterns of procedure when the weight of a leader was not cast on the scales—a base line for judging of deflection in the Big Man cases. They show matters unaffected by reasons of state or possible worry over political effects of hewing to the line or breaking over. They show, finally, things more likely to have been in the day's work and living of the tribe—things which did *not* become news for the whole camp. The personal experience cases are therefore needed. And their quantitative weight is to be multiplied in the degree to which their individual qualitative weight is reduced when they are compared with the cases of the Big Men. Finally, and in respect of the juristic level of the net law-way of a culture, the work of the police courts is as vital to a people as the "constitutional decisions" of the Highest Nine—not more vital, but as vital—in Cheyenne as in the United States. And in no culture can the one be judged by data from the other.

There are two further matters which need mention, both of which bear on theory of investigation.

First, there is Grinnell's material and the relation of the present work to it. He who asks sharper questions in any single area has hope of coming out with sharper answers. We were led to ask sharper questions on the subject matter of this study than Grinnell had asked, because theories of significance of dispute behavior, of plurality and alternative norms of procedure in trouble-cases, and the case lawyer's theory of how to work cases into a fuller scheme of social norms—all focused inquiry and gave finer calibration to insight in this field. In no instance has there been occasion to challenge Grinnell's positive report of a particular case, as fitting fact. There is almost never any occasion to doubt the presence of solid data under the relatively few positive generalizations on legal matters in his work. What we repeatedly find, however, is that his work shows no sign of having turned up material of a type which came to light for us in our specialized inquiry. It becomes clear, further, that Grinnell's generalizations and even his case reports are cast in terms which for legal purposes are blunt and undiscriminating. If taken literally they could read as evidence on the wrong side of a discrimination which the nicer noting of the legal data has forced into light. But in each case it is a discrimination which Grinnell did not have in mind, and to which neither his interest nor his language was addressed. It is as if a lay observer might report of the modern United States: that "their law is made by bodies called legislatures, and they have a doctrine of separation of powers which bars their judges or executives from making law." Whereas the records of such an observer upon American politics, or press, or social life, or economic system might well yield a later investigator background and stimulus as grateful and indispensable as Grinnell's has been for this study, yet the particular hypothetical passage would have to be regarded as simply not addressed to such a nicer problem as the degree to which American judges or administrators do shape and reshape law, in the teeth of the doctrine of separation.

The last matter is concerned with the likelihood that a theory of investigation may dictate what one sees and makes use of, and may dictate also a general frame into which the data may be squeezed —though without conscious intent—in order to make them fit. And it will not have escaped the reader that in regard to the validity of the present data we have leaned on the consonance of the data with general theory as one test for such validity. And in distinguishing the more solid from the more shadowy pieces of an account, recourse has been had to "essential" aspects of pattern and solution, with the criterion of the "essential" hidden somewhere in the background.

On this we wish to be neither mystical (say, about "just getting the feel of the culture") nor yet blind (say, concerning the dangers of conditioning eyes by a prior theory or by an appealing *ex post facto* theoretical frame). The sound line of effort does consist in starting with a theory of investigation as clear as one can get it. That speeds work. But it is our belief that the plan of inquiry into cases of dispute or trouble, followed through *as cases*, provides as quick and as uncomfortable a strain toward correction of theory as has yet been devised. Cases (enough of them) do make an intractable body of behavior, to be seen and to be recorded, whether it "fits" or not. It is our experience, further, that patterns, attitudes, and strains which are peculiar in the culture make themselves felt rather rapidly in the trouble-cases. The felt strains and stresses then give leads for inquiry not foreshadowed in the anticipatory plan. From this point on, one follows the given culture as it reveals itself; but one follows no less, and tests constantly against the cases, the general theories which other work has made persuasive as hypotheses. As to the job of ultimate reconciliation of the data —i.e., put baldly, of the job of creating a theoretical scheme to hold them—we can say only this: it is art, thus far incommunicable art, and something goes into it which has been rightly called "feel for" "the feel of" the particular culture concerned. There is also another thing which goes into that art, a thing which ought to be called "feel for" "the feel of" the particular *aspect* of culture in general which is under scrutiny: in this case, "feel" for the ways of law-stuff. What any man or men can bring out will be a gamble. There is one good hedge against self-deception, and only one: the cases must be not only gathered, but recorded, bare and in full, especially the ones with most uncomfortable corners. The shrewdest and most accurate observer's generalization or interpretation is no substitute for the cases on which it rests. Cases are of course themselves no substitute for sound theory; but they are the writer's and the reader's only means for checking on the theorizing.[9]

[9] Certain further points on theory of investigation, which require more specific material for their discussion, are dealt with at the close of Chapter VIII.

Chapter III

PRIMITIVE LAW, AND MODERN

W HEN Law comes to take on the form most familiar to us, that of authoritative rules and doctrines expressed in their own queer, technical language, gaining precision from the operations of technical specialists at work in their own peculiar context of technique, then Law becomes a world of its own. It is a world like Alice's Looking-Glass—both difficult to break into, and difficult, once one has become acclimated to it, to break out of. Beside the layman who does not know anything about Art, but does know what he likes and is mildly apologetic about insisting on what he likes, there stand a hundred of his brethren who do not know anything about Law, but do know what is right and who insist without any apology at all that they ought to have it. They are baffled, frustrated, angry, if Law and right persist in being different. But they do not see what to do, nor how to take hold. They cannot break in. Even the specialists of the social disciplines find the self-contained world of authoritative legal doctrine a sort of unchartable fourth-dimensional space. Effort after effort at synthesis of the social disciplines over the past ten years has made worth-while headway in all phases, except that of integrating law-stuff with the rest.

The authors hold that the obstacle here is closely akin to that which has stood between the study of modern law and the study of primitive. The obstacle is the acceptance of the realm of Law as being of a different order; for if of a different order, then it sets its own premises and becomes impenetrable on any premises except its own. But the only thing about technical Law which is different in the sense of incomparable is that it has a technical field of discourse, one of legal correctness and incorrectness—discussion of which can of course be based only on premises of doctrinal Law itself. But if this technical side of Law be moved out of the central position and set into its relation to other things—if it be viewed merely as a batch of tools to get jobs done in a culture, then every item among those tools becomes at once familiar instead of different. For we are familiar enough, outside of Law, with Authority as a fact; and we can view it as a tool. We are familiar with norms and imperatives, and with whole systems of each, or of both, as conditioning facts; we can view them also as tools. We are familiar with processes of handling trouble and of channeling behavior. We know procedures and institutions for accomplishing these things. We know ideological systems with their clustered concepts, again as conditions given in fact and as capable of study as to how well they serve their functions.

In order to make contact with the social disciplines, with the problems of the common man, and with primitive law-stuff, the technical Law of the modern state requires only to be viewed as a world of working tools measured against a body of stated objectives and problems not posed by it, but *given to* it for solution. It requires only to be seen as part of the machinery of functioning legal institutions and then to be set, together with the rest of the lawmaking machinery, against what both the technical Law and the legal institutions are for. This is so obvious that the only wonder is why men should for decades have understood it, in regard to law-at-large, and in regard to constitutional law in particular, without having approached the rest of the body of more detailed legal doctrine in the same terms.

When seen thus, each legal concept becomes a candle to illumine the working of society. It became a concept because some type of problem has recurred often enough, has required to be wrestled with often enough, to be not only felt, but seen, as a type of problem. Every legal concept represents then in first instance an effort at diagnosis of a recurrent social trouble of some particular kind. It represents what W. I. Thomas[1] might call an effort to define a

---

[1] E.g., William I. Thomas and Florian Znaniecki, *The Polish Peasant in Europe and America* (New York, Alfred A. Knopf, 1918), Methodological Note.

situation of perplexity. Comparative study is to this extent a study in comparative diagnosis, if really similar problems have occurred in different cultures.

This aspect of a legal concept as an effort at significant diagnosis of a recurrent problem has been obscured by the other aspect of a legal concept: its prescription for cure. For each legal concept also, and simultaneously, represents the clustered result of sustained efforts at solution of the problem concerned, efforts which are sometimes superb, sometimes merely adequate, sometimes purblind, occasionally puerile. Nowhere can one study more effectively the partial conditioning of solution by the manner of diagnosis, or the amazing ability of man to muddle through despite inadequacy of diagnosis. Nowhere, either, have records been gathered to enable so effective a study of the interplay of those conflicting urges characteristic of any specialized department of culture. The one urge is for the institution to build further, as if *in vacuo*, on what have come to be its own premises. The other urge is to modify the most definitely fixed internal premise so as to achieve net results which can meet the audit from without.

Only in a third aspect does a legal concept begin to present itself as impenetrable to the non-lawyer. This is when it stands as a datum which, because it is legal, is held for that reason alone to be correct and authoritative for legal thought, and free of need for inquiry into either its basis or its consequence. And even in the extreme case, that of litigation before an authoritative tribunal, modern jurisprudence has made unmistakable that such inviolate nature is very partial. Even in the courtroom, the authoritatively given doctrine has proved to call for complement and supplement.

A few illustrations will make the point. There is, for instance, a terrific welter of rules, some of them very tough indeed, clustered around the legal concept of "jurisdiction," which is the technical way of posing the question of what official organ has official power to deal with a situation. The underlying problem is difficult to answer, but it is not difficult to see—it is simply that of allocating the "say" in a situation. You can have the problem naked, with most of its complexity vibrant, when Christmas is at Grandmother's and

Grandmother has announced that the lid is off, and Father is coming to the conclusion that the children are getting out of hand, and Grandmother is not Father's mother. Holmes, on the Supreme Bench, was great in good part because beneath all rules and precedents which a judge must face, he never lost sight of just this homely essence of it all; not even when faced with some history-ridden problem of Uncle Sam's jurisdiction under the Federal Constitution. So, in the Cheyenne homicide cases, the structure of government itself trembled and threatened to shift as soldier societies arrogated or sought to arrogate to themselves a "say" which in tradition had been the Great Council's (Chapters IV and V).

Or turn the matter not to illumination of modern law by a primitive problem, but to illumination of the primitive by the modern. In the procedure of the modern lawsuit, modern legal theory distinguishes the "operative facts" which have always occurred before the lawsuit starts, and which confer a legal right in theory and in claim, but which do not of themselves walk into court. Such operative facts are a basis of effective legal rights, but merely a basis. Enforcement is another matter, and it is not automatic. There must follow, first, the setting up of legal "proceedings" in proper form, with notice of the claim to interested parties, and with official "proof" of the claim, and opportunity for challenge. There follows then an official "judgment" which crystallizes the right in a new and now almost unchallengeable form. And people today insist on preservation of a "record," that the matter may be remembered and may stay settled, so that the officially established right may rest thenceforth as on a rock. Now the Cheyennes had no such analytical apparatus; nor had they any such elaborately structured procedural machinery. And in the matter of the high war honor of the "coup," both the Cheyennes and their translators and the literature of comment use the phrase "count coup" quite indiscriminately to mean the actual striking of any enemy (if dead, striking him as one of the first to do so) or ceremonial recitation of the story of the deed. This can become confusing. But by the capitalization of modern legal analysis to give suggestion, there appears a fascinating order in the handling of this war honor—an order which would come to attention only by accident were it not for the stimulus of modern legal theory. There is the actual deed, which is the "operative fact." There is a claim made, a public claim, of a character and on an occasion to elicit any challenge; there is "proof" by personal testimony, perhaps by witnesses, sometimes by more solemn means. The case of Lone Wolf (CASE 23) tests this out. There is then public recognition, "official" allowance of the honor as rightly won. How this was done and how regularized its doing may have been, is not known. It may have been at the informal meetings of warriors after battle. But there is one set of claimants to coups who were held disqualified, and who saw the effective "judgment" award the honor elsewhere (CASE 21). Finally, there was among the Cheyennes and other Plains peoples in very truth a "record," and a record of a character to make the judgment "roll" of a modern court look weak: The recognized coup-striker was called upon on ceremonial occasion after ceremonial occasion to tell and act out the story of his officially accepted honorable deed. All this the reader will see in its Cheyenne context when he reads Chapters VI and IX.

This type of illumination of perennial problems offers itself from any modern legal concept or theory. A later chapter indicates, in application to the Cheyenne law of homicide, the bearing of the problems which underlie such modern concepts as "justification," "excuse," "responsibility," "causation," and even "person." Others indicate the bearing of the problems which underlie, say, "intestate succession," in contrast with "testamentary disposition" and "gifts *causa mortis,*" or of contractual obligation on the level of "gentlemen's agreement," in contrast with clearly legal contractual "obligation." A final illustration here is one which applies to a major difficulty of all law—the problem of really getting a fresh start in relations between litigants after disposition of a trouble-case. This is the problem not only of keeping settled what has been legally settled, but of killing off the grievance tension. A piece of this totality, the piece that has to do with effective authoritative settlement, may be summed up in current terminology under the heads of "day in court" and *res judicata.* The first of these, "day in court," is a makeshift device for rendering the net result of the second both possible and moderately just: namely, a chance, a due and reasonable chance, so far as arrangeable, is to be offered for a litigant to be fairly heard; and then—"the matter has been finally adjudicated"; it is *res judicata*. But this means only: adjudicated for official purposes and by authority. The lasting grievance of the loser, the continuing taunt of the winner, may remain; the problem of mediation, conciliation, and the desirable outcome in *working* adjustment is too often sacrificed over the more imperative bare-bones need for achieving the fresh start. This last is, indeed, in itself a tremendous social achievement. So, too, is the accomplishment of it without a ritual so complicated as to be an unwieldy, crushing burden. Early Germanic procedure was hamstrung for centuries by the technical hurdles which stood between a litigant and any effectively *final* judgment "at law." Chagga litigation on the village judgment-green, on the other hand, has difficulty in reaching any finality. The Chagga are found dragging into discussion the "settled" cases which lie back through the generations of remembered family history, seemingly not only for what the modern advocate would call "atmosphere," but with some expectation of more directly influencing the new decision.[2] One of Schiller's Coptic documents, recording the close of a dispute, heaps penalty-obligation upon curse and self-curse down through sons and sons of sons who may reopen the matter.[3] This is evidence enough of how difficult a matter it can be to close a case and keep it closed. And the Paris, or Mexican, or Reno divorce can still (in American culture) wobble or give in a divorcee's home courts under "collateral" attack on the methods of getting the decree.

Thus not the least of the legal achievements of the Cheyennes is the degree of settledness of any grievance which did come to open adjustment among them. Indeed, not the least of the attributes of "the legal" about any of their open adjustments is this character of completeness and of permanence. Not the least of their juristic

[2] Bruno Gutmann, *Das Recht der Dschagga* (Munich, G. H. Beck, 1926).
[3] A. Arthur Schiller, *Ten Coptic Legal Texts* (New York, Metropolitan Museum of Art, 1932).

feats is the freeing of such settledness from preconditions of tortuous ritual. Moreover—and be this noted—wherever the pipe was called into play, or differences of policy were worked out by the processes of deference to another's judgment, one finds in addition to the *res judicata* type of finality that further and hardly less functionally important outcome which so few systems of *law* have managed to guarantee at all, i.e., a working harmony on into the future.[4] Indeed, the Cheyenne cases could profitably be recombed and reclassified to show how much more satisfactory the double achievement of settlement plus satisfaction proved than did mere settlement.

But against the conscious development of the pipe procedure into the exclusive type of settlement stood the whole drive of the career patterns and the self-dramatizing urges of spectacular pleading-by-action and outfacing. For if a law technique is to make its way without the aid of centralized will and force to drive it through, it must not only be effective socially, but must also make personal appeal to the individuals who may be concerned in its possible use. The spread of a pattern or process—or rule—by growth and contagion, by what one may term the more democratic processes, is quite another matter from its spread by way of authority. One can match the delay in the contagion of the superior Cheyenne technique of chief-and-pipe with the non-success or slow spread of many of the finest pieces of case-law hit upon in the last half-century by one or another of the multi-headed courts among the United States.

"Tort" and "Crime"

Against such a background of the problems which force law-men to devise law-ways, law-concepts, and law-rules, many of the common "contrasts" between primitive law and modern lose much of their seeming contrast; and they gain understandability thereby. There is, for instance, the conception that primitive law runs much

---

[4] The sole recorded apparent exception to this is not a full exception. It is Pawnee's continuing grudge against the Bowstring Soldiers (Case 2). There cannot be said to have been a formal settlement. On the other hand, the flavor of the occasion should have killed the grudge.

more heavily to "tort," i.e., private wrong, than to "crime," or public wrong. Viewed purely as a matter of procedure, there is truth in this. But it is when viewed as a matter of substance and function that the truth takes on its needed perspective. The fact is that in any group or culture *any* wrong concerns the Whole to some extent at the same time that it gives concern to the more particularly Aggrieved. If it did not concern the Whole, the Aggrieved would be looked upon as an aggressor, not as a redresser, when he undertakes his redress. If, for instance, men did not today dimly or strongly deem breach of contract something against the public interest, they would not provide courts and sheriffs for contract-plaintiffs' use. That public officials are not used to prosecute criminally for breach of contract or to jail the contract-breaker; that no official undertakes to force plaintiffs to bring private suits for enforcement whether they will or no; that plaintiffs are allowed to compromise their claims at will—these things indicate only that the persons immediately aggrieved are managing enough stiffening of the general practices of contract performance to satisfy the sense of general need. Indeed, they have been found a touch too insistent for general comfort. Constitutional restriction has been undertaken against debt slavery, which rests in contract; courts lop away penalty clauses which promise arbitrary (and so "penal") damages in case of breach; and the same courts refuse to enforce some deals which they see as too lopsided and provide by "constructive conditions" some rather material mitigations of seeming express promissory obligation. More than this, the national legislature offers luckless promisors a refuge in bankruptcy. At the same time, and on the other side, people today do turn to the criminal law; they set public officials to prevent or to prosecute certain types of abuse of the contract institution, running notably in the general area of "fraud," but covering also the maintenance of proper reserves against bank deposits or insurance obligations. The net picture is one of the public interest playing upon the private at every turn, and of *administrative convenience* as the focus for determining the allocation of initiative.

Precisely the same scene opens in the field of non-contractual wrong. To take simple cases, "indecent exposure" is a direct grievance to any person shocked thereby; robbery is an injury to the robbed as well as to the public; and treason is a personal affront to each individual patriot in his individual person. So that "crime" differs from "tort" not in kind, but in the effective predominance for purposes of administration of the public or the private elements, *both* of which are always present, to some degree. The old English attitude toward theft is a lovely example: suit for recovery of the stolen goods was allowed only after criminal prosecution of the offender. The administrative arrangement looked to channeling the aggrieved's individual interest into public service as a stream is diverted into a millrace.

What distinguishes primitive from developed law in regard to "public" and "private" enforcement thus becomes the range and clarity of available administrative machinery. Homicide under a feud regime is therefore ill conceived as pure tort. It is better conceived as what it is in a modern society, crime plus grievous tort, except that among feuding peoples there is no machinery available to take care of the first aspect either directly, or comfortably, or preferentially. How else is one to explain the pressures and procedures and limitations which emerge again and again in society after society to limit and control and finally to end the feuding? How else is one to explain the explosion which occurs when some at-length-become-intolerable repetitive killer, in a non-feud regime, is suddenly lynched, or is speared from behind by a delegate of the community?[5]

The reason why sustained insistence on this approach is justified is not only that it keeps to the fore the perennial common ground of the law-stuff of all societies, but that it also reinforces, for study of primitive and modern legal institutions alike, the way in which

[5] The authors concur fully with Ralph M. Linton's conception that one line of crime among primitive peoples is the achievement of a status of the finally intolerable. The equivalent modern concept is that of Public Enemy No. 1. The riveting of legal attention on a particular offense exclusively is a deposit in our law of constitutional efforts to control arbitrary and despotic officials. The parole, psychiatric, and juvenile court approaches reintroduce the attempted coping with the whole man (the offender rather than the offense), which is the other primitive approach. For, of course, primitives also react to single offenses.

the available administrative machinery conditions both the diagnosis of a problem and the attack on it.

Group Responsibility and Diverse Levels of Law-Stuff

This fact of administrative conditioning is brought out by meditation upon another focus of "contrast" between primitive law and modern: that of "group responsibility." It is trite that primitive societies are likely to show much more highly developed kin structure than modern, in relation to the other given types of organization; and the relative absence of political authority resting on an other-than-kin basis emphasizes the role of kinship in legal trouble-cases. So far, good. From this point on, however, the lines of usual contrast slide off the track. It is true that "the individual" does loom large in modern law, if the mind be centered upon the ideology of Western Law at the period of its emergence from feudal thinking into the pre-industrial mercantile phase. And law books are indeed still written about A and B and C. Further, current criminal law wrestles with individual responsibility as distinct from "attainder of blood" and consequent extirpation of the culprit's branch and root.

Yet the cumulation of these lines of thought gives no true picture of modern law at work. All legal theory avails nothing to remove from a family the stigma of a convict within it, and today's official law (quite apart from recrudescence of reprisal upon family "hostages") relies for its deterrent efficacy quite as much upon this threat to family as upon the threat to the offender. Whereas on the civil side (and with overlappings into the criminal) modern law has been moving uninterruptedly into expansion of group relations and of group responsibility: the party, the corporation, the union, the coöperative, workmen's compensation, and *respondeat superior*. This should give pause to simple "contrasts" built in terms of individual versus group responsibility. It does not mean that we lack individual responsibility. It means that along with family groups (which today are once again increasingly coming to be dealt with even by Law as units, as in housing and relief) we are carrying also some types of more purely individual responsibility, but that the dominant picture is coming more and more to stress groups, other-than-kin groups, as the legal units. The persisting ideology of individualism is not to be taken literally; what it means is that neither our legal thought nor our general thought has wholly deconfused the actual scene.

But if with these things in mind one turns to a primitive culture, he will commonly find less contrast than parallelism—not exact parallelism, but enough to dispel any notion either of mere "group" responsibility, or of kin groups, as the only legal type. Consider the phenomenon of extrusion or disowner, a marked type of individuation occurring among primitives. Beside ways of bringing an outsider into kinship status, such as adoption and blood-brotherhood, there stand ways of disowning, of producing forfeiture of such status for one born to it. And finally, one finds in many primitive societies in which group responsibility appears on the surface to be the exclusive "legal" phenomenon that the meaning is only that what happens to have been selected as "the law" is a single portion of "the law"—to wit, the law of *intergroup* relations. But in modern courts, too, individual stockholders are barred from rowing out the differences between their corporations. Only "the corporations," and these only by their official "managements," and in the main, these only by their counsel, have standing to manage an intercorporate dispute. The same is true of individual nationals in many of their claims against other states: only through their governments can their claims be heard. The body of the Law which is concerned is not the whole of the Law which there is. It is no more than the immediately relevant portion or aspect of the Law. And it must be defined in terms of what grouping it is whose law is in question.

Similarly, ancient Rome is badly understood if the paterfamilias be looked upon as once was common, to wit, as being the only subject of "legal" rights. For there was another kind of "law" at work in Rome—that within the gens and within the familia. It was a kind which we believe to have had much generality as well as much variety, in much the same way that there is today another kind of "law" regulating the relations of a national with his own government, or of a stockholder (or a laborer) with his own corporation.

It can be put this way: If the level or nature of what is taken as in first instance the Law or the Legal is such as to cover only a limited class of relations (such as those between particular kinds of groups), then the going total "legal" structure of the culture is to be understood only by getting on down into the intra-group regulations as well. This is indeed different and therefore to be distinguished, but it also exists and therefore must be taken into account. What is more, the total picture will demand inquiry also into any portions of intragroup or cross-group relations which may escape direct contact with what may perhaps properly be taken as the Highest Official Law.

This study is not concerned with the names to be given to such different coexisting types or levels of effective regulatory and trouble-settling devices (e.g., "international" versus "municipal" law; or intercorporate law versus corporate directors' rules and other Bylaw within the corporation, such as announced conditions of employment, etc.). It is concerned with the various types of law-stuff which go to make up a complete picture. It is concerned with the need for discrimination in terms of which entirety (social group) provides the context, the order, against which the units concerned work out their relations. Modern trade-usage may be, for instance, law-stuff for the trade and may require to be seen as such, but law-in-court it is not. It works itself into court recognition only as an element of an agreement-in-fact. That needs noting, carefully. Only such careful noting can avoid confusion which will mislead. But worse confusion and worse misleading would be the inevitable outcome if the Bylaw-stuff operating in the trade should be ignored because it does not happen to be Class A Law-stuff for official courts.

This matter of there being diverse and sometimes conflicting levels of control-systems (we should say "law-stuff") within any complex social scheme has been made familiar by contrasts between "law" and "custom" and between "law" and "morals." Without any attempt here to anticipate the general theoretical discussion of Chapters X and XI, it is well to sharpen the connotations of such contrasts by emphasizing two points. The first is again, that what in the official and technical thinking of an official legal scheme is "merely custom," is yet likely to be the controlling bylaw material of some particular subgrouping. What is loosely lumped as "custom" can become very suddenly a meaningful thing—one with edges —if the practices in question can be related to a particular grouping. If they can, then within that grouping, any practices which make for conflict avoidance will commonly be found to have their own "bylaw" sanctions. The anthropologist or sociologist or student of government must reckon with these as being what they are: not "mere" anything, in a particular hierarchical order of official legal thought, but those effective devices of group self-regulation without whose aiding presence the devices of official law would falter and fail.

The second point is that only by inquiry into *whose* practices or *whose* standards of rightness may be concerned in any material labeled "custom" or "morals" does one set the stage for effectively differentiating between matters which a given body of Official Law-stuff leaves, so to speak, to differential "local self-government"—those in which it relies on buttressing parallel pressures from the other systems and levels of control-stuff—and those in which there is cross-purposing (as with the modern legal duty to inform of crime, the friendship and generosity duty to give aid and succor, and the persisting boy-gang *mos* against tattling.)

Thus the subgroup structure of a complex group is likely to be a key not only to matters of responsibility in intergroup relations, or relations between members of different subgroups, but, no less, to the organization of the different levels of law-stuff.

An illustration may properly derive from a contemporary controversial field: labor relations. Prior to the Workmen's Compensation Acts and the Wagner Act, the only high official Law there was dealt rather less with the substance of labor relations than with limitations on the manner of working out such substance. The Workmen's Compensation Acts covered one area of substance; the Social Security Acts have moved further into substance. The Wagner Act has somewhat modified the basis and manner of reaching adjustment on the rest; but for present purposes, it has reached only a single point of substance: it has dictated something as to the type of unit "legally" to be recognized on one side, and something as to the how of organization of such a unit. Now against this, set the picture of the real regulation as it goes on. At one pole is the almost statelike industrial organization achieved by the Amalgamated Clothing Workers with Hart, Schaffner and Marx, with arbitration not a phenomenon of legislative character, but of judicial—not of what is to go into the agreement, by a board chosen for the occasion, but of the agreement itself, by an established board handling cases "under" that agreement. New agreements are worked out in a process reminding one more of partnership than of economic war: "If your economists agree with ours that a reduction of output and a wage-cut is foreshadowed, then it is your responsibility, not ours, to sell that to your People. We will, however, manufacture for losing inventory, if you insist." At the other pole is anathema to any organization, in three phases: the first, the Grand Old Man, with his workers behind him because they and their children love him, and for cause; the second, the employer who brooks no man's interference and consults no man's interest but his own; the third, and definitely tragic, case: the would-be Grand Old Man who goes to his old employee's christenings and thinks he knows "his men," but has acquired a seventy-five per cent roster of South Europeans lacking We-ness with him.

If conduct-regulating machinery in these United States were to be investigated by an ethnologist, that ethnologist would be unwise, in the field of labor relations, to rest content with the Court Law or the statute Law. Whatever the Official level which he might choose, there would be other levels which, in appropriate cases, would need distinguishing and exploration. In the labor relations field, these have, indeed, of very recent years been finding a modicum of official Legal recognition as being effective contract, though contract of a sort which, a generation ago, would have lacked technical enforceability. But it is not that recognition which makes them pertinent.

A second illustration can be brief. Present-day official Law forbids wife-beating and requires support, allows a married woman her own earnings derived from work outside the home, and leaves the husband otherwise in general legal command of the household income. The actual regulation of "the" same household income begins perhaps with the farmer whose wife's "egg money" long ago won official legal recognition. It continues through the papa-and-mama shop where mama works at papa's financial mercy unless he decides to expand "in his wife's name." It passes on into the complex variation of the bourgeois groupings and into the wage-earning household in which practice and decency call for an "unopened" pay envelope to be turned over, with only an allowance to the husband. The quantitative incidence of any of these "patterns" simply is not known. Neither is it yet known how far they *are* patterns, nor what sanctions any of them may have. What can be stated with definiteness is that a canvass of the official Law, alone, would give a silly picture of the going regulation of this phase of our own society. And one can state, with no less definiteness, that the regulation which is now going on does not depend upon the judges' or legislators' officially recognizing the (divergent) "moralities" involved; and that levels of effective normation other than "morals" are plainly in the picture.

Religious "or" Secular Origin

A third point on which there has been unnecessary controversy concerns "the" origin of law as resting in the general secular, the political-secular, or the religious. Legal historians, with a particular eye on Rome, have tended to lay down too flatly "the" origin in religion. An understandable counter-emphasis has tended to insist too flatly upon "the" secular original base of law. The given fact seems to us to be that, as a body of trouble-easing and conduct-channeling devices, law-stuff begins in three things: first, in any *order* which a group may have. "What goes on, what is done," unspecialized and general, is the matrix. Upon this plays, second, the "litigant" individual's action, the experimental, the often unpredictable, the that-which-happens-to-get-done-*this*-time. Third, there is the tendency to cluster further problem solution around any machinery or competing bodies of machinery which happen to have arisen anywhere in the culture, for that purpose. We deny any exclusive, single line of origin, on the evidence. We deny any exclusive, single sequence of development, on the evidence and on the probabilities. Indeed, we put forward as highly probable the thesis that any existing institution or recognized personnel which once begins to acquire authority of a character capable of extension into the legal field is likely to attempt such extension or have claimants attempt it. In this the legal differs in no wise from the governmental. In both the impulse to harness the force of the Whole, in order to serve particular interest, is recurrent.

Now to the evidence. We have denied any exclusive and single line of origin of law-stuff. The report from the Hopland Pomo,[6] which Dr. Bert Aginsky has been good enough to give us in conversation, will serve as a base line. He gives, first, a picture of secret sorcery, accompanied by overwhelming fear. One of the writers (Llewellyn) was sitting in on Aginsky's field work when an informant—who had "adopted" Aginsky—flatly broke off a discussion of sorcery because another Pomo (a friend, too) had appeared within earshot. There is secret vengeance-sorcery; there is secret hit-him-first sorcery; there is secret sorcery in vindication of one's own rejected aggression; and there is secret sorcery so complicated in its alleged motivations as to leave the observer as bewildered as the "objects" of it were dismayed. But side by side with this cloud of uncertain horror go three other things, in Hopland Pomo, as Aginsky carefully reports. The first is that sorcery is not centralized. And up to the present day, no machinery for organizing the supernatural into the sole legal structure has worked out. It could have, but it did not. What would have been needed was the man to put over his position as an avowed "poison-doctor," starting a trade, a guild, a blackmail, and a system. But an alternative to sorcery which Aginsky reports is a recurrent sequence of self-help, of personal, secular action in redress. Highly developed, this was not; in embryo (or better, in a succession of eggs laid for possible hatching) it was and remained present. Still a third alternative present is intervention by "the civil authority." In one aspect, he appears as

[6] These are the Pomo Indians of Hopland, California, studied by Dr. Aginsky.

peacemaker: "When you fight thus, it is not you who are struck; it is I." But in another, he appears as the seizer of initiative and the organizer of a governmental move. Six young men who have become unbearable are, on the chief's initiative, bidden (if not ridden) out of camp forever.

All of these lines for possible development sit thus side by side in a culture still in process of gaining a definitive legal form. Who shall say whether a dominant chief was to come along, or a dominant and aggressive self-helper (one man even is recorded as having gone successfully after a poison-doctor) or a dominant poison-doctor, and so to throw the three or four latently possible lines of given legal growth into a single one? It is against such a scene as Aginsky's groping Pomo that one must see Gutmann's Chagga. There the civil authority has achieved the upper hand and can put sorcery remedy under severe control. Or compare with ancient Rome, where the semi-miracle of correct decision had gravitated (not without secular influence) into the hands of a priesthood manned by the sound, old families. Or consider Homeric Greece, where the old men and the oracle seem to have continued side by side for some time as judgment-givers, and successful self-help remained also one way out. We entirely concur in the feeling of the modern writers that too much stress has been laid on supernatural, religious, and sorcerous sanctions in primitive law. We concur especially in the feeling that use of these sanctions is peculiarly likely to be filling a gap in the work of secular legal devices, especially in resolving those doubts on secret facts which so bother a close-knit community. We do not at all concur in any suggestion that the supernatural aspect of the matter can be belittled or can be regarded merely, or a priori, as a late priestly intrusion.[7] Nor must it be forgotten that even in our own culture any effective organ of judicature and the Whole System of the Law, still have and hold

[7] See the conclusions of Arthur Sigismund Diamond, *Primitive Law* (London, Longmans, Green & Co., 1935). Diamond's code materials derive from too advanced a stage for persuasiveness concerning his basic contention on this point. His more directly ethnological material is handled in breadth too sweeping to be meaningful. The test lies in the fuller and more careful monographs.

a mystic flavor in the public mind. In a religious context, this would mean a religious flavor.

The Cheyenne cases also make obvious the need for rejecting any hypothesis which too much belittles the religious in law's possible origin. Cheyenne homicide law must be regarded as most anciently affected by the supernatural from the time of its recognition by the tribe. And every indication is that the secular aspect moved into the later forefront largely because of the existence of secular administrative machinery. On the other hand, Cheyenne law on theft is as clearly a secular growth as one could find—yet even there dreams were used for detection. Adultery, rejection of a sister's accepted husband as one's own husband, and perhaps even elopement of a wife, present a less clear picture, secular in appearance, but with the practice of "putting a woman on the prairie" offering some suggestion of possible older supernatural influence.[8]

It is not necessary to solve this particular insoluble problem. It is enough that cheek by jowl in a single culture sit supernatural-based and secular-based elements of the law. The urge of law-stuff into the hands of political authority is enough to explain rapid secularization or the development of the original secular element, if it ever gets under way. The drive of any institutionalized personnel for power is enough to explain an important supervening religious influence, if ever the relevant personnel both have the vision and acquire the opportunity.

We thus find insufficiency and difficulty in the concept of a single-line and inevitable sequence. Rather do the buddings which work out into law-stuff seem capable of emerging in any of the sequences, or all together. Lines which in due course both indicate and limit proper redress may develop out of mere incident, memory, and repetition. The Comanche material carries a definite flavor of an unmentioned, vaguish standard beyond which a husband really has no business to go, in dealing with an eloping couple.[9] It carries also, especially when contrasted with the relatively formless incidents from the related Shoshone,[10] a sufficient variety of ways of

---

[8] See pages 202 ff.
[9] Hoebel, *Political Organization . . . of the Comanche Indians,* 49 f., 96-103.
[10] *Ibid.,* 135-42.

proceeding to make clear that patterns of redress-procedure were still in process of formation and crystallization and to make probable that some one (or some set) of them would in a hundred years have worked its way into more definitely "prevailing" character. Gillen's cases from the Barama River Carib[11] look on the surface like nothing but a fight, when a wife's lover came to be detected. Yet it is very queer, if that be the whole story, that husbands are not reported getting hurt in such fights, whereas lovers are. One cannot help querying whether such "mere" fight may not be working out into a pattern in which it is the lover's part to limit himself to saving his own skin. Certainly in other cultures the fight has come under all kinds of regulation, from a requirement of notice before attack, or a regulation against certain lines of combat (e.g., house-burning), or a handicapping of the causer of the grievance, to the near-ritualization of even group combat. In none of these cases does the driving formative factor appear to have been with any regularity either secular authority or any variety of the supernatural; secular the procedures are, indeed, but specialized secular practice rather than an offshoot of secular government. On the other hand, for example, the Ifugao custom of wrestling duel-and-ordeal for boundary-marking has all the appearance of a precisely parallel development, with a good bit of supernatural tinge thrown in.[12] Finally, and in terms of the attitudes of the participants, what we call "secular" and what we call "supernatural" have their own ways of flowing into each other—as when an "ordeal" by champions staying under water finds friends at hand to literally roast a champion back to consciousness and "supernatural" victory.

In a word, not only multiple schemes of normation grow in a culture, both within groups and across groups and from mere manners on through to what one conceives as law, but law itself may grow up in complementary or rival systems, each clustered around

[11] Gillin, "Crime and Punishment Among the Barama River Carib," 331-44.

[12] Roy Franklin Barton, *Ifugao Law* (University of California Publications in American Archæology and Ethnology, Volume 15, 1919), 1-127. Ifugao law presents buddings from almost all conceivable roots, including even the semi-professional mediator who is not otherwise a political authority.

such own machinery as may be its root, or organ, or both. There will develop then nice questions as to which system of law-stuff a litigant can wangle himself into or under, making careful anticipatory weighing of the advantages to himself. Such a jurisdictional scheme any central political authority will proceed to remodel to its own interest, as the English kings did, and as can be followed in the works of Gutmann[13] and Rattray.[14] One of the things which lends to both Malinowski's study of the Trobriands[15] and Barton's first monograph on the Ifugao[16] a surface confusion which the material internally denies is that this problem of jurisdiction among the various coexistent, and often essentially competing, legal schemes is not brought into deliberate focus. *What is clear is that one has no business expecting of any primitive culture that its law shall have achieved the official and doctrinal unity allegedly found in the modern state.* But by the same token, it pays then to take a fresh look at the modern state and so to discover how artificial, how well confined to the world of paper doctrine and to the particular forum of the official courts is this same official and doctrinal unity of law. For that unity is achieved and achievable even in doctrinal theory only by excluding from consideration all the law-stuff of the culture except that most formally centered in court and statute. Today, for instance, administrative regulation presents a difficult technical legal problem precisely because it is so like official law as to cry for attention together with it, yet it finds no comfortable pigeonhole in the orthodox conceptual scheme which has been built without thought to its emergence. Who, for that matter, would attempt to integrate into the doctrinal unity of law the effective work done daily in a well-handled juvenile court?

This same matter of multiple budding leads to a further observation which the American official regime of precedent tends to obscure, and which the older emphasis of the social disciplines upon

[13] Gutmann, *Das Recht der Dschagga.*

[14] Robert Sutherland Rattray, *Ashanti Law and Constitution* (Oxford, The Clarendon Press, 1929).

[15] Branislaw Malinowski, *Crime and Custom in Savage Society* (London & New York, Harcourt, Brace & Co., 1926). Contrast the later study of Hogbin, under Malinowski's aegis.

[16] This is corrected in *The Half-Way Sun* (New York, Brewster and Warren, 1932).

"patterns" and "institutions" also tended to hide. We refer to the phenomenon of the unsuccessful precedent, and of the tendency or urge which does *not* develop. An admirable instance from the Cheyenne will be recalled in the use of the pipe in settlement, with its magnificent possibilities both of working adjustment and of the relevant chief's influence upon what it would be proper to do. Such a device has in it, in germ, everything up to and including deliberative consultation of all the chiefs before one of them would undertake a mission, and up to becoming the exclusively available device. Not only is it found that neither of these possibilities was developed, but our judgment is that their development would have been most unlikely. The growth bud had shifted to the military societies; in addition, the self-dramatizing career patterns of the Cheyenne stood across the path.

It is thus of fundamental importance, in the emergence of legal institutions, to be on the lookout for the reasons for non-recurrence of an incident, for non-establishment of an incident as a precedent, for variation upon, instead of the following of any one emerging possible pattern. This is peculiarly true in regard to law-ways. The dramatic and memorable character of the trouble-case, the manner in which an issue shapes, draws into itself, and is then reshaped by, the particular personalities concerned as wholes and the latent strains or tensions in the culture—these give to the trouble-case a peculiar possibility of making patterns with speed. Whereas in other matters one may say that the emergence of a pattern calls for explanation, in the handling of trouble-cases it is almost as if the non-emergence is what requires understanding. And we suggest that no body of material sheds more revealing light upon man's practices of generalization. The trouble-case, with its aspects of normation and legality, is indeed perhaps the most potent stimulus to generalization known to culture. The question becomes then, first, whether it will be generalized; and second, how it will be generalized. It is in the matter of the *how* that the juristic flavor of the culture will reveal itself. Legalism builds upon generalization (and distinction) undertaken in terms of unmistakable, but non-significant, external marks. Juristic beauty builds upon generalization (and distinction) undertaken in terms of function and significant reason. This holds, whether the law-stuff be cast into elaborated verbal form, or not. It goes, however, not primarily to the verbal forms, if forms there be; it goes much more deeply to the use of them—to the nature of the juristic method.

Juristic method itself lies partly in personal artistry, but it lies more in transmissible, but often unspoken, practices and norms for practice. The pieces of it which are concerned directly with the mechanics of handling of legal doctrine are commonly not the major part of it; "legal tact," for instance, which rarely is taught directly, is more important. And as one turns back to modern law-stuff from the primitive, the question which rises is: How much more is there of this unspoken, primitive stuff within the very gears of our own elaborated legal scheme itself—supplying oil, and it may be supplying fuel, and even direction, as well? The reference here is not to the law-stuff of our society outside the official legal system of the state—of which, as has been seen, there is enough in all conscience. Rather, it is to the official legal system itself. We have in mind such things as the amazement of Cardozo at discovering that when, after years on the Court of Appeals, he came to sit as chief, his voice in consultation had suddenly acquired treble weight,[17] although in law the judge's vote is nose-counted—one judge, one vote. We have in mind the effects on a court of a severe damper on dissenting opinions, by the chief or by the tradition of that court; or of a regime wherein the chief assigns the cases and can build a quasi-party within the court by manipulation of the reputation-making opinions and can flavor the law which is to be, by his allocation of the drafting of its statement or restatement in opinions. We have in mind the difference between a court in which each judge prepares a memorandum, and one in which only one judge works up the case. We have in mind the effect and effectiveness of a solicitor general who makes himself in truth an officer of the court and argues cases which should be lost, in a manner to lose them, gaining thereby threefold power for his argument in cases

[17] Cardozo to Llewellyn, in conversation.

which need winning. We have in mind also the whole range of those creative and shaping factors which rest in the *crafts* of law-work, coloring, infusing meaning into, doctrine and its operation.

If the study of primitive law-stuff can open eyes and minds to such things and help men to see them as needing study, to see them as something which is as much and as necessary a part of a modern legal system as are courts and rules of law themselves; if it can help men to come to manage and to use them effectively and not by chance, then modern law can well be grateful to the primitive.

Such is a first indication of the background of general thinking against which we have sought to set the law-ways of the Cheyenne; further treatment of general theory appears in Part III. But we have striven to let the Cheyenne material appear also in its own form, with its own flavor, distinguishable always from our interpretation.

PART II

Cheyenne Law-Ways

Chapter IV

THE COUNCIL OF FORTY-FOUR

ONE reputed trait in the polity of the Plains Indians is its amorphous character. But in this thinking the category "Plains" is taken too broadly. If one takes the Plains in terms of the Comanches,[1] or even the Crows, then the formlessness of government may be marked indeed. This is not so, however, if such a tribe as the Cheyenne is under consideration, for the Cheyennes as a tribal unit possessed a governmental organization with delegated functionaries of two orders: the tribal chiefs who made up the Council of Forty-Four, and the military societies. The Council of Forty-Four formed the formal façade of government in the tribal constitution, and had real powers. The military societies were in a theoretically subordinate position. But, as is so often the case with political and social institutions, the operating powers of civil and military units of the government abetted and over-lapped each other to such a degree in practice that the reality did not wholly conform to the Cheyennes' "legal" theory of the relationships.

As a political and legal force the Council appears to have crystal-lized some time before the military societies began to function as important agents of social action. The reasons for this impression will become clear to the reader as the materials of this and succeed-ing chapters unfold. It is still clearer, however, that the military societies were becoming more and more potent as lawmaking and law administering powers during the period of the last century which is covered by the time span of the present data.

Cheyenne legend has it that the state organization of the Chey-ennes was due to the work of a woman. Myth as historical

---

[1] For comparison, see Hoebel, *Political Organization . . . of the Comanche Indians*.

"evidence" is not sound, since primitives have a way of erasing the uncertainty of unknown origins by an act of fiction which, when hailed as truth, gives sanctity to prevailing mores. Civilized men are not innocent, either, as the critically disposed have vaguely felt, and as Frazer in his *Folklore in the Old Testament* has shown for modern religious mythology, while Thurman Arnold has turned the same leaf for American economic myths with the sounder portions of his *Folklore of Capitalism*.[2] And while the migration legends of the Cheyennes can be substantiated by historical and archeological fact,[3] the tales accounting for the origin of the chiefs enjoy no such buttressing. Nor can they even lay claim to plausibility; they remain pure mythology.

James Mooney tells in his brief monograph based on data recorded from the Southern Cheyenne that a captive maiden showed the Cheyennes the manner of chiefs in her tribe and that the Cheyennes followed the pattern she described to them. Mooney was willing to accept this story as fact, hazarding a guess in which he put 1750 A.D. as the approximate date of the inauguration of the council system.[4] George Bird Grinnell gives a version in which a Cheyenne maiden is captured by the Assiniboines, with whom she lives for a number of years. At last, upon making her escape, she returns to the Cheyennes to impress upon them the effectiveness of the Assiniboine system of chieftainship. So well does she impress them that the Cheyennes forthwith adopt the Assiniboine system.[5] But alas for fact, there is no evidence that the Assiniboines ever had such a system of chiefs as this Cheyenne legend ascribes to them.

From Black Wolf comes yet another version which turns on the far-flung and only half-Cheyenne theme of deserted children who even in their revenge upon their faithless parent embody the hope

[2] Sir James George Frazer, *Folklore in the Old Testament* (abridged edition, New York, The Macmillan Co., 1923) ; Thurman Arnold, *The Folklore of Capitalism* (New Haven, Yale University Press, 1937).

[3] See especially George Bird Grinnell, *The Cheyenne Indians* (2 volumes, New Haven, Yale University Press, 1923), I, 1-146.

[4] James Mooney, *The Cheyenne Indians (Memoirs of the American Anthropological Association*, Volume I, Part 6, 1907), 357-99.

[5] Grinnell, *The Cheyenne Indians*, I, 345 f.

of youth for solution of men's problems. It is presented here in all its rich literary and psychological detail.

« « « I once asked Elk River, when he was an old man, about that question. "Now we have chiefs," I said to him. "I wonder how we got those chiefs. Can you tell me? And how did we come to get the law against killing our own people?" This was many years ago and there were many people in the lodge when Elk River gave his reply.

"Yes," Elk River answered, "that was a long time ago, many years before our time, that this thing of which I shall tell took place."

This is what Elk River told.

People used to wander about the country in those days. There was one old man among them who took his family away from the main band to camp out alone. He stayed out here with them—his wife, his daughter, and a small son—for a long time, until one day he killed his wife and deserted his motherless children.

The orphan children wandered alone about the countryside seeking their tribesmen and shelter. At last they spied the main camp of their people in the distance. The first lodge they came to was that of an old woman of whom they asked news of their father. The old woman did not answer, but went to the lodge of an old man who was a camp crier to tell him that the children of Bull Looks Back had returned to the camp seeking after their father. This old man went out and announced the news to all the camp.

Bull Looks Back was right there among the people. When he heard the news he ran crying to the announcer, "Those monstrous children of mine killed their own mother out there and have eaten her flesh. That is why I left them. Tell the people that even though they are my own offspring, I say they should be staked to the ground and abandoned." [This is our only Cheyenne reference to cannibalism. This dispute of fact is "decided" without notice, hearing, or comment, and the "decision" turns sour. Is there, in what ensues, a legal moral? None is mentioned; but the culture moves as if there had been one.]

The camp crier[6] repeated all that Bull Looks Back had said. "In the morning we must tie them to the ground and move camp as early as we can. We must not leave a living thing with them, not even dogs."

That night the people prepared green rawhide in rope lengths. The next morning they tied the boy and the girl to stakes driven in the ground and waited, sitting watching, until the thongs had shrunken tight and firm. Then the camp was moved.

[At this point the train of the narrative was broken when Black Wolf was asked whether a soldier society had carried out the deed. In response he gave the polite rebuke, "No, I asked Elk River that same question. 'I am telling the story,' he said. 'I'll come to that.' "]

There was one great, black dog. Maybe it had pups. At any rate, it had packed some stuff, meat and sinew, into a hole near the camp site. Toward evening the hapless siblings saw the dog coming up to them. It wriggled and scratched as a dog does and then went right to work chewing on the rope which bound the girl's wrists until they came free. The girl then untied her brother. They followed the dog to its hole in the creek bank, where it crawled in, and when it came out again it was dragging dried meat and some tools. They all ate and sat there.

During the night someone walked up to them, but the sister did not look up, for her head was hung in sorrow. This person addressed her little brother.

"Over there you will see a wikiup and an arbor. Go to it!"

"Sister," the little boy cried, "look over there!"

"It will do me no good to look," she murmured. "They have been telling lies about us. This person has not come here to speak the truth."

"Look anyhow," the boy insisted.

So she raised her head, and she saw it was true.

Then the stranger spoke again, "In the morning—at daylight—a herd of buffalo will come. Have your sister look at them."

---

[6] "Crying" to the camp was an official job, with edges of authority not too clearly marked. This tale suggests the degree of influence of a crier, in determining substance and tone of his announcement.

At daylight the buffalo came as the stranger had said. "My sister, look on those buffalo," the boy cried in delight.

"That herd won't die if I do look at them," she morosely replied.

Even so, she had medicine power from the man who had been there, though she did not know it. She looked, and at her glance all the buffalo fell dead! After that the boy and girl went to the wikiup.

A bear and a mountain lion were living there. Three beds were made up in the hut, so the boy and girl took the extra one.

Again the strange visitor appeared before the outcasts. He spoke to the boy as before. "Tell your sister she must butcher all those buffalo. She must look after all the meat and take care of all the fat. A big crow will come to one of these trees. When she has done her butchering she must put some kidney fat in the branches for it. That will be on the third day."

In the end, when the girl had finished her butchering, a crow flew down and looked at them. The sister spoke to it, because she now believed in the stranger. "Here, come get this fat. Fly with it straight to our people's camp. Fly right through the opening [in the camp circle]. Fly low about the circle. Then drop this in the center before the lodges. Tell those people it is from the children they left on the prairie to die."

When the people saw this, and understood the crow to mean that the two children had plenty of meat, they made ready to move the camp back to them, because they had been unable to find game for some time. [This is straight Cheyenne: a sign, in time of trouble.]

The boy and girl heard a man come singing. He was singing Elk songs.

"That is my father," the girl told the lion and the bear. "Do not harm him until he has eaten, but when he leaves this lodge, take him."

When the father came in, he was given the place at the back of the lodge. The girl sent word to the approaching people not to move in too close to her.

"I shall see you tomorrow," was her order.

When her father finished eating, the lion and the bear killed him for her.

She now sent for the men, and the women too, because she had cooked up a lot of food. When they had eaten she spoke to the men.

"Tomorrow you move down on this flat and put yourselves in a nice circle. We are going to make chiefs. You people know I have been accused of killing my mother. That is not true. Now, however, I have killed my father through animals. We shall make chiefs, and hereafter we shall make a rule that if anyone kills a fellow tribesman he shall be ordered out of the camp for from one to five years. Whatever the people decide."

When they had arranged the camp circle they took two big lodges and made one in the center. She asked them to move five other tipis into the space within the circle. These were put in the medicine wheel arrangement. When everything was finished she packed a large bundle and walked around the circle to enter it before the big lodge. First, she took some dirt from the north side of the lodge. Carefully patting it she arranged it in a mound in the center of a cleared space. It represented the world. Next she set up five sticks representing the men she would choose as head chiefs. She filled her pipe. She held it to each stick, showing the people what would be expected of them.

"You will have to swear," she said. "You will have to take an oath that you will be honest and care for all the tribe."

Following the instructions she gave out, her brother purified himself in the smudge of the sweet medicine grass. Now she told him to go out to walk four times around the camp.

"When you go out you have a starting place. Go around until you come back to it. Do this four times," she ordered.

He had already been told what men to select. After the four circumambulations he sought out the first man, leading him into the lodge. Then the other four were brought in like manner.

When they were seated the sister told them everything. She had all she needed in that bundle. She told them she was going to make them chiefs to rule the camp. And this is what she said.

"You have seen me put up five sticks here. You shall have to do this to the others who come after you. Now you five men are to be the chiefs of the entire tribe. You must rule the people. When the tribe comes to renew the chiefs you must put up these five sticks again. If anyone of you still lives, and the people want him again, then you must call him in to take his old place."

Now she has finished telling them. [Changes of tense are the narrator's.] She is going to swear them in. She is holding the pipe herself, in both hands with the stem out. They smoked. The pipe is smoked for peace. That was done so that if some persons ever used strong words to the chiefs, they would have strong hearts and not get angry. The sweet grass was used on all of them.

Then the big crowd came in. Enough more were in the lodge to make forty-four men. She did the same to each of the rest of them. When this was done she told them to pick two men to sit on each side of the entrance.

"Some day you will have a lodge of your own," she informed them. "Then you can use these two. They can cook for you, or you can send them out on errands. They shall be your servants and messengers."

These two could not be of the five.

"Every ten years you must renew the chiefs. But each time keep five of the old ones," the maid continued.

She had a parfleche for the stuff they used in the ritual.

"When you move camp," she exhorted them in closing, "keep out in front of the people. Stop and rest four times with it [the chiefs' bundle] on the way.

That is the way they came to have chiefs. There were a big bunch of people in the lodge when Elk River told this a long time ago.   »   »   »

The Cheyenne chief was thus not just a fine old man who got that way because everybody respected his wisdom and loved his genuine geniality. He was a mature man, yet vigorous, who had been appointed to his station because he approached the ideal qualities of leadership—wisdom, courage, kindness, generosity, and even temper. His chieftainship had a definite beginning and a definite ending. There was form to Cheyenne society.

The Council of Forty-Four was a self-perpetuating body of

tribal trustees; each chose his own successor. Each generation saw a double turnover of the Council, tenure of chieftainship being ten years. In the winter of each tenth year, word was passed among the bands that there would be a chief-renewal the coming spring. The chiefs themselves had declared the rendezvous. As the snows melted and game again was plentiful, all the Cheyennes from the far-flung territories began their annual drifting together. Within a few weeks, band after band converged; there was the great ingathering. Each group came marching or riding into the camp, whooping, shouting, and singing as they circled the lodges, while those already there cheered and applauded. The groups arranged their lodges in a large circle by bands, each in a traditional position.[7] (It is to be remembered that through the fall, winter, and early spring months the Cheyennes, like the other nomadic Plains tribes, lived in widely separated bands. Though the authority of chiefs of the Council carried over into the band camps, the structure described at the moment applies to the summer organization of the society primarily, for this was the only season during which the whole, or most of the tribe, could risk living together. Concentration lacked economic base, in winter. Whether it would have resulted, if economically possible, there is no means of knowing.)

The cleared space in the center was a good mile across, and when all the Cheyennes were present, there were five or six hundred lodges, each facing east. The circle itself was a symbolic tipi with the open door to the rising sun. When all was ready, a huge chiefs' lodge of double size was raised in the very center of the circle. To this all those who survived of the forty-four repaired. They sat in the order their bands had taken outside in the great camp circle.

The ritual of renewal of the chiefs was an event of great sacredness, the ceremony being connected in all its phases with Sweet Medicine and with the supernaturalism of Cheyenne cosmology. It was under the direction of the five priestly chiefs who served as the head chiefs of the tribe.

For the supreme order within the Council was that of the five sacerdotal chiefs, commonly called the head chiefs. These sanctified

[7] Grinnell, *The Cheyenne Indians*, I, 88 ff.

ones served in both a political and a religious capacity to the tribe. Chief among them was the one representing Sweet Medicine (referred to by Dorsey[8] as the Prophet). He manipulated the medicines of the chiefs' bundle and presided at meetings of the Council. Though looked upon as the most holy man in the tribe, he reputedly had no consequent special political authority. The Sweet Medicine chief was symbolically associated with the center of all directions —the heart of the world. The others, according to Dorsey's report, included an accomplished shaman, who had served as a Sun Dance priest, and a priest who had functioned in the Massaum ceremony.[9] This does not complete the roster, however, for Black Wolf and others of the Northern Cheyenne informants were adamant in their insistence that there were four priest-chiefs in addition to the Sweet Medicine Man—a total of five sacerdotal dignitaries. These were detailed as the Crazy Lodge (Massaum) priest, who sat in a position at the southeast portion of the lodge, where he was vaguely associated with the Spirit Who Rules the Summer; the Wolf Cub Man (i.e., a priest who had performed the Wolf Cub Ceremony), who sat on the southwest side and was linked to the Spirit Who Rules the Ages; the priest called *na'oeta* (untranslatable), who sat on the northwest side and was associated with the Spirit Who Gives Good Health; and the Crooked Pipe Man, who sat at the northeast, symbolic of the northern lights—Where the Food Comes From, the spiritual home of the Big Holy Ones, the mythological teachers of the Cheyennes.

Of a lower rank, but still higher than the great body of the Council, were the two door men, or Servants. The remaining thirty-seven of the Council were undifferentiated among themselves in the matter of their formal, as distinct from personal, status within the Council.

When a priest-chief had lived out his term, he chose his own successor from among the retiring forty. Should a priest-chief have

[8] George Amos Dorsey, *The Cheyenne* (2 volumes, Field Columbian Museum Publications, 99, 103, Anthropological Series, Volume IX, numbers 1-2, 1905) ; Part I: *Ceremonial Organization;* Part II: *The Sun Dance.*

[9] Variously called Crazy Dance, Animal Dance, and Buffalo Dance. A fine description and interpretation of this ceremonial is given in Grinnell, *The Cheyenne Indians,* II, 285-336.

died during his incumbency, then the remaining chiefs of the priestly grade talked long over the one they would choose as his successor. A priest-chief not yet senile could step down to a lower rank of chieftainship when his term was up. Brave Wolf spoke to the Council at the last renewal in 1892 telling them how he had served the people, how he had been through many ceremonies for them, how he now wanted to step down from his office. The Council agreed; one of the retiring ordinary chiefs gave him his place. This was "holding him in the lodge." When the Massaum priest who sat in the southeast position stepped down to take a place on the north side of the lodge, an old man prayed to the sun for him asking forgiveness for his sin, for "forgetting that he represented that territory."

It is said to have been a regularly observed rule that one member of the Council of chiefs was always an alien Indian—notably, a Dakota. Today the Cheyennes have no explanation to offer for this rule. It is possible that the principle is derived from the inclusion of Those Who Eat With The Sioux among the Cheyenne bands, thus serving as a constitutional measure guaranteeing formal governmental representation to the Cheyenne-Sioux.

When the choosing of successors was over and the four days and nights of ritual in the chiefs' lodge were done, there was much gift-giving and celebration throughout the camp. The poor profited handsomely, because it was an esteemed gesture to give horses and robes, or whatever else of value to any person, especially the poor.

Immediately after the inauguration, the camp was also busy with ritual scenes of "payments" by the newly installed chieftains to their predecessors. For it was expected that each newly installed incumbent "paid" his nominator an equivalent in gifts to what the retiring chief had paid his predecessor.

Calf Woman reports having had a (very dubious) hand in one of these doings in the last chief-renewal, on the Reservation. Little Wolf had sent for Sun Road, Calf Woman's husband. The men were remotely related, both Sutai.[10] Little Wolf, as the sponsor, gave instructions. He told Sun Road to lay a fire in the center of the camp

10 Sutai: a formerly alien, but cognate, tribe, incorporated in the Cheyennes.

circle. Because the camp was not in a circle as it should be on ceremonial occasions, he said, "We'll just take this spot, and say it is the center." [Inventiveness and legal fiction are not limited to conscious jurisprudence.] Four pieces of calico were laid radiating out from the fire to the cardinal directions [this was the ceremonial number four and the sacred cross]. A plug of tobacco was placed by the fire, and two gift horses were staked nearby. Only men were supposed to carry out the preparations, but Calf Woman put a finger in it. Then said Little Wolf (allegedly) to Sun Road,

"You are supposed to make it, but she helped. Now we will have to include her."

Wherewith Calf Woman gave two horses of her own and became what she calls "chief's wife."[11] Sun Road's daughter, to honor her father, also added a horse.[12] Thus the "payment" was raised to five, which would have been the minimum sum for Sun Road's successor, had they ever again renewed the Council.

When the new chiefs had finished these "payments," there followed the inaugural ball, the Chief Dance. All the chiefs had to be there, old and new alike. To start it a holy song was sung; then a single brave was called forth to dance—a man of proven bravery. When he had finished his steps, he recited all his coups, ending his recital with a proclamation to the chiefs, "As I have done it, so must you protect the people." The whole tribe rose in a shrill chorus of praise, whereupon they all danced together. After four dances the pipe was filled for all the chiefs to smoke, the old and the new.

Then a second warrior was asked to recount his coups and dance. This was one who had saved a comrade whose horse had been shot from under him. Right then relatives of the new chiefs would come

[11] Probably not a regular Cheyenne form. This, so far as can be ascertained, is most likely an invention of Calf Woman's. Her later information disclosed no knowledge of what went on in the council.

[12] At this point in the recording, the daughter, now a woman of sixty, who was standing to one side, burst into loud words of anger. Calf Woman is a garrulous hag of eighty-six and wholly without sensitivities. She is a big boaster where her self is concerned, a mine of information, but one which needs checking on some points. So hot was her comeback to the daughter that the interview had to be stopped for a cooling-off. The interviewers were disturbed because they were afraid the daughter was accusing her mother of lying. It turned out, however, that the daughter had vowed at her father's death never again, out of respect, to speak of him. Her feelings were hurt by having this incident described in her presence.

in to give away horses. The people praised the dancer's deeds, and themselves took to dancing again. This cycle was repeated four times; then followed a great feast between the old and the new chiefs, waited upon by the two new doormen.

Because each chief was a dominant figure in the family groups which made up the Cheyenne bands, the chiefs were in effect public opinion itself. They were inclined as well to listen to the opinions of the women—via their wives. The female influence, however, was informal. It is a bit of a stretch to state as does Grinnell that, "Women are the rulers of the camp."[13] Yet it is clear that their position was not without power.

A nice balance of stability and vigor resided also in the structure of the Council. The decennial turnover prevented oligarchical permanence; the discouragement of sons as successors must be taken to have worked in the same direction.[14] The carry-over of the five priest-chiefs from the preceding Council gave a continuity and a gentle aura of supernatural sanctity to the functioning of this governing body. Since there were never more than four thousand Cheyennes at most, there must have been a representative on the Council for every one hundred persons or fewer. Contact could not help but be rather direct, in general. And, as the cases show, it was carefully implemented, on crucial occasion.

Beyond his official duties the tribal chief was expected to be an exemplar of good conduct, as was usual for Plains peace chiefs. No standard for conduct is more clearly fixed than that the chief must not be angry—that he must be aloof from personal irritation. It was only when a chief had been four times wronged by the same person that he is said to have been free justifiably to climb off his pedestal of virtue to act. But no chief within present memory was ever so provoked.

[13] Grinnell, *The Cheyenne Indians,* I, 128.
[14] A retiring chief might or might not choose his own son as his successor. Though Grinnell explicitly states that retiring dignitaries often chose their sons as successors, citing the instance of Bull Hump, who declined his father's nomination of himself in 1883 on the grounds that chiefs were no longer needed (Grinnell, *ibid.,* I, 341), some of the informants declared it was contrary to good form for a chief to name his own son. It seems more probable that Bull Hump was conserving the accepted decencies even against his interests, his father, and the people, who wanted him in his father's place. Later, indeed, Bull Hump became a chief, but not as his father's successor.

The tradition of good behavior required of chiefs caused some men, not sure of their tempers, to reject the office. Thus when Little Wolf offered Sun Road the chiefs' medicine in 1892, he refused, according to Calf Woman, in these inelegant words:

"When a dog is running after a bitch in heat—if my wife is chased by another man, I might weaken and open my mouth. Then it would be well if another had the medicine and not I." Though this reason is plausible in a Cheyenne context, it is in this case an excuse to cover the real reason, which lay in the pollution of the medicine by Little Wolf's killing of Starving Elk (see page 183 f.).

A chief who was sore beset was wont to seize his pipe to smoke and renew his pledge not to speak harsh words. A head chief who weakened would be despised by the people, it is said. The check was effective, if the almost entire lack of cases of transgression is an indication.

Further, the chief was expected to be a paragon of generosity. Whatever was asked for or hinted after he was expected to bestow as a gift. It was greatly to his honor if he succored the poor as did High Backed Wolf so handsomely in the case of Pawnee (CASE 2). Now that white civilization has taught the lesson of greed, some Cheyennes hang back from the possibility of chieftainship, because they feel the chief's obligations are too great an imposition upon their possessions.

Should a chief of the Forty-Four fall short of the standards of his office, he was still unimpeachable. Tenure of office was not to be abridged. This put the tribal chiefs in special and favored positions, for soldier chiefs, the Sacred-Hat Keeper and the Arrow-Keeper were all impeachable, as cases show. But the enunciated principle is that a tribal chief could not be deposed, no matter what his conduct might turn out to be—a pretty instance of law, coupled with reliance on extra-legal restraint, but working itself out still as Law, if ever the social and extra-legal safeguards failed. There is a "case" in antiquity given by Calf Woman to substantiate the generalization. It has the flavor of accuracy in essence, despite one's doubts as to many details.

《   《   《   This happened so far in the past, I can hardly
remember of it. My grandmother told me this thing happened when
I was only three years old (1855). One of our chiefs killed a man. I
do not remember why, nor can I recall his name. But it happened.

The people talked against him. "We will take him out of his
place," they said.

That is what they wanted to do. But the Indian law stopped it.
Even so, the chief and his wife and children were banished from the
camp. [We read this as meaning: they went with him, as of course;
not by *legal* compulsion.] But he was still chief, though all by
himself.

One day his wife came poking her way into the main camp to
plead with the soldier chiefs. "We're in pretty bad shape out there,"
she told them. "There is no game, no food. My poor children are
starved to skinny bones. Pray have pity on us, you warriors. Take
pity on me and my children, I beg you and your children, your
mothers and your fathers, all. Forgive and forget! Let us come
back!"

The soldier chiefs heard her words. They all called meetings of
their troops. The Foxes, the Dogs, the Shields, the Elks, and all the
others—each met in their chiefs' lodges to consider this thing.
They were all meeting separately to decide what they thought about
it. Still, none of them could come to a decision. They did not send
her away, however. They told her to bide in the camp until the
morrow. Then they would take it up once more.

That next day they had a big meeting of the tribal chiefs, the
soldier chiefs, and all the warriors in conclave. Some man (I don't
know who) talked for them. He said this thing, "It is enough. They
have been away two years now. He is one of our chiefs. Let us
permit them to return."

All agreed that he had said the right thing.

The people made a little collection of food then, and other
things. They gave these to the woman, and told her to go home and
wait. Two days later the people went out with food and clothing to
find them. An emissary was sent to the chief from the big council
to bid him come in. This chief had been mean and quick-tempered,

so the emissary spoke to him in this way, "Now you are coming back. The people ask of you only that you be temperate and good. You may move right in."

He changed his ways after that. Did he give presents to the relatives of the man he had murdered in order to keep them quiet? Well, maybe, but I don't remember. He didn't have to, though, because the soldiers had given him an awful pounding at the time of the murder. He was still a chief, too. He had his position in the chiefs' lodge, and he used it; he had a right to talk, and he did so.   »   »   »

Except for the matter of the soldiers' having given this man "an awful pounding at the time of the murder," and for the meeting of all, *together,* (which sounds to us like dramatic heightening of an event concededly not remembered with accuracy), this case matches the other material point for point, though it may be fiction. What ultimately follows in the train of this beating—Calf Woman equates a pounding by the soldiers to satisfaction of the murdered man's relatives—sheds light on the degree to which in her eyes the soldiers had come to serve in place of the aggrieved in matters of criminal law. At this juncture, however, the striking thing is that though exiled from association with his fellow men like any ordinary murderer, the killer's character as holder of chief's office—though in banishment—is alleged to have been maintained. The immediate reaction of the populace is revealing also. "We will take him out of his place," they said. Then in some manner the "Indian Law" was read; they were told that an impeachment would be unconstitutional. Law, as distinct from other lines and levels of normation, is revealed in the pinch. The law defined the situation, it was appealed to, and it was heeded and obeyed. This in no manner, moreover, nullified the regularly recognized law of homicide, which placed the ban of exile upon a murderer.

There is no doubt that age and chieftainship swung the weight of public opinion to final compassion for this sinner and his wife and children, when the wife sought reinstatement for him after so short an exile as two years. The doubt goes only to legal effects on his official position. Note, too, that the mechanisms of control which had been socially applied are said to have effected, here as in other cases, a real contrition. The quarrel is with the premise: how could "a mean man" be chosen as chief? But this—as will appear—fits one line of Cheyenne rehabilitation of likely men. You may *impose* a new frame of behavior on him, by making him a chief. This time, it seems to have failed, at first.

Here, then, a reorganization of personality resulted. "He changed his ways after that." The social end had been effectively attained. No more could be asked than this. It fits Cheyenne ways that his chieftainship should then be also validated by way of his resumption of participation in tribal counsels and in the great Council itself.

There is one thing lacking, however, in the story. The investigators neglected to inquire whether this man could smoke the chiefs' pipe with the others and whether he was allowed to be present at the Medicine Arrows ceremonies. By the tribal law of homicide he would be forever barred, and hence could never reëstablish full citizenship, a full council-participation. The case of Little Wolf half answers the point.

Little Wolf was one of the grandest Indian leaders of all time, of whose supreme accomplishment George Bird Grinnell has written: "In 1877 the Northern Cheyenne had been transferred to Oklahoma by order of the United States Government. There they starved and suffered the ravages of a new disease, malaria. With brutal obstinacy, officialdom refused their pleas to allow them to return to their homelands in the high plains of the north. Finally the Cheyenne openly announced their intention to go north, and did so in the fall and winter of 1878. There are few sagas to compare in heroic qualities with this.

"We have heard much in the past years of the Nez Perces' march under Chief Joseph, but little is remembered of the Dull Knife outbreak, and the march to the north, led by Little Wolf. This march was over an open country, where there was no opportunity to avoid pursuers or to hide from them so as to get a little rest and respite. The story of the journey has not been told, but in the tradi-

LITTLE WOLF

tions of the old army this campaign was notable, and the men who were stationed on the plains forty years ago are likely to tell you —if you ask them—that there never was such another journey since the Greeks marched to the sea.

"Of the three hundred Indians sixty or seventy were fighting men. The rest were old men, children, women, and boys. An army officer once told me that thirteen thousand troops were hurrying over the country to capture or kill these few people who had left the fever-stricken south, and in the face of every obstacle were steadily marching northward.

"The war department set in operation against them all its resources, but they kept on. If troops attacked them, they stopped and fought until they had driven off the soldiers, and then started north again. Sometimes they did not even stop, but marched along, fighting as they marched. For the most part they tried—and with success—to avoid conflicts and had but four real hard fights, in which they lost half a dozen men killed and about as many wounded."[15]

This was the Little Wolf who killed Starving Elk in the winter of 1879-80 at Fort Keogh after the long march was done. Twenty years previously, Little Wolf had ordered Starving Elk to keep away from his wife. Bad feeling had smouldered. Now they were at an army cantonment after the northward flight. Little Wolf's great job was done, but the taste of power lingered. Unchieftain-like, he let himself meddle where he ought not, by trying to stop a card game in which his daughter was playing and gambling for candy. Because it was none of his business, and because he was slightly "full," the players paid him no attention. Enraged, he shot and killed Starving Elk, who was standing by.

The act sobered him. "Well," he said, "I am going up on that hill by the bend of the creek. If anybody wants me, I'll be there."

This was the invitation for judgment or revenge, as might be. There Little Wolf sat alone and foodless for a couple of days. Starving Elk's relatives had set about to destroy his goods (chop-

---

[15] Grinnell, *The Fighting Cheyennes*, 383 f. The heroic and tragic details of this episode are recorded in full, 384-411.

ping the tongue of the new wagon the government had given him and ripping down his tipi), but they were dissuaded by other Indians. William Rowland, an adopted white Cheyenne, persuaded the chief to leave his self-imposed exile to seek protective refuge in the army post. Public pressure was put on Starving Elk's kinsmen to agree that they would not attack the chief if he were released from the army confinement. Because Little Wolf had been drunk, and because they admitted he had cause for the grudge, they agreed to it. So little Wolf was set free after several months of confinement. Forthwith, he withdrew his family to Tongue River to settle upon the present tract of the Tongue River Indian Reservation, to which the government was then trying to entice the tribe. The following year other Northern Cheyennes began to drift into the reservation and settle about him, for his influence was still great. He was still a chief and treated as such by his people, but he on his side continued his withdrawal. He had little to say to the Indians.

By 1892 the reservation was well filled. Then it was that somebody, now forgotten, called attention to the fact that the renewal of the chiefs' council was long overdue. There had been so much trouble that this thing had not been done.

When the surviving chiefs met in council to choose their successors, they met an impasse. There they were. And Little Wolf, the possessor of the chiefs' medicine, the sacred bundle of Sweet Medicine, was absent. He was the supreme priest-chief, the one who symbolically was Sweet Medicine, the culture hero. Ever since he had done murder he had kept aloof from the people, and now he had not come to the renewal. He alone could bring the medicine bag; he alone had the ritual right to open it; and he was not at his place at the back of the lodge. They needed that medicine to rub on their limbs and bodies, starting in the traditional manner with the "servant" who sat at the left of the entrance, passing it about the circle from man to man, following the course of the sun from east to west by way of the south. Sweet Medicine had given this bundle to the people in the beginning when he blessed them with the Holy Arrows. "Don't forget me," he had told them. "This is my body I am giving you. Always think about me." (This is reminiscent of the Last Supper.) Without that medicine—and Little Wolf—the chiefs could not proceed.

In ritual situations the Cheyennes can show ingenious fiction and adaptability at need, as when Little Wolf spoke to Sun Road, "since the camp is not in a circle, we'll just say it is so." Equally ingenious was Black Wolf's purchase of ten boxes of Cracker Jack for the Peyote meeting over which he was to officiate, a purchase which caused us to wonder whether our friend could be taking advantage of us, until, when the Cracker Jack appeared in the ceremonial breakfast, he apologized:

"We are supposed to have parched corn. But there is no corn in this country this summer." [It was the drought year of 1935.]

Nevertheless, when Little Wolf was needed with the Sweet Medicine, there was no substitution, because Little Wolf was available. The Council sent him their runner, telling him that all the chiefs sat waiting. It availed not.

"I've done wrong," he replied. "I killed a man, and I don't think I ought to sit with the chiefs."

"We need you," was the Council's reply. "We can't proceed without you."

Still Little Wolf hung back, while the whole tribe waited, and the stalled Council sat frustrated. The people are said to have gossiped to one another, "Maybe he is ashamed to come in to sit where he was once a great man." [The people had one main portion of truth firmly by the tail.]

After a day's holdout, the chief came in to take his place. The renewal was completed, and the new chiefs installed for the last time.

Thus Little Wolf, though a murderer, remained in law a chief until, by due process, he formally appointed his successor in Sun Road. To him the murderer's stigma stuck, nevertheless, and because of it he could not touch his lip to the pipe with other men. From the fatal day on, he did not eat from other men's bowls. The greatest man of all the Cheyennes, the hero of his people, a chief to the end of his term, because a chief could not be deposed, was yet a man apart. Custom and the law made it so. His deed was a tribal calamity. The Sweet Medicine itself was suspected to have taken on the "murderer's stench." That was why Sun Road at first refused it. He confessed to Calf Woman later, "I didn't want to say it, but he wears that medicine over his shoulder slung under his left arm. I think it has begun to smell." When Sun Road later succeeded Little Wolf as a member of the Council, he took the chiefship without accepting the Sweet Medicine bag. [This is radical innovation; it is almost like taking office as a judge, while denying responsibility to precedent.]

The whole tribe came to believe the medicine was corrupted by Little Wolf's misdeed, so that there was actually talk in the Council of doing away with it. Grasshopper forestalled tribal action. He accepted the medicine from Little Wolf, and when Grasshopper died, it was gone—no one knows where, but the guess is that he buried it.[16]

The situation here presented, baldly and without solution of the extraordinary problems with which it was pregnant, is worthy of more detailed canvass. It is known that the office of first chief was associated with possession of the Sweet Medicine, that such possession was an attribute of the office, and that the Sweet Medicine was of peculiar tribal value. That Little Wolf, though he deemed himself fallen from grace, still carried the Sweet Medicine on his person, evidences no less clearly than the Council's action in insisting on his opening the renewal of the chiefs, that his office persisted despite his offense and his banishment. One is faced first with the question how, if times had been normal and the Council in regular function, the Council could have gotten on without the Sweet Medicine and its priest. One can assume that measures were available, for head chiefs had died in office, and head chiefs may have been absent for reasons other than banishment; still, cases of the Council's operation in the absence of the Sweet Medicine are not on record (though the legend attempts to compass the problem—Case 6).

[16] The data in this history are from High Forehead, who was present at the Starving Elk shooting, and to whom Little Wolf offered a daughter as wife in return for his aid in smoothing the affair; from Calf Woman, who was a party in the doings; and from Walks Last (age 81) and Stump Horn (age 86), who were on the reservation at the time of the chief-renewal in 1892.

What presents a totally novel aspect, however, is the situation on Little Wolf's return. As sacred a thing as the Sweet Medicine must be deemed to be strong against corruption, and might be reasonably deemed to have inherent curative powers. Even murder by any but the priest did not sully it; only the Sacred Arrows suffered thereby. There was, for instance, no known procedure for renewing the Sweet Medicine, as there was for renewing the Arrows. For the first time, then, this great medicine now came into bodily contact with the murder odor. The murder odor, on the other hand, seems (so to say, on principle) never to have faded out if it once attached itself to a man, though the pragmatic treatment of return from banishment shows that it must have become reduced to bearability.[17] The new conjunction of the Sweet Medicine with the body of a stinking murderer had no result which could be predicted as a necessary one in the Cheyenne culture of the time. The cultural elements at work left a clear possibility of the matter passing over without crisis or particular notice—as is indicated in the summoning of Little Wolf to open the renewal council. But, were attention challenged and the matter tested, this unprecedented case might, within the Cheyenne patterns, have worked out as well to make the Sweet Medicine for once purify the murder odor (which had never happened before) as to make the murder stench pass into the Sweet Medicine (a thing which likewise had never happened before). For Cheyenne religion shows no easy predominance of ill things to corrupt the good; if anything, its tendencies run the other way. The interesting thing is that in this situation (which has in it the germs of constitutional crisis—for how, with the Sweet Medicine corrupted, destroyed, or hidden, is the Council to proceed or to be renewed?)—in this situation, as in any crisis of constitutional law, the outcome hinged in some part, neither measurable nor demonstrable, but as tangibly present as if it were, on the play of personality and on the play of events which were in themselves irrelevant to the *legal* form taken by the constitutional issue. If Little Wolf's own sense of unworthiness had been less dramatic; if the grandeur from which he had slipped had been less conspicuous; if, finally, the issue had taken

17 See pages 137 f. below.

shape in good times, successful times, rather than in defeat and during painful readjustment to reservation bleakness, then the outcome from the net culture matrix might well have been wholly different from what it was. We do not, in a word, read the case as indicating, for instance, that the murder odor was so powerful that it would corrupt even the Sweet Medicine, if that were worn by the murderer, or the like. We read it rather as indicating that even the unimaginable could be construed to happen, if there was sufficient tribal misfortune seeking for an explanatory cause. Though the case does make clear in no uncertain terms the power of the murder stench.

The prompt desuetude of the Council, or its lack of notable and remembered matters to deal with—even the ordering of new marches being now out of possibility—has left students without light on the solution of how to get on without the Sweet Medicine.

Today the Northern Cheyennes feel stirrings within themselves toward the appointment of new chiefs and the formation of a new Council in the hopes that "it will bring better times to the tribe." (Commissioner Collier's conviction that a revival of the Indian's sense of self-worth through allowance of self-dependence is taking root and, here, pushing up a sturdy plant.) The reluctance of some influential men to show a willingness to accept a chiefship because they fear the generosity obligations of the post, and the lack of current knowledge of the ritual sanctions and procedures of the Council are obstacles in the way of bringing the stirrings to a head. The Peyote Cultists pray for guidance in their meetings. We venture the prediction that no Peyote revelation will disclose a procedure for reinstitution of the Council which will fail to contain directions for provision of a substitute for the Sweet Medicine and any other lost ritual elements whose lines or names are remembered. We have seen enough of Cheyenne accuracy to become clear that without accuracy, the wise Cheyennes halt; enough of Cheyenne ingenuity to become clear that no obstacle can overcome felt necessity; enough of Cheyenne skill to feel that no measure will be proposed which will not elicit the approval of the People.

Though the chief could not be removed, he who had stumbled was not asked to succeed himself. Yet he retained the right to name his own successor. Bear Runs Out was an example of this. As a young chief he took a horse from a man whom he had seen flirting with his wife. He was let out at the end of his term. Yet, because he was a "great protector of the people in war" (and had learned the needed dignity?) he was renamed to a place on the Council after the due ten years had passed.

The Case of Sleeping Rabbit (CASE 16) substantiates the non-removal principle as well. In spite of his criminal action and the violent treatment he received from the Fox Soldiers, he remained a chief to the end of his term. Chiefship was a *status*, then. It was a status with teeth. Even infraction of the duties left the status—and so the duties—live. There is no case of double infraction.

Camp-moving was properly the chief's affair. "In the usual way," according to Stump Horn, "some chief gets the urge to move. It is evening; the people are in from the day. He sends out for three or four fellow chiefs to come to his lodge. They eat supper. He will tell them why he has called them. He will tell them he would like to go to the Arkansas River, then to go out the West Trail. They agree.

"In the morning the crier goes around crying the news to the chiefs. All the camp can hear it, so they know what the chiefs will take up. [Note the wherewithal to "reach your Congressman."] All the chiefs rise, if they are in bed, and hasten to the lodge of the man who has the thing on his mind. His wife has already been preparing food. If the chiefs agree to what is proposed, then it is harangued to the camp at large, giving details of the route and the time intended for each stopping place so that those who go off to one side will know where to find the camp."

This is what the crier said, "We have passed on what we have taken up. Today, tonight, and tomorrow, we move camp. The first camp will be on Powder River. The Dog Soldiers are selected to go in front [i.e., to police the march]. When we break camp on Powder River, we move to Crazy Woman. When we move from Crazy Woman, we move on a little creek across Clear Creek. This moving is for the purpose of hunting buffalo. After we get to Crazy Woman, two men will be sent ahead to see if they can see any buffalo or bulls."

In addition to the matter of camp-moving, and determining thereby the time and place of the communal hunt, it is seen in the crier's words that the naming of the soldier society which was to undertake the direction of the camp-moving and the control of the hunt was a function of the Council. In this respect the military were nominally under the discretion of the civil Council, and served as its police arm. And though the soldiers were thus in charge of the march resulting from the Council's decision to move camp, the chiefs of the Council did not remove their fingers from the pie. The two scouts who were sent out by the Dog Soldiers when the tribe reached Crazy Woman, in accordance with the predetermined plans of the chiefs, found lots of buffalo on Clear Creek. They then reported back to the Council, with the recommendation that the tribe stop before reaching Clear Creek.

The chiefs agreed to this, ordering their crier to announce the plan *to the Dog Soldiers*—but in a loud voice so that the whole camp could hear it.

"This is what the scouts recommended. What do you think of this plan? This is what your scouts said. Of course, you may do as you want to, but this is the thing they say."

Though the "legal" decision now lay with the Dog Soldiers, could anyone doubt what the Council felt? This is a phase of Cheyenne juristic technique, to be watched throughout: *the procurement of general acceptance* of a decision.

The movement of the individual bands during the months when the tribe was split up was directed by the band chiefs separately. Yet here, too, initiative could come from the followers. For as Black Wolf expressed it, "Perhaps there are three or four Elk Soldiers in a band. They get together and have a notion as to where they would like to see the band go. They tell the chief."

Often the chief approved; sometimes he called for a séance such as Grinnell describes.[18] It is said that if a medicine man who had

[18] Grinnell, *The Cheyenne Indians*, II, 112-17.

powers as a spiritual medium was in the camp, he was usually called up before a decision was announced. This rite must have been exceedingly ancient among the Cheyennes, for it is an Algonkian ritual similar to the lodge-shaking séances of the tribes of the northern woodlands. The performance shows also a startling resemblance to the séances of the Greenland Eskimos described by Peter Freuchen.[19]

The sanction for neglecting to follow instructions given by the séance spirits was disaster. There were, of course, people who would go too far. "It must be that way with all people," opines Black Wolf. "But the tribe believed it, because it always turned out as the spirits said." It is said that there were many different spirits who might come to the lodge. Each one usually announced his name, but before giving instructions these spirits always left to consult Badger, who was regularly referred to in high-sounding metaphor.

In general the picture, as between the tribal chiefs and the soldier chiefs, is one of mutual deference—and of careful politics. The former had the weight of seniority and social recognition of their position and wisdom on their side (for it was deemed more honorable to be a tribal chief than to be chief of a soldier society). The latter were in a strong position, however, for they were the men of direct action, and those to whom most of the fighters bore peculiar allegiance. As Dog put it, "They are the ones who will have to do the work." And throughout, one will find Cheyenne recognition of him "who strikes the enemy"—a needed man, in the period in hand, and perceived as such.

Grinnell's account of the peace with the Kiowa tribe effected in 1840 is the prettiest of all examples of such relations between tribal and soldier chiefs. Against this relatively quiet pattern, later tension-cases must be set.

《   《   《   A war party of eight Cheyennes, on its way south to take horses from the Kiowas, Comanches, or Apaches, was stopping at a large Arapaho camp. At the same time some

19 Peter Freuchen, *Arctic Adventure* (New York, Farrar and Rinehart, 1935), 132-38.

Apaches came to visit Bull, an Arapaho leader. The Apaches told their host that the Kiowas and Comanches were seeking peace with the Arapahoes and Cheyennes. Bull took the opportunity to bring the eight Cheyennes together with the Apaches in his tipi; he filled his pipe and offered the smoke. The Cheyennes declined, Seven Bulls, the leader of the war party saying, "Friend, you know that we are not chiefs. We cannot smoke with these men, nor make peace with them. We have no authority; we can only carry the message. I have listened to what you say and tomorrow with my party I will start back [He has authority to call off his own raid.] to our Cheyenne village, and I will carry this word to the chiefs. It is for them to decide what must be done. We are young men and cannot say anything, but we will take your message back to the chiefs."

When Seven Bulls reached the Cheyenne camp with his companions, he told of the Kiowa-Comanche proposition. That night a crier went about the camp calling for the chiefs to convene the next day. The big double-sized chiefs' lodge was pitched and early the next morning the chiefs all gathered there. Seven Bulls and his companions were sent for to deliver their message officially. The proposal was then on the floor.

After the first speakers had sat down, it was evident that there was no ready agreement at hand within the Council, so the proposition was made and accepted that the Dog Soldier Society should be asked to render a decision to the Council on the question.

High Backed Wolf, who was the directing head chief of the Council, sent one of the door-servants to bring in White Antelope and Little Old Man, the bravest chiefs of the Dog Soldier Society. When these two had been greeted in the chiefs' lodge, High Backed Wolf told them about the order of business, describing to them the state of opinion in the Council. "Now, my friends," he concluded, "you go and assemble your Dog Soldiers. Tell them about this matter and talk it over among them. Let us know what you think of it. Tell us what you think is best to be done."

When the Dog Soldiers had assembled, White Antelope laid the problem before them. "The chiefs are leaving this matter to us," he told his followers, "because we are the strongest of the military groups. It is my own thought that our chiefs are in favor of making peace. What do you all think about it?"

Said another of the Dog Soldier chiefs, "I think it best to leave the decision to you two, White Antelope and Little Old Man. Whatever you say will please us all." All the Dogs agreed to this with one assent.

The two men accepted it and declared for peace. Leaving their troop, they went back to where the Council was waiting for them, to tell the Council that they would make peace with the enemies. The chiefs all stood up at this and gladly said, "Thank you, thank you, Dog Soldiers."[20]   »   »   »

The procedure which has just been described is a typical handling of an important situation in the Cheyenne manner. The proposition, the reader will realize, was no simple one. The Cheyenne had become dependent upon the horse, and any warrior's path to glory and wealth lay most easily and quickly in raids upon the rich horse herders of the south, these same Kiowas and Comanches. Acceptance of the proposal meant that the young men would be blocked in one of their main and favorite avenues of activity. Hostility with the Kiowas and Comanches had been unceasing for at least half a century. The alternative values to the Cheyennes are not clear to us, unless they lay in some scheme for trading horses, on which we lack information. The soldier interest in the case is obvious; no less obvious is the fact that it had the favorable aspect of coinciding with the interests of the whole Cheyenne tribe. In the light of this one understands the diplomatic reluctance of the Council of Forty-Four to reach a decision by themselves. So smooth a delegation of an important decision, inverting the pyramid without any bickering, yet with the machinery at all points for the sensing of opinion in widening representative groups, is an act of social beauty. From the Council to the Dog Men, from the Dog Men to their two most

[20] This version of the peace decision which was made by the Cheyennes in 1840 is adapted from Grinnell's detailed history of the event. Mr. Grinnell's account continues with a vivid description of the ensuing meeting of the Cheyennes with the allied Kiowas and Comanches for the formal dedication of the peace, a peace which was never broken from that date forward. See Grinnell, *The Fighting Cheyennes*, 60-66.

outstanding warriors, to a momentous decision binding on the entire tribe! Nevertheless, the Council at no time gave up its authority; the decision, be it noted, was reported for announcement back to the Council, which then discharged the Dog Soldiers with thanks. This is also a superb face-producing, as well as face-saving, procedure. The actual announcement of the decision for peace was made to the camp at large by the head priest-chief himself.

Such interaction between the Council and the military societies was not unusual; rather, whenever there was an important problem of tribal policy (new policy in general or in particular) to be decided, it was the ordinary thing to see the chiefs' and the soldiers' messengers moving back and forth between the meeting lodges, sensing, reporting, and subtly influencing the state of both "expert" and "lay" opinion until the decision was accomplished. In this way, the legislative knot was cut without resort to dictatorship or friction.

But what happened when there was an irreconcilable opposition within the body politic? Then the governmental authority could act with force. It acted also with tact. It moved sometimes in involution. Power was present, form was not always achieved. Note, however, the Cheyenne drive for form, if repetition of situation makes it possible, if time serves, if dramatic urge finds—even for a sole occasion—an inventive voice. Seven Bulls was called on for an "official" presentation of a proposal the camp had buzzed with for a night. Little Wolf was "required" to be present. Compare the careful staging of Pawnee's rehabilitation. It is not too much to argue that *drama* is a vital *line* of reconciliation hit on by the Cheyennes, between their urge toward form (pattern, ritual) and their urge toward individualizing self-glorification. If this be sound, it suggests a relation between aesthetic balance and soundness of working institution, or of the individual's work in and with an institution, which deserves inquiry.

Walks Last was moving with the tribe one time when it was drifting westward toward the Big Horn Mountains. There was considerable disagreement over how the mountain barrier should be tackled. A minority of the populace was vociferously for detouring around the mountains, while a stronger number wished to cross over the range. A Council meeting was held to decide the issue, with the outcome that orders were issued to take the over-mountain trail. Like the States Righters of '61, the Around-the-Mountain faction packed up and seceded. The Council then called on the Shield Soldiers to drive the secessionists back into the fold. These latter when confronted with the military force of the executive Council returned without cavil. But—the die-hards among them still had a way to attain their end, as they packed their tipis in the night and stole off into the dark without hindrance from anyone. The challenge to tribal authority which they had exhibited in their daylight defection was dissipated by their capitulation before the eyes of the majority. Their sneaking off in the night permitted them to attain their goal, true, but at the same time the face, if not the ultimate power, of the legal agencies was saved. Since such a method of flaunting authority was veiled and hardly valiant, it was not likely to set a precedent which many Cheyennes would wish to emulate.

On a similar occasion, Dog was with the tribe when it was moving down the Tongue River, in Montana, when the following incident took place.

《 《 《   Some of the people wanted to split the camp, but the Fox Soldiers, who were in charge of the march, said that all the people were to stay together. White Bull, one of the chiefs of the Elk Soldier Society, was the leader of those who wanted to break off to go visit the Dakotas over to the east somewhere. Being a chief, White Bull moved out. The Fox Soldiers went down and blocked his way. "You go one step further," they threatened him and his followers, "and you'll go afoot. Just move that way you are heading, and we will kill every horse you own."

White Bull came back; he was just taking a chance on getting through. When a move was made to enforce the law, he called it quits. If he had wanted to go ahead, though, there would have been quite a fight. Those Fox Soldiers would have found it just like hitting a grizzly bear to try to take him.   》   》   》

Dog, the teller of this tale, has a high reputation among the Northern Cheyennes as one who has always been a very reliable citizen; today at the age of eighty-two he is probably the most respected person among the Indians on the reservation. Far be it from one of Dog's qualities to want to see the tribe stirred up by trouble, yet he would have delighted to have seen these Foxes try to carry through their pronouncement if White Bull had not been bluffing them. With a twinkle and an amiable chuckle he now reminisces on the discomfiture of Red Eagle, an old Fox Soldier, whom he accosted a few years later with the taunt, "Do you remember that time we were moving into Tongue River? You brought back White Bull. Did you hit him yet?" Red Eagle said never a word.

It is clear that success of the soldiers in carrying out orders in such matters of march discipline, and the acquiescence of men of White Bull's caliber to their control, built rapidly into precedent and rule; and that such an incident not only shows, but *builds*, a regime of law of the march which controls even the personally and politically powerful.

The chiefs were not immune from a bit of leg-pulling either, especially if a chief's brother-in-law was around. Walks Last was dawdling about camp one time, when the crier went by calling for the chiefs to gather. "Don't call them chiefs," bellowed out Bull Head. "Call them fools. There are too many fools with the chiefs." (The loungers who were in the tent listening to the talk passing between Walks Last and Hoebel roared with laughter as he told this.) There was no blasphemy in the taunt. Everyone knew that Bull Head had a brother-in-law on the Council, and the limits on the privileged joking relationship which was customary between such relatives were wide.

The chiefs' crier has appeared on these pages several times. Cheyenne criers were usually retired chiefs with unblemished records and stentorian vocal chords. There was always a number of qualified criers about the camp, serving the regular chiefs, and also the soldier chiefs. A regular chief of the Forty-Four could do his own public haranguing if he wished, but a soldier chief did not enjoy this privilege. Except on the buffalo hunt or in battle, where orders had to be given directly and with dispatch, all soldier orders to the camp at large had to go through a crier. It would appear that this materially aided in keeping the military power subordinate to the civil government. A "voice," when it is an exclusive voice, has power, as the history of the English kings can show. And the Cheyenne crier comes out of the "civil" government tradition, with his absorption of that tradition documented by appointment.

The crier's position was one of respect and rank with an aura of sacredness about it. He is not to be thought of as the village crier in the Anglo-Saxon tradition. Stump Horn hung back from giving a representation of a crier's harangue because "people are superstitious about doing what they did not have a right to do in the old days." Indeed, in antiquity, each public announcement of a crier was given a formal ritual sanction by either the Keeper of the Sacred Arrows or the Keeper of the Buffalo Hat, and failure to obtain such a sanction was believed to cause great wind storms.[21] All criers were appointed by the tribal Council; they served the Council and not the chiefs individually. A man who had murdered could never qualify as a camp crier because "his breath stank."

Cheyenne chiefship, it may be concluded in summary, was highly institutionalized. A Council of definite size comprised the body of civil chiefs. Accession to, and departure from, chiefship were ceremonially marked with sacred ritual.

Though the Council is plainly the supreme official civil authority, there is too little evidence of its functioning for one to be able to lay out with any clarity the limits of its powers or indeed to fill in the full measure of its functioning within those limits. Its internal procedure, for instance, is not known, save in a few cases. The extent of the religious functions and functioning which its very constitution shows to be so important, is not known. One can surmise, however, as he looks into the material of subsequent chapters, that the close association of supreme civil authority with religious office provided one main bulwark of the civil power when the newer and much more largely secular powers of the military societies came

[21] George Bird Grinnell, "The Great Mysteries of the Cheyenne," *American Anthropologist,* Volume 22 (1910), 565.

to develop, during the white wars. One can see that the directly legal activities of the Council, which centered on cases of intratribal homicide, dealt with aspects of law in which religious sanction was even more to the fore than secular, and in which religious sanction persisted (as with the murder odor) even after secular sanctions were exhausted, even after the Arrows had been renewed. With straight secular law matters—whether of the older sort or of the newer and emergent—the Council was little concerned; it is not shown to have been even consulted when the military societies made and policed new criminal offenses. On the other hand, it is clear that the Council's supreme position was continued, and was assured of continuance, by use of a fine sense of political tact—not only feeling out the state of tribal opinion and of important group opinion before delicate decisions, but watching with care over the preservation of forms which made acceptance of decision preserve the fact and law of the Council's authority. We hazard no opinion as to how long, in continued turbulence and stress of external misfortune, this situation might have maintained itself against the impact of an unbroken succession of unruly military leaders. We note, however, that the machinery was at hand for going far to coöpt into the Council a sufficient number of such leaders to maintain a running balance of prestige against brute power. There was wisdom in the Cheyenne way, and understanding of need as well as of tradition.

Chapter V

THE MILITARY SOCIETIES

THERE were six military societies among the Cheyenne Indians—the Fox Soldiers, Elk Soldiers, Shield Soldiers, Bowstring Soldiers, Dog Men, and Northern Crazy Dogs. These were free associations in which membership was voluntary and at the discretion of the individual. Open to all men of all ages, they were of the ungraded type. Alternative names were used occasionally by the Cheyennes for various of these societies, and these names have been used somewhat interchangeably by several previous writers without clarification of the identities. Error, too, has crept in when writers on the Cheyennes have carelessly included groups which were not military societies within the roster of such associations. Such are the Chief Soldiers of Clark,[1] who were in reality the Council of Forty-Four, and the Inverted Soldiers of G. A. Dorsey,[2] who were the familiar Contraries of the Plains Indian tribes, of whom Grinnell has properly written, "There was no band or guild of these; they were merely brave individuals bound by certain beliefs."[3] That the confusion concerning the Cheyenne societies may be resolved, it may be well to equate the names most consistently used by the Cheyennes for each society with the alternative names which have been used by earlier authors.[4]

The Fox Soldiers have been dubbed Kit Fox, Swift Fox, and Coyote by others. The Elk Soldiers may be found as the Elk Horn Scrapers, Hoof Rattle, Crooked Lance, Headed Lance, and Medicine Lance. The Dog Soldiers are Dogs or Dog Men to all Cheyennes

---

[1] William Philo Clark, *The Indian Sign Language* (Philadelphia, 1885).
[2] Dorsey, *The Cheyenne: Ceremonial Organization*, 15-30.
[3] Grinnell, *The Cheyenne Indians*, II, 79.
[4] Clark, Dorsey, and Grinnell, *ibid.;* Grinnell, *The Fighting Cheyennes*, 209, 360; Mooney, *The Cheyenne Indians*, 412 f.

and to all writers on the Cheyennes. Equivalents for the Shield Soldiers are Red Shield, Buffalo, Buffalo Bull, and Bull. The Bowstring Society was limited to the Southern Cheyennes; it is sometimes called Owl Man's Bowstring, but more commonly the second name for the society is Wolf Soldiers. The Northern Crazy Dogs were limited to the Northern Cheyennes and are sometimes called simply Crazy Dogs or Foolish Dogs. The Crazy Dogs and the Bowstring Soldiers were two societies of recent origin which were formed by the fission of an older Wolf Society after the separation of the Southern Cheyennes from the Northern. The Wolf Society itself was a nineteenth-century innovation which sprang from the vision experience of Owl Friend, a Cheyenne warrior who lived during the first quarter of the century.[5] In spite of its relative newness among the Cheyenne military organizations, the Bowstring Society, as will be seen from cases, functioned as a notably powerful unit in Cheyenne life. Of all the Cheyenne societies, however, the Dog Soldiers were the most unique, and until the period of the white wars, the most influential. This is because the Dog Men, of all the military societies, were the only ones who also formed a band unit within the tribe; hence they camped together in the tribal camp circle, while other societies, which had their members scattered among all the other bands, did not. By some remarkable process that bore fruit sometime before 1850, all the male members of the Flexed Leg band had joined the Dog Soldier Society, so dominating it that the distinction between band and military society became lost. Thus the Dog Society became a band—a band which was governed not by the usual band chiefs, but by the military chiefs of the society. This extraordinary feature endowed the Dog Society with a unique cohesiveness and gave rise to a situation pregnant with great—but largely unrealized—possibilities of governmental formation. One main problem of theory, had the times been less disturbed, would lie in how such a unit could escape developing new and dominant governmental aspects.

The ceremonial and ritualistic behavior of the associations, which

[5] See Grinnell, *The Cheyenne Indians*, II, 72-78, for a detailed description of Owl Friend's experience.

were social fraternities as well as military orders, their costumery and special idiosyncrasies have all been treated by Dorsey[6] and Grinnell.[7] The functioning of these societies in matters of intra- and intergroup control is the subject of special attention here.

First, let us consider the organization of leadership and control within the group. This is the formal organization which was operative when the Cheyennes were living on the tribal basis during the summer months. Then and only then were members of any particular society (save the Dog Men) to be found living in the same encampment. At other seasons of the year they were divided throughout the many scattered bands and camps into which the tribe was broken.

The war chiefs of the Cheyennes consisted of the officers of the military societies, of whom there were two headmen and two "servants" in each organization.[8] The two headmen in each society sat at the back (or west) side of the tipi, opposite the door, in the customary place of honor, whenever the fraternity was in session. The two servants sat on either side of the entrance way, "because in the breastworks they will be at the mouth" (i.e., the post of danger). These two ranked next to the head chiefs in status. It was not their custom to participate in the society discussions in normal circumstances, since leadership in policy was left to the headmen. It is said by our informants, however, that if matters came to a deadlock, the decision was given to the two servants for making; whatever they decided, nothing more was to be said. This is what happened in the peace-making decision which was described in the previous chapter (CASE 9).[9]

In theory, according to Stump Horn and others, the chiefs who sat at the four points were elected for life, but several factors kept

[6] Dorsey, *The Cheyenne: Ceremonial Organization*, 16-30.
[7] Grinnell, *The Cheyenne Indians*, II, 56-79.
[8] Dorsey, *The Cheyenne: Ceremonial Organization*, 16, 18, ascribes one chief and seven assistants to the societies. The authors' informants unanimously contradict this, agreeing in their testimony on the four described here.
[9] Grinnell simply called the two men (Little Old Man and White Antelope) "chiefs"; but since they were the ones called upon to carry the message between the Council and their society, there can be no doubt that they were the servant-chiefs of the society. That the decision was passed along to them to make was in accordance with the rule just enunciated.

the tenure limited. First, as in all the military societies of the Plains Indians, the leaders were "chosen to die." If, however, a chief did become advanced in age, he did not look too seriously upon the rule of life tenure. Rather, when he knew he was getting too old for his active position, when he saw that a better young man had risen from the ranks, he appointed the younger warrior to fill his place. In the same way, any other member of a society who wanted to be relieved from active duty simply stated to his group that he was giving another man his place. He was still a club member, free to participate to the end, but free from responsible duty as well. Though it is difficult to determine the average age of retirement, it seems to have been at about fifty. A chief who died during incumbency was replaced by a successor chosen by the entire membership of the group.

Soldiers, other than military society leaders, were not barred from chiefship in the Council of Forty-Four. This was necessary, of course, if the quality of the Council was to be held at a high level. But a soldier chief was never permitted to be a tribal chief at the same time. When a soldier chief was selected by the tribal Council to fill the place of a deceased head chief (one of the five priest-chiefs) as was frequently done (Little Wolf was the last to be so honored), he automatically retired from the leadership of his society and gave up all affiliation with his military brethren. The Cheyennes reiterate that the appointment of tribal chiefs is elevation to a position of responsibility to the entire tribe. We interpret the rule which separated the supreme tribal and the military chieftainships, preventing the vesting of the powers of the two types of office in any one individual, as a constitutional device designed to forestall undue accumulation of power by any special interest group. It served to guarantee the principle of checks and balances as between the military and civil branches of the social organization.

Unlike the tribal chiefs, the chiefs of the soldier societies were subject to impeachment for malfeasance in office. The earliest of the recorded cases goes back to Buffalo Chief, who was in charge of the Dog Men when the occasion arose to punish a culprit who had gone out to hunt buffalo in secret at a time when hunting had been forbidden. While the Dog Soldiers were destroying the miscreant's tipi, the owner resisted and struck a brave. Buffalo Chief shot the man dead and, when the criminal's wife ran forth with a knife in hand, he shot her to death as well.

Quoting from Grinnell's account, "Buffalo Chief was now ordered to leave the camp. He gathered together all his relations and friends and they went off and for a long time camped by themselves, for now Buffalo Chief was an outlaw [we should say: exile]. At length, after they had been out away from the main camp for a long time, the people of Buffalo Chief's camp began to avoid the other people whom they met; they were shy about speaking to them. Hence they were called *Tatoimanah*, the shy or backward band."[10]

Little Wolf, though his murderous act arose from a purely personal grudge, was not deposed from his office as tribal chief, nor was the unnamed chief whose history was given by Calf Woman (CASE 7). When Buffalo Chief killed—though in the line of duty —his violation of the Cheyenne prohibition against the killing of a fellow Cheyenne was an overreaching which both exiled and deposed him. (Compare the threat to White Bull's *horses,* page 95.) The prestige and power of the man, however, is seen in the result of his magnetic influence in drawing a large number of innocent Cheyennes into exile with him. In this action may be seen also one way in which a new Cheyenne band was formed—a powerful and popular leader followed into involuntary (in this case) or voluntary separation from the tribe, plus an occasion, such as the prolonged exile-for-murder period, for continuing the new grouping until it had acquired a cohesion of its own, and its members had lost their older ties. In this case, too, in spite of a personal loyalty so strong as to override the Cheyenne revulsion for a murderer, the followers of Buffalo Chief recognized that Cheyenne revulsion and manifested the recognition in their bashful self-consciousness. Though this tragedy was enacted more than a full century ago, the

[10] Grinnell, *The Cheyenne Indians,* I, 98. Grinnell also describes a subsequent series of killings (*ibid.,* 99 f.) which he attributes to this same Buffalo Chief. Walks Last has insisted, however, that the second Buffalo Chief murders took place about 1865, and were committed by a Buffalo Chief with whom he, Walks Last, was personally acquainted. This Buffalo Chief was also named Mica. According to Walks Last the first Buffalo Chief killings took place many years before his own birth.

descendants of these people are marked among the Cheyennes on the Tongue River Reservation as the "Bashful Ones" to this day.

Last Bull, also, whose combination of bullying arrogance and philandering had become unbearable, was impeached by his society of Fox Soldiers—a pregnant history free of the murder-complication, which is developed at a later point in this chapter (CASE 15).

The coercive authority of the military leaders bordered on the dictatorial in the hands of some of the fighting leaders. The function of fighting (and during the last two decades of their aboriginal existence the Cheyennes were fighting desperately) and policing in emergency lends itself readily to the development of summary power; and the qualities which brought a leader to the fore in Plains warfare were not exclusively those of balanced judgment and patient self-restraint. Nor is it clear that the ideological pattern of "As I struck the enemy, so I strike you" runs off without a vicious thrust toward striking "you" as "I" ought to strike the enemy. The ideological connection is, in any event, clear. The fact that some arrogant soldier chiefs "were just as mean to the enemy as they were to the people" is what caused them to be suffered. Willful leaders among them were not reluctant to use physical force. Cheyenne warriors submitted to whippings where it would have been inconceivable to a Comanche. Not all leaders were as tough as Last Bull, but even Little Wolf quirted his men.

There is evidence which indicates that any order of a military society chief had to be obeyed if the order had been issued. The authority of the office was supreme. Nevertheless, one sees the Cheyennes always struggling to keep officialdom within bounds, because the dictatorial tendency of egotistic officials was dangerous to Cheyenne principles of freedom. Yet an authoritative officialdom was needed and sought by the Cheyennes to hold in check the impetuous individualism which Cheyenne military practice nourished and which the Cheyenne sense of order feared. The discrimination which western medieval Europe found so difficult to work into clarity, that between the office and its occupant, the Cheyenne legal genius felt and marked throughout. Their method, however, was not the modern American method of limiting the powers of the office. It was, instead, one of developing machinery for anticipatory pressure on the officer.

Thus the Dog Soldiers in 1863 forbade Bull Bear, their chief, to accompany Elbridge Gerry, emissary of the United States Commissioner of Indian Affairs, to attend a treaty council with the American Commissioners. Bull Bear had expressed a willingness to go with Gerry, but of his followers Grinnell wrote, "it is apparent that they did not trust their chiefs and thought that they had been bribed or cajoled into signing the treaty of 1861. They said that the treaty of 1861 was a swindle."[11]

This warrants a moment's meditation. It is clear from the Seven Bulls story, anent the Kiowa peace proposal, that political "authority"—i.e., here, power to bind the People by treaty—was a Cheyenne concept. Seven Bulls knew he did not have it. What is lacking is a developed concept of a power-with-a-limitation-of-extent. Limitations of *kind*, in regard to powers, one will find implicit and recognized all through the material; the Medicine Hat and its Keeper will serve as an example. Limitations of *degree*, however, flow much more easily from a background of varied economic transactions (as, the Anglo-American "special agency"). Cheyenne government builds not out of economic life primarily, but out of social life; one gets rather naturally a regime of powers to be used when needed, and with *social* checks upon their improper use. But it will not do to dub these social checks "extra-legal"—as they would be in the American system. The Dog Soldiers "forbade" their chief to go. He—the normally "autocratic" chief—recognized the prohibition. A legal limitation of power by occasion, and with a machinery, emerged.

More spectacular was the check put on Tangle Hair, chief of the Dog Soldiers, in 1879, when Dull Knife's people were being cruelly starved-in the unheated and freezing confines of the barracks prison at Fort Robinson. Captain Wessels, hoping to break the Indian spirit in his attempt to carry out his orders to force this group of Cheyennes to agree to return to the Indian Territory, from which they had just fled, cut off their food and fuel supply in midwinter.

---

[11] Grinnell, *The Fighting Cheyennes*, 127 f.

The desperate Indians were stubbornly awaiting death, resolved to die on their own land rather than go south again. On the last day, an army officer announced that Tangle Hair was free to leave the barracks with his family. His followers threatened his life if he attempted to accept, and Little Shield, who was spokesman for the others, declared, "This man cannot go out; he owns us and can do what he likes with us."[12] They were afraid that he in his freedom would order them to capitulate.

In this terrible crisis a soldier chief's order was held to be so immutable that his followers deemed it necessary to threaten to kill him rather than run the risk of allowing him freedom with which he might enter an agreement against which group conviction was set.

But the case presents difficulties. It is not clear whether the threat is to be taken as meant in full seriousness. It may have been—as so often was the case with show of disciplinary or vengeance violence —a dramatic indication of the depth of the speaker's feeling, an outlet in word and gesture for emotion (at this time many of the Cheyennes were mad with hunger, anger, and despair), and, finally, a trading on the decencies to bring the other party to give up lest by any chance the calamity of intratribal killing *might* occur. But if the threat is to be taken as wholly meant, a double question arises: first, why could the society not limit and bind its chief? The answer here plainly lies in fear lest, under pressure and without the sustaining influence of his fellows, Tangle Hair might in breach of duty, but in exercise of power, take such action as the soldiers feared. As indicated above, the *concept* of limited-degree power is not at hand. The second question is more puzzling: why could the Dog Men not depose him, instead of threatening death, and then let him go? Possibly impeachment could not occur without cause. Tangle Hair had not as yet given cause.

Note, however, in both cases the Cheyenne result. It is the right result. Artistry in legal concept is deficient; artistry of managing available legal concept to the needed end, is not.

Professor Lowie has focused attention on the role of military

[12] *Ibid.*, 410.

societies among the Plains tribes as effective territorial unifiers. The policing of the buffalo hunt he emphasizes as the specific cohesive function which acted to counterbalance the centrifugal forces residing in interassociation rivalry and frictions. The importance of such police activity is notable because it so sharply contravenes current general conceptions of individual freedom of action and lack of centralized authority among the Plains Indians. Still, in harmony with the general culture patterns of the area, the police functions have been thought to have been limited to the vital and short period of the great hunt.[13]

Two paragraphs sum up Lowie's exposition. First, "With amazing uniformity as to detail the police functions just described have been recorded for a dozen and more tribes and for a period of two hundred years. The personnel of the constabulary varies with the tribe; the duties may be linked with a particular society (Mandan, Hidatsa), or be assumed by various military societies in turn (Crow), or fall to the lot of distinguished men without reference to associational affiliations (Kansas). But everywhere the basic idea is that during the hunt a group is vested with the power forcibly to prevent premature attacks on the herd and to punish offenders by corporal punishment, by destruction of their property generally, and in extreme cases by killing them."[14] [For Cheyenne culture, this last needs somewhat more delicate drawing. The threat to the "criminal" is unambiguous, as appears in Grasshopper's case, and Buffalo Chief's. But the Cheyenne police had no business to kill, even to enforce hunt-law. As Buffalo Chief discovered. And as the case of Sticks Everything Under His Belt reinforces. "There ought to be ways, without that" comes close to summing up the Cheyenne best.]

Lowie, in being the first to catch the state-growth significance of the military societies and the potential governmental significance of all types of associations, has contributed a point of potent interest to the ethnology of government. The way in which preëxisting associations with primary interests in mere sociability and warfare

[13] Robert Harry Lowie, *The Origin of the State* (New York, Harcourt, Brace & Co., 1927), 76-107.
[14] *Ibid.*, 103.

(not war as an instrument of national policy) could take over secondary governmental functions of extreme importance, and thus work for the general societal welfare, is an exciting phenomenon. The sudden and sharply limited assumption of authority for a precise occasion at the moment of need, coupled with a hasty and clean-cut relinquishing of this same authority at the instant the moment of need had passed, excites first admiration, and then wonder. One begins to ponder concerning the nature of man. Can men, for two hundred years, thus assume and drop organized authority? And what lines of penetration would police authority follow if it were ever to break over the sharp usage which appears to confine it to the immediate occasion of the communal buffalo hunt? Given first opportunity for expansion and development, where would it go? Would Plains Indians find themselves subjected to an increasing governmental tendency growing out of this germ, or was the exalted individualism of these peoples sufficient to prevent any centralization of power? Such are the questions which arise as one reads Professor Lowie's *Origin of the State*. These were some of the questions which were to the fore as we began our investigations of the Cheyenne ways. Indeed, these and the "ordeal" problem led us to the Plains. The Comanches gave light on supernatural decision of doubts of fact, but almost none on this more important matter. The Shoshones gave little light on either. The Cheyennes?

Indicators that the military societies of the Plains had actually penetrated many phases of tribal life beyond the food-getting emergency of the buffalo hunt were indeed already at hand. Lowie's report on the Hidatsa had recorded that the pipe-bearers of the Blackmouth Society, the policing unit of this tribe, functioned to adjust quarrels and preserve the peace, to restrain cherry-pickers from going out if enemies were reported to be near, and to restrain war parties from setting forth if for any reason the sortie was considered inauspicious.[15] And on the basis of the shreds of data which are scattered throughout the several monographs on the Plains

---

[15] Robert Harry Lowie, "Societies of the Hidatsa and Mandan Indians" (American Museum of Natural History, *Anthropological Papers*, XI, 1916), 278 f.

military societies in the American Museum of Natural History volume,[16] Lowie himself had once written of Plains Indian justice in general, "The police society also restrained men from inopportune raids, preserved order on the march or on ceremonial occasions, and in general exercised authority when the success of collective undertakings was at stake."[17] Doctors Provinse and MacLeod, working quite independently with such materials as are already available in the literature, have both felt constrained to go beyond what may be called the "classic" judgment. Provinse concludes, "Though the policing of the buffalo hunt has been frequently remarked by Lowie, Wissler, and others as the primary duty of the police officers, their duties as keepers of the public peace during tribal gatherings appear as important as regulation of the hunt. In fact, if one can judge the relative importance of the police functions by the number of references to each kind found in the reports, police duties in connection with settling disputes, punishing offenders, and maintaining order in the camp generally would seem to surpass in importance the police duties at the communal hunt."[18]

MacLeod has covered an even wider range of material than Provinse, to the result that he sees the police activities of the Plains societies not as a creation to meet the special emergency needs of the communal buffalo hunt, but as a historical heritage carried from a more ancient condition of social organization, such as existed before the buffalo-hunting tribes had ever gone into the Plains. "Among most or all the bureaucratically organized tribes of North America the police function was performed by special groups or individuals. We cannot here go into the data for other than North America. But we should observe . . . that it becomes evident that the particular development of police in the plains is a Plains variation of police control as it existed among the Plains peoples at the time they lived in the Minnesota woodlands before their eighteenth century migration into the bison-filled Plains. Our first note of the

[16] *Ibid.*

[17] Robert Harry Lowie, *Primitive Society* (New York, Boni and Liveright, 1920), 415.

[18] John H. Provinse, "The Underlying Sanctions of Plains Indian Culture," in Fred Eggan (editor), *Social Organization of North American Indians* (Chicago, University of Chicago Press, 1938), 348.

police of the Dakota, curiously enough, is Hennepin's, recorded in 1680 at a time when the Dakota had not yet left the woodlands. The police organization, and, in fact, the entire political patterning of the central Algonkian and Siouxans of the north central woodlands is fundamentally similar to that of the peoples of the southeastern woodlands of North America."[19]

Whatever their derivation, the Cheyenne military associations, certainly in the era from which the information for this study chiefly comes, present the most dynamic aspect of the governmental and regulatory, and indeed of the social, order of the tribe. They are found to be at once the machinery which tightens, and the machinery which disturbs, orderly government. The question of whether the older institutions would, in the continuing crisis of unsuccessful warfare (against the whites) and vanishing buffalo, succeed in controlling and harnessing the restless, creative, but often arbitrary impulses which tended always, through the soldier societies, to gain continuity and institutional form and sanction —that question is live in almost every page of the present material. Case after case requires to be viewed as one in which, now in this direction and now in that, some novel aspect of the new and needed balance was worked out, in which some possibility was wholly or partly foreclosed, some set of tensions in unstable equilibrium was given often by a single incident a partial resolution and sometimes a definitive new direction.

Except under most unusual circumstance, the military societies functioned as units only during the summer months when the whole, or most, of the Cheyenne tribe was camped together to observe the ceremonial season of the Sun Dance, Crazy (Animal) Dance, or renewal of the Medicine Arrows. None of these ceremonies was annual, but one or another, or even several, were given each year, each ceremony being followed by a great communal hunt, or in extraordinary times, by a tribal movement against an enemy tribe. When in the fall the Cheyenne tribe broke up into its many band

---

[19] William Christie MacLeod, "Police and Punishment Among Native Americans of the Plains," *Journal of Criminal Law and Criminology*, XXVII (1936), 199. See also his "Law, Procedure, and Punishment," *Journal of Criminal Law and Criminology*, XXV (1934).

segments, all the military societies (save the Dog Men) were disbanded until the cycle of the seasons brought the tribe together again. Yet one sees in many instances that such tribal chiefs and soldier society members as happened to be in any band camp could, when the occasion demanded, gather unto themselves something of the initiative which they were trained to show in time of the great tribal gatherings.

The occasions when some particular military society acted with explicitly delegated police authority fell at the times of the great tribal ceremonies, the communal hunts, and at such times as the tribe was on the march as a body. On ceremonial occasions, such as the renewal of the Arrows, the Sun Dance and Crazy Dance, the military association of the pledger of the ceremony automatically assumed charge of the camp policing for the duration of the ritual. On hunting and marching occasions the authority for police control was vested in one of the societies by pronouncement of the Council of Forty-Four. The functioning of the military societies as policing authorities, their interplay upon the tribal law and tribal behavior, the ways in which they made law, and the ways in which the police themselves were restrained from overreaching—all these come out in the cases-in-action which follow. Numerous histories of hunts wherein one or another of the military societies was in charge have been given us by the Cheyennes. One finds that it was the universal practice, when a soldier society had been placed in charge of a hunt, for the chiefs of that society to send a crier about the camp calling out that when the buffalo had been sighted no one was to go out to hunt alone. "This rule is for your own good," the crier reminded them every time—a reminder that seems to have been needed, if the frequency of violation is an indicator of the strength of a temptation too strong for some Cheyennes, in whom the impulsive and individualistic drives of the culture had failed to acquire balance from the other phases.

The punishment of the two sons of Two Forks and the consequences which followed in its train may serve as a typical action on the hunting scene.[20]

[20] Informant: Stump Horn.

«   «   «   The tribe was moving in a body up the Rose-bud River toward the Big Horn Mountain country in search of buffalo. The Shield Soldiers, who were in charge on that occasion, had their scouts out looking for the herds, and when the scouts came in with their report, the order was given that no one should leave the camp or attack the buffalo. Nobody was supposed to shoot a buffalo until the signal was given.

All the hunters went out in a line with the Shield Soldiers in front to hold them back. Just as they were coming up over a long ridge down wind from where the scouts had reported the herd they saw two men down in the valley riding in among the buffalo. A Shield Soldier chief gave the signal to his men. They paid no attention to the buffalo, but charged in a long line on the two violators of the rules. Little Old Man shouted out for everyone to whip them: "Those who fail or hesitate shall get a good beating themselves."

The first men to reach the spot shot and killed the horses from under the hunters. As each soldier reached the miscreants he slashed them with his riding whip. Then some seized the guns of the two and smashed them.

When the punishment was done, the father of these two boys rode up. It was Two Forks, a member of the Dakota tribe, who had been living with the Cheyennes for some time. He looked at his sons before talking. "Now you have done wrong. You failed to obey the law of this tribe. You went out alone and you did not give the other people a chance. This is what has happened to you."

Then the Shield Soldier chiefs took up the talk. "Now you know what we do when anyone disobeys our orders," they declared. "Now you know we mean what we say." The boys did not say anything.

After that the chiefs relented. This was not alone because of the fact that the culprits were Dakotas. They called their men to gather around. "Look how these two boys are here in our midst. Now they have no horses and no weapons. What do you men want to do about it?"

One of the soldiers spoke up, "Well, I have some extra horses. I will give one of them to them." Then another soldier did the same thing.

Bear Standing On A Ridge was the third to speak out, "Well," he announced, "we broke those guns they had. I have two guns. I will give them one."

All the others said, "*Ipewa,* good."

Meanwhile, someone had been counting up the men. There were forty-nine in the troop at that time, and now it was noticed that five or six were not at hand. When they began looking around, they saw these men way down the creek chasing bison. "Now we will give them a good whipping," shouted one of the chiefs. "Charge on them and whip them, but don't kill their horses."

They all leaped to their mounts to see who could get there first. When the slackers saw them coming, Big Footed Bull, who was among them, took off the blanket he was wearing and spread it on the ground. It was one of those fine Hudson's Bay blankets which the government used to issue to the Indians. He stood behind it with his friends, because he meant it as an offering to the troop. Last Bull, who was one of the Shield Soldier chiefs at that time, called to his men to halt. They stopped, and then they split into two columns which rode slowly around the men by the blanket and circled around to the front again. The soldiers dismounted and divided the blanket among themselves, tearing it into long narrow strips of cloth to wear as tail pieces when they were having a dance. They finished by cutting an ear off each of the horses of the culprits. That was how they punished them.   »   »   »

This laying of the blanket was not bribery or buying off. It was open recognition of error, submission, and a good-will offering. It stayed the beating in good part, as we see it, because it removed the flavor of defiance about the insubordination; but it did not stay all the penalty. The duty of all the members of a society to participate in the administration of punishment and the liability of all members to discipline in case of neglect were stated by all informants as generalized rules and are borne out in several cases.

The rehabilitation of the miscreant hunters by the very police who had despoiled them is not to be looked upon as a freak happening, for this is reported as a widespread practice of the Plains Indian police. If people had to be punished, it was done for the common-weal. Nevertheless, it ran against the generosity grain of a Plains Indian warrior to leave a fellow citizen in straitened circumstance. So long had these men, who were police of the moment, been trained in helping the poor and destitute, that after meting out punishment they meted out goods. The lesson having been driven home, they were satisfied. In the instance described above it was not because the culprits were Dakotas among Cheyennes, either. The Cheyennes granted that the police would have done the same for a Cheyenne, and we agree, for it is in keeping with a pervasive (though not universal) attribute of Cheyenne administration of criminal law—keeping punishment or vengeance from obscuring a basic purpose of reform, of richer living; an amazing flexibility and sensitivity in adjusting the available devices not only to the end of maintaining order, but to the greater end of a finer life for all.

Nevertheless, these military societies maintained discipline within their own ranks with a rigor which could be harsh. One tribal rule was for the soldiers of the society of the Sun Dance pledger to march afoot before the tribe when they were making the ceremonial move preparatory to giving the Sun Dance. When the Crazy Dogs were marching because their comrade, Old Wolf, was giving a Sun Dance, one of their number rode up on his horse. He had as an excuse his sore knee, which was badly swollen, but they had no pity on him as they pulled him from his mount, destroyed his saddle, and made him walk. If he had stayed away because of his sore knee, Spotted Elk says they would have killed his horses. On lesser occasions, a member not wanting to go on duty with his comrades might succeed in securing a release by a promise of a feast or a large bag of tobacco given to the chiefs of his society for use in the association's meetings. But there is not enough information to know whether this ever worked out to give a rich member an unduly easy berth. We doubt it; such an outcome would have strained the functioning machinery of a society not only in a degree, but in a direction, which does not fit the "feel" of Cheyenne.

The details of discipline in actual war, either within the societies

FROM THE BUREAU OF AMERICAN ETHNOLOGY

CHEYENNE WARRIORS AT THE SUN DANCE OF 1892

or by them, are exceedingly unclear. On the one hand there are repeated breakings-over of the restraints, cited in Chapter IX. Nor are these instances accompanied by mention of disciplinary action.

On the other hand, Grinnell gives the following as "an example of the way in which" the soldiers "treated those who neglected or disobeyed orders": Six Cheyennes and Sioux were sent out with instructions to locate a Pawnee village which was thought to lie in the vicinity. They were explicitly told that if they accidentally came upon any Pawnee on the prairie they should kill him so that no news could be carried to the Pawnee camp. They came on a lone Pawnee warrior who repulsed their attack so bravely that they drew off with one wounded. When the scouts reported, they hid the story of their frustrated attack, until Wolf Mule, the wounded one, unfolded under questioning. The Sioux Soldiers whipped the Sioux "unmercifully," and the Dog Soldiers did likewise to the Cheyennes. Note the careful division of "jurisdiction." Wolf Mule was spared for informing—state's evidence![21]

We incline to the conclusion that set practices had not developed, although clear standards had, for right action. We incline further to the belief that the general policy of keeping up the fighting spirit of young warriors, and a general understanding of the emotional effects of dances and of the career urge, must have worked so repeatedly to lead toward the overlooking of offenses as "understandable," that penalty-practices remained unsettled.

Before the final disintegration of Cheyenne government, no prestige or standing was sufficient to permit a man to do as he pleased when the soldiers were on duty. Old Bear was considered one of the bravest men in the tribe at the time the Shield Soldiers found him butchering buffalo when a no-hunting decree was in force. They whipped him but did not destroy his goods or kill his horse. They stopped at the latter, opines Stump Horn, because he was such a brave man. Little Wolf, in the days before he had become a chief, stole out with some cronies to hunt against orders when the

[21] Grinnell, *The Cheyenne Indians*, II, 54 f.

Cheyennes were on Crow Standing Creek, cold and hungry. He and his company of friends received a good beating for their pains.

It is in the situation which arose when a hunter was suspected of having brought in buffalo taken by stealth when the "no-hunting" word was out that one first begins to note the contagion of the policing powers of the Cheyenne soldiers. The setup is, to be sure, still a part of the hunt complex, but it is an important additional step to allow a searching party to enter a man's lodge to look for evidence, for this is a social policy of a much more deliberate nature and fraught with greater possibilities for limitation of individual liberties. The concern of the American bills of rights with search and seizure is evidence of deep-rooted distrust of the investigating power of police. Search of residence represents a machinery not merely for policing, but for detection and conviction. It represents among the Cheyennes a lengthening of the attention-span of the secular arm into the phase of deliberate and sustained work unaccompanied by any excitement of the mounted charge on the red-handed lawbreaker. Above all, it represents a clean-cut recognition of the privilege of a proper law enforcement staff, in the public interest, to move upon and into the individual's private sphere not only of action, but of living—his very lodge.

Consider the case of Man Lying On His Back With His Legs Flexed, as told by Stump Horn, who was one of the Shield Soldiers at the time of its happening.

《　　《　　《　　The Shield Soldiers were having one of their dances. The order had been given to the people that no one was to go out to hunt buffalo. Man Lying On His Back With His Legs Flexed needed something to eat for his family, so he let it be known to the Shield Soldier chiefs that he was going out to hunt small game. There was no objection to this, but when Man Lying On His Back With His Legs Flexed got into a herd of buffalo (without really looking for them), he could not restrain himself. He shot just one fat cow and butchered it. Someone saw him and reported to the chiefs of the Shield Soldiers when they had finished their dance.

When the Shield warriors appeared at his lodge, Man Lying On His Back With His Legs Flexed did not rush out to protest his innocence as he saw them coming. The soldiers went right on to the next step, ripping a gash down the back of his tipi. In spite of this warning, Man Lying On His Back With His Legs Flexed sat inside saying nothing. Then they knew he was guilty, and so they destroyed his whole lodge around his head.   »   »   »

Not so, Low Forehead. He was peached on one night, though he had not offended. When the soldiers approached, he rushed from the lodge holding high his hands, calling upon them to stop. He denied the charge and invited a search. Last Bull and Wrapped, two chiefs, entered and hunted about. They emerged and said it was all right. At that the soldiers left him unmolested.

The proper patterns, according to the informants, are clearly established. If innocent, one came out holding up the hands in protest. A search followed. If guilty, one made no move and the penalty followed. But here as always in Cheyenne, there were variants; and here as always there was machinery which served commonly to keep even irritant and counterirritant from forcing a legal issue into social crisis when the pressing of formal law too far came to threaten law's fundamental purpose. The case of Last Bull in his treatment of Grasshopper is a clear instance.

«   «   «   The Fox Soldiers had issued the "no-hunting" decree. Grasshopper ignored it, and was informed on. Blood was on his horse before his tipi. Last Bull as chief of the Foxes rode up and shot the horse without further inquiry. This fanned Grasshopper's mother to such a state of indignation that she cut several gashes in the chief's tipi.

At this Last Bull called out all the Foxes. "Friends," he said, "we're going over there and ruin everything those people have."

On learning this intent, the father of Grasshopper loaded his gun and took vigil. It was his announced intention to shoot the first man to touch a thing. The Foxes drew bead on him with their weapons, telling Last Bull to destroy the lodge while they covered the old man. Then one soldier spoke up with soothing counsel, saying that the incident was not worth all that trouble. They would have killed the whole family—a half war. The advice was accepted; the old man announced he was going to move off to one side to camp and hunt by himself. The soldiers let him do it.

People said Last Bull did just right; he had a right to "clean up the whole family to enforce the law." » » »

That it was for the commonweal he acted was recognized by the informant, Calf Woman. When asked if she would have informed if she had seen Grasshopper coming in, the answer was, "Yes. The soldiers were not working for themselves; they were working for the people."

When questioned, "If he had been a relative?" the answer was, "I'd lie low. Some one else would tell anyhow." The conflict between kin and community ties resolved!

It may be added that though sentries were not posted against enemies, there were always soldiers lurking about the fringe of the camp when the no-hunting rule was invoked. They observed who left the camp. If the absent one was not back by early evening, they began to tell each other that he must have killed a buffalo; then a special watch was kept to see whether the suspect returned clean-handed. Also, women might observe the infringement and report.

This case is further discussed in another context in Chapter XI. Here it is enough that one more dramatic precedent to clinch police powers was established. Whether the losers had also made good in part what one sees as the point of their protest—the right to a hearing, even by the guilty—this incident does not alone reveal.

In another field of civil action, too, the soldiers had penetrated deep as the police arm of the community. Murder was crime, sin, and tort to the Cheyennes: sin first, crime second, and private wrong, third.

Calf Woman brought out a crucial case which tests the position of the soldier police in the murder situation.

«   «   «   Somebody found an aborted fetus in the vicinity of the camp. The discovery was made known to the Council.

They believed that the fetus was that of a Cheyenne, but nothing was known about it. The soldier chiefs were consulted, and by them a plan of investigation was produced. The two head chiefs of a soldier society convened their group, while the society announcer was sent out to broadcast the order of the soldiers for all women to assemble in public. When it was seen that all were at hand, the women were ordered to expose their breasts for inspection. The soldier chiefs looked closely at each one to note lactation enlargements of the breasts as a sign of recent pregnancy. One girl showed symptoms, and she was charged with the crime, judged guilty, and banished from the tribe until after the Arrows had been renewed. » » »

Calf Woman claims to have been present, but to have escaped the inquisition because she was too young to have been pregnant. This would place the event in the 1860's.

Three salient points are to be noted here. First, that the unborn child had tribal status and insofar a legal personality; abortion, too, was murder which tainted the tribal medicine. Second, this was a situation wholly religious and criminal, for the violence had been done within the most intimate family unit possible. Blood-feud was precluded. Third, the murder was a secret crime demanding detection of the criminal—the only secret killing in the present material. A technique was ingeniously invented to meet the situation. Here, as throughout, one meets the Cheyenne legal elasticity—a quick adaptation and invention rare in any people, primitive or modern.

Clearly, the military associations were well along toward establishment as a civil power and organ of government. Further cases will prove that this one is not an isolated exception. The next of these involves Last Bull and his temporary eclipse.[22]

« « « Two Twists filched a bowstring from Last Bull, a distant relative, and chief of the Fox Soldiers. Two Twists denied the guilt, but the day came when Last Bull caught him with the bowstring. He was accosted by Last Bull and given a beating with a club until blood flowed from his head. People ran to separate

[22] Told by Calf Woman, confirmed by Stump Horn and High Forehead.

them and had managed it when the Elk Soldiers swooped down on the scene. They had given their rallying cry the moment the quarrel broke out and they were coming to give a whipping to both men. But the spectators were for keeping things smooth; Last Bull and Two Twists were hidden away where the Elks could not find them. So thwarted, the Elks turned to Last Bull's tipi and slashed it to shreds.   »   »   »

Ordinarily the soldiers would not destroy a man's home for fighting in the village, though to stop a quarrel the soldiers would, "if they were on duty." But with Last Bull the ax fell. "He had whipped many a man in his line of work." Furthermore, and in particular, it is certain that Last Bull both enjoyed inflicting punishment, and showed it. He was a "mean copper" and resentment had simmered long. "They had always been waiting for Last Bull to slip so they could get him," observed Calf Woman. Yet the spectators managed to get the culprits hidden—and one notes that Last Bull preferred being hidden to being on the receiving end of mean copper's work. But we do not believe the spectators saved Last Bull because they loved him. We believe they feared, rather, that for the police to catch him might prove fateful. For the Elk Soldiers are said to have had a special grudge against him, for causes unknown to the informants. This grudge may conceivably have stemmed from the incident of the night before the capture of Dull Knife's village by Colonel Mackenzie on November 25, 1876. Last Bull, then chief of the Fox Soldiers, had forcibly put over his countermand of the order of Crow Split Nose, chief of the Elk Soldiers, for the people to move camp to a safe place. He and his henchmen had cut the packsaddle cinches of the loaded horses and forced the people to stay at the camp to dance through the night. The attack came just at dawn, to the complete route of the Indians with heavy casualties and the total destruction of the camp. Besides arrogantly superseding the authority of the Elks, who were in charge of the camp at the time, Last Bull had impugned the honor of Crow Split Nose with insulting taunts.[23]

[23] The exciting details of the whole affair are skillfully given by Grinnell, *The Fighting Cheyennes*, 360.

The Two Twists imbroglio kindled a fire against Last Bull. He was deposed by his own society. There, too, the fuel had been accumulating. People were attaching odious sobriquets to the Foxes. They had dubbed them the "Beating Up Soldiers," for Last Bull's violences, and "Women Soldiers," for his notorious philanderings, which latter were certainly not in any Cheyenne pattern of sound conduct. Because they felt they were getting a bad name, his own society thus "ordered him from his position at the back of the lodge."

This history is potent in revealing how the control authority with which the societies were becoming invested could lead not only to arrogance and tyranny, but also to internal frictions and corrections, as social pressures outside and inside the group were put to work to reëstablish decencies in their action. Again one notes the all-or-none approach to governmental powers. Last Bull is not limited, but deposed.

But the reasons for the deposition are exciting. There may have been resentment inside the society at an unduly arbitrary commander. But the nub which did the work lies elsewhere. Last Bull was endangering the society's reputation by abusing his position to personal ends partly of a kind (philandering) which was obnoxious. No man can say with certainty which factor, if any, was dominant. No man can doubt that "departure from social function, too outrageously far," is the essential grievance.

Wholly extraordinary remedies can get out of hand; a single event, in conflict-matters, tends toward precedent. Buffalo Chief's deposition was a necessity forced by his exile, and carried no danger; but Last Bull's packed the social TNT of successful mutiny on the high seas. Cheyenne legal and governmental philosophy, implicit as usual, was as usual accurate in immediate action: Last Bull's successor, hardly chosen, explained brutally to his soldiers that Last Bull's rigor of control would be as nothing, against his. No objection is recorded. If any hotheads were thinking of license in prospect, they perceived that the constitutional innovation meant not loosening, but tightening, of discipline directed to the society's true social functions. But the strong words of threat, needed to hammer home a position, are again not to be taken literally. Case reports of authority's further abuse do not turn up. Procedure and effect are of a piece with Grasshopper's case (pages 117 and 118).

"Social function" is in lesser cases not clear. What is advantage to the tribe may be disadvantage to the particular society, and vice versa. Professor Lowie has discussed the centrifugal forces in the formal rivalries of the Crow societies.[24] Here is an aspect in which rivalries pull together, because they rest on the welfare of the entire tribal group directly. According to Grinnell, Last Bull by his obstinacy and high-handedness seems at the time of the capture of Dull Knife's village "to have cowed not only the chiefs of the tribes, but also the owners of the two great medicines of the Cheyennes and the chiefs of the other soldier bands."[25] That was disaster. It called for cure. The pressure on his men of name-calling, and an overt challenge by the Elk Soldiers when he beat Two Twists, finally put a check on him. Internal conflict was avoided, however, only because the Fox Soldiers retained some sense of propriety in their intertribal relations, and found the initiative, in last resort, to meet the crisis with impeachment.

Another instance given by Calf Woman will further the demonstration of police penetration of civil life by the soldier groups.

« « « The people were moving camp through a deep snow in dead winter. Even though I had a stick to lean on I could hardly walk, it was so bad. Bird Face, a Dog Soldier, came upon his niece, Elk Woman, struggling exhausted through the drifts. He sang a Dog Soldier's song, "In any fight I protect the people." To this he added, "This is a cold day, I'll do the same thing." Whereupon he told Elk Woman to mount his horse behind him.

They rode on until they overtook Sleeping Rabbit, husband of Elk Woman.

"There is one thing I don't like," Bird Face upbraided him, "that is leaving a woman in the deep snow. I don't know what would become of my nieces if I were dead. How would they get through the deep snow?"

[24] Lowie, *The Origin of the State*, 98-101.
[25] Grinnell, *The Fighting Cheyennes*, 355.

He made no threats, but Sleeping Rabbit's rejoinder was to draw his bow and shoot an arrow into Bird Face's left elbow. Bird Face pulled the shaft loose, but the head stuck fast in the wound. Red Eagle, son-in-law to Bird Face, came up and took Bird Face home. Then he set after Sleeping Rabbit with his gun, but when he could not find him he turned back.

Meantime, Bird Face was having difficulties. Attempts to extract the arrowhead failed. The lower arm gradually blackened until amputation was thought necessary. In the face of this, Red Eagle called the Fox Soldiers together to see what they would do about it. The decision was that they would apprehend Sleeping Rabbit and beat him until he was as sore as Bird Face's arm.

Though Sleeping Rabbit was informed by a friend, the Foxes caught him. They punched him, they kicked him, they beat him with sticks. They threw snow balls in his face; they pushed him in the snow. But they did not kill him. During the melee, a Fox called out that any who failed to beat him would have to give a Contrary Dance. Everyone spared the expense with a vim.

Nevertheless, the arrowhead was still in Bird Face's arm. So the Foxes told Sleeping Rabbit he had to remove it. Compulsion gave him strength where others failed. He managed it. The arm was now so bad that they ordered him next to amputate it.[26] And he was condemned to sit up with the patient every night until he was well.

Public feeling ran high against Sleeping Rabbit. Other soldier bands were agitating for running Sleeping Rabbit from the camp.

Contrition saved him. He had five good horses which he presented to the Fox Soldiers, saying he had done wrong. These men took them to a trader in a deal for a barrel of whiskey. Then they set up a feast and invited all the military clubs to a good binge. They had a good time and no harm was done.   »   »   »

The whiskey is said to have pacified the warriors, and the matter was considered settled. Sleeping Rabbit served his chiefship until the expiration of his term. He attended the Council meetings, but

[26] The situation must have been serious, for Grinnell categorically states that the Cheyennes never practiced amputation, that no man was willing to lose a limb, nor would any doctor undertake the responsibility. Grinnell, *The Cheyenne Indians*, II, 147.

was, of course, not given the signal honor of being asked to become a head chief. He lost his wife, however, for Bird Face declared her divorced from him.

Though Calf Woman was in the camp through all of this, she cannot remember that Sleeping Rabbit gave gifts to Bird Face. It appears that there was no composition. The penance did not inure to Bird Face's benefit, though the divorce must be regarded as a private sanction. The "fine" was paid to the "government." And with it, its functionaries were socially rewarded for their arduous labors. Note especially the growing sense of public duty among the soldiers. Not only was the punishment, by sheer invention, adapted to the crime by the Foxes (important is the fact that this was not Bird Face's own society; this is not a case of a military society avenging a harm to one of its own—community responsibility is at work through a soldier society), but "other soldier bands were agitating." This may mean merely that other soldier societies were tempted to keep the Foxes from monopolizing a popular issue, but more than that it most certainly means assumption of policing responsibility by the soldiers and assumption of lawmaking power.

Further analysis of the case of Sticks Everything Under His Belt (CASE 3, in which he proposes to violate the no-hunting decree, and is banished therefore by the combined council of tribal chiefs and military societies, until reinstated by the Sun Dance which was given by his brother-in-law) throws further light on the lawmaking and social adjustment powers of the Cheyenne council and soldier societies. The problem there to be met by the Cheyenne authority was what to do with a person who set up an open anticipatory claim to personal immunity from the tribal law, though proposing to maintain his position within the tribal community. It was not unusual for Cheyennes to violate the hunting law, but such violations as have been previously met with were all secret and clandestine. Sticks Everything Under His Belt, however, proclaimed his defiance of the law flatly, and in advance. Such announcement was in itself no breach of the law. There was no existing weapon in the Cheyenne legal armory to deal with this. Cheyenne law was built to deal with action, not with intention. Yet the plan of Sticks

Everything Under His Belt threatened tribal disruption and was such a challenge to authority as the Cheyennes were unwilling to pass by.

What was there, then, to work with? Banishment for murder was known, but only for murder; and the banishment had no flavor of Germanic "outlawry," which made the culprit a wolf's head, to be killed on sight, a true out-of-law. Disowner of a daughter by a father was known, for defiance of her brother's choice of husband—i.e., expulsion for a type of action which was also repudiation of family government; but such expulsion had been only from the subgroup, the family, never from the tribe. Neither sedition nor treason can be located as offenses which are in any sense crystallized, though active defiance of the public force has been outfaced and put down, and Grinnell's stories give cases of attitudes which could readily develop into the recognition of something akin to treason.

The extraordinary council proceeded to solve the matter *as if* by logical conclusion from the dissident's own declaration of a new legal concept, and of himself as flat within it: He says he is Out-of-Tribe; so be it—Out-of-Tribe he is. Further: not explicitly, but by plain implication, the road to recantation, readmission, rehabilitation is made clear. And still further, that road is by way of sacrifice of wealth and gain of prestige by an interceding person, and by way of a ceremonial occasion apt for the purpose of marking death of rebellion and the assumption by the offender of a reformed personality. None of these things is explicit in the evidence, and other pieces of evidence are such as to make one believe that a goodly number of them may never have been explicit even at the council meeting. But how a solution could more closely fit into the going institutional structure, and at the same time carry that structure forward, we cannot see. Nor can we imagine more effectively individuated reform treatment, or more unforgettably dramatized record for the young.

The sanction imposed to line up the outcast's friends and relatives is the equivalent to that so often used by the soldier band upon its own members. He who failed had to sponsor a ceremony. The sole pressure in such a sanction was its cost. To pledge a Sun Dance or other ceremony was a great honor to the giver; the ceremony was always a delight to the tribe. The sanction was not, therefore, so much a penalty imposed upon the individual as it was a sort of super-restitutive payment to the society at large, which brought social pleasure and benefits to both wrongdoer and the "gang," even as we make the loser "throw a feed" for those who triumph. Yet all sit at the board together.

It should also be observed that the one who broke the banishment for the pariah did it according to good social form, not in defiance, but in coöperation with society. The unanimous alacrity with which the chiefs gave their assent to the outcast's return seems to reveal the discomfiture of the tribe in the extraordinary position of Sticks Everything Under His Belt. It is another instance indicating the dominant and effective drive of Cheyenne action in criminal cases toward not only reform, but rehabilitation of the offender.

But policing was not confined to the hunt alone. The policing which was done at the Sun Dance and Arrow renewals, of course, had nothing to do with the hunt and was of a different kind. Order seems not to have been difficult to maintain at such times, however, for only one of the present cases of military police action took place at such a time. This occurred at the Sun Dance of 1880 in Oklahoma. The soldiers were out moving in the people for the ceremony. Some of the Southern Cheyennes refused to obey the Northern Cheyenne police. These latter simply went to the windward and set fire to the prairie. As for the obstinate ones, "they moved fast."

Grinnell has noted another such instance, however, in which the soldiers were completely confounded. One of the greatest and bravest warriors among the Southern Cheyennes, Big Ribs, had been a scout with the American army, and his experience with the whites had undermined his faith in the efficacy of the Sacred Arrows, so that he refused to join the camp for the ceremonial renewal. When a band of soldiers came to force him in (as tradition required), he met them with his rifle, declaring that he would kill several of them before they would be able to kill him. The soldiers considered the offer and declined it, retiring in order and defeat.[27]

[27] Grinnell, "The Great Mysteries of the Cheyenne," 547.

This is the sole instance of which we have record where Cheyenne techniques were utterly unequal to the occasion. Other Cheyennes before Big Ribs had challenged the tribal authority, but it had always worked out that someone followed the cue to intervene, allowing the dissenter his face-saving gesture, but giving "authority" the end it sought. It is possible that the corrosive effect of acculturation to white ways was already eating into the old Cheyenne order, when the days of fighting and living the old life were done. It is possible that an unbeliever—a new problem—seemed a dubious addition to a ceremony of faith.

Nevertheless, the reach of the soldier societies was wide, and widening, as the reach of active governing officials tends always to be. Not only in such matters of direct public concern, not only in the initiation and execution of needed charities, but also in matters relating to personal property, they could and did serve as law agents. Furthermore, in this field as in those previously discussed, they made law and enforced it. With two last cases this point may be closed.

In the first history there is Wolf Lies Down, owner of horses.[28]

« « « While Wolf Lies Down was away, a friend took one of his horses to ride to war. This man had brought his bow and arrow and left them in the lodge of the horse's owner. When Wolf Lies Down returned, he knew by this token security who had his horse, so he said nothing.

A year passed without the horse's return, and then Wolf Lies Down invited the Elk Soldier chiefs to his lodge, because he was in their society. "There is this thing," he told them. "My friend borrowed my horse, leaving his bow and arrow; there they are yet. Now I want to know what to do. I want you to tell me the right thing. Will you go over and ask him his intentions?"

The borrower was in another camp well distant, yet the chiefs agreed. "We'll send a man to bring him in, get his word, or receive his presents," they promised.

The camp moved while the messenger was gone, but he knew of

<hr>

[28] Informant: Black Wolf, to whom this story was told by Elk River.

course where it would be on his return. The soldier returned with
the borrower, who was leading two horses, "one spotted, one ear-
tipped." He called for the four Elk chiefs on his arrival. The chiefs
laid before him the story told by Wolf Lies Down.

"That is true," the man assented. "My friend is right. I left my
bow and arrow here. I intended to return his horse, but I was gone
longer than I expected. I have had good luck with that horse,
though. I have treated it better than my own. However, when I got
back to camp I found my folks there. Our camps were far apart and
I just could not get away. I was waiting for his camp and mine to
come together. Now, I always intended to do the right thing. I have
brought two good horses with me. My friend can have his choice.
In addition I give his own horse back, and further, I am leaving my
bow and arrow."

Then up spoke Wolf Lies Down, "I am glad to hear my friend
say these things. Now I feel better. I shall take one of those horses,
but I am giving him that one he borrowed to keep. From now on we
shall be bosom friends."

The chiefs declared, "Now we have settled this thing. Our man
is a bosom friend of this man. Let it be that way among all of us.
Our society and his shall be comrades. Whenever one of us has a
present to give, we shall give it to a member of his soldier society.

"Now we shall make a new rule. There shall be no more borrowing of horses without asking. If any man takes another's
goods without asking, we will go over and get them back for him.
More than that, if the taker tries to keep them, we will give him
a whipping."   »   »   »

Thus was a situation fraught with possible friction brought to an
amicable close through the good offices of the chiefs of the society
of an aggrieved member.

Far more important, however, was the crystallization of a new
social policy, the formulation of a law making it a crime henceforth
to borrow an owner's horse without his expressed permission. The
old custom of free utilization of another's goods, providing one left
an identifying "security," was apparently creating friction as it

came to be applied to horses. What between good friends could develop into a tense situation—as evidenced here by the resort to soldier chiefs as spokesmen of inquiry—could become immediately and actively disruptive if the concept "friend" were loosely interpreted by a borrower, or the horse not cared for, or if the unnotified borrowing broke in upon the owner's plans, or one owner became the recipient of too many such evidences of friendship. Pawnee's case of horse "borrowing" and its punishment (CASE 2) shows the degree of social irresponsibility which the older practice, left unguarded, could engender. Black Wolf stated that the soldiers, and even the tribal chiefs, had been for some time talking about means of putting a stop to the practice. The Elk Soldier chiefs on this occasion took the opportunity to make the step. After declaring the case at hand settled, they moved into general policy. They did not mix the two. Note also, as a soldier society moves into the very unfamiliar matter of legislation, their sound technical attention to what they shall do, if. . .

Wolf Lies Down died a half century ago, an old man of over eighty years. By rough interpolation this ruling must have been made a bit less than one hundred years ago. This means, of course, that the circumstances as recounted do not make first-hand evidence. But that the story is so clearly told after three generations is indicative of the importance of the step in the minds of the people. Such distinctive legislation was uncommon.

The last case to be referred to in this field is the impressive one of Pawnee (CASE 2). Not only does this history detail the action of the soldiers in the legal field of individual property rights—a field of tribal order, but not one in which any emergency can be conceived—but it shows as well how their treatment worked in the rest of the institutional setting. In the history of the reformation of Pawnee is another of those cases in Cheyenne life wherein corrective measures publicly administered cured the chronic malbehaviorist. Here again kindly treatment after harsh chastisement rehabilitated the wrongdoer to make a decent citizen. Here was a soldier-made law operating in full vigor. Here was a young peace chief rising to the full duty of his position. Here were the forces of Cheyenne society working at their best. And none are such ardent converts as those who have rolled deepest in the gutter!

The military societies will recur in the material which follows. But as one looks back upon even this one series of cases involving the soldier-police, it becomes increasingly clear that for the Cheyennes the military societies had truly become an ever-ready arm of a state "towering immeasurably above single individuals," not only on the particular occasion of the communal hunt, but in internal private and civic affairs as well. Though, in general, subordinate to the tribal Council in policy-making, the military functioned importantly in meeting individual situations of tribal concern.

When a company on duty handled a violation of the law, it rolled police, judiciary, and correctional activities into one breathless action. Their law was anything but dilatory. What is more, it was usually effective in restraining a people not used by custom to restraint. But patterns of gracefully submitting to the new policing, or carrying it out, had not yet had time wholly to crystallize. Impulse and individualism—and a touch of resentment at the innovations—were still at work. Else, there would not have been the numerous instances to record which so nicely reveal the law, nor could the existence of law have been so clearly tested.

This, and the law of homicide, make clear that the Cheyenne state was a reality of soundness and permanence. One may argue as to whether there was even a germinal state to be found among such lowly peoples as the Great Basin Shoshones.[29] With the Cheyennes, however, enough advance has been made to find organized government definitely established and growing. The Cheyenne Council, as an executive and deliberative instrument, existed to serve a necessary end in attaining political unity. The system of ungraded military societies was unquestionably borrowed in part from other sources, and its original main purpose was fraternal and

[29] The reader interested in comparing the advanced and organized Cheyennes with the rather anarchistic Shoshones should refer to Julian Steward, *Basin-Plateau Aboriginal Sociopolitical Groups* (Bureau of American Ethnology, *Bulletin 120*, 1939) and to Hoebel, *Political Organization . . . of the Comanche Indians*, pages 129 f., and Appendix A.

ceremonial. The utilization of the military societies in the growing scheme of government was probably an afterthought, a happy expedient, a vigorous and successful experiment, but one which came soon to color—as an organ of government both flexible and close must color—every phase of Cheyenne life and law. "The soldiers" were the police, a legislature, the voice of the People. The marvel is that, in the continuing emergency, the "office" aspect took shape as definitely as did the aspect of "power." The further marvel, for a modern, is to see this happening with almost no reference to known, phrased, "rules" of law.

Chapter VI

HOMICIDE AND THE SUPERNATURAL

THE homicide record of the Cheyennes—sixteen recorded killings within the tribe in two generations (1835–1879), or an annual rate of almost one killing to a theoretical ten thousand of population—is another evidence of the conflict between the aggressive personal ego of the individual male and the patterns of restraint which were also ideationally promulgated by the culture.

The killing of one Cheyenne by another Cheyenne was a sin which bloodied the Sacred Arrows, endangering thereby the well-being of the people. As such it was treated as a crime against the nation. (The belief yet actuates Cheyenne imagination, though the criminal aspect, insofar as the Cheyennes are free to deal with it, is gone.) Much of the crystallization of Cheyenne community consciousness into political reality was due to the action of this social catalytic. Fear of supra-social consequences and the resultant efforts of the Cheyenne community to purify itself from the stain of Cheyenne blood on Cheyenne hands are most probably what brought homicide under the public law. Killing became a crime; its criminal aspect came then to dwarf its aspect as sin, though by no means to displace the latter; and the criminal aspect had in law gone far to actively displace the private wrong concerned: homicide had ceased to be legally a matter for blood-revenge. So far as concerns total discountenancing of blood-revenge, this is a logical consequence of the social calamity of bloodying the Arrows. But there is no reason in logic, and no premise in the culture, which with any necessity stood in the way of purifying the Arrows, say by ritualized and consecrated execution of the offender. The ancient Hebrews were struggling through a similar problem, to reach a

solution curiously similar in spirit (the cities of refuge, the for-
bidding of composition, the limitation of blood-vengeance where
"killing" was not "murder"), yet utterly different in detail—and
less neatly engineered.

When murder had been done, a pall fell over the Cheyenne
tribe. There could be no success in war; there would be no bounti-
fulness in available food. "Game shunned the territory; it made
the tribe lonesome." So pronounced Spotted Elk; so assent all
Cheyennes.

There is thus a branding synonym for "murder" in Cheyenne,
(he'jɔxowɜs), *putrid*. Such was the murderer's stigma. With murder a man began his internal corruption, a disintegration of his
bodily self which perhaps contrition could stay, but never cure.
About the killer clung the murderer's smell, an evil mantle eternally
noisome to fellow men and the sought-after animal denizens of the
plains. Though the tribe, after ridding itself of the murderer's presence through banishment, could purify itself by the sacred ritual of
renewing the Medicine Arrows, the murderer was tainted beyond
salvation. Hence, the immediate consequence of murder was a
conference of the tribal chiefs—such as were in the population of
the band at the moment. By them a decree of exile was given.

It is too often said that in primitive life banishment from the
group is tantamount to a death sentence. That depends on the
conditions of physical and social environment. For the banished
Cheyenne circumstances were relatively kind. The friendly Dakota
or Arapaho would seemingly receive him with open hospitality and
no questions asked. Among these well-disposed foreigners his stink
did not disturb the delicate sensitivities of the herds! Though he
had become a man of no standing in his own community, though he
was forced to rend his life-long ties, he was accepted by the friendly
alien tribes without voiced opprobrium. Yet homesickness seems
to have played an important part. Again and again the remission of
banishment was preceded by eloquent presentation of the wretched
condition of the banished man and his family, cut off as they were
from association with the tribe.

The ceremony of purifying the Arrows is in itself of no direct legal significance; the compulsion to perform the ceremony is. For the murderer's transgression *the tribe* paid penalty, until the ceremony was performed. The control significance of such a penalty must not be overlooked. It must not be overlooked, even though active references to it when a killing seemed toward, are not found. For instance, people intervened when men quarreled violently. What they said was "You must not." "You must not be a murderer." "You will disgrace yourself." "It is not worth it." This is the language of law and morals, reputation and horse sense, not of religion and sin and supernatural visitation upon the people. But we hold the shadow of this latter to have been present and felt, despite the powerful secularization of overt expression. When Sweet Medicine gave the Holy Arrows to the tribe so many generations ago, it is told that he then instructed the Cheyennes in the rituals of purification. They were to keep the Arrows forever sweet and clean.[1] This the Cheyennes have faithfully done. Were there to be a murder among either the Northern or Southern Cheyennes today, an abridged form of the renewal ritual would be performed in Oklahoma, well shielded from the prying eyes of white men. In the old days, the renewal occasioned the presence of every living Cheyenne, except murderers, their families and followers. The military societies saw to the presence of all citizens in good standing and enforced the absence of the others. Surely this division of the goats from the sheep was a painfully potent form of ostracism. Surely it impressed upon the minds of all the values in good conduct. Of course, unification of the tribe was cemented in the sentiment of social solidarity, so engendered in mutual sharing of the awesomely wonderful rite of the Arrow-renewal. To the Cheyennes, as well as to the Ontong Javanese of the Southwest Pacific, Hogbin's words may be appropriately applied:

"The effect that many of them [the tribal ceremonies] produced was an intensification in each individual of the feeling that he and the rest of the community were closely linked together. He thus

[1] The four days of ceremonialism are described by Grinnell in his article, "The Great Mysteries of the Cheyenne," 542, and by Dorsey, *The Cheyenne: Ceremonial Organization*, 4-10.

became mindful of his fellow-men, and paid more respect to their rights, at the same time, too, fulfilling his obligations with greater consideration."[2] In a ritual so carefully controlled as the Sacred Arrow Ceremony the tribal nature of existence was made even more explicit. Quarreling and even undue noises were expressly forbidden and are said to have been summarily punished by the vigilant soldier patrols.

So, for the Cheyenne one notes the significance of the Arrow-renewal as a social binder. But the more direct importance of the Medicine Arrow complex for law lies not in the ceremonies, but in the associated notions. These notions brought forth not only measures punitive and measures absolvent; they engendered preventive measures as well. When violent emotions were brewing, "the thought of the Arrows kept lots of people back."

In the case of Bull Hump and Starving Elk, the need to keep the Arrows from defilement served in our view as the presupposed focal point for the restraining pressures put upon the turbulent ones by interveners.[3]

« « « Bull Hump and Starving Elk returned from a foray to find the camp in a state of seething excitement over an outbreak of violence which had resulted in the death of their friend, Sharp Nose. The two braves boiled for revenge.

When they went to rally Spotted Elk to their cause, the latter's father subjected them to a lecture. "Don't do it. In our tribe killers have a bad name. You are men of reputation. Your names are well thought of. Don't spoil them!" When Starving Elk refused to listen, there came two chiefs bearing a pipe and an offer of two horses provided by the murderer's relatives. When finally the revenge-seekers capitulated to the chiefs' plea for peace, they were showered with the two leaders' thanks. They refused to profit by the "bribe" of the horses, however. They let them loose for anyone to take who would. [No contaminating their virtue with sullied blood-gifts!] But when the father of the dead Sharp Nose embraced them, pro-

2 Hogbin, *Law and Order in Polynesia,* 200.
3 Informant: Black Wolf.

fusely thanking them for not causing trouble, they acceded to his request, that they take their pick of *his* horses.   »   »   »

Thus one sees pressures marshaled from three sides: Spotted Elk's father bearing down on their reputations, tribal chiefs applying the pressure of their office and backing it with proffered "blood money," and finally the father of the murdered youth giving rewards and thanks because their impulse to avenge the death of his son was not followed! The only thing lacking in this instance was intervention by the military societies to *enforce* the peace (as happened other times).

Immediately after murder was done, such tribal chiefs as were in the group at the time met to pronounce the sentence of banishment. The procedure on such occasions should be of crucial interest, but unfortunately we learned nothing about it. Was there a trial? What was done about evidence? These are, thus far, unanswerable questions. The deficiency does not rest on failure to inquire. Though an informant could cite the color of the horse the victim rode, he could not (possibly, would not) state the way in which the High Court took its action. No living Cheyenne has participated in a session of the Council of Forty-Four when it was giving consideration to a sentence of banishment. There seems to have been no public knowledge of what took place. Since in cases of forthright murder the evidence is unequivocally clear, there may have been little need for court procedure in the ordinary case; but questions of fact did arise. The Council had to determine whether one killing was murder or accident. And there was one murder case in which it was necessary to seek out the criminal (CASE 14), and a military society functioned as a court of investigation.

On that occasion both technique and procedure were invented —but outside the Council. Indeed, legal inventiveness and intuition were at a peak in the Cheyenne law of homicide—a context in which some of these cases are again discussed in Chapter XII. Here the emphasis is on what the law was, not on the process of its production.

The native view is that it was the function of the soldiers to enforce the chiefs' decree of exile, an act which, however, was never necessary. The criminal always went.

Banishment of the murderer was not for life. In theory the sentence was to run for five or ten years. Actually, the ban was in the nature of an indeterminate sentence with commutation possible on a number of grounds. First of these was absence of intent. In peculiar instances, as will appear later, this removed homicide from the category of murder, as evidenced by the chiefs' failure to "convict" in such cases. In some such instances, however, the soldiers invaded the chiefs' sphere of jurisdiction. This happened in the case of White Bear, who accidentally killed his mother when drunk. According to Dog and others, White Bear was not at first exiled. But when the time for the great communal hunts was at hand, the soldier societies began to fear bad luck. On word from them White Bear departed with a few of his friends. In the fall when the hunt season was over, it was decided that because White Bear's misadventure was accidental, he could be permitted to rejoin the community. This homicide took place on the North Platte River in 1874. The real legal problem, which was the tribe's source of perplexity in this situation, was the question of the personal culpability of the drunken man. Could a drunkard who has revealed no malice aforethought be excused for an accidental homicide? This was a new problem to the Cheyennes. In this case the chiefs apparently deemed banishment unnecessary. The Arrows, however, were renewed for White Bear's mother almost immediately. Manslaughter, intentional or not, was a sin to be cleansed; at least, any doubt there might be was too grave to be let continue. The military acceded to the killer's presence at first, only to raise misgivings when the time for the great hunt came. Hence the semi-banishment. The first season successfully met, the probationer was allowed to return. Even though reinstated, White Bear for many years could not eat from other men's dishes, nor could he put their pipes to his lips. That this held "for many years," and not for life, evidences in our view that the religious point was one of doubt, rather than of conviction, that the Arrow-renewal, like the uncleanliness tabus and the soldiers' half-hearted action, rested on precaution rather than on certainty. The legal and secular side of the case could be dealt with, decisively, according to the purpose of the penalty; but, lacking a vision, the supernatural uncertainty was handled as a lawyer should handle a matter of moment, by charting the safe course against even the unfavorable event. This case is further discussed in Chapter XII.

It would appear certain that absence of premeditation or intent was at least a mitigating factor in homicide, reducing manslaughter of this type to the "second" or "third" degree. However, since the sole cases of accidental homicide were intrafamilial, empirical data are lacking for determination of what would have followed if a killing involved more than one family.

When a Comanche killed his wife, for cause, it was not murder.[4] In Cheyenne culture, whatever the disposition of the woman's kin toward the husband, the expectation would be that this form of homicide should be looked upon as murder, and it was. It would furthermore follow that wife-slaughter among the Cheyennes ought to be less common than among the Comanches. In contrast to the relatively common wife-killings of the neighboring Comanches, only one such instance could be found for the Cheyennes. This story has in it a peculiar twist of vision compulsion. According to Stump Horn, whose account is offered, there was little choice for Dying Elk.

      «   «   «   He was a holy man [medicine man]. Maiyun kept telling him he would have to kill his wife. Maiyun said not to send her away, but to kill her. If Dying Elk had failed to heed Maiyun, he would have died, or have gone crazy; he did it to save his own body.

He was mean to his wife. It happened one day that she did not hear him call. He kept bawling at her, but she was gossiping with a bunch of women. When she came back to his lodge, he was waiting with his gun. She died there.

The soldiers ordered him out; it would be a terrible thing to have him in camp. He went to the Sioux for two years, and then went south to other tribes. In his absence he was lost track of,

[4] Hoebel, *Political Organization . . . of the Comanche Indians*, 73.

until he turned up after five years had passed. The Dog Soldiers had it announced that he should be received in camp. He returned, and as long as he was with his family he could eat from their dishes, but not with the public; he could not smoke from the common pipe in gatherings of the men; nor was he ever allowed in the Sacred Arrow Lodge, though he could go to the Holy Hat Lodge.   »   »   »

This case, alone, might indicate that killing one's wife was a slightly attenuated crime. Distinctly more probable is the view that the supernatural urge to do the killing was held to make Dying Elk slightly less responsible, or to give him somewhat mitigating circumstances. The fact is not determinable.

But one notes in the account a point of grave legal importance. "The soldiers ordered him out." In White Bear's case the soldiers' suggestion was proper interstitial policing precaution, and the case went to the competent authority. Had the soldiers in Dying Elk's case arrogated to themselves the solemn jurisdiction of the Great Council?

Commutation of sentence for a murderer whose case was clear-cut and simple was not a matter for government alone to decide. The action in such instances shows ever so clearly the survival of kin urges to do damage to the murderer and the public's recognition of the kin's feelings in the matter. The handling of Cries Yia Eya, slayer of Chief Eagle (CASE 4), shows this.

That case revealed the survival of the law of kin retaliation enmeshed in the wider law which made murder into crime. Permission of the soldiers and Council—communal agencies—*and* of the father of the murdered victim had to be sought. The direct approach was to the governmental officials. In winning their approval the crystallized force of public opinion represented by the state was enlisted to exert pressure on the kin group. It responded in letting the ancient law of retaliation rest. Composition did not enter here. The tobacco offering was again more in the nature of a propitiatory offering, an expression both of repentance and request, than a customarily regulated payment for wrong done.

(As was Sleeping Rabbit's gift of horses to the Fox Soldiers.) Its rejection by Chief Eagle's father compels this interpretation. He did not accept it as a wergild which was his due.[5] Note also that Bull Hump and Starving Elk (CASE 18) refused the gifts proffered them not by the murderer, but by his relatives interceding on his behalf.

If the power of the government was not so supreme as to make unnecessary the consultation of a dead man's kin in the process of commuting a decree of exile, so also was it too weak wholly to prevent the outbreak of blood-revenge. What was once law and now illegal was still present, and human, with a lingering touch of customary right.

The Walking Coyote case as derived from Mr. Grinnell's account is an astounding example of the flare-up of the principle of retaliation and the degree to which departures from the standard murder penalties might on occasion occur. Unfortunately, no checks on the accuracy of this history could be obtained among the Northern Cheyennes. These calamities befell the Southern people some eighty years ago; the details are not clear to the Montana people.

«   «   «   In the year 1854, White Horse, then chief of the Fox Soldiers, stole the wife of Walking Coyote, who was very fond of her and brooded much over the trouble. He sent word to White Horse to send back the woman, saying that if he did not do so he would kill him. No attention was paid to the message, and after a time Walking Coyote went to Yellow Wolf, who had adopted

---

[5] It appears that Mr. Grinnell went astray in his treatment of this point. In *The Cheyenne Indians*, I, 354, may be read (referring to murders), "If he saved himself by flight, the council considered the case, and the chief called in the relatives of the dead man and from them learned how much it would take to satisfy them for their loss. The relatives of the slayer were then called together and the penalty stated to them. When they had paid this fine over to the dead man's relatives, the slayer might return to the camp." The available cases do not bear out this statement. It is an admirable instance of a bluntly perceived pattern (composition—penance tendered for a wrong, as in the absconding cases) leading to misinterpretation of superficially similar overt behavior. To compound for kin-blood was not Cheyenne practice. Nor were the victim's kin in essential control of the legal machinery; though they were attended to, they also were controlled. Further questioning, out of a background of general theory plus the context of the culture, would have forced Grinnell to perceive such differentiations. A similar error in the authors' inquiry is noted just above in ambiguous record on a point only later perceived to be vital, that of the interaction of soldier society and tribal Council jurisdiction.

him, and said: "Father, as you know, White Horse has stolen my woman and I have sent word to him many times to send her back, but he does not do so. Now I intend to kill him, and I ask you not to interfere with my trouble, not to ask me to refrain from killing this man."

Walking Coyote knew that Yellow Wolf loved him better than he did any of his own sons and daughters, and he suspected that Yellow Wolf might ask him not to take revenge on White Horse, and if Yellow Wolf asked this, Walking Coyote felt he must obey him.

One day in the summer of 1854 Walking Coyote with War Bonnet rode up to St. Vrain's Fort (on the South Fork of Platte River in Colorado) from their camp twenty miles below. White Horse was living in a camp of Cheyennes there. Walking Coyote rode into the fort and saw White Horse and his wife—not the woman who had been stolen—sitting on a bench in the hall of the fort. When the two saw Walking Coyote, they arose and walked toward the men's messroom, and Walking Coyote jumped off his horse and shot White Horse with his gun, the ball passing through the upper part of the chest and killing him at once. Then Walking Coyote and War Bonnet led their horses outside the gate of the fort, and sat down there, and Walking Coyote said, "If anyone has anything to say to me, I am here."

After they had sat there for a short time, Little Wolf, a cousin of Yellow Wolf, came out and said to Walking Coyote, "This is all over with; you should now go back to your camp." The two men mounted and rode to camp.

Shortly after this the woman returned to Walking Coyote's lodge. After this killing, Winnebago (*Nähk to wun*) renewed the arrows because of the killing. A little later he stole from Walking Coyote the woman that White Horse had stolen and went up north with her.

Walking Coyote sent word to him, saying, "I am not going to kill another man for this woman, but I shall take your wife, Spirit Woman (*A si mon i*)." Before Nahktowun returned from the North, Walking Coyote went to Nahktowun's lodge, and, entering, took Spirit Woman by the arm and said, "Come along now!" She went with him, for she feared him.

When Nahktowun returned from the North and found what had happened, he was angry, so that night he took his gun, went to the lodge of Walking Coyote, looked in at the door, saw him sitting on his bed, where he was resting after returning from the buffalo hunt, and putting the muzzle of his gun through the door he shot Walking Coyote, killing him.

Next morning he went again to Walking Coyote's lodge, took Spirit Woman, and made her go back to his lodge.

After the killing of Walking Coyote the arrows were renewed, perhaps by Red Moon.

One day, eight years later, in the spring of 1863, Nahktowun was sitting behind his lodge filing arrowpoints, which he had fastened into a cottonwood stick to hold them. While he was doing this Kutenim came up and began to discuss with him the question of a horse, the ownership of which had been in dispute between the two. Kutenim was a distant relative of White Horse. As Nahktowun was working away, Kutenim became more angry at him and abused him, and finally Nahktowun jumped to his feet and raising the stick which he had been using to file his arrowpoints, struck Kutenim on the head with it and knocked him down. Kutenim jumped up and ran to his lodge, which was near by, to get his rifle, while Nahktowun strung his bow and took a handful of arrows from his quiver. Presently Kutenim ran out of his lodge and fired at Nahktowun, and the ball passed close to his head. Nahktowun drew his bow and shot Kutenim in the left breast. Kutenim dropped his gun, and drawing his butcher knife, rushed at Nahktowun, who ran away, but Kutenim overtook him and slashed him on the arm, and then fell dead.

The men round about, seeing what had happened, did not go near the two. Only old women and old men ran up to them.

The Bowstring Soldiers, who then had charge of the camp, wanted to punish Nahktowun for killing Kutenim by whipping him. They consulted the chiefs, who advised them not to notice the affair at all, and nothing was done to Nahktowun.

The Arrows were renewed not long afterward.

In the summer of 1864 Nahktowun was living with the Arapa-

hoes. He had an Arapaho woman, and some people began to talk
as if Rising Fire, *Ho ist ó ha a* (Smoke Rising), were trying to steal
the woman. This made Rising Fire unhappy, and the more he
thought of it the worse he felt, and the angrier he became toward
Nahktowun. Finally he said to some of his friends, "I shall have
to kill Nahktowun; he killed my cousin and now he is talking
about me."

His friends replied: "You ought to do so, because if you do not
kill him, he will kill you. He has already killed two men and is an
outlaw, and if he feels like it he may cut your throat or shoot you."

Not long after this, Nahktowun, who was a Dog Soldier, was
invited by one of the Dog Soldiers to come over and eat at his
lodge. He therefore moved over from the Arapaho camp near Fort
Larned on the Arkansas and camped with the Cheyennes who were
on the Saline. On the day of the feast he started, with Little Robe
and Good Bear, to walk to the lodge of the host. On their way they
passed the lodge of Rising Fire, who was sitting inside looking out
the door, and as they passed he shot Nahktowun with a gun and
broke his spine. When Nahktowun fell, Little Robe and Good Bear
stepped to one side, and Little Robe called out to Rising Fire,
"Well, you have begun your work; now come out and finish it."

Rising Fire took an old brass-mounted horse pistol, walked over
to where Nahktowun lay, and blew out his brains. *Meh him ik*
(Eagle's Head) renewed the arrows on the Solomon.[6]

»   »   »

In interpretation four things stand out. The first is the persistence
of the vengeance urge, community and religious notions to the contrary notwithstanding. The second is the possibility that where
there was sufficient provocation to murder, banishment did not
necessarily follow, even when the Arrow-renewal did. Walking
Coyote seems not to have been exiled; nor are the events leading
to his own death easy to understand save in terms of his continuance with the tribe.

There are many obscure angles to Winnebago's (Nahktowun's)

---

[6] Grinnell, *The Cheyenne Indians*, I, 350-53. The case is presented verbatim as
given by Grinnell.

role in the case and his final demise in the story as Mr. Grinnell has given it. There appears, in the first place, no adequate reason for his killing of Walking Coyote. Nothing is said of Winnebago's reinstatement in the tribe, but it will be noted that eight years elapsed between his first killing and his reappearance in the narrative. This was time enough for the banishment to have run its course. When Winnebago killed a second time, two years elapsed before he appeared again, but this time he was among the Arapahoes —from which we infer he was in exile. Thus, though Grinnell observed that "nothing was done to him," he was apparently out, and the soldiers had put to the chiefs the question of whether they might not whip Winnebago. This it would seem was thought of as a punishment for brawling in the camp, for his consequent murder of Kutenim could conceivably be regarded as self-defense, and it was hardly in the character of the soldier societies of the time to delay a whipping in order to consult the tribal Council, if the cause for whipping was unequivocally clear. It is more probable that the soldiers were making a wholly novel proposal to the chiefs at the time they were holding their meeting to consider the banishment of Winnebago, namely, that whipping be added to the traditional and solemn decree of banishment, where the murderer was guilty of brawling.

And finally, there seems to have been a distinction between Cheyenne attitudes toward murderers and bully-murderers, i.e., between decent men who happened to kill and mean, bullying men, who in their overbearing conduct kill. It is clear that in a quarrel the murder stigma could be called upon to put the murderer out of countenance. Bear Louse, in his quarrel with the murderer, Buffalo Chief (page 101), cried out, "Ah, I have been looking for you ever since you took to killing people. I have been to war in my time and have beaten enemies over the head with my whip. I shall have this horse, which is the one I want. I will knock you senseless, too."[7] Such a taunt, however, could bite two ways. It could stiffen the bully-murderer into a very bad man indeed; Buffalo Chief answered Bear Louse with a shot that killed.

[7] *Ibid.*, I, 100.

The key to the discrimination between murderer and bully-murderer is plainly given in the feel of the whole Cheyenne material and in the particular expression of the murdered man's father in the case of Cries Yia Eya (CASE 4), who was a "naturally mean man": "If ever his voice is raised against another person . . ." The father was then insisting that penalty and disciplining produce the proper effect, as a condition of readmission of Cries Yia Eya into tribal life. Cries Yia Eya had been a mean person, an abuser of decencies, a trader on other people's unwillingness to come to open violence. The danger in admitting him back into the tribe was, as it may be with any other such person, that he would take even further advantage, that in order to make an adversary back down even from a just claim, he would capitalize his reputation as one who kicks over more quickly than does the normal man. There was the danger that he might move into outrageous "diplomatic" victories because others confronting him would feel that he would be more than likely to disregard the right and known restraints which governed others when they built up their pleading-by-action toward apparent (but not necessarily intended) violence. This possibility the wise old man nipped in the bud—Cries Yia Eya was not even to "raise his voice" against another.

Winnebago with his two murders had gone so far beyond the Cheyenne pale that his position had become precarious and untenable—both for himself and for other Cheyennes. As the Central Eskimo murderer is reported to become shifty eyed from watching for the ever expected attack,[8] so Grinnell says that Cheyennes of Winnebago's status "often" developed chronic nervousness. Once when Winnebago was out hunting, he screamed and fell over backwards when his wife touched him without warning; he had been thinking of Walking Coyote and how someone might kill him at any time.[9]

The actual destruction of Winnebago reveals how well founded his fears were, and it shows how far some of the Cheyennes could go in ignoring the religious injunction against killing when there

[8] Franz Boas, *The Central Eskimo* (Bureau of American Ethnology, *Report VI*, 1888).

[9] Grinnell, *The Cheyenne Indians*, I, 357.

was a Cheyenne around who had twice demonstrated that the religious and legal injunctions meant nothing to him. The circumstances of his death have all the marks of a social conspiracy. Suggestion and public gossip built up a grudge ("he is picking a fight") feeling on the part of Rising Fire toward Winnebago, which was compounded with a blood-grievance and fear of what Winnebago might do. The invitation of the Cheyenne Dog Soldiers for Winnebago to leave the Arapaho camp to visit them is an amazing invitation. It is too amazing for coincidence that Winnebago should be escorted right past the door where Rising Fire sat waiting for him. Even more amazing is the remark of Winnebago's two Dog Soldier companions when he fell, if they were, or were acting as, his friends; or even if they were concerned, as soldiers and citizens regularly were, with heading off killings within the tribe. The only credible interpretation is that Winnebago was lured into an ambuscade for his assassination, that this was deliberately planned by members of his own former military society, and that Rising Fire was more or less deliberately built up psychologically to be the trigger man. If this interpretation is right, then the final removal of Winnebago is on a par with the extraordinary justice of the Star Chamber, called upon when ordinary criminal law had failed.

Porcupine Bear, like Buffalo Chief, was another Dog Soldier leader who was exiled for murder. The homicidal history of Porcupine Bear, told in its entirety, sheds clear light on the Cheyenne attitudes toward their Sacred Arrows and murder, showing up the inconsistencies of their attitudes which result from the lack of complete integration of cultural ideals. This case goes back a hundred years, and what can be learned from the Indians of today is no more than vague hearsay, but from Mr. Grinnell's account of the events leading up to the battle with the Kiowas and Comanches on Wolf Creek in 1838, the essential details are fortunately available.[10]

«   «   «   About 1836, six years after the capture of the Arrows by the Pawnee Indians, a renewal ceremony to purge the

[10] Grinnell, *The Fighting Cheyennes*, Chapter V.

stain of a tribal murder was called. It happened at a time when the
Bowstring Soldiers were anxious to be off on a raid, but Grey
Thunder, the Keeper of the Medicine Arrows, was delaying the
service because he thought the time and place not propitious. [The
exclusive "voice" was not only exercising power, but was perceived
to be so doing.] This irritated the soldiers, who had by right a
certain control over the Keeper, for he was occasionally appointed
to his position by the united action of the military societies. [It has
been stated by Dorsey that these same societies had the power of
impeachment.][11] At any rate they did not consider the Keeper inviolate, because when Grey Thunder remained obdurate to their im-
portunities, the Bowstrings set on him with whips. He gave them the
renewal, but as Dog told us, he cursed them [predicted ill-fortune]
for what they had done. The pledger of an Arapaho Sun Dance,
which the Cheyennes were visiting at the time [possibly Grey Thunder's reason for wishing to delay the Arrow-renewals], prophesied
disaster also. In spite of these supernatural warnings, small groups
of Bowstrings stealthily left the camp, until they made up a war
party of forty-two men. The whole company was annihilated by the
Kiowas and Comanches, not one surviving to tell the tale.[12]

The next winter Porcupine Bear set out to muster a revenge
expedition. He was going from camp to camp carrying the pipe in
the traditional manner of a war-party leader. And he also carried
a barrel of whisky to help whip up the fighting spirit in the camps
he contacted. In one camp a big carousal resulted. A cousin of Porcupine Bear began fighting with Little Creek, rolling and tussling
on the ground. The chief's cousin called for help, but for a long time
the drunken Porcupine Bear paid no attention. He just sat by with
his pipe, quietly singing songs, until suddenly he arose and whipped
out his knife. The blade sank into the unprotected body of Little
Creek, while Porcupine Bear called on his relatives to follow his
lead. They did, and when they were done, Little Creek lay dead.

[11] Dorsey, *The Cheyenne: Ceremonial Organization,* 11. No cases of impeachment
of the Arrow-keeper are known. Grinnell, in "The Great Mysteries of the Cheyenne,"
554, declares succession was hereditary.
[12] The story of the battle as told by the Kiowas is given in Grinnell, *The Fighting
Cheyennes,* 45 f.

Porcupine Bear and all his guilty relatives were subsequently banished from the tribe, but instead of going to an alien territory, they tagged along with the main camp, always staying a couple of miles behind—exiles, unexiled.

Now the work of inciting the Cheyennes to revenge was taken up by Little Wolf. By fall all the Cheyenne bands had ingathered, so that the whole tribe was there, but the onset of winter delayed the expedition, and they had to lie over until spring. The experience of that bitter season shows why the organization by bands prevailed throughout most of the year—why the tribal aggregation was normally only a summer trait. When the deep snow of winter came, this large camp of Cheyennes nearly starved. There was neither game for the people nor forage for the horses. Some of the horses died of the famine. When spring did come, the tribe had finally so scattered in the search for food that it was necessary to send out messengers to collect the various bands once more.

Early in the summer, they all moved south and east, finally to attack a large camp of Kiowas and Comanches on Wolf Creek in northwestern Oklahoma. All this time Porcupine Bear and his exiles had been following the main camp. On the day of the battle, when the main war party moved down from their camp on Beaver Creek to find the enemy, Porcupine Bear and his group of six fellow-exiles dropped south, too, moving on a parallel course ten or twelve miles west of the main force. When half way to Wolf Creek, the exiles spied a group of thirty Kiowa hunters and women out after buffalo. Porcupine Bear hid his men and signaled to the Kiowas as though he had spied buffalo. The ruse worked. The unsuspecting enemy came hustling up, and then to their surprise, they were set upon by the seven Cheyenne warriors. There was a slaughter which nearly evened the loss of the Bowstring braves. The attack was so sudden that the Kiowas made no defense. Porcupine Bear himself killed twelve, Crooked Neck killed ten; the others accounted for the remaining eight or nine.   »   »   »

It was a superlative accomplishment. And it took place at least an hour or two before the fight began at the main camp. But it did not wipe off the exiles' stain. Officially, their deed received no recognition. The great honor of first coup in the battle went to Walking Coyote, who struck it at the main camp. The exiles' coups were invalid. As exiles, they were disqualified—a disability to acquire war honors which is comparable to loss of civil rights on conviction of some crimes today.

Whether his loss or decrease of civil status had other effects upon the exile's civil rights, as in regard to marriage contracts, inheritance, or any other privileges beyond claiming coup, is not known. We doubt any effect on matters other than prestige and position.

It has already been seen that within the meaning of the law a fetus possessed recognized legal status (CASE 14). What of the alien resident with the tribe? Mr. Grinnell considered the killing of an adopted alien as noxious a crime as the slaying of a full-blooded tribesman.[13] Stump Horn disputed this as a principle, citing by way of substantiation the death of Eagle Bird, who accidentally shot and killed himself while dismounting. The Arrows were not renewed for him because, in Stump Horn's words, "he was an enemy [alien]." But it strikes us that Grinnell was right and Stump Horn wrong. A Cheyenne did not have to be a lawyer, or gifted peculiarly in the direction of law, to *feel* the sound decision. But to get the decision put on a sound, explicit ground is an art and a gift in any culture, and doubly so in one in which legal institutions are peculiarly inarticulate in relation to their development. We have noted repeatedly the elaborate Cheyenne mechanisms, in case of actual dispute, for eliciting the *precisely* correct answer by consultation, by dramatic suspense until the precise solution came to utterance. Here Stump Horn had only the result. Two better lines of *ratio decidendi* lay in the culture: first, suicide was not, within the meaning of murder-law, murder, unless it was *forced* suicide, forced by intolerable grievance; second, accident was not "killing." The case of Eagle Bird was thus not one of murder; it was not even suicide—it was accident; and accidental killing, even of another Cheyenne, was at worst a border case, both legally and religiously. Stump Horn added a third reason, but his qualifying statement is

[13] Grinnell, *The Cheyenne Indians*, I, 356.

enough to show how loosely his first phrasing had run. Yellow Nose was a Ute taken captive when six years old, later to become one of the great warriors of the Cheyenne tribe. Stump Horn thought they would have renewed the Arrows if he had been murdered "because he was a big man and had saved many Cheyennes in the fights."

A speculative question of an amusing turn is a consideration of the possibilities of the law of homicide as applied to the Contrary Warrior. No Contrary is known to have committed murder, but what would have been his status at law if one had? Stump Horn believes a Contrary would not have been expressly exiled because a decree of banishment would have been taken as an invitation to remain! The special position of the Contrary was such that it is believed he would have been induced to pay composition to the kin of the dead. The message from the Council would have been phrased in this way: "Those people don't want you to send them any horses. They don't like your horses. They want you to keep them all. The truth is, they want you to have your horses a long, long time. And they don't want you to send them six horses. They don't want them." So the six horses would be sent. If he had two good horses especially desired, they would have phrased the message so as to get them. "Don't send those two nice greys you have. They hate those terrible nags." If they had said, "Send them some horses," he would have been happy and clapped his hands exclaiming, "That's fine; they don't want anything."

CASES 4, 7, 8, and 14 all demonstrate other phases of the effect of homicide among the Cheyennes. Little Wolf and his pollution of the chief's Sweet Medicine (CASE 8) will be recalled in conjunction with the murder stigma concepts. The reformation and tribal regeneration of murderers was effected by exile and readmission to the body of Cheyenne polity by the Council and the soldier societies, upon the qualified approval of the immediate kin of the deceased (CASES 4, 19). This is the important goal which was sought throughout by Cheyenne criminal law, though instances of failure are not lacking, by any means.

Justifiable homicide did receive recognition by the Cheyennes, though in their strict theory any killing of a fellow tribesman was an evil act. Doubt as to the right course of action is reflected in the situations which revolve about homicide for "justifiable cause" (e.g., CASE 32), because though the Arrows were renewed in any event, banishment did not inevitably follow by pronouncement of the Council of Forty-Four. When the buffalo failed of procurement, however, then the doubts simmered to the surface, and one notes some soldier society "advising" the slayer to leave camp until the meat supply had been obtained.

The evidence has thus far formed a picture of supernatural factors playing a powerful role in control of Cheyenne non-religious behavior. But only at this one point does such a conception hold true. Conditional curse, or self-curse, for instance, while an existent mechanism in Cheyenne legal techniques, was not extensively used for legal purposes or otherwise; nor does vengeance-sorcery loom at all large in the culture. But disputants sometimes swore upon the Holy Hat, especially if adultery was involved.

Thus, the prevalent conception that "ordeal is not found in the New World" requires qualification. The elements lumped to make up the "ordeal" concept include appeal to the supernatural to determine a disputed question of fact, of legal import, the procedure being known and standard and conclusive. That much—which might be thought the heart of the concept—appears in both Cheyenne material and in Comanche. What appears in neither is the element of priestly administration, with its possibilities of manipulation (toward justice or toward injustice). And the Cheyenne cases show no machinery for inflicting the test on a wholly unwilling person, nor for shaping penalty to outcome.

Owl Head, for example, accused Chief Eagle and Stump Horn's friend, Brady, of intimacy with his wife. The accusation was expressed through action; Owl Head just came up and seized the defendants' horses. Chief Eagle gave up his; Brady refused and denied the implicit charge. He led Owl Head to the Medicine Hat Lodge. Chief Eagle acquiesced in the still implicit joinder of issue: he went along. When they entered the lodge, they were asked no questions, for it was naturally a place for people to gather. Brady spoke to the Hat-Keeper, telling him the story, asserting that he wanted to swear on the Hat. The Keeper said nothing, but led them outside, where the Hat, in its bundle, hung on the pole. Both Chief Eagle and Brady addressed it as though talking to Maiyun, saying, "They have accused us of being with that woman. It is not true." No names were mentioned.

Owl Head did not swear, says Stump Horn, because he knew they were guilty and would get their just deserts. But Chief Eagle got back his horse. Legally, the oath cleared him. Stump Horn knew that Brady was guilty, too, for he was Brady's friend. As they rode away, he asked Brady why he had done it. Brady made no answer. He had challenged one of the fundamental beliefs of the Cheyennes, the power of the Buffalo Hat. Now his friend reproached him with his anxious question. There was nothing to say.

The dogma of the Hat was substantiated when Brady was wounded in the next fight with the Crows. In the second fight Chief Eagle was killed, though he stood a long way from the firing.

Suspected wives were not forced to take an oath or conditional curse, as Comanche women were,[14] though if nagged by a suspicious husband, women sometimes declared their intention to swear by the Medicine Hat. Stump Horn insists that they never did so, however, for the husband was wont to drop it then with the feeling that "this woman is going too far; she must be a true wife." The total absence of such cases in our recordings would seem to substantiate him.

Other symbols were used for oaths, as well. A pipe or four arrows, said to represent the Medicine Arrows, or a specially painted buffalo skull to represent the Holy Hat[15] could be used as the equivalents of the modern Bible in oath.

Mr. Grinnell has presented a nice description of oath in settling coup disputes.[16] It should be qualified only insofar as the impression is left that oath rituals were frequent. Stump Horn never saw

---

[14] Hoebel, *Political Organization . . . of the Comanche Indians*, 96 ff.

[15] Grinnell says the Medicine Lodge (Sun Dance), Grinnell, *The Cheyenne Indians*, II, 34.

[16] *Ibid.*, II, 33 ff.

a coup dispute so settled in his time. Dog could tell of only one instance which he knew from experience.

《   《   《   The claimed coup was Lone Wolf's and it was denied by an observer, who declared that Lone Wolf's spear had been too short to have touched the Crow as the latter fled across the creek. There had been several in a position to see; one spoke. Lone Wolf, as he lay wounded, "touched the pipe" and reiterated his claim. Next day the wound on his leg burst open; on the subsequent day he died.   》   》   》

Note that here was no disputant motivated from self-interest to make the challenge. The observer was apparently socially motivated in denying Lone Wolf's right to a great social honor, though he may have had a hidden grudge seeking satisfaction in exposing Lone Wolf. On the psychological side, this case leads to fascinating speculation. Lone Wolf embodies, in the excitement of battle and the irresponsibility of fever, the young man's *need* to fit the military-glory pattern fixed for the young Cheyenne. "What I wanted to do," "what I must have done," "what I rightly and gloriously did do," come into fusion. Temperament, on contradiction, must have played its part; but this hopeless oath is an amazing testimony to the driving and shaping power of ideals. For there can be no doubt that Lone Wolf responded quite as powerfully to the tradition of the pipe.

Certainly in Stump Horn's mind, the effect of the oath was in itself a consumption of the grievance, of whatever sort. The oath "merged" the claim as a judgment at law does in modern legal magic. It then proceeded to operate justly, and when it had operated, everybody knew what the truth had been. He cited, with grave approval of the machinery, the use and effect of an oath by the whites in recent years which, the claim being false, had had proper Cheyenne effect. A good machinery to have available, said Stump Horn. He showed no concern at all that the grievance in question had not been cured. His satisfaction lay, so far as we could see, in that the facts had become clear, and the supernatural had intervened to rebuke. Stump Horn, of course, is of the type of the conventional gentleman, and a dweller in a realm where good taste and correctness count more than personal advantage. Not every Cheyenne would be thus satisfied.

In one of the most amazing pictures of defiance of a tribal constitution and daring of the supernatural which even an imaginative mind could create, there rises a stirring history which demonstrates supernatural sanction at low ebb as an effective preventive of antisocial behavior. This is the astounding mutilation of the Buffalo (Holy) Hat by Ho'ko, wife of Broken Dishes.[17]

«   «   «   When Half Bear, the then Keeper of the Hat, died about the year 1865, his wife, Crooked Woman, acted without orders from the soldiers. [It is said that the military societies took successive turns in appointing the Hat-Keeper. This point, however, cannot be considered wholly substantiated.] She hung the bundle containing the Hat before the lodge of Broken Dishes, thereby making him its Keeper. [Indicating the leeway of the tribal constitution, as distinct from its guidance,] it was declared, "Since the thing is done, let it stand."

Still, it could not stand [and the wisdom of the more considered appointive practice was made tangible, for Broken Dishes' character was profoundly affected by the circumstances of a changing world]. He became one of those despised, a "Sioux-dweller" and an "agency Indian," one who stayed with the Dakotas to the east, hanging about the government agency where one could be an easy parasite. Though the tribe moved on the plains, it moved without the protection of the Hat. For where Broken Dishes stayed, there stayed the Hat.

Dissatisfaction among the people became such that the Shield Soldiers felt moved to depose Broken Dishes. Several horses loaded with gifts were sent to him along with the notification that he should surrender his office. [The sending of the gifts is indicative of the

[17] Corroborating accounts were independently obtained from Walks Last, Calf Woman, and Black Wolf. Mr. Grinnell's version, given in "The Great Mysteries of the Cheyenne," 555 f., differs somewhat in details.

fact that Broken Dishes had rights in the holding of the Hat which were not to be wholly ignored. It is also typical of the culture that any type of change, whatever the form of expression, should be initiated by way of offered gift.]

Broken Dishes said nothing; he took the gifts. But Cheyenne women must be reckoned with. There was Ho'ko. She poured counsel of resistance into his ear. That night the two of them fled with the Buffalo Hat bundle. On the White River a band of Sioux were met. These people, by what inducement is not known, agreed to throw a mantle of protection over the pair. So it was that when the pursuers arrived, Sioux resistance was set. The Shield Soldiers dismounted to enter the Sioux camp afoot. [This was probably an indication of peaceful intent towards the Sioux.] They were received with gunfire. Stopping only to slaughter Broken Dishes' horses and dogs, the Shields retreated.

The affair had now become an issue of tribal safety. Was the Sacred Hat to be lost? The entire available fighting force of the Cheyennes was marshaled to advance upon the Sioux camp in support of the Shield Soldiers. Each society advanced as a unit.[18] The Sioux women fled. Battle impended. At the very moment of crisis Broken Dishes cracked. The slaughter of friends would be his responsibility. Appearing before his lodge, he announced the surrender of the bundle. Let someone come remove it from the pole where it hung as customary beside the tipi door! Cold Bear, father of the deceased Half Bear, had been named as the Hat's next Keeper. He made his way forward, watched by wary Sioux and Cheyennes, packed the bundle on his back and triumphantly marched away, followed by the Cheyenne braves. War was averted!

But joy was soon alloyed. Cold Bear was disturbed. The Holy Bundle was restless on his back as he carried it from the camp. When his wife took over the duty, she, too, was bothered. "Perhaps," he mulled, "it is unhappy over the shooting. It does not like

---

[18] This is unusual, for we have the explicit statement that the military societies were not comparable to army units. What this means would seem to be this: inasmuch as the military societies deliberated matters of tribal policy as separate units (see pages 91–94), the pattern carried over in this constitutional crisis. Each society felt its self-being in relation to the welfare of tribal-being.

the bad way things have gone." He called on a crier to announce his misgivings to the people. The soldier societies sent their criers about ordering everyone to convene. Forthwith, without the usual ritual, the bundle was opened "by the old people" in the view of all. Inside, the Hat was upside down, with one horn missing. Mutilation! The incense herb was gone as well. Ho'ko had vented her spite.

Four scouts back-trailed. They searched every article of Broken Dishes' lodge. Their report was, "It is not to be found." [With that amazing Cheyenne adaptability when faced with an impasse,] an imitation horn was affixed to the Hat, new incense was substituted. The Hat was at ease. No longer did it sit uneasy on the bearer's back.

At the century's turn came an aftermath. Ho'ko died in Oklahoma. The Southern Cheyenne people prepared her for burial. There in her bosom, worn like a pendant, was the missing horn. That was a thing to talk about! Messengers were dispatched to Montana. Wounded Eye, Cold Bear's successor, was sent southward to fetch the horn. On his return, a ceremonial opening of the bundle was held and the horn was enfolded with the Hat, but not put on to replace the substitute. [This was tentative action, akin to the soldiers' tentative move after the accidental killing, page 138.] Nevertheless, doubt existed, doubt persisted. Just what was the proper course? This was a matter for appeal to the supreme source of power. Consequently a séance was held.[19] The very voice of Maiyun spoke in the lodge. This horn now before them, it said, was not the real horn. The horn they had got back was only the husk. The "real" horn had become angry long ago at being apart from the Hat; its spirit had departed and left long since. It had gone home. Because the husk of the horn was lifeless, said Maiyun, it should be taken to the hills and buried.[20] It had no place in the sacred bundle. So came the horn to its end.   »   »   »

[19] As described by Grinnell in *The Cheyenne Indians*, II, 113 f.
[20] This statement unintentionally defines the pure nature of all fetishism. The material object is not revered, but the spirit (whatever it may be) which resides in the object is alone of mystical significance. Thus, though Congo wood-carvers make many images, only those which have received potency from a medicine man are worshiped. Robert Harry Lowie, *Primitive Religion* (New York, Boni and Liveright,

Though an effective substitute was thus finally confirmed by Maiyun, supernatural displeasure had not been wholly avoided. It seems utterly out of keeping with the strength of Cheyenne law and belief that Ho'ko went unpunished throughout her life. True, she lived an exile among the Sioux for most of her remaining years, yet she did die among the Southern Cheyennes. The wrath of the Hat has fallen on others. Her children, save the one son who disavowed his mother and father, soon died. This is said to be her punishment. The tribe, too, suffers because one of its people so defiled a sacred object. No Hat-Keeper now lives long. The last ten years have seen three successive Keepers. With this knowledge in mind Sand Crane, before whose tipi the Hat bundle now hangs (old-time objects with adhering old-time beliefs must be treated as of old, hence the Keeper must forego a house), refused the office when the Hat was brought to him. When lightning struck his house, he changed his mind.

Here, too, the sanctions of the supernatural operated and still operate, though in a manner not wholly consistent with good sense and social policy. But in Maiyun's revelation there is a point of significance no less legal than religious. Healthy legal form never forgets its function. Neither its presence nor its absence must be allowed to defeat its function. The form of horn, out of place, is husk; the substitute, in place, is holy! Maiyun's voice in the séance was true to the legal genius of Maiyun's people. (See pages 319 f. on legal fiction.)

It has now been seen how clearly religion had solidified community sentiment to such a point that matters regarded as a subject for kin-vengeance by most primitive hunting peoples could no longer, for the Cheyennes, be considered such in law. It has been seen how the machinery of tribal government supervened with a secularization of sanction which, while wholly harmonious with the religious, gave a tangibility and flexibility of power and beauty.

1924), 269. This is affirmed by Father Wilhelm Schmidt and substantiated by further authority in Schmidt's *Origin and Growth of Religion* (London, Methuen & Co., 1935), 59.

These factors, rooted as both were in the tribal world philosophy, combined with the developing police activities of the soldier societies to advance Cheyenne society far along the road to statehood. Over this road the society was traveling fast from the primitive law which rests upon the powers of the kin group to the more advanced law wherein authority directly responsible to the society as a whole prevails. In this combination, in the authoritative discretion of the chiefs to pardon and arrange the return of the culprit; in the invention of fact-finding machinery in the abortion case (CASE 14), in the sureness of legal attitude and device, of which these are but instances, the Cheyennes attained a juridical level degrees higher than any Plains people of whom we thus far have evidence—except possibly the Omahas.

The device of exile combined with an almost certain ultimate commutation was a technique of multiple excellence. By removing the murderer it lessened provocation to revenge; it disciplined the offender; allowance was made for the return of the culprit; but only when dangers of social disruption were over. Whatever the superstitious basis in bloody Arrows and discriminating olfactory senses of bison, the result was sociologically sensible, and the recorded handling of the cases compares in effective wisdom not unfavorably with that more familiar to the reader in his own society.

Suicide is self-inflicted homicide and very much a cultural fact expressing definite social patterns rather than a mere individual urge. While to the Pueblo Indians of the Southwest the notion of self-slaughter is so alien that one is reliably informed that the Pueblo imagination cannot even formulate a conception of the act,[21] among the Cheyennes, as with other Plains Indians, suicide played an important social role. Death courted on the field of battle could be sought as an act of great public service (Two Twists in CASE 1), as a means of self-effacement when life appeared empty and pointless, and above all as a face-saving and protest device with legal repercussions; so also, death by self-violence.

All the present cases of direct suicide, and some of the glorious

[21] Ruth Fulton Benedict, *Patterns of Culture* (New York, Houghton Mifflin Co., 1934), 117.

death type, involve a grievance within the closest family and
amount either to sacrificial reëstablishment of own and family prestige, or to an appeal to the public for redress of a wrong beyond the
cognizance of existing tribal law. Suicides could indeed occur over
trivial matters without consequent repercussions.

«   «   «   On the Little Horn River, Hankering Wolf
used his sister's horse in a buffalo hunt. When the kill was brought
in, the sister took two hides for the use of the horse, but Hankering
Wolf's wife objected. Reappropriating the hides, she remarked
that her sister-in-law could look elsewhere for hers. That night the
sister disappeared, not to be seen again until in the leafless fall her
body hung exposed on a skeleton tree. Hankering Wolf, it is said,
no more than reproved his wife.[22]   »   »   »

The incident illustrates one typical phase of primitive law: when
the bargaining (or shall we say the haggling) pattern is absent,
then refusal of any person's offer constitutes a rebuke, sometimes
unbearable, and occasion for fight or flight. In such a situation, a
person has a social obligation to diagnose what is right beforehand,
and not only that, but what will be acceptable. The Cheyenne patterns were all built to make the first offer reach within the range of
decency. In this instance they failed, in tragedy. In the economist's
language, there existed in such situations only a "quasi-market"
—guess and pressure on both sides, but not "bargaining." (For
parallels one may consider the Icelandic Sagas on marriage offers,
in all aspects.)

In several other recorded cases there was no marshaling of community forces to chastise the one who had so aggravated as to cause
a suicide. Indeed when Goes To Get A Drink hanged herself because
Morning Star, her husband, took a Pawnee captive to wife, her own
grandmother remarked that she was foolish to hang herself over
such a little thing.

It here seems to be another conflict between a sane general social
organization and an individualism never tamed. The individual's
machinery of protest was live and available, but, as will show in

[22] Informant: Spotted Elk.

the succeeding histories, it produced results only in circumstances which stirred the social body. The cases to follow show that growing and trusted social organization was suddenly perceived not only to have failed to produce the results desired, but somehow to have missed badly. This means, it would seem, that suicide as a pattern of protest, or as the case may be, of release from shame, or both, was existent, but in social consciousness was definitely uncertain in response. The Cheyenne nose *for cause,* which runs through the entire picture, was at work, even when this older (?) formless type of pressure was used. The people responded, or did not respond, according to their judgment on what was in effect an extra-legal line of protest about law. As to any particular grievance, the grievance was required to outweigh the Cheyenne tendency to find an authoritative answer. So far as concerned effective protest, suicide gambled a life for a crushing effect. But the Cheyenne public was not to be stampeded into such an effect by unreasonable melodramatics.

Thus one comes to the suicide which effected the desired result: an aroused social sympathy and shocked reaction.

«   «   «   When Red Owl's daughter eloped, the infuriated mother went after her. As she drove the girl home, lashing her with whip and tongue, she declared, "I hate that family of his. If you go back, I'll beat you to death." At home, her scolding annoyed her son. As his sister sat silent under their mother's tirade, he declared he was getting out.

Soon Red Owl also shuffled out, grumbling. Then two shots were heard, and people came running. The girl was dead. Seeing what had happened, Seminole, who was standing by, smashed Red Owl to the ground with one blow. The brother ran up, and in horror, he forgot that Red Owl was his mother; he too knocked her down. It was the needed release for the crowd. In mad frenzy they beat her with everything at hand, with fists and tearing fingers. Only the persuasive intervention of her faithful sister saved her from death.

When they were through with her, she was forced out of the camp. She was made to live by herself in the willows. "I used to see her peeping out at us," said Calf Woman. "Whenever she ventured forth, people assailed her with bad names. They would say, 'Oh, there is that loose woman. There is that nice woman.' " After many years, they gradually let her partake again of community life. But whenever she ventured to offer an opinion, she was quashed with a summary: "Oh, you are a nice one to be speaking. You killed your daughter. Sit down!"   »   »   »

Though ostracized, she continued to be abusive. She berated her son for generosity. So nasty was she that he, too, attempted suicide without success (possibly, only intended as a threat). This near-calamity at last brought a change of personality. Red Owl became a decent person and a respected storyteller among the young.[23]

In this instance, causing the daughter to take her life was akin to taking her life. The Arrows were renewed for the girl by Holy Bear. The shedding of Cheyenne blood by another Cheyenne is murder. Though, in fact, the daughter was the killer, in the public emotion (and by its action, in the law) the mother, as the responsible party, was the murderess. This reaction was given expression in law, for Calf Woman states that a soldier band (Elk or Fox), declaring that Red Owl's smell scared the buffalo, placed a ban of exile upon her. In order to support her, her family had to leave the camp to take abode with her in exile. This suicide occurred in the 1860's.

A parallel tragedy produced parallel results at another time.

«   «   «   A girl who had left her husband was indecently beaten and berated by her mother for joining a young people's dance. The girl found surcease in self-hanging. It is said the women of the camp threatened the mother's life. She was charged with having killed her daughter. Her husband did beat her, so she fled. The Arrows were renewed for the girl, as well, and a decree of banishment was pronounced.[24]   »   »   »

In all probability, the distinctive factor in both cases, the fulminate of the public reaction, was the beating of the daughter. Such behavior was contrary to all Cheyenne standards, sufficiently so

[23] Calf Woman's version.   [24] Informant: Calf Woman.

as to verge on the criminal, as a matter transcending familial self-government.

The suicide pattern of self-sought death at enemy hands was not so strongly institutionalized among the Cheyennes as it has been found to be with the Comanches.[25] In marital imbroglios such suicides were much less common, probably as a result of the fact that because Cheyenne settlement techniques normally involved no face-to-face weighing of individual prowess, there was no call for face-saving on the part of the defeated litigant. Only among brothers whose sibling authority had been flaunted by eloping sisters (CASES 30, 31), or young men, harshly spoken to by shrew-tongued mothers, were personality wounds because of women found to be so deep as to require release in the "glorious death."

This glorious death, rooted as it was in a military culture, was adequate compensation for the most damaged prestige. It could also be sought by those who had suffered no prestige-loss, but who sought more prestige (or notoriety) and were willing to go over Niagara in a barrel to get it.

The demise of the two sons of Red Robe in an attack on the Crow Indians gave rise to the situation which provided Two Twists with his opportunity for action of this kind (CASE 1). This colorful case, presented in the opening chapter, also needs consideration in the present context.

It is entirely probable that the extravagant and obstinate display of mourning by Red Robe was aimed right at the result it produced. The motive, if this was so, was hidden under the conventional pattern of parental behavior, for the Indian commentators denied any ulterior motives to Red Robe. "He loved his sons," was their comment. "He was showing them respect." But the more astounding thing was the action of the soldiers. They could not prevent him from disposing of his property, but they could and did put themselves forward as the sole claimants in response to his open invitation for all persons to help themselves. They made themselves self-appointed executors, or trustees, to hold his goods until he should return to a state of emotional balance. Just why the

[25] Hoebel, *Political Organization . . . of the Comanche Indians*, 112-16.

WOLF ROBE

soldiers did this is again not obvious. But who could dispute them? Red Robe's act was the admirable thing to do. He was acting with perfect propriety and with broad gestures. The soldiers did not need to be concerned with his well-being in this manner, for Red Robe and his family would have been adequately helped back when their period of mourning was over. In this respect, interference in such a non-crisis situation is all the more illuminating of the social influence of the soldier societies. One suspects here, too, that they were playing the game with Red Robe. The warriors were wanting a go at the Crows, and a vengeance expedition, properly stimulated and sanctioned on a grand scale, would be the very best way of working up a really satisfying emotional state and of socially justifying a wholesale undertaking against the despised Crow. In order to move Red Robe to reconsideration, it was necessary for all the fighters of the tribe to swear to get him vengeance. Since it seems to us most unlikely that everyone in the tribe was so concerned over Red Robe's condition, we suspect it was the desire for a grand war party which led the soldiers to interfere in the case.

Finally, this history offers an incidental instance of how war undertakings could subjugate the entire tribe to the leadership of one man. This was effected by the entire tribe's changing its normal constitutional status to become nothing more than a war party in which war-party constitution prevailed. It was Two Twists' party, for he had carried the pipe to all the societies—hence he was its supreme leader. By this coincidence, though not a tribal chief, he became for the time being a supreme leader of the tribe. There was of course no carry-over of this authority when the expedition was done.

Though the individual initiative of Two Twists looms large in this scene, he was the carrier for the moment of a culture pattern well established among the tribes of the western plains. His was the Cheyenne counterpart to the more highly developed analogous institution of the Crow Indians, the Crazy-dog-wishing-to-die, so admirably described by Professor Lowie.[26] Two Twists exemplified the

[26] Robert Harry Lowie, *The Crow Indians* (New York, Farrar and Rinehart, 1937), 331-34. By happy coincidence Professor Lowie has presented a most vivid description of the emotional tension and preparations in the Crow camp the night before Two Trists' affair. *Ibid.*, 230 ff., 332 f.

prestige and more purely military motives underlying this type of suicide. That the Crows failed to bring death to Two Twists, when he exposed himself so courageously to danger, merely brought release from his suicide vow and raised his prestige to exalted heights.

Scalp Cane in his misadventure revealed the drive of world-weariness and sorrow, when upon the death of his brother at Crow hands he publicly announced his intention of joining his beloved sibling.

《 《 《 When the whereabouts of the Crow camp had been reported, Scalp Cane mounted an old man on his horse, and together they rode up and down the Cheyenne village, the old man crying for all to hear, "Here we have Scalp Cane with us today. Look at him now, ye Cheyenne. Tomorrow he will have left us. Behold him! Tomorrow he will be with us no more." From then on Scalp Cane could take meat from anybody or whip up any laggards on the march. People were a little afraid of him, for they considered him already dead because he had given his life to the enemy.

The next day they charged the Crow camp in the morning, fighting until the sun was low. The Cheyennes and their Dakota allies were driven back and back. Scalp Cane was running, too, not dying as he had vowed he would. Some boys caught him a pack horse with two saddles to change for his own winded charger. So he outstripped the pursuing Crows. After that day the standard greeting for Scalp Cane was, "Hello, you are back? You don't look like a ghost. How do you like riding two saddles, eh?"[27] 》 》 》

Death was not thus the inevitable result of the declared intention to die in battle. And the Cheyennes did not demand it when the end to be served by the announcement of the intention had been fulfilled (note also CASE 42A). But what a difference is seen in the social reaction to the circumstances under which death was missed without honor. Scalp Cane was ridiculed and shamed—not released. (One thinks of the Crow woman's warning to her brother, "If men become Crazy Dogs and are not killed, they become a laughing stock, . . . they are said to be worthless.")[28]

[27] Informant: Walks Last.

Possessed of more fortitude than Scalp Cane was the maiden of whom High Forehead's father-in-law told him long ago. Her lover was killed charging through the enemy. She dressed in her best elk-tooth dress and walked backward off a cliff, singing, with her face to the camp, of the greatness of her love and the barrenness of life without him whom she loved alone.

Touching, too, is the story of the old blind man, Spit, who at the Wagon-Box Fight with the United States Army said he was always looking for just such a chance to die, for he was tired of only half seeing his way; where were the soldiers? Young ones took his hand, lined his face toward the firing enemy. Serene, he walked toward death, until a bullet brought it to him. Whenever we led Walks Last by the hand, he in his blindness muttered, "If only I had been brave as a youth, I would never have come to this." He would have died in glory, in his prime.

These last suicides and glorious deaths or glorious exposures are not legal in flavor; but they are necessary to round out the picture of similar behavior when it rests not on act of fate or the public enemy, but on act of a fellow-Cheyenne, and more intensely, of a family member. One can imagine protest suicide, in substantially similar default of the event of strikingly unjust action of the organs of the law. But Cheyenne suicide as a legal, or better, extra-legal proceeding, involved more than shame or grief or weariness or glory; it was an appeal, direct and extreme, to justice beyond the law—and so, in its groping way, for better law.

Aftermath[29]

THE CHEYENNE LAW OF KILLING

Following is a somewhat modernized and consciously articulate statement of the norms, as they appear in action, in the recorded cases and opinions. [NOTE: *A question mark accompanying a*

[28] Lowie, *The Crow Indians*, 331.
[29] This method of formulation is inspired by Professor A. L. Kroeber's concise handling of the Yurok data in his *Handbook of the Indians of California* (Bureau of American Ethnology, *Bulletin 78*, 1925), pages 20 f.

given phrase means that the point is indicated in the material,
but not definitely established.]

ARTICLE 1. Definition and Effect of Homicide.

Killing within the tribe is a crime, and a sin, but it is no longer even a fully recognized tort.

(a) The killing of a Cheyenne by another Cheyenne is a sin which bloodies the Sacred Arrows and endangers the people; it is a crime against the peace and the people, and normally within the exclusive jurisdiction of the tribal authorities.

(b) The rule that the kin of the victim of a killing are privileged to seek self-redress in their own right, or to retaliate, is no longer law. However, the authorities are directed to take due account of the natural feelings of the victim's kin.

(c) It is the expected duty of every citizen, and especially of the military societies, to intervene in disputes before they reach the stage of killing.

(d) Within the meaning of this Article, the person killed is a Cheyenne:

(i) if it be a recognizable fetus, carried by a Cheyenne woman;

(ii) if he be a resident alien [or captive?] substantially identified with the Cheyennes and notably deserving of the people.

(e) Within the meaning of this Article, such outrageous treatment of a daughter [child? family member? person?] as must be viewed as causing a suicide in protest, constitutes killing.

ARTICLE 2. Jurisdiction and Punishment.

(a) The chiefs present in a body of Cheyennes at the time of a homicide shall have exclusive jurisdiction over the offense of killing, if they exercise jurisdiction; but, in the absence [pending ?] of a ruling by the chiefs, a military society may take such [minor ?] measures as

they may deem required, including temporary banishment during a hunt [or even a general banishment ?].

(b) Save as provided in Article 3, the chiefs shall decree
the banishment of the killer. Unless otherwise expressly
provided in the decree, the banishment shall be for a
period of ten [five?] years.

(c) Banishment involves permanent disability to attend
renewal of the Arrows, or to eat or smoke from a Cheyenne utensil without polluting it. It involves during the
period of effective banishment disability to acquire
coup honors [or other civil honors, or to officially perform acts of chieftainship ? but not disability to effectively engage in ordinary civil transactions of marriage,
gift, and the like?].

(d) The chiefs present in a band or in the assembled tribe
or tribal division may at any time in their discretion,
but not in general in less than two years' time, on being
persuaded of the penitence of the culprit and of the
safety of his return, remit any banishment. Provided,
however, in the interest of public order, that no such
remission shall be ordered without prior consent of the
several military associations and the representatives of
the kin of the victim.

(i) Remission of banishment involves readmission to
performance of tribal function, except for such
permanent disabilities as are provided under sec-
tion (c) above.

(e) Non-murderers who band up with a murderer in banishment incur the murderer's disqualifications with regard to coup by voluntary choice. Even signal service
allows no relaxation of this rule.

(f) Visitation of corporal penalties by the authorities upon
a killer is improper; but spontaneous expression of
general indignation at a particular offense, not resulting in death of the offender, is itself no offense.

(g) No person, not even a military society, shall impose other and further punishment specifically for killing, save with the consent of the chiefs in the camp.

(h) When any further dispute arises with an obnoxious killer, the other party to the dispute may properly raise the tone of his demands and conduct.

ARTICLE 3. Exceptions and Mitigations.

(a) A killing is justified:

(i) Where necessary in self-defense against incestuous rape; or

[(ii) Where necessary to remove a homicidal recidivist generally felt to be dangerous to the people; ?] or

[(iii) Where utterly and absolutely necessary to military police in the execution of an important duty?]

(b) A killing is excused if [within the family, and?] demonstrably accidental.

(c) Provocation, drunkenness, seeming necessity for self-defense, or other mitigating circumstances, are for consideration of the authorities in admeasuring, or later, in remitting banishment.

(d) The authorities may adjudge the killing secularly excused or justified and yet take such measures as may seem to them desirable in pursuance of communal safety, in regard to possible supernatural effects of a killing. Only in extraordinary cases are the Arrows not to be renewed.

[(e) Voluntary withdrawal by a notable head chief who has killed under extenuating circumstances may serve in lieu of banishment?].

Chapter VII

MARRIAGE AND SEX

COURTING and marriage customs are not in our view family law. Much loose usage of so-called marriage law, or family law, is attributable to anthropologists who, for some reason, look upon the folkways and mores entering into the institution of marriage as having *ipso facto* a quality of effectiveness which justifies their being dubbed "law."[1] Marriage customs which operate without the aid of legal sanctions have what legal character they may possess as thinly diluted as the modern social rule which leads people to eat peas with the fork instead of with the knife or fingers. Marriage norms, however, which are stanchioned with legal sanctions, make clear marriage *law*. They command attention.

For details of marriage and courting customs of the Cheyennes, the reader is referred to George Bird Grinnell's full treatment.[2] Cheyenne marriage was distinctly a contractual arrangement and was, as such, of legal interest. Whether accomplished in the formal way or reached through elopement, the marriage union was validated by exchange of gifts.

Acceptance by the girl's family of the proffered first gift of horses, sent by the suitor's family through a female intermediary, bound the troth. Acceptance or rejection was expected before the first sunset. Inasmuch as the preceding courtship was frequently extended over four or five years, it was generally well known

---

[1] A series of examples of this may be observed in the writings of the contributors to the recent German compendium, *Das Eingeborenen-Recht*, editor, Schultz-Ewerth (2 volumes, Leipsig, 1929-31). In fact, this follows the bent of the whole German school of comparative jurisprudence of Post and Kohler.

[2] Grinnell, *The Cheyenne Indians*, I, 131-37. Cheyenne kinship terminologies and practices have been further analyzed by Dr. Fred Eggan, "The Cheyenne and Arapaho Kinship System," in *Social Anthropology of North American Tribes*, 35-95.

beforehand what the disposition of the girl's family would be. In theory, the girl had no voice in the matter. In practice, she sometimes did; that was a matter of internal family arrangement. Her eldest brother living regularly at home was the first authority, and if present, the clear *legal* authority; then the mother and father, and then the other "brothers", which included her classificatory brothers or close cousins. In some instances the brother decided; in others the parents, alone or in conjunction with the brother; in others, the brother with his cousins. Factors of personality seem to have determined the relative influence of parents and brother in any particular case, but always the brother's word was at least formally deferred to. Whether the brother called in his other brothers seems to have depended on his will. The pattern was there to use, as a matter of sound family practice, but it was not compulsory.

The correct etiquette in regard to the girl's approval and consent is as clear as it is distinct from either the legal powers of her disposing brother or the social norms intended to produce satisfactory individual adjustments. Correct etiquette in Cheyenne required the disposing family member to put the matter up to the girl, who then, if the marriage was to go through, put the matter back into his hands. In ancient Iceland, where refusal of a suitor was a short road to a feud, this procedure was used to take the onus of a concerted refusal off the fighting members of a family; and it may have been so used in Cheyenne. And unquestionably the practices and norms of proper family life called as clearly for a girl's welfare to be considered as they did for the girl to leave as many of the arrangements as possible to her family. Her duty to submit is quite plain, however; and it was a duty not merely sanctioned within the family by disowner of a girl who eloped in defiance of her brother's disposal of her. It also gave the "husband" permission to penalize her for refusal to go to him. It was felt to affect the brother's tribal relations so severely that, on the girl's flouting of it, he could be moved into protest suicide. Under such circumstances his authority must be regarded as legal within the meaning not only of family arrangement, but of tribal law.

The stake of the near relatives was made tangible by their participation in the property exchange. When an acceptance was made, the male relatives of the girl were summoned by the brother to come to choose of the horses and gifts which had been received. Each took according to his ability and willingness to return a gift of equivalent or greater value. On the next day, or soon after, the bride dressed in her best, was mounted on the finest horse, the goods were packed on others, and the bride was led by a non-related female to the home of her husband.

When the road of the suitor to his heart's desire was not smooth, the choice of female intermediaries was an important element of success. These women, usually non-related, provided a subtle means of bringing the pressure of the "public" to bear. This is neatly turned in Calf Woman's account of how a wife was procured for Medicine Bird.

《　　　《　　　《　　　Medicine Bird wanted to marry Walking Buffalo. I can't remember which two women were sent first, but the horses were sent back several times. Finally, they [it is the boy's family, not the boy, who is negotiating] came to me. I refused, for I was afraid that I might be turned down, too. Not that people would talk about me, but I would feel badly.

My daughter and her husband were the ones who went up and made it stick. They had let it be known they were coming with horses. When the day came, it was storming and blowing, but they went the fifteen to twenty miles up on the divide to Walking Buffalo's home. They took the two running horses which Medicine Bird was offering.

Walking Buffalo's people were objecting to the marriage because Medicine Bird was sickly. When my daughter and son-in-law arrived, they tied the horses and entered the house. My daughter told her husband, White Dirt, to go out to talk to the father while she went in and warmed up. [Even when assisted by a man, the woman seems to have remained the leader in such ventures.]

She talked thus to the mother, "Medicine Bird has been running around trying to get people to bring horses here. My mother was asked to do it. Instead, we are taking her place. He just begged us to do it for him. Please don't refuse us. Say yes!"

The mother wept. The girl had no brother to decide it.

But the father said, "I shall speak to my daughter to learn her will. I don't want to force her to do this thing." His name was Lion. "Daughter," he said, "what do you think? These people have come here on this cold day. Do you want to marry him?"

"Father," she modestly answered, "I leave it up to you. Whatever you say."

"There was an old woman sitting there, Twin Woman. "One thing you have to look into!" she called out. "Those two children there are the children of chiefs. They are not supposed to be refused. Whatever they say, you should do."[3]

Lion agreed. "I'll say, 'Yes,' to you two. You may go home with the word." This made them feel happy, for they were the only two of all who had come who had made it fast.

After a couple of days, when the weather cleared, the girl and two horses were brought to Medicine Bird. They were led by Twin Woman, for Lion had said to her, "You are the one who led us into this; you will have to take her back." Then many people came bringing goods. All the extra things were taken back to be distributed among her people. The girl's mother made them a tipi and provided household goods.   »   »   »

The acceptance of proffered gifts by a girl's guardians was legally binding. For instance, Sets Like A Man, according to Walks Last, was giving horses to the parents of Brings Something. These were accepted by her parents, but she refused to go to him, so he cut off her braids. Her parents made no protest to his action.

Elopement made impossible an exchange of gifts before marriage. Even so, care was taken to validate the marriage by gift exchange at the earliest possible moment. Cheyenne girls sometimes eloped to escape the suitor favored by their brother or parents.

[3] The authors have no other evidence of any such attitude toward children of chiefs. The touch of embroidery fits with Calf Woman's development of herself in the otherwise unknown status of "chief's wife" by alleged virtue of alleged special ceremony (page 77).

Such a challenge to fraternal authority was not to be taken lightly. Serious as elopement could be as an offense against the girl's family, it was not true that the eloping pair might be pursued by the father *or brother,* as Grinnell has written. Nor could any substantiation be found for the solemn statement that "more than once men have been killed on this account."[4]

High Forehead, who regularly interpreted for Mr. Grinnell over many years, was quite bothered by this statement. "I never interpreted that for him," he maintained. "The fact is, a boy would never chase after his sister. The women or her father could, but never a boy. I know that. One of my 'Indian sisters' [i.e., a classificatory sister] ran off one time. An aunt came to me and asked, 'Will you go look for her?' and I could only answer, 'I will not. Those young fellows will laugh at me.' "

This study turned up no cases of family pursuit of elopers. What usually happened, in mere elopement, accompanied by no prior disposition of the girl, was that after three or four days a "feeler" was sent to the girl's parents. This was an old woman who went to sound out the family's temper—"especially the mother's. If the mother is happy, they'll send her over." If all was well, the girl was mounted on a horse given by the boy's relatives and, accompanied by other horses loaded with gifts, she was led back to her parents' tipi. The parents kept an eye out for them, and when the party approached, they went out and took the reins to lead their daughter in. This was the act of reconciliation. Or, they lifted her from her mount to carry her into the camp on a spread blanket.

Then the girl's "brothers" were sent for. Her various relatives spoke for their choice of the goods—men the horses, women the dresses and utensils. As in pre-nuptial exchanges, they were expected to return with gifts in equivalent value, after which there followed a feast. This done, the boy's relatives carried off their presents. Thus, if everything went smoothly, the exchange binding

---

[4] Grinnell, *The Cheyenne Indians,* I, 139. The writers incline to believe that Grinnell has here confused pre-marital and post-marital elopement. Both are ways of avoiding one husband and getting another; but the sanctions differ. It is also possible that the protest suicide of a brother whose authority was flouted may lie in the background of the statement.

the contract and validating the marriage was accomplished. This type of elopement did not, as Grinnell implies,[5] eliminate the conventional exchange of gifts.

Stump Horn got his wife in this way and his history is considered according to type by other informants.

To challenge the statement that brothers pursued sisters who eloped is not to imply that brothers were not sometimes aggrieved by such contravention of their authority. Nor fathers, either. Drastic action was sometimes taken. But that was in cases where the girl was not simply assuming to choose a husband, but was defying a brother's prior disposition of her.

There is the case of Pushed By Everybody, with its tragic drama.[6]

《 《 《 Pushed By Everybody was given away by her brother. She was told by her mother [in accordance with principles of brother-sister avoidance], "Your brother has given you to so-and-so."

But the girl cried, "That's just the man I have no love for." That night she ran off with a Southern Cheyenne named Stitching.

Her brother was named Bang! [the sound of an exploding gun]. He took his gun and shot himself dead, for it was a disgrace that his sister had failed to obey him. Word got to her that she would be killed, so she fled to some Siouan tribe.

After a year, she had left her lover and started drifting back to the Cheyenne. Another of her brothers heard that she was nearby. He sent out word to her not to come too close—his heart was still paining for his dear brother who was dead. 》 》 》

We take the threat of killing implied above to be the usual Cheyenne warning that a deep grievance existed, not a true threat to pursue and kill.

《 《 《 Pemmican Road, daughter of the famous chief, Iron Shirt, suffered in another way for her intransigence.

[5] Ibid., I, 139.
[6] Informant: Calf Woman.

A good many years ago Iron Shirt's son was receiving horses from a suitor for his sister. She did not follow her brother, but ran south with Chief Comes In Sight.[7] Her father denounced and disowned her.

It was in 1882 when the girl came back up here. People went to Iron Shirt, telling him his daughter was returned. But he said to them, "I do not know how many years have passed since I disowned her for disobeying her brother. She is not my daughter. I do not want to see her!"

She went back to Oklahoma. Later, she returned once more, but they never took her in. Pemmican Road died without father or mother.   »   »   »

When Calf Woman was probed on the state of public opinion in this matter, she replied that everyone knew Pemmican Road was no longer his daughter, in fact, that Iron Shirt had threatened to shoot her. It was true, she admitted, that some people had gone to Iron Shirt when she came back to the tribe, telling him that it was a long time since the girl had done wrong and that he should forgive her. He was a strong man, however, and refused, for her brother had been killed in battle, after her elopement, and people thought that he had let himself be shot for shame. That is what made Iron Shirt adamant.

In response to further questioning, Calf Woman explained that there was no ritual performance in the disowner of Pemmican Road. Her father just spoke it out in his lodge. Then people spread the word around. At which point High Forehead departed from his customary strict adherence to straight interpretation to interject, "Some women make good newspapers."

It was on the death of Chief Comes In Sight that Pemmican Road attempted to return to her people. In further detail, it was said that she found a brother and told him, "I have come back home." But the brother, too, refused to recognize her. "I don't know where your home is," he answered. After the death of Iron Shirt, it is said people began to urge Rising Sun, her surviving brother, to take

[7] One of the outstanding Cheyennes at the Custer defeat.

her back. Nevertheless, he, too, was unmoved, and to this day none of her relatives will claim her as kin.

These cases make it clear that fraternal-paternal authority in relation to a girl had legal teeth, which could bite. So far as the cases go, it appears that the teeth closed when a girl eloped after her brother had by act or word betrothed her elsewhere. To anticipate a brother's decision was one thing; to flout it when he had contracted, was another. In the two specific cases which are recorded above, the protest suicide of the brother resulted—one by self-inflicted violence, the other presumably by battle-courted death. Each instance resulted in permanent extrusion of the erring daughter from her family, one began before the suicide of the brother, the other after. In each case also, the girl was threatened. But it was not against elopement, it was against contravention of authority, that these sanctions operated.

The attempts of the public to effect a reconciliation indicate a desire, even there, to smooth the path again. And as High Forehead said, "I don't think I would hold it so long. Sixty years is a long time. Most people felt they were too hard."

There were no determinable supernatural sanctions for sororal disobedience.

The preceding data indicate that getting properly married was taken seriously by the Cheyennes. This is so, and Grinnell has not exaggerated in writing that "the women of the Cheyenne are famous among all western tribes for their chastity. In old times it was most unusual for a girl to be seduced, and she who had yielded was disgraced forever. The matter at once became known, and she was taunted with it wherever she went. It was never forgotten. No young man would marry her."[8] This is true, though there was a way for a fallen woman to be redeemed by ritual purification (page 210 f.).

Cheyenne girls wore a chastity belt which was assumed upon puberty. It consisted of a thin rope placed about the waist, knotted in front over the abdomen, with the free ends passing down between the thighs to the back, thence down around the legs to the knees.

[8] Grinnell, *The Cheyenne Indians*, I, 156.

It was worn always at night, as well as during the day when away from the home lodge.

Its respect was law. To disturb the rope, or to assault a girl, was a private delict of first magnitude. Unless the offender fled into temporary exile, he stood in danger of death at the hands of women relatives of the outraged girl.

As Dog stated it, the women[9] relatives, when informed by a girl of her misfortune, charged the lodge of the boy, and laying about right and left, destroyed whatever of his goods came to hand and killed his horses. If the father of the boy was at home, he came out of the lodge and stood to one side to let them at it. Even the parents could lose thereby. Dog avers he has seen this done. He probably refers to Lone Elk, who forty years ago untied a girl's rope, according to the testimony of Black Wolf. In this case the mother destroyed all the property of the boy's parents.

Trifling with the rope was nearly as bad. Dog told of Big Foot, a medicine man, who used to take a daily stroll before sunrise. A woman was bending down scooping up water at the creek. A man stole up behind her and ran his hand up her legs. She jumped and spun around in surprise. The rude disturber was walking away, his head hidden in his blanket. "I know you," she cried. "You are Big Foot."

The man turned and, speaking Sioux, denied it.

When the woman started telling other people about it, they cautioned her, "You ought to be very sure before you lay a charge like that. Big Foot is a great man; he would not be up to such tricks."

The matter never went farther than that. Yet if she had been certain it was Big Foot, says Dog, the woman would have torn up his tent.

When factors of this variety and intensity are caught in cross-play, an understanding of resultant behavior, in any adequacy, calls for intimate first-hand knowledge. In our own culture, elopement

[9] Grinnell (*ibid.*, I, 131) reported that the male relatives did the punishing. However, in the case he describes the girl and her mother were the sole survivors in the family line; these two waylaid the transgressor in a surprise ambush, pounding him nearly to death with heavy stones.

is likely to set up a complex of tensions for whose resolution there is no single pattern. If, for instance, in a skilled mechanic's family, there be what there so often is, a combination of severely bourgeois morality with a strong sense of headship of the house, the elopement of a daughter sets up on the one hand a potent pressure to be stern, on the other hand a potent pressure to manage a face-saving regularization of the situation. We possess what the Cheyennes lacked, a preacher or justice of the peace whom the young people can so enlist as to make unambiguous the essential nature of their action; but in the absence of an official marrier, it is clear that both the sense of parental grievance and the drive to get things straightened out must grow more intense. Something of this sort is presented by the Cheyenne elopement, though so far as the cases show, the eloper's intentions were always assumed to be toward marriage. It is true that Cheyenne marriage did not have an irrevocable character, nor is there found any clear indication that a union would not be recognized socially as regular in essence, if for some reason exchange of gifts failed to occur. But it does seem clear that elopement tended strongly to force the hand of the respective families; and the hand thus forced seems to have been effectively forced, for no cases were found of a girl's relatives undertaking to declare a speedy divorce.

It may well be in such considerations that one finds an explanation of the case of not freewill elopement, but girl-stealing—though with honorable intentions. We have only one such case (from High Forehead)—two girls simply found by warriors at a trader's store, and liked, and lifted. "There was nothing they could do." Here the whole thunder of the law of rape rolls in the background. The matter worked out as if it had been a regular elopement. But had the girls refused consent and later escaped, one has no picture of which of the dice faces would have rolled uppermost.

Not one case turned up of the abduction of a married woman without her agreement, unless the retaliatory taking of Winnebago's wife by Walking Coyote be such a case; and the whole Walking Coyote story is deviational (CASE 20).

The incest prohibition was a social norm which approached, and may have had, legal status. Public opinion was dead set against its violation, but there does not seem to have been any direct public legal sanction attached to it. Yet even killing, in self-defense, where rape and incest combined, was recognized as utterly blameless. Since there are only three cases of incest, it is impossible to determine any regularity or institutionalization in legal sanction. But this is what happened in two historical cases.

«   «   «   High Forehead was with a portion of the tribe on Beaver Creek, in Oklahoma, when Comes In Sight stabbed her father, Bear Rope. "He was a mean man trying to make a wife of her." Though she disemboweled him as he attacked her, there was no sympathy for Bear Rope. The Arrows were renewed for the killing of him, but the girl was not exiled or treated as a murderess.   »   »   »

This is a startling exception to the otherwise universal legal and supernatural effects of homicide; the more so, as the case of the abortion (CASE 14) shows that the exception is not due merely to the intrafamily character of the killing.

A good many years after Long Jaw had cut off the scalp lock of Brave Wolf for suspected adultery (CASE 37), Long Jaw got involved in incest with his own daughter.

«   «   «   Brave Wolf heard of Long Jaw's transgression. "Here is my chance," he cried. "I will kill him. He is the fellow who did that to me."

Then he started sneaking around.

"I will give him what he did to me," he kept saying.

But the people tried to talk him out of it. "Forget it," they urged him. "That was years ago. Forget it, you are men now. Let him do what he wants to."

His own wife kept him back. "Let him be," she ordered her husband. "You are not married to that girl."

"I know I am not," he agreed, "but he is doing something wrong. I'll get him."

But he never had the chance, for Long Jaw left that night. It was true that he was committing incest with his daughter. His wife caught him at it and she had cautioned her daughter to marry the first boy who offered himself.

But the girl was afraid. "No," she wept, "my father is threatening to kill me if I marry."

All the boys who came to court were run off by Long Jaw, but finally it got out. One of the wooers, after holding her in the blanket, [the Dakota courting practice adopted by the Cheyennes, in which a boy ran up and threw his blanket around his sweetheart, holding her fast while he talked to her of this and that] told the others, "I think our sweetheart has a baby in her."

After that they all quit her, and when it became known, the family broke up, two sons leaving home to stay with other people. Long Jaw fled from Brave Wolf's threats. The mother counseled her daughter, "I am ashamed to stay here. Let us leave our tribe!" They did this and went to live with the Sioux.

People talked a lot about Long Jaw. They said he was crazy —not a good man. The girl seemed to have got rid of her baby, for it was never born. But even so, no Cheyenne boy would ever have married her. People would have said of him, "He married Long Jaw's daughter-wife."   »   »   »

This last case makes it clear that incest was in first instance an intrafamily matter. "Let him do what he wants to." Nevertheless, it was heinous misconduct, and public disapproval was strong. It is interesting to note again (see Pawnee, CASE 1) how the man nursing a grudge desired to make of himself a self-appointed public guardian of tribal morals, to seize upon the occasion as an opportunity to get personal revenge in the name of community righteousness. He wanted to make a quasi-criminal act out of Long Jaw's transgression. Yet in spite of the moral censure of the community, there was no support for Brave Wolf's proposal. As his wife reminded him, "You are not married to her." In other words, "This private transgression is none of your business." In law Brave

Wolf's urge had no clear standing, yet the pressures were enough to induce Long Jaw to leave the territory posthaste.

The position of the Cheyenne woman in the marriage bond had considerable strength. In the first place, there is her near guaranty of status. Consider the amazing concept, "daughter-wife," immediately *supra*. Its use (or invention) means that she who lives in a man's lodge and has sex relations with him is a "wife" almost by virtue of the lack of any term like "concubine" to give her a lesser status. This has its bearing also in the pressures toward regularization of elopement. The legal disabilities which a woman suffered were few, while there were effective positive checks against malicious cruelty on the part of the husband, for such was good ground for divorce; and in the case of Last Bull's sister, this was made the occasion of depriving the husband of his inheritance from his wife.

The fate of Bird Face (CASE 16) and Carries The Arrows (CASE 45) shows that a wife's relatives who were grossly displeased with a husband's behavior could directly declare her divorced from him and remove her from his lodge.

A wife displeased with her husband's conduct went "home to mother." Her parents would remind her of her agreement to live with the man but had no authority to force her to another try at the marriage.

Fraternal authority still held, however, though the brother took no notice of his sister's presence unless the husband sent over a horse. This signalized a request for the return of the wife. It was the prerogative of the brother and any of his "brothers" who had been in the gift exchange at the marriage to decide the woman's fate. They put her through a cross-examination to determine her grounds for divorce. If they were weighty, the disunion was allowed. It is said that the brothers did not like to send back the same horse, but this they did if they declared a divorce. On the other hand, if they sent the woman back, she went on a horse provided by a brother, who in turn kept the horse sent by the husband. Calf Woman's brother sent her back to her husband on his best horse. Such a horse-exchange is a mirroring of the first marital exchange. It indicates a renewal of a contract relation which had been broken off for cause.

When a husband left his wife, there was no privilege accorded her to send a horse to get him back. However, a legal disclaimer was published by the deserted wife's brother, closing the ex-husband's interest in the wife. According to Black Wolf, the brother sent word to the deserting husband through a comrade in the husband's soldier society to the effect that when the woman remarried, the husband was not to put in a claim for her. This action clarified the status of the woman and checked possible future legal action against the wife.

The legal position of Cheyenne women, combined with their strong spirit, gave them an unusual power over their warrior husbands. An erring husband betimes suffered much at the hands of indignant females.

She Bear stepped into such a she-hornet's nest one time.[10]

«   «   «   She Bear had been off on a trip in the winter. When he came home, his lodge was empty—no fire, no food, no wife: she had gone home to her mother. She Bear went after her. When he entered the tipi, he struck her in the face. His mother-in-law turned on him, and bawled, "I never said anything to you before. You have been abusing our child ever since you married her, but I never knew whom to blame. Now you have gone too far. Now you have come here to beat my daughter. The world won't come to an end if I beat my son-in-law."[11] She pounced right on him, knife in hand, and stabbed him in the back.

The girl's father cried, "That's enough! You have stabbed him once!"

She Bear screamed, "I am killed." [Told with gusto and laughter.]

The daughter joined in, seizing a club and beating him.

"Now you get out of here," the mother ordered. But when She Bear still showed fight, she grabbed a branding iron from the fire,

10 Informant: Calf Woman.

and chased him to his lodge, where she tore everything down, scattering his goods all over the place.

"Here, you can come and get them," she said when she was done.

The pair were separated for a long, long time. She Bear began sending horses, but they were always refused. He was sending them to the mother to make peace with her, but at last he began to send them to her brother. The brother told the emissary, "I was never going to let them remarry, but he has kept begging all this time. Perhaps he is a changed man. I will take these two horses, but you tell She Bear that this is the last time. If he abuses my sister again, I'll be right there with her."

The mother, when she heard of her son's action, was very much put out. "I know what that son of mine wants," she is said to have remarked. "He wants to make a murderess of me, giving my daughter back to that man. If that son-in-law of mine makes trouble for my daughter, I'll just do worse to him than I did before."

But it stuck. No one ever heard of their having trouble in that family again.   »   »   »

Brave Wolf (he of the Long Jaw affair) also had trouble with his women. He was beaten by his nieces for beating his wife. He was beaten again when his wife returned. He had to humble himself in serving her brother on a raiding party (done of his freewill), and he had to give his very best horse before he could get himself reinstated.

Bull Head's misadventures with his spouse were a comedy and a lesson. It, like the last case, is from Calf Woman, and it does not err in undercoloring of the report.

«   «   «   We were going toward the lower Missouri when the men went hunting. Bull Head was along with them. He was coming in with his meat when, looking down from the top of a hill, he saw his wife riding along with the other women, sitting on top of her pack and dragging a travois with their camp goods. He

[11] Here is one more instance to indicate that Cheyenne mother-in-law avoidance was not legal in character, and not absolute; and no supernatural sanction seems to have been attached to it.

rode down and gave her the meat to pack into camp. While she was transferring the meat from his horse to hers, he sat down to wait. Just when she crossed behind the pack horse, it kicked out and hit her hard. She went down, and the horse stampeded. Her child burst out wailing, "My mother is killed."

Bull Head came running, all solicitous. "Where are you hurt? Where did he kick you?"

"Keep away from me," his wife screamed. "Don't you come near me. You men! You lazy fellows! It is not far to the camp, and yet you make me pack the meat. It is all your fault."

But Bull Head did not heed her as he went to help her up. She just took his war spear and broke it over his shoulders, wherewith he went off to look after the runaway horse, while she came hobbling after.

They found the horse mired in a mudhole. "There, see what you did," she yelled. "You stay away." Then she tried to get the lead rope, but could not reach it. She ordered her repentent husband into the mudhole to get it himself. He obeyed her, but the horse reared, stepping on his foot. He disappeared from sight under the water, going right under the horse's belly and coming up on the other side—a mess. His wife plucked a handful of mud and hurled it just as Bull Head turned his face. It smeared him; he threw some back—and they were at it.

In the meantime the horse was drowning. Hawk rode up, and while they were fighting, he lassoed the horse and pulled it out. Then he yelled to them to help him and stop ducking each other. When it was over, the meat was ruined.

When they came into the camp late, Sharp Nose, an old woman, invited Bull Head to stop and eat. "Why don't you wash your face?" she asked him curiously.

"I did," was his reply. But no, he had only smeared the mud around.

Then the daughter came over there.

"What is the matter with your parents?" was Sharp Nose's query. "Everyone has her lodge up, but your mother has nothing."

The truth is, that wife of his refused to put up the tipi or cook for him. Her mother tried to soften her, saying, "Maybe you are wrong."

But then she remained stubborn, "Not until my arm is well will I do a thing for him."

Whenever the mother-in-law gave the little girl a bit of food to take to her father, the injured wife seized it and threw it to the dogs.

Bull Head had to go rustling food from camp to camp. "I am being punished," he told the people. "My wife won't feed me."

But after some time his wife took him back. This man had a good war reputation and a great medicine for curing snake bites.　　》　　》　　》

The submission of strong men to such usage as this indicates the semi-legal, indeed legal, rights of the woman and of her family that she be fairly treated in the contractual wedlock.

Yet, in spite of such checks, the balance of legal prerogatives weighed in favor of the men. While a woman could leave an adulterous husband (her family accepting this as a ground for divorce), she had no regularized legal right to punish him, nor could she prosecute the correspondent for alienation of affection. The husband, on the other hand, enjoyed these privileges with embellishments.

First, a husband could divorce his wife on the drum—a great disgrace for any woman. And he could do it even without important cause.

Drum-divorce was a public divorce, which notified everybody that the husband was giving a quit-claim to all his rights in the woman. The event took place at the dance of a soldier society (the husband's own), or in later years, at the dances of the Omaha Society. In earlier years, the practice was for the husband to inform his troop of his intention, so that they would sing the "Throw-away" song. Then the husband danced by himself, holding a stick in his hand. Dancing up to the drum, he hit it with the stick. Boom! "I throw away my wife." If he threw the stick among the men, whosoever it struck was bound to take the wife. In later years, at the dances of the Omaha Society, they had a regular dance in which all men who had so thrown off a wife got up to dance. Even though this was a man's ritual, glorifying man's prerogative, the women were not completely downed by it.

«   «   «   Forty or fifty years ago, Round Stone was living peacefully with his three wives. On the day of an Omaha Dance ceremonial, he happened to make a request of a wife, which she saucily refused. He slapped her; she struck him back. While they fought, another wife joined the fray against him.

"I never knew a woman to pull my hair," he roared. "I am a big chief. They don't get away with that."

When the time came for the men to dance who had drummed a wife away, he got up and danced with them. It is said there were about ten men dancing at the time. At the end of the dance, each man was to give away a present to whomever he wished. The turn to give came to Round Stone.

"I have nothing to give," he told them, "but on my word, I never knew a woman to pull my hair." Boom! "I throw her away." Boom! "I throw two away. I keep back Sharp Nosed Woman. The other two are gone."

A number of people, including the women, were standing about as spectators.

Sharp Nosed Woman yelled at her husband, "You fool, let each of them have a horse to go out with." [The horses would have gone to any person Round Stone named.] "Hit that drum again and throw me out, too," she screamed at him.

He gave her no answer. Sharp Nosed Woman was his first wife, while the other two were her classificatory sisters. Then these two, Buffalo Wallow and Looks Around, joined in with more ado. It is claimed they used such words as these, "You great, big-nosed, hog-eyed, hanging-lipped thing, why don't you hit the drum and throw her out, too?" There were forty or fifty women looking on, all laughing at him, so that Round Stone picked up his big eagle-wing fan and hid his face behind it for discomfiture.[12]   »   »   »

[12] Informant: Black Wolf.

A variant of this drum ritual was for a brother to throw away his sister when he was made an Omaha Dance leader. Medicine Bird and Lone Elk were two men who did this. Yellow Tangle-Hair got the stick from Medicine Bird. He did not know it was coming, and so was caught by surprise. It was his duty to accept the girl, if only for a few days; otherwise Medicine Bird would have been insulted. As it was, he lived with her until her death, which was not long after.

In contrast to throwing off a wife, the throwing of a sister was for her a great honor. "It was like giving away a fine horse, only more so." Cheyenne husbands were not prodigal in voluntary disposal of wives, however. They generally thought too well of them for that. A spendthrift Elk Soldier chieftain once triumphed for his fraternity because he was a careless deviator. The Elks and Bowstrings were engaged in a drinking, generosity, and coup-counting bout. Each society was in its own lodge. When it had a present to offer the other group, the gift was presented and a coup recited by the giver. Then the giver took the convivial whiskey barrel back to his cronies, who drank full measure of its contents until a reciprocal coup-counting and shower of gifts took it back to the opposition. Little Shield had no more horses to give, so he put up his household —wife and all! "The recipient had only to go in and lie down, and there he was."

Then the Bowstrings were beaten. They said, "We love our wives and our homes, and we can find no one among us to equal this thing you have done. We are overcome."

There were thus some men who valued the reaching for prestige more than the keeping of their wives, but not many. That rare warrior who would not wait for a settlement offer when his wife eloped or philandered (CASES 41, 42, 42A) was also of this order.

The relatively strict morality of the Cheyenne women and their famed chastity carried deep into the marital situation. Adultery seems to have been exceedingly uncommon. An indication of its rarity lies in the fact that though all informants stated that a man could cut off the braids or nose of an adulterous wife, yet the total of mutilated women known to them was one; and that was a case where the penalty was incurred not for adultery, but for refusal to go with a husband of the brother's choosing. Walks Last had been told of a few long ago by his father, but he knew none of them himself.

Cheyenne morality was so strict that suspected adultery was enough at times to set a husband to seek a violent revenge on the supposed seducer. Part of the incident of Brave Wolf and Long Jaw has been described (Case 33.) The preliminary action which led up to the friction between the two men deserves its exposition here, for it centered around suspected adultery. This is a famous action known to all informants. Calf Woman's version is given here.

«   «   «   Brave Wolf had quite a reputation for hanging around women. One he especially liked was Road Woman, sister of Two Moon and wife of Long Jaw. Long Jaw found Brave Wolf at his lodge one time, so he suspected things.

He accused Brave Wolf, but Brave Wolf always denied it. The woman told her husband that Brave Wolf had not even spoken to her. Still Long Jaw kept it up. Brave Wolf could have taken the oath to prove his clear conscience if he had wanted to, but he used to tell the people he had nothing to take an oath about. "That woman is a sister to me,"[13] he would point out to them.

Nevertheless, Long Jaw was out to get Brave Wolf. One night he saw him waiting to talk to a girl, squatting there beside a lodge with his blanket drawn about him. He crept up and jumped on Brave Wolf, forcing his face into the dirt while struggling to draw his knife. In Brave Wolf's twisting and turning, Long Jaw gashed him in the back. Then Brave Wolf's hand came back in such a way that Long Jaw seized it with his teeth. This freed him, so he could cut off the scalplock he was after.

Then Long Jaw got up. "Friend," he advised the disheveled adversary, "I don't want your horses. This is the satisfaction I want (dangling the scalplock between his two fingers). Now I have

[13] Classificatory sister. He meant to imply by this that the incest imputation was enough to indicate the absurdity of the charge. Since Brave Wolf is reputed later to have married the woman, this remark is inconsistent; it is a "litigant's" favorable argument of his case.

it, I shall bother you no more. You may have my wife now. I do not want her. No, not I. Go over and get her." She had gone home to her parents. Then he started to walk away, but turning, he added, "Friend, I have cut up your back. That was beyond my intention. Come over tomorrow, and I will give you a horse to ride. You may have it with my wife."

Long Jaw was mighty proud of that scalplock. You could see the bare place on Brave Wolf's scalp for many years. » » »

In spite of all this, Brave Wolf does not seem to have lost status greatly in the tribe, though he was thereafter called Red Back of the Head. In later years, he was one of the outstanding Cheyenne fighters and thus his status was maintained. Possibly he was guilty, and this may account for his submitting to such indignity. Or it may have been that he desired the woman enough to consider her acquisition fair compensation for the rough handling he received. Yet, even after years had passed, his resentment was not dead and he did his best to seize opportunity to even up with Long Jaw (see above, pages 179 f.).

It is in keeping with the strong position of Cheyenne woman, that so far as could be determined, no husband had (or revealed through use) the right to force a confession from his wife by third-degree methods such as were used by the Comanche spouse.[14] Nor was there any special oath or conditional curse which the husband applied to the suspected wife. In fact, no informants knew of a wife's ever having been put to oath. But men, by suspicious husbands, though not forced to the oath, were placed in positions that urged in that direction. (See Cases 22, 23.)

A tribal chief who had been made a cuckold ideally ignored the adultery, as he should also the much more respectable procedure of desertion by his wife with another man. They had a phrase for it—"a dog has pissed on my tent"—whereby it was implied that the matter was beneath notice.

14 Hoebel, *Political Organization . . . of the Comanche Indians,* 66 ff.

«   «   «   Shoots Left-Handed [in the one case of adultery known to Black Wolf], though not a tribal chief, met the situation in the dignified way, for he was an Elk Society chieftain. When this man returned from a long absence on the warpath, he found his wife was fat with child. He asked the name of her lover "in a good way." She revealed it as his friend, Sharp Eyes. Shoots Left-Handed convened the Elk troop to lay the matter before his soldiery, asking for their advice. In the meantime, Sharp Eyes' father had engaged a chief to take horses to Shoots Left-Handed, saying, "I am going to send my son to join his troop." [This, because the offender was an Elk Soldier as well; he apparently had been ostracized from the lodge.] When the emissary found Shoots Left-Handed in the society lodge, the husband refused to smoke the pipe until the soldiers had acted. "I won't have a word to say, because I have turned it over to my soldiers. Whatever their answer may be, that shall be mine," are his reputed words.

Sharp Eyes was sent for. He was first given a pipe, and then was addressed by another chief. Was he guilty? Sharp Eyes confessed, offering to make amends by aiding Shoots Left-Handed in the care of the child after its birth. The society then informed their aggrieved chief that he should accept the offer and keep his wife. True to his word, he followed their judgment.   »   »   »

Absconding seems to have been much safer than adultery among the Cheyennes—and more common. There was nothing immoral in a woman's changing marital status through desertion for cause; and there appears to have been nothing immoral in deserting to another man, becoming the latter's wife, although that did involve a matter for legal adjustment between the men. It did not fit a Cheyenne warrior's ideal conception of dignity to chase a woman who did not want him. There are found cases of resentment against such a woman. One finds cases of husbands, in spite of considerations of dignity, making steady pleas to a woman's family to return her. What one does not find is her ex-husband pursuing her after she had taken another man. Consequently, husbands usually gave little external evidence of emotional tension when wives sought new spouses. There was none of the slaying of the wife before the eyes of her would-be husband, which so often happened in Comanche cases. Cheyenne abhorrence of intratribal blood-spilling was of course a severe check to such violence; killing a wife was murder.

Neither was the absconding pattern of the Cheyennes woven into the war-party complex as it was with the neighboring Comanches. The Cheyennes long ago faced and solved this problem as described in the opening chapter (CASE 5). Many Cheyenne histories have delighted us in our work; this was one of the most delightful. The probable date for the happening is not far from 1820. Walking Rabbit, the principal, was Elk River's brother, who told it to Black Wolf, the informant.

It will be recalled that the warriors on this raid stopped to hold a council when Walking Rabbit turned up with another man's wife; they decided to send Walking Rabbit and the woman back and voluntarily offered to put up a lavish gift-restitution to the aggrieved husband on behalf of Walking Rabbit. In this they were as good as their word. However, the gifts did not go to the ex-husband, since Walking Rabbit's father had anticipated them; instead, they were sent to the girl's parents and relatives as a wedding payment.

From that date to the end of the raiding days there were no more attempts to abscond with war parties. Informally a decision regarding substantive law was reached and handed down to remain an unaltered part of the tribal constitution. It was constitution, not merely law, because it dealt with allocations of powers. War parties were definitely barred from participation in divorce-and-remarriage procedure. The case itself is an example of the almost unique Cheyenne legal resiliency. In how many other cultures would a clear rule and precedent of non-participation in divorce proceedings be accomplished in a case which was itself one of historic and ceremonial active participation?

Other factors made absconding with parties really unnecessary. Cheyenne legal procedure placed great restraints upon the offended husband. Where the Comanche husband was forced by opinion to go after an absconder in person, the Cheyenne husband was expected not to do so. A chief, it has been seen, was expected to pay no attention whatever to his wife's infidelities or defection. So also the owner of a scalp shirt. "His fellow-chiefs would think less of him if he weakened." How nice a connotation, this "weakened"! Cheyenne custom here stripped the most powerful men of use of the powers which might place undue coercive sanctions in their hands.

Any husband who followed the best code did as a chief would do. He did not press the absconder for settlement. He, like the chief, waited. Custom and the social pressures, which induced men to act decently, made up for the deficiency, however. Within a few days, the absconder took steps to set things right. He invited one or more chiefs, or other men of influence (possibly medicine men), to his lodge and prepared the pipe for them. He laid his case before them and spoke of what he intended to send the husband by way of composition—one horse, or two or more, possibly a blanket or gun. One of the chiefs accepted the commission to act as intermediary to settle the case. There was nothing of the champion or even arbitrator here. The issue did not turn on the balance of relative strength, nor was the amount of damages to be paid a matter of bargaining. The payment was ordinarily set by the absconder. Its size seems to have been determined largely by his resources and the esteem in which he held the woman he had taken; perhaps also partly by his relation to the aggrieved husband. The function of the go-between was to bear the pipe to the husband, along with the horses or other "gift" the absconder was offering. He attempted to induce the husband to smoke in acceptance. The conformer to good usage smoked without resistance; so the case was settled. The changed status of the woman was legally validated; the husband had received payment in consideration of release of his rights in her.

A chief was chosen as intermediary "because a person ought not to refuse the request of a chief." The pressure came then, not only from the principal party, but acceptance was made a sort of personal favor to, or better, status recognition of, the third party—the chief. In a mild manner this brought the pressure of the "public" to bear. It was a definite constraint toward smooth and peaceful settlement of a private wrong by a type of community action. For the chief was a tribal official, and it was by his special position as a community representative that deference was due his wishes. Nor would one lightly ask a chief to go with a gift unduly niggardly. There is no evidence on whether the chief could, or ever did, move to raise the ante.

An example of the way this general pattern worked in a specific instance was given by Stump Horn from his own experience.

« « «   My wife ran off with a certain man. For a while I said nothing, but simply studied the best way to do. To the other people I simply carried on as though not a thing had happened.

Then one day I saw a man coming my way leading a spotted horse. It was Crazy Head, a chief. I would not say anything to a chief. Crazy Head said he was pulling [using his influence] for me not to cause trouble. Would I accept the horse and settle it?

I said to him, "Do not talk about such things" [i.e., the causing of trouble]. But I did tell Crazy Head this, "I am very sorry you brought that horse. I would much rather have had a saddle and some blankets. However, since you have brought the horse, I shall take it."

So we smoked, and I took the horse, and that other man had my wife.   »   »   »

What appears as the first deviation from the ideal conduct (which we take to be no deviation at all from the normal real pattern of conduct) is the fact that Stump Horn did have in his mind's eye a picture of what he would have liked to receive in composition. Though overtly conforming to the pattern of indifference, he had gotten around to thinking covertly in terms of what might be had.

Calf Woman claims to have heard of cases in which a disgruntled husband told the intermediary to turn around and go back. "That woman has done more harm to me than that," he would say. While no details were obtainable on any such instances, the stories of Walking Coyote (CASE 20) and of the hard-bitten warrior-husband (CASE 42A), are suggestive.

From further cases comes the revelation of a second pattern of procedure, one which would normally be followed, if, within the lapse of a few days, no emissary and no composition had been sent. Then the aggrieved husband could take the initiative by sending a chief to the absconder with a statement of his demands. Thus Bear Tusk, when Round Stone ran off with his wife, sent a chief specifying the two horses which would give him satisfaction. "I am not going to stir this up," he said. "Send those two horses and it will be settled." Round Stone, who was himself a chief, had just picked his chief to send, but he accepted the request of Bear Tusk's emissary. This act, which was unusual and not in accord with the generalized statements of the informants, is more easily understood in the light of what Mr. Grinnell writes on the subject; one reads that the intermediary asked the aggrieved husband what it would take to bring satisfaction.[15] Though this was certainly not always the case, the actuality of its practice provided a point of departure from which a demand upon the absconder could be made —in fact, by Bear Tusk, or, in fancy, by Stump Horn. This held for compensation felt as compensation. But the form of compensation could be turned to other uses. Mr. Grinnell cites that when Roan Bear's wife ran off in 1877, Roan Bear smoked when the pipe was sent, and when the emissary asked his will on the settlement, he answered that he would have a dog—a woolly dog to eat. Such was the way he scored the woman.

A second deviation from the ideal standard, providing a third pattern of normative conduct, was for the husband to take his pick of the absconder's horses. This bolder step might, or might not work, and whether it succeeded or not depended on the temper and quality of the principals involved.

《   《   《   When Young Two Moon ran off with the wife of Black Coyote, nothing was said on either side. Black Coyote after a while simply went to the place of Young Two Moon's relatives, calmly selecting the three best horses for himself. One of the horses belonged to Black Bear, father-in-law to Dog and an uncle

[15] Grinnell, *The Cheyenne Indians*, I, 154.

of Black Coyote. This uncle, a mother's brother, sent a messenger to Black Coyote saying, "I am your uncle. I am related to that other family only through marriage. Can't you give me back my horse?" Black Coyote had not known the horse was his uncle's; he gave no reply, but set the horse loose, so that it went back to its owner.[16]   »   »   »

Interesting here are the manifestations of kin liabilities—loose in outline, but real—the privilege of taking horses from relatives of the wrongdoer, and the fact that consanguineal ties, as would be expected, outweighed the affinal. The delicacy with which the mistake was rectified is also in the best Cheyenne manner. These are points incidental to the main issue, which was the *taking* of the horses as settlement for a wrong done, followed by acquiescence of the defendant. This procedure reversed the usual method. The aggrieved party initiated the steps leading to a readjustment, and the procedure was direct, without the peace-preserving intermediary chief.

The outcome of such procedure was different, however, when there was a willful person standing on the side of the wrongdoer. High Forehead tells of how he frustrated an attempt to collect from his classificatory brother. "I started it in fun, but I had to carry out my bluff." This is what happened.

«   «   «   This "brother" ran off with Two Moon's wife in January, 1880. He had had her a week or ten days without attempting to make a settlement. Then the mother of Two Moon came visiting to tell High Forehead's family that they had decided on having the young man's three horses—they were good ones. High Forehead, who happened to be present, announced that the horses would not be sent, nor could they come and take them. The old lady went away. High Forehead went into his tent to put on his cartridge belt and bring out his carbine. He was a sergeant in General Miles' Cheyenne scouts, a fact which probably helped to build up his braggadocio. Thus prepared, he announced to all

[16] Informant: Dog.

about him, "I don't intend to kill anybody, but I also do not intend for them to have those horses. If they come here to take them, I'll shoot the horses dead. They shall not have them."

At sundown, he was still awaiting developments. Folks were hanging around to see what might come. The "brother," who had taken the wife, was staying discreetly in his lodge. Quite innocently, a straying dog came sniffing around. "Look here!" High Forehead called out. "If they come over here for those horses, I will do it just like this." Crash! His gun roared; the dog fell dead. Nobody came for the horses, then or later. The young man lived with the woman until he died.   »   »   »

These situations show the extremes of conduct which occurred when the aggrieved party took steps to gain satisfaction through his own action. Just what would have happened if the aggrieved had attempted to push through to his goal when resistance was expressed on the other side cannot be said. Investigation brought out no cases of this sort. The most informants could offer on it was that there would be trouble, which means a building up toward violence, perhaps unaverted.

Still another variant, in which the wronged man took steps to get his justice, was a more drastic modification of the last. When She Bear took Iron Shirt's wife from her husband's lodge to his own, She Bear said nothing, according to Stump Horn. Nor was the pipe sent to Iron Shirt. After a few days, when it happened that She Bear's horses were being brought into camp, Iron Shirt put on his blanket, and going over to the herd, he shot the two best horses. No overt reaction was noticed from She Bear. The deed was accepted.

This is the only case portraying such an action, but its general acceptance as a type is indicated by Grinnell's mention of such conduct as a possibility in wife-absconding settlements;[17] its motivation is a combination of the desire to show scorn evidenced in the woolly-dog demand of the warrior who would show that he is no man to be lightly meddled with, and of release of built-up tension by vio-

[17] Grinnell, *The Cheyenne Indians*, I, 154

lence directed into safe channels. We are inclined to believe that the aggressor's failure to send a mediating chief had in it an element of additional grievance. Attempts to obtain judgments of natives concerning whether it was more estimable to accept settlement or to kill an absconder's horses as a gesture of balancing the account were of no avail. If things took the most ordinary course, the killing of horses did not occur. If the wrongdoer did not take steps soon enough, then the aggrieved could take whichever of the paths he chose, and the public seems not to have praised or blamed one or the other.[18]

Finally, there were the rare cases in which the husband proceeded violently against the wife-taker. Taken together, they leave no doubt that while the pattern of divorce and remarriage by action was clear, and was recognized, the wrong to the husband was deep, and the legal devices and social pressures which had been developed to work out the transition of status for the woman played over a volcano. In two instances the violence occurred because the husband came upon the pair in the act of absconding—which flavored the situation with adultery. In the case of Little Son, he shot and killed both the wife and absconder. But Little Son was an Arapaho living among the Cheyennes, so this case is doubly atypical. He went back to his people. In the case of Red Eagle, Coyote, the absconder, escaped after he had received a beating from the husband. Red Eagle went home for his gun, but could not find Coyote. It was the next day, when the camp was on the move, that he discovered him.

《   《   《   Red Eagle was with the Fox Soldiers, who were marching in a bunch singing. He ordered the Foxes to keep marching, while he dropped out of the ranks. Coyote saw him at

[18] A good deal of the discussion of Comanche killing of horses due in restitution (Hoebel, *Political Organization . . . of the Comanche Indians*, 56) will apply in explanation of Cheyenne motives leading to similar conduct. An incident at the Tongue River Agency in 1936 shows the survival. One of the Cheyennes had petitioned the relief director for foodstuffs for his mother. When the request was refused on the grounds that the applicant had a horse and so was not destitute, he left the office. Then he got his horse and rode it right up to the door of the agency where he shot it, exclaiming, "So I suppose they think I can eat my horse." Then without going in to ask for relief, he strode off, leaving the carcass for the agency to dispose of.

that moment, so he rushed in among the soldiers. Red Eagle rode up pointing his gun. "Move!" he cried to the soldiers, "move, so I can shoot him." At first the soldiers scattered a bit, but as soon as they recovered, they closed in on Red Eagle and seized him. They argued with him. They said, "You are one of our chiefs. We think a lot of you. Don't do this thing. You will spoil your reputation."

Red Eagle answered back, "If there is one thing I hate, it is to see a man let another get away with his wife." But the soldiers held him in check.

Red Eagle's own Foxes then sent an old chief to him with the pipe, but he refused to smoke. His threats toward Coyote continued. After he had refused several chiefs, the Foxes advised Coyote [who had been in hiding under their care] to leave the camp. This was ten years before the Custer fight. Coyote went south and did not return until a few years ago, long after the death of Red Eagle. In a joking mood he began to say to the folks, "I am looking for that wife of mine. Where is she?" She, on the other hand, announced that she hated him for the trouble he had caused her. For though Red Eagle did not mutilate her, and kept her as wife, he beat her regularly until she wounded him in the armpit with her six shooter."[19]   »   »   »

Naturally, in the light of Cheyenne attitudes toward murder, public pressures would be directed against homicidal vengeance in absconding ventures. Here there is another example of the specific peace-time, non-hunting activities of the military associations as stabilizers and controllers of intratribal conduct. It focused the community sense of order, which was also secondarily expressed by the free advice offered in scoldings given Red Eagle by "the people."

The tragic results of the taking of Walking Coyote's wife by White Horse (CASE 20) reveal in stark terms the practical reasons for checking homicidal revenge. Four men lost their lives in successive murders because White Horse failed to return the wife of Walking Coyote in compliance with the husband's demands.

[19] Informant: Black Wolf.

An old-time case given by Black Wolf shows a Cheyenne husband in a markedly un-Cheyenne, but very Kiowa- or Comanche-like, frame of mind, pleading his case, however, with all the finesse of the best of Cheyennes.[20]

《   《   《   One time one man's wife ran off with another. Before anything could be done, the husband sent word over to the absconder.

"Don't try to send me any gifts! Send no chief to tell me a story about what you are going to do to get this thing settled," was his message. "I want nothing from *you*."

Then he went on talking to his friends. "That man thinks nothing of me," he told them. "He thinks I am a coward who will do nothing. Well, some day we are going to meet the enemy together. There is where I am going to see my friend. If he shows any cowardice then, there is where I'll come in."

The husband was a noted warrior among the people.

The camp was moved to the south, down toward Oklahoma. It was a big camp, for they were getting all the tribe together. When they got in the south country, a big war party was made up.[21]

After the declaration of the husband, that wife-taker always went in war parties in which the husband was not a member. This time the husband hung back several days before starting out, then trailed down the group the absconder was with. When he overtook them, they were at rest in camp. They saw him coming and heard him singing a soldier song—a death song. When he got into camp, he rode right over some of the men as they were sitting there. That meant he intended to charge right into the enemy breastworks. If the campers ran into a lodge, they were safe from him, but if he came upon one, he struck him hard with his whip. That was the way he would count coup on the enemy. He could take whatever meat he wanted from any pot.

[20] Cf. Jane Richardson, *Law and Status Among the Kiowa Indians* (Monographs of the American Ethnological Society, No. I, 1940).

[21] The informant is talking of the occasion of the tribal move against the Pawnees, undertaken as a revenge expedition which was spoiled by the unexpected presence of a party of Potawatomies. This was in 1853. See Grinnell, *The Fighting Cheyennes*, 80 ff.

The absconder looked scared.

Three days later, he walked up to the husband. "Friend," he said, "as long as we are on this war party, it is my desire to look after you. I want to make your camp, to cook your food, to look after your horses. I know what you have declared as your intention. You are on this war path, never to return."

He got no satisfaction from the other. Came the rebuff, "I haven't finished this thing yet. You acted as though you did not think so much of me when you were making off with my wife. You put on as though you were the better man then. I still think I am good. I could have accepted gifts from you. But that is not what I want. Now we are out to see who *is* the better man."

That began to worry the absconder. "If I turn back, he'll kill me. If I go on, I must die before the enemy."

In his dilemma he went to the leader of the war party and to the Holy Hat Keeper to see if they could do something. He was asking them if they would not carry the pipe to the husband.

Again he was rebuffed. "No," they told him, "the pipe is still filled. But, even so, we'll go talk to him without a smoke. We'll see if he won't agree to leave some things out which he has in mind. That kind of man is hard to handle. It will take a lot of talking."

They went to see him as they had said. And they told him the old-time history [way of doing things]. "In the old times," they pointed out to him, "people went to war like you to get killed. That is all right. But you are up to something else. You want to scare him so he'll run off by himself where you can kill him. Can't you leave our friend alone?"

"Well," said the husband, "I'll leave him alone on this trip. But you chiefs know how it is when a man steps in and induces your wife to run off with him. He acts as though you were nothing. That is what makes me angry—for him to act as though he were not afraid of me! Now what I want to know is, is he the better man? When we find the enemy, I am going right in. If he leads me in and counts coup before I do, I am satisfied."

When they charged the enemies, the husband counted two coups, but the enemies were well armed and turned the Cheyennes to rout. When the wife-taker lighted out with the others, the husband took after him and quirted him. "Just as I thought," he yelled, "you are no man. When we get back, I take my wife from you."

But when he started to do this thing, his father-in-law intervened, saying that his daughter had made a poor wife. Now he had another who had come of age and he was giving her to his son-in-law instead. 》 》 》

This husband was obviously a man who was touchy about his war status and personal prestige position in a way which did not concern most Cheyennes. Where a peace chief merely shrugged his shoulders and made a customary remark about the habits of dogs, where a war chief could ask for a "woolly dog to eat," this man—who was neither peace chief nor war chief, and yet a great warrior—took occasion to see personal affront in the wife-taking. Among the Cheyennes the giving of settlement gifts did not carry with it the least flavor of submission to any dominance position of the aggrieved. But that is what this aggrieved husband wanted. To get it, he laid his successive moves perfectly. He forestalled the bringing of the pipe by announcing that he was not of a mind to accept a settlement and by letting it be known what he intended. The absconder strove to postpone the issue, but in this he was neatly outwitted. The aggrieved riveted attention of the public on his case by his actions in the camp, which set him out as a man dedicated to the glorious death. Private settlement was out. The relative worth of the men was to have its public demonstration.

Looking backward, one can summarize the factors of law pertaining to the violation of the marital rights of a husband through wife-absconding. Six patterns of action have been noted: (1) There is the basic and ideal norm—according to which the husband made no move, but waited for the emissary, usually a tribal chief, to come from the aggressor bearing the pipe and, (a) bringing horses or other goods acceptable to a man, or, (b) asking the husband what he desired in way of settlement. Smoking the pipe meant acceptance; the matter was closed, and the status of the woman in question changed. (2) When the aggressor failed to carry out his legal

duty, the wronged husband occasionally sent a chief with a statement of his demands. (3) The aggrieved might take his pick of the
herd of the aggressor or his relatives. This was either (a) acquiesced
in by the aggressor, or (b) blocked by him or a relative. Or, (4) the
husband shot horses of the aggressor. (5) Rarely, the husband was
so angered as to kill (or try to) the absconder without any attempt
at legal settlement. This must be regarded as illegal. (6) The husband could demand the return of his wife. This last may have been
old law; but practice had so set against it that it cannot be safely
regarded as still a right. There was found no case in which the
demand was honored, or in which attempts at its enforcement were
unambiguously approved.

The Cheyennes did not recognize the sororate claim as a right.
They looked upon it as a potential privilege which might be made
available to a good son-in-law. However, a Cheyenne husband seeking a second wife could, and often did, take the initiative in seeking
his wife's younger sister to espouse. By giving horses to his parents-
in-law, he made his desires clear. Acceptance of the horses by the
parents established a legal claim upon their second daughter. So it
was that because Sets Like A Man had been giving presents to the
parents of Brings Something, when she refused to live with him, he
cut off her braids. Yet her parents did not upbraid or attempt to
punish him in any way. Failure to meet the brother-in-law's ripened
claim apparently made a younger sister subject to sanctions.

There was dispute over the nature of the sanction which was
legal in such instances of a sister-in-law's refusal to accept marriage.
A husband-claimant, with the coöperation of his soldier comrades,
applied the "free woman penalty" as proper. The blood relatives
of the girl, male and female, violently denied its applicability; and
public opinion seems to have been with them on the point. To make
a "free woman" of an unfaithful wife was agreed to by the informants as a right of the husband, if the woman had committed adultery
more than once. The practice is called *noha' sɛwɔstan,* literally "any
man's wife." It is also referred to as "on the prairie," because the
husband, after inviting either his soldier band or his cousins to

assemble at a certain spot on the prairie for a feast, brought them his wife.

«   «   «   Big Laughing Woman, who died in 1910 a reputed centenarian, deserted her husband as a young girl. He threatened to give her to his soldier society—and did. All the unmarried men of the club who were not related to her had intercourse with her on the prairie. It is said there were forty or fifty of them. The girl survived, but no man ever married her afterward; she was not molested after the one experience, however. In later years, she became the favorite storyteller of the tribe. High Forehead says that in his youth the boys sat quietly the whole night through, listening to her tales of the great days of old. Although her experience made her a woman apart, there is little evidence that she was morally looked down upon because of it[22]   »   »   »

When One Eye tried the same thing on his young wife after surprising her in illicit relations with her former sweetheart, he experienced a fervid backfire from her family. They recoiled at the horror of the act and saved their daughter.[23]

«   «   «   One Eye gave her to his brother soldiers in the Elk Society. He had said to her, "We are through, you and I." Then he left the tent.

The girl was the younger sister to Buffalo Woman, his head wife. Buffalo Woman told her to hide. "Our husband has gone to invite the soldiers," she said. So the younger wife went to the lodge of her old girl friend. One Eye found her there and dragged her off. A little boy saw what was going to happen, and he ran to the girl's mother to tell her the place on the prairie where her daughter would be found.

The mother cried for Red Bird, her son. He came. In anguish, she told him what was befalling his sister.

"I'll shoot to kill," was his answer.

"No," his mother cautioned, "shoot only to wound in the legs. We do not want you a murderer."

[22] Informant: Black Wolf.
[23] Informant: Dog.

"I vow death to them when I get there," he repeated.

But he did not have to shoot. When the Elks saw him coming, they scattered without fighting.

Still it was not all over for One Eye. Buffalo Woman divorced him. More than that, before she left his lodge she cut all his goods to shreds. He could not even claim damages from the adulterer, because he had tried to make a free woman of the girl. No offering was sent him either. Later, the girl grew up to be a fine, good-looking woman, and she married Corn Tassel.   »   »   »

In this case, it was the family of the girl who checked the action, and went on into retaliation as for a wrong committed against her—and this even though it was the girl's husband punishing her for a misstep. Certainly, brutal over-punishment is an independent countergrievance.

Indeed, it is difficult to read the recurring instances in which a new wife sets up sex relations with "a former sweetheart," without strongly suspecting the presence or emergence here of a social, and perhaps even quasi-legal, escapement-valve recognizing some privilege in a young girl to control the choice of her husband. The girl here is not treated as a seduced young girl would be, if there were no marrying in the picture. Nor, in these circumstances, does adultery (here a first step toward prospective elopement and remarriage?) seem to carry the normal stigma.

In the case of Stands Different Colors, which follows as told by Calf Woman, the intervention was by outsiders, indicating the degree to which public sentiment was shaping, or had shaped, to counteract the practice of "the prairie."

«   «   «   There was a Bowstring Soldier, Carries The Arrows, who had an elder sister to wife. His parents-in-law had been accepting his presents, so they let him marry her younger sister, too. This was Stands Different Colors. She hated him. It was because of this that when her mother, Owl Woman, took her over to her husband's lodge to make her stay, she refused to bide with him.

Carries The Arrows got disgusted; he told his Bowstring companions he was going to invite them to a feast—but it would be a woman. Then he got Last Bull to capture the girl for him. When they were moving camp one day, Last Bull seized her horse's bridle and led her off. She knew something was about to happen. Last Bull led her over to her brother-in-law-husband. This one said, "Get off your horse and get up here with me." She was willing and they rode off.

After they got out there, all the Bowstrings began coming up. "Here is the feast," Carries The Arrows declared. "Take her!"

The girl threw herself on her husband. "Oh, take me home," she pleaded. "Please, please, let me go back with you. I will love you forever."

He was hard with her. "No," he grunted. "It is too late now. When this is over you will never think yourself too good for me again." He turned from her and rode off, not staying for the fun.

Tassel Woman and her husband, Blue Wing, cared about this. They were worried for the girl's sake, and they were plotting how to save her. After they had worked out a plan, they rode up to where the Bowstrings were gathered. The soldiers were suspicious of them, but Blue Wing told them he wanted to get in on it too. Well, they thought that was all right, so they told him he could go over to the girl for the next turn. They had her over a ridge and were taking her one at a time. Blue Wing rode over with his wife. They found the girl on the ground. She could just raise herself, and she barely answered when they hailed her, "Are you alive?"

Then they worked fast. Tassel Woman was a good rider on a fast horse. "Change our saddle, quick," she told her man. "Now put her up behind me."

"Now hold on for your life," she warned the girl. "I am letting this horse run free. It is your one chance."

They surely traveled.

After a while Blue Wing went back alone to the soldiers. "Did you do anything?" they eagerly quizzed him.

"Oh yes, I am through with her."

"Where is your woman?"

"Oh, she wouldn't stay to see me with that girl." So he talked to them, stalling for time. "Let her rest a while," he interposed, when one of them wanted to go next. Then after a bit he asked for another chance, so he went down once more and fiddled about.

All at once he whipped up his horse, dashing up out of the gulch. "She is gone," he cried. "I have been searching for her, but she has got away." The soldiers rushed down and all about, but by this time the girl was in camp with her folks.

The girl's brother learned of it when he came in. He loaded his gun and took his father to attack the Bowstrings. They almost had a real fight, but the soldiers scattered before them.

Then Carries The Arrows had cheek enough to come back to his lodge. It was right beside his parents-in-law's. [Carries The Arrows had been raised an orphan.] He had seemed such a good, quiet boy that his mother-in-law had told the first daughter to marry him, so they could have him to live with them. That was all over now. The brother ordered his older sister back to her parents' lodge. "He shall no longer have my sister for a wife," were his words. Besides this, he cut up the lodge and destroyed all the property with it. The parents drove Carries The Arrows from their camp, although he did not have to leave the band.

As for the soldiers, they had nothing to say; they never go two times for the same girl. The people, however, praised Blue Wing for his work. The women gossiped with Tassel Woman about how she had done it, and Blue Wing received a horse from the father for what he had done. The girl never recovered though, and I don't know whether she married. 》 》 》

A similar attempt to make a free woman of a girl on the basis of a sororal claim, but this time one less valid, was frustrated by the wife of the Medicine Hat Keeper and the courageous anger of Crooked Nose Woman. Crooked Nose Woman, who is now old and nearly deaf, gave her account to check against that of Calf Woman, who was also a principal actor in the event. It centered about Little Sea Shell, who was Calf Woman's girlhood chum.

《 《 《 One night as we were idling in Little Sea Shell's tipi, there came a tap on the hide from the outside. "I want to speak to you," whispered a mysterious voice. "Tonight or tomorrow night, I don't know which it will be, but they are going to get one of you. Now is the time to escape."

"It is I," Little Sea Shell whispered in alarm. "Buffalo Hump wants to marry me. I hate him. I won't marry him, and he said he was going to give me to his friends."

Buffalo Hump was married to Red Leaf, elder sister to Little Sea Shell.

The next day, when the whole tribe was moving, the wife of the Medicine Hat Keeper was trudging afoot with the Holy Hat Bundle on her back. They were on a ceremonial march to reach a dance site where the Crazy Dance ceremony would be held. Suddenly, Buffalo Hump and his gang of cousins rode over a hilltop and down on us.

"Run for the Hat," I shrieked.

Little Sea Shell got to the Holy Hat woman and cried, "Take me in, take me in. They are chasing me." The woman put her arms out in a circle for her to step into. [It formed a symbolic lodge for the Buffalo Hat—the lodge in which even an enemy found asylum.] I was holding off the men with a threatening spear. They tried to scare me by saying that I had a good figure, too, they would take me instead of Little Sea Shell. But it did not move me!

Buffalo Hump then got off his horse and strode over to the Holy Hat Woman. He grabbed the girl and started tugging at her.

"Don't you touch me," the Holy Hat Woman warned him.

Buffalo Hump in utter recklessness snarled, "I'll do anything I please."

Whereupon, the Hat Woman retorted, that if he wanted to be crazy, she could be as crazy as he. So saying, she reached over her shoulder to pull a long stick from the bundle. She stuck it into the ground and held on with both hands, arms around the girl. At that Buffalo Hump stood off. [We could never get a full explanation of this. Crooked Nose Woman says it is because it would bring bad luck for the Hat Woman to stumble while packing the Sacred Hat. For this reason, she carried a staff to help her over rough ground. Buffalo Hump, she says, was afraid that if he upset her it might cause him ill. However, it would not seem a "crazy" thing for the Keeper's wife to do, unless it were an act of exceedingly great sacredness—as setting up a fictional, "symbolic" lodge of asylum might well be.] It was at this point that Crooked Nose Woman entered. She was my "sister" and also "sister" to Little Sea Shell. The night before, we had hidden in her lodge. When she heard all the noise, she came pushing her horse over the ridge top, waving a six-shooter. She started right off to shoot over their heads, at which danger the braves scattered. Then Crooked Nose Woman mounted my badly scared and scratched friend on her horse and rode off snapping her fingers at the men.

Even that was not the end. When Strong Eyes, Little Sea Shell's father, heard the news, he went into a rage. He stripped to his breechclout and prepared for war. The gang was in camp now, so, armed with his gun, he led his daughter over to where they were playing the hand game, trying to act as though nothing had happened. The women, seeing him coming, uttered squeals of excitement. "Here comes the thunder. A bear is coming over the hill." Strong Eyes stood before the soldiers, daring them to come and take his daughter. He got so terribly angry that he called out, "Just to show you people how I feel, this is what I would do to Buffalo Hump if he were here." With a loud explosion of his gun, he shot his own horse. After that he had to walk back to his camp.[24]

It took some time for things to calm down again. When Red Eagle, our uncle, came in from the hunt, he also raged against Buffalo Hump. Strong Eyes gave a terrific beating to his second wife, whom he blamed for wanting to give Little Sea Shell to Buffalo Hump. He ended it by divorcing her.

Buffalo Hump seems to have got the idea that his right to Little Sea Shell had been established because he was giving presents to Little Man to help him in the Crazy Dance Lodge, which he had pledged. Little Man was a distant "brother" to my friend, Little Sea Shell. Everyone in the camp talked about the absurdity of Buffalo Hump's trying to take a girl upon whom he had no claim. Even the men gossiped about it.   »   »   »

[24] Crooked Nose Woman says she cannot confirm this act.

In the scenes described above one sees what is probably the most glaring example to be found in the social organization of a Plains tribe of public disharmony over the justification for, or even acceptance of, a prevailing social norm. Here was a point where a people split widely on the matter of the legality of a supposedly legal sanction. It was a question of substantive law. Women were against the practice. Most men accepted it—except when it struck into their family. Actually, even the men were ashamed of it. For the women in their aggressive way hurled the shame of it into the teeth of men, and the men winced. "There is one of those young men there—taking a poor girl out on the prairie. Do you feel it yet? Have you gotten back your strength?" This the cry of the women. It is said the men never replied, but dropping their heads, turned quickly around a tipi. Some men would deny stoutly that they had anything to do with the deed. It was not, then, a deed which the men themselves held free of taint. Their readiness to scatter when a wrathful relative came shooting is another evidence. Yet the act persisted. As a gang of individuals reinforcing each other in some off-the-line activity, also possibly, as a release of sex antagonisms by which men could make a woman suffer for her defiance of male authority, it was possible for men to do collectively that which they did not individually hold to be honorable. We suspect that the right of the husband to this particular penalty was old and may even have had some sacred significance. Grinnell mentions a warrior before a desperate combat "vowing a woman to be passed on the prairie." The whole Cheyenne tribe at that time was moving against the Pawnees with their Sacred Arrows and the Buffalo Hat in the great revenge raid of 1853. While the great Medicine Arrow Dance was being performed just before the attack, Long Chin obtained the Sacred Hat from its Keeper to wear in the battle (this privilege had been denied Two Twists twenty years previously, it will be remembered, because he had pledged himslf to die in the attack [Case 1].) As Long Chin was tying on the Hat, its string broke. To expunge the bad luck, "Long Chin publicly pledged himself to give a woman to be passed on the prairie."[25]

[25] Grinnell, *The Fighting Cheyennes*, 88.

One suspects that the relative frequency of the practice in application to claimed sororal rights, short of established consummation of the marriage, has two roots: one, the perfection for the scorned would-be husband of "You'll never think yourself too good for me again"; the other, the opportunity the old practice offered to rally company and strength, with a tinge of right, for retaliation or aggression against the woman which a man left to himself could hardly carry beyond the cutting off of braids. One suspects, finally, that except for the rise in power and effrontery of the military societies, the practice might have completely disappeared.

A loose woman among the Cheyennes was without social status. Evidence makes it clear that a woman who has been divorced four times became any man's bait. Calf Road, according to Black Wolf, was one such; a lost woman, but redeemed. She was a lass with more beauty than virtue. The Cheyennes say today that the usual Indian maid pictured on the calendars must be Calf Road. At one time she was one of the Elk Society virgin maidens.[26] When she disgraced herself, they cut her hair and turned her loose. She could get temporary liaisons with some men, but no presents were given for her in marriage. The salvation for such a girl was to throw herself on the mercy of an oldish, single man. If he cleansed her by giving a great religious ceremony before he married her, she became a respectable, if not wholly respected, matron.

Calf Road got a Samaritan to pledge her a Sun Dance. Then she, according to form, renounced her past life before the tribe. Her champion danced for her in the ceremony. The priest of the Sun Dance prayed to Maiyun to give her a new life. The holy pipe was smoked several times. When it was done, the leaders told her to go home, never to think or speak of her past. After the Sun Dance for Calf Road was given about 1865, she lived faultlessly with her husband for many years.

Women gossiped about her, but not to her face. So faultless was she that she irritated. "Look at that woman," the others whispered.

---

[26] Each soldier society had an honor corps of four virgins to assist in their ceremonies.

PRAIRIE CHIEF

"She used to be the biggest whore in the tribe. Now she thinks she is the only decent woman here." Some men were even nastier to her. When she blankly ignored their obscene hints, Black Wolf avers they threw it in her face, "Well the only thing that saved you was that ceremony. By now you would be bulled to death." She never answered; it was the medicine men's instruction not to. The women's gossip here fits into any human frame. The men's remarks were out of line with general Cheyenne attitudes toward the rehabilitated. Perhaps the general prevalence of chastity was a little burdensome to the men. Perhaps the purification ceremony was too unfamiliar to seem solid—though, in general, ceremonial assumption of a new and law-abiding personality was familiar enough. Perhaps Calf Road had become too potently and aggressively a prig.

Chapter VIII

PROPERTY AND INHERITANCE

GRINNELL summed up Cheyenne property disposal after death: "When a man died, all of his property not placed with him—and often that of his father and even of his brothers—was given away, and to people who were not his relatives. As soon as his death became known, the whole camp was likely to gather near the lodge. All the relatives were crying. The widow herself, or perhaps one of her sisters, began to carry out the property within the lodge, and to throw the things down on the ground before the various people standing about who were not relations. Then the lodge was torn down and given to someone, and soon everything was gone, and the widow perhaps retained only a single blanket with which to cover herself. This distribution took place immediately after the body was removed from the lodge, and this was always as soon after death as possible. Thus if a man died leaving a widow and two or three children, they retained nothing."[1]

Yet Stump Horn declared that the regular thing to do was for a widow, after several weeks had passed, to call upon the brothers of the deceased spouse asking each to come and take a horse. This indicates that not all horses were disposed of at the death and that property could be given to relatives. Walks Last independently corroborated this statement with the case of Sly Dog, whose deceased brother's wife instructed her son thus, "Go to your father [classificatory father]. Invite him to come to choose a horse from our herd." In this, and in other points, the statements of informants and the conclusions of Mr. Grinnell might seem to be widely discrepant. The key to the dilemma is found, however, in the

---

[1] Grinnell, *The Cheyenne Indians*, II, 162.

application of the principle of pluralism among the levels and types of prevailing normative systems which controlled one or another case.

First, there are the rules of "strict law." By this is meant the rules to which *legal* sanctions definitely apply—the rules which control, if they are appealed to. Second, the quasi-legal pressures upon survivors relative to the disposition of property are to be delineated. Third, the definite social and personal pressures are to be conned, which, though non-legal in contrast to the strict law, yet condition inheritance distributions. The important fact is to recognize that there was no single legal rule of inheritance controlling all situations among the Cheyennes, nor any single line of *practice* under any of the legal *rules*. As one proceeds from the first to the third aspects noted above, one moves from stringent norms to greater variability—a movement from delineation in bold lines to lighter etchings.

"I am generalizing old customs from what I know," Calf Woman cautioned. "Some families did differently than others."

The death of the married man may be considered first. A husband's possessions were split two ways. To his body and soul at the grave went one full equipment of his best. The corpse was dressed in the deceased's finest garments, wrapped in robes, tightly bound, and carried out to a rock cleft or tree for burial. Here he received his armaments—bow, arrows, gun, war club, knives—and his pipe or other very personal belongings. Upon his grave his dearest horse was slaughtered. These things were his and his alone. As to enforceability, this law was probably on the first level; i.e., a brother of the deceased could probably have forced a widow to follow it through against her will. But as to performance, in the opinion of the authors this provision was on a level even above the rest of "strict law." Departure was simply inconceivable.

More could go into the grave with him. Just what and how much apparently were at the widow's discretion, as affected by her desire, or personal pressure from his relatives, and therefore not strict law. This was especially true of extra horses, for frequently more than one horse was killed. The medicine bundle of a shaman went to the body likewise, unless it had been previously "willed" to a friend or son through teaching that person the mysteries of its use. As Lowie has so aptly made clear, the significant property aspect of a medicine object is not the material tangible, but the incorporeal powers and rituals which accompany it.[2] So it is that unless the ritual of a Cheyenne bundle had been imparted, the bundle was valueless; worse than that, it was dangerous, because to misuse a medicine object could bring disaster. Thus to impart the formula, while withholding the bundle, was to give title in futurity, thereby willing it. That is why in some cases the bundle was buried, and in others it was "given" to a friend.

The residue of the property of a married man dying intestate went to his widow. But a man could make anticipatory gifts, seemingly *ad libitum*, which bound; although there is here no case in which such gifts were made outside the family. As with the medicine bundles, goods designated in testament went to the beneficiary without regard to the will of the widow. Mere designation for the event of death on a war raid rarely occurred, if ever. Disposition through will and testament seems to have been limited pretty much to men approaching death by old age or sickness, at home. However, this point is not certain.

According to High Forehead, Elk River, when an old man many years ago, called in his children and grandchildren of both sexes. He divided all his horses among them, save one for himself. High Forehead's wife, who was Elk River's youngest daughter, got seventy-five horses, while for the others the number dwindled down to ten. Elk River was ninety years old at the time. He lived to be one hundred.

Today Jim Brady is the oldest living Cheyenne. Six or seven years ago he divided all his one hundred cattle among his children, the largest share going to his daughters.

The pattern is an old one. Calf Woman cited the case of Man Lights All Over The Ground. "Many years ago, I heard one morning that he had divided his horses among his children. It was said

---

[2] Robert Harry Lowie, "Incorporeal Property in Primitive Society," *Yale Law Journal*, XXXVII (1928), 551-63.

that he said, 'My children, I am old. I cannot take care of it all!' He named his horses off and divided them among them. Before he did this he confided his intent to his wife, and she agreed." Again the girls got the biggest share, "because they could not go out and steal them from the enemy like their brothers."

This last statement explains why the male offspring got the short end of "wills" so regularly. The explanation is reasonable enough. Another generalization of the informants was that the eldest son was often designated as executor of his father's testament. The death of Morning Star, Bull Hump's great father, in 1881, provides a positive test of this rule. The widow said, "We shall give away every horse to the people." Bull Hump, the only son, objected, "No, it is not right to give them all away. I have sisters." The son, mother, and daughters had been in the lodge when Morning Star died. It was said that Morning Star told Bull Hump, "Keep these horses. Don't do away with them. Keep them and give them to your sisters; they have need for them." The brother did not have unlimited continuing power, however. The horses once given to his sisters became theirs, not his, to administer. Later on Bull Hump wanted to sell his sisters' riding horses, but they rejected the idea. He had three or four hundred wild beasts left in the herd, so he sold these instead. The money he divided with the four girls.

Such were the testamentary dispositions which could exclude certain properties from the widow's control.

Now what of the pressures operating on the widow regarding disposition of the surplus of goods not buried and not willed? The first of the definite, but quasi-legal, usages was that a son should be given a horse to give away, preferably to his dead father's brother. At times the son, "to show his love for his father," invited an old man to sit with the corpse. The old man said a prayer and comforted the mourners. For this, he got the horse. It has already been noted that Sly Dog's widow told her son to invite his dead father's brother to come and take a horse from "our" herd. The uncle's answer was fittingly modest. "My son,"[3] he replied, "I did not want any of my brother's things. But now that you mention it,

[3] The classificatory term of reciprocal address.

I am glad. I will come right over and take any horse you think I ought to have." This man was a person of delicate restraint. He did not press a claim, though he was readily willing to accept his due when the subject was broached.

That the widow's title to her husband's horses was "law," while the brother-in-law's right to share was only implied in "good usage" was finally established for us in the perplexing conduct of Red Sash, brother to Crane. As the history was first recorded from Last Walker, Crane was killed by lightning, after which his brother appropriated all his horses. "People," said Last Walker, "thought he was a fool for robbing his brother's children." His conduct was clearly not exemplary to this observer.

Yet, when told from the other side, the case becomes understandable. From Red Sash's intelligent granddaughter, Bessie Standing Elk, the following facts were gleaned.

«   «   «   The band was camped in the valley where now stands Sheridan, Wyoming. As storm clouds piled up over the Big Horn mountains, Crane, who since childhood had had a psychopathic fear of lightning, dressed in his best regalia. He had always said he would die by lightning, so now he sang his death song and prayed to Maiyun. When he was done smoking, he mounted and bid his family good-by. His mother begged him not to go; yet he went. Red Sash, his elder brother, followed after. Yet Crane refused his plea.

"I must go," he said.

Red Sash returned to the family. As they all stood watching, Crane rode over the hill. [All his grandchildren and even great-grandchildren are taken to this hill and told the story.] Then the skies opened. Tipis toppled in heaps. A great crash splintered the howling atmosphere. Then it was over. Red Sash rode over the hill. Crane and his horse lay dead upon the ground. Red Sash rubbed out the smouldering ashes of his dead brother's shirt, after which he led the new-made widow to view her husband's corpse.

"Let him be buried as he is," she said. "He was dressed for death." Crane's widow thereupon told Red Sash to take her husband's horses and to dispose of all his properties. A person killed by lightning could not be touched by relatives. If it was a man, as in this case, the comrades of his soldier society must serve. For this they received gifts. To them Red Sash gave most of the horses, it is said.   »   »   »

Thus, his descendants maintain that the widow had expressed her will; his actions were in accordance with law.

But that the procedure was unusual stands forth in the admission of Mixed Berries, daughter of Red Sash, that Red Sash's "enemies" charged that he had confiscated the horses. And even to this day the widow's side of the family declares that it was mean of Red Sash to take the horses.

The legal principle, however, is affirmed from all sides. A deceased male's brother was the executor of his estate only if so commissioned by the bereaved wife. The moot point in the Crane-Red Sash affair is thus one of fact, only. Had such commission been given?

If after meeting the definite legal and quasi-legal demands, there was still a residue of property left in the hands of the widow, she was under definite pressures to go further. If she loved her husband, if she wanted to do him full honor, she showed it by conspicuous giving to non-relatives. If she wanted to vent her emotions in highest Dionysian display, she carried the mourning largesse to self-destitution. She gashed herself until the blood flowed and caked. She cut short her hair. She left the camp, protected only with her blanket.

This was the grand display. It was a matter of family prestige and social approval. Grinnell found it so frequent, or so conspicuous, as to lead him to lay it down flatly as the only way.[4]

The widow who wanted to go the whole way in grief display did do these things. In addition she camped alone away from the main village for at least a month—if steadfast in her mourning, for a year. Gradually, her friends, or her husband's relatives, began to move out around her until, after they had absorbed her into their

[4] Grinnell, *The Cheyenne Indians*, II, 161 f.

own social life and provided her with new equipage, she could be induced to return to the community. Then she washed off the dried blood; her tresses grew once more.[5]

The widow who did not wish to *show* great love for her husband, could stop with the burial of his goods. She did not isolate herself from the camp. Instead, she remained quietly with the people, with her hair cut short. Most women carried out the full pattern, driven by great grief, love of the dramatic, or obedience to good form.

A woman who had deserted her husband had, we believe, no claim on his goods. As to the husband's claim upon her properties, presumably he retained his legal right until after he had smoked the pipe, thereby relinquishing his rights in the marriage contract. A woman who was at her parents' home attempting divorce was not among her husband's inheritors. This is of course to be distinguished from the case in which, with the husband away on a raid, the woman moved into her parents' lodge. Under those circumstances she testified her loyalty to her husband by periodically visiting his parents to do chores about the household. Her father-in-law "babied" her by dicing her meat at meals and bestowing on her solicitous attention. The rules of inheritance indicated in this paragraph are, however, all probabilities, as there were no test cases available.

Upon the death of an unmarried warrior the disposal of his goods was the work of the parents. Like the married warrior, he was dressed in his best to be buried. His body was accompanied by his favorite horse rigged in its best paraphernalia. The horse was shot to be his soul-companion, but the accouterments were not buried as in the other instance. The officiating shaman prayed to Maiyun "to take pity on the trappings," saying that they were going to give them away now. This, of course, was an act of purification, the shedding of the touch of the dead. Then the giving away was

---

[5] Compare the motivation to that which begets "decent" burials for the dead among New York Irish and Italians. The average Irish funeral puts $452 into a burial, dissipating forty-two per cent of the net family assets. The Italians throw fifty per cent of their family assets into a funeral. See John C. Gebhardt, "Funerals," *Encyclopedia of the Social Sciences*, VI (1931), 528.

announced, in which any non-relative who wished could step up to take the goods.

Whatever remained of a youth's goods was held back by his parents for alternative paths of disposal. If the son had been killed in war, the disposal was made to obligate someone to obtain a scalp "to make the father happy." The deceased's best friend might be called in to eat. He received the goods and carried out his mission. Thus the acceptance of the goods (and no decent youth would refuse) bound him in a quasi-legal contract, sanctioned only by informal pressures. If the slain warrior was a member of a soldier society, it was customary for the parents to go wailing through the camp displaying the goods of their son, as they sought the lodges of the chiefs of his military society to give them the property for distribution among the fellowship. Or perhaps they invited the entire society to their home for a feast and bestowal. One of the chiefs prayed over the goods and eulogized the boy's deeds and virtues. Then one of their number was picked out to do the distributing. One fine piece was kept to be given to the next recruit who joined the company and filled the gap left by the deceased. For the soldiers, too, such an act was a bid for a revenge scalp-taking raid. But who in the band was obligated to go was not determined.

Had the youth died a natural death, either of the above procedures could be followed without incurring the scalp-taking obligation. In such circumstances, the single recipient incurred a socially implied obligation which was hardly on the level of contract. Nevertheless, at some dance soon following, the new possessor exhibited the goods to all spectators. Then he publicly announced the bestowal of a horse on another party, this done in memory of his dead friend.

Thus, the obligation was not one of reciprocal economic exchange. The parents, in return for gifts given, received the satisfaction of further public recognition of their loss. Yet a poor man who had been their son's friend was not obligated to so memorialize. Only those who were in a position to make a public display needed to do so. Of course, any who could would, because it was an act of grace beloved by all Cheyennes.

Parents, like a wife, could—but it was not nearly so incumbent upon them—give of their own personal property in addition to that of their son. They could even give to destitution. But this was most unusual and could evoke remarkable responses when it did occur, as the case of Red Robe (CASE 1) so amply demonstrated.

When a daughter died, the clothes not buried with her were placed in a heap; then her best chum was called in to receive them. There is no record of any general gift-giving beyond this for girls.

When a wife died, the situation was again a bit more complicated. In strict law, her male horses went to her husband. The tipi, which she had made or received as a gift, was her property. It went to her female relatives, as did her rawhide bags and utensils. Her best raiment was buried with her, the rest given away (to non-relatives?). The husband was under definite social and personal pressures, non-legal in character, to go further. He, too, was constrained to show grief and devotion by large giving, by giving to non-relatives, by giving to the point of near-destitution. The devoted husband, responding to the social code, withdrew from the community with his children. He wailed, and in his despair cut strips of flesh from his arms and chest. He took with him into his exile his hunting outfit and war gear, his blankets and a minimum of utensils for his needs. A horse he kept for himself and one for each child. Beyond these reserved requirements he gave away as many of his surplus horses and goods as he desired. The mares which had been his wife's, in strict law, went to the female relatives of his wife, who cared for her body in the funeral preparations.

A nice case of dispute, related by Calf Woman, centered about this last point, and shows the notorious Last Bull in another of his peace-shaking ventures.

《 《 《 Last Bull's sister died, leaving a surviving husband, Point. Last Bull demanded her horses.

Point refused. "If you had ever helped your sister, it would be all right, you could have them. But you never did a thing for her, so what are you coming around here for now?"

"I brought in horses once," Last Bull refuted him. "I let her have the pick of the herd."

"You have paid her no attention since she married me," countered the other. "Now you are coming here."

"Yes," Last Bull retorted, "but I treated her fine while she was single. And what have you done? You abused her. You were her husband, and I said nothing when you beat her. But I said my chance would come. Now I have it. I shall take a horse."

"No." Point was firm.

Then Last Bull got angry and stalked off.

That evening Point gathered in the horses to change pastures. Last Bull came striding over, and *bang,* he shot the horse he wanted.

His brother-in-law screeched at him. "You didn't do a thing for your sister after her death. Did you put anything in her grave?"

Last Bull pulled the trigger on him, but the gun missed fire. Grabbing his gun, Point yelled, "If you love your sister so, then go to her."

But before he could fire, people seized him, and the quarrelers were taken away from each other. That night Point slunk away, leaving his herd standing, for fear Last Bull was watching it. He took another man's horse to make his escape.

Last Bull went to the herd in the morning. Bang, bang, bang! He killed the mare and two colts belonging to his sister. "I'll show my brother-in-law he shall not own them," he proclaimed. "Furthermore, when I meet that fellow, I shall kill him."

He hunted hard for Point, but he was nowhere to be found. Last Bull came back to the Fox Soldiers. "I know you think I am a fool for what I have done. Well, I have raised myself one notch higher [referring to his other acts of unusual behavior] and I am going on. I have studied over how he abused my sister. It makes me burn. When I visited them, she acted as though I were non-existent. It was his fault. Let him come back here, and I'll kill him. Mark that!"

Last Bull then went to his niece, the daughter of his dead sister, to ask her which of the horses [the mares?] in the herd were hers [those which had belonged to her mother]. These he gave to her, also replacing the ones he had shot. He gave one horse to the man who had lost his when Point rode off. The rest he kept for himself. There were two little children left. Last Bull put them in the care of an unmarried aunt, his sister. He gave her some horses to go with them, and always helped her with food.

People praised Last Bull everywhere, saying he had done just right. They had seen Point thump her.

Point was a man without family; they had died in the great cholera epidemic.   »   »   »

Answering questions whether the presence of relatives would have made a difference, Calf Woman gave the simple answer, "Nothing stopped Last Bull." Which is true enough.

Though Last Bull was mean and obstreperous, Point was mean and small, and handled his case stupidly, where Last Bull was shrewd. Point's previous conduct gave Last Bull the excuse he needed for calling the former in his otherwise legal attempt to appropriate his wife's estate. And whether or not the claim was legal, Last Bull's demand for "a horse" cut too close to the decent claim of a brother to a memory-gift to be wisely refused. Last Bull was, in all conscience, late in coming to his sister's protection; but he focused the official dispute on the horse he had a moral claim to, swept aside with his gun Point's effort to expose the weakness in Last Bull's own position, and, with Point once driven out, he had the sense and decency not only to fulfill the family obligations he had been neglecting, but to move in the grand manner. He—the generous Last Bull—became the distributor to his niece of what was hers. He cared for the children. He replaced the horses destroyed. His making good for Point turned the latter utterly into the rascal; it was magnificent pleading of the case by Last Bull. Because of his conduct, Point got no sympathy, and having no relatives, he got no support—a man without family was a social orphan. Family or no family, Last Bull would have gone through with his purpose, but the ultimate outcome would most certainly have had further ramifications. Last Bull received praise because he was upholding one important social usage which Point was disregarding—sound treatment of a wife. Here, as so often in primitive law, the public judged the dispute upon the total situation in its net effect rather than on the narrow legal issue: character, power, past relationships, the shaping of the controversy—all came in to flavor the strict law of inheritance.

Through the consideration of inheritance, the existence of private-property rights among the Cheyennes has been clearly revealed. With the Cheyennes, as indeed among all American Indians who had them, horses were individually owned. Even when acquired through such group action as a raiding party, the spoils were individually divided. Unless it was agreed otherwise beforehand, each horse went to the man who first struck a coup on it. This gave great advantage to the man with a fast horse. To equalize this, the Cheyennes often agreed before the raid to divide equally, in which event the leader of the raid took first choice, then named the succession of choice for the rest of the party. There was no notion of the spoils' belonging technically to the leader, to be shared with the others because ethics of generosity demanded it, as Professor Lowie has reported for the Crows.[6] If there was no agreement calling for equal division, then a man who saw horses off to one side, and ran them in himself, took all for himself without any obligation to divide. This was Stump Horn's dictum. No cases were obtainable to prove or disprove it. Again, in the absence of the equality distribution, scouts out on duty who missed out on the take, missed out on the booty! Nor did the cooks receive any special preference for their labors. These two last stated norms are queerly out of keeping with the general utilitarianism of Cheyenne law.

Disputes over who touched a horse first were reputedly rare, and it is said they were settled by witnesses. When witnesses could give no clear-cut solution, we were told, there was no resort to determination by oath; what did happen, if such cases arose, cannot be said because no such cases were obtainable.

[6] Lowie, *Primitive Society,* 208.

A nice distinction in the claiming of enemy horses existed, too. When a group was traveling, but not on a horse-taking raid, the person first to sight the tracks of a stray horse laid claim to the animal. He stopped his companions and called their attention to the tracks. This rule seems to have been socially recognized, but was perhaps not fully established as law. At least, there was dispute over its validity when challenged by a forceful man such as Bull Kills Him.[7]

« « « Somebody, I have forgotten the name, found the tracks of some horses. But when he got to them, Bull Kills Him had come upon the horses from another way and had claimed them.

There were five horses, and that other man thought they should be his. He kept insisting that he saw the tracks before Bull Kills Him saw the horses. "You saw me trailing them down," he complained. "If you had left them alone, I would have come on them myself."

"Well, I don't see where you think you got any horses," was Bull Kills Him's logic. "You just got the tracks. The horses are better than the tracks."

"No," the other countered. "The tracks come first. And I am going to have those five horses."

"Oh no you don't. You think you'll get them. You shall have none of them." So saying, Bull Kills Him mounted his horse. Drawing five arrows from his quiver, he rode over and shot the horses dead.

The other fellow kept his mouth shut. People talking to Bull Kills Him said, "You did wrong, killing all five of those horses. That was not right."

Bull Kills Him excused himself saying, "Well, if he hadn't been so selfish, it would not have turned out that way. If he had wanted to divide up on them, I would not have done that thing. But he could not have them all." » » »

What happened here was that two rules of property rights crossed. From Bull Kills Him's last statement and the comments of

[7] Informant: Stump Horn.

the people, it was clear that the track-finder's claim was recognized. It is possible that its full recognition had not been extended beyond the claims of others than the tracker's own party. But Bull Kills Him set up a claim in another orbit, independent and supervening, as first horse-finder, and impishly announced that a horse in hand is worth two on the prairie. Possession may have borne legal weight. Nevertheless, the track-finder's claim would seem to have been the stronger—though it may have had need of modification for this unusual case—for Bull Kills Him maintained it was up to the other man to divide the finds; and when he was unwilling to share, Bull Kills Him as a willful and important warrior deprived him of all his game, daring him to complain at the violence. The single case leaves unresolved whether the reaction of "public" disapproval went merely to Bull Kills Him's high-handed methods, or included his claim; it is a classic of the occasional ambiguous precedent, made and left in what one may call the worst Cheyenne manner.

Another interesting point is found in the question of what happened to an owner's title to his horse when it had been stolen by enemy raiders and later recovered. The law was simple. If horses were recovered in pursuit, before the enemy getaway was complete, they went back to their owners. However, the owner of many horses, if generous, gave at least one horse to the recoverer for his pains. If the theft was successful, the title passed to the enemy, so that whosoever recovered a stolen horse became its full owner. But a personal bond lending a moral right was recognized. The former owner of a recaptured horse, if it was a favorite, went to its new-captor with a good blanket or other bundle. Placing the bundle on the ground before him he said, "Friend, I love that horse. Pray, will you give him to me again?" Stump Horn and High Forehead say they have never known a man to refuse such a request. Since the blanket or goods were not usually so valuable as the horse, a residue of proprietary right where sentimental attachment existed was recognized. There was no seizing a bargaining advantage in the former owner's desire to recover.

The desire for social approval and the self-regarding pleasures of altruism led some men to return horses beyond the demands of strict legality. Hairy Hand, who was a great taker of horses, used to give back recaptured horses to their former owners "to make them pleased." Black Coyote once recaptured some horses from the Americans. He had the crier call for all people to come and take theirs from the group, though "he did not have to do this; the horses belonged to the soldiers when he got them."

Appropriation of another's property seems not to have been too uncommon. Calf Woman says that lots of times she heard the crier haranguing about the loss of an article by somebody, asking anybody who found it please to send it back. No "finders keepers, losers weepers." If it was not brought back, nothing was said. That is, unless it was something the owner wanted badly. In that case another crier was asked to make the rounds calling for it, and a horse was offered. As an example, Deaf Ear lost his entire buckskin suit. A crier made the announcement. Still, no suit. A second crier offered a horse. "It is a well-marked suit. Any member of the family will know it. You'll feel badly if you are caught with it on," he warned. The suit was returned, and the thief (unnamed) took the reward, "because it had been promised." It is said that he was not reprimanded.

It really was not good taste to make too much fuss about "stolen" articles of minor value—or "borrowed-stolen" articles. (It is difficult to get into brief English phrasing the slightly vague edges of Cheyenne "private" property in chattels in the face of a non-possessor's want or need.) Calf Woman says many butcher knives used to disappear in the old days. If they were taken in the daytime, nothing was said, but night filching—"that is stealing and not liked." If one found such a transgressor, one upbraided him in public and shamed him by saying, "If you had come in the day, I would have given it to you." Which, it will be noted, does not necessarily bring back the knife.

Calf Woman laughs with self-pride when she tells of how her chieftain husband reproved her for her unbecoming conduct in seeking to recover stolen goods. Engraved Woman took a knife from their camp; Calf Woman, following, took it away from her.

Sun Road rebuked her, "You are like a dog. If another dog takes a dog's meat, he follows it up and takes it away. If she had asked for it we would have let her have it, so you should let it go."

A chief more than any other person was expected to maintain such an attitude. In responding to questioning about the use of the supernatural in thief detection, Calf Woman told how her husband sang songs to see if Maiyun would tell him who had ransacked their house. He dreamed of a person who pointed up the creek, but did not speak the name of the culprit. He spoke to Calf Woman of it, saying, "If I were not a chief, I would go up that way and search every tent. Being a chief, I can't. So just forget what has been taken. I have been given all my children [the tribespeople]. I do not want to go to search their tents. When I was selected, the whole tribe elected me. It would be bad work to go searching my people." Not that such action would impair his medicine power. Rather it would hurt his chief power. People would not think so well of him.

In general, there seems to have been no real legal mechanism for handling petty thieves. For three generations Cold Bear's family have been kleptomaniacs. "Everything stuck to their hands." When people complained to Cold Bear, he whipped his children, making them give up the goods. Parental whipping was extreme punishment, not to be borne by most Cheyennes. Cold Bear's children, however, would not commit suicide because of it; they were "foolish" people who did not mind being whipped. They were scolded by their relatives, and people talked to their faces, but it did no good. People simply covered their goods when they saw any of that family coming.

But for larger matters, especially horse taking within the tribe, it has already been shown what special remedial steps were formulated to correct Pawnee (CASE 2) and to effect the return of the horse for Wolf Lies Down (CASE 17).

The give and take of chattels as a part of the rituals which signalized ceremonial shifting of social position from one person to another, as in succession to the tribal Council (Chapter IV) or as in marriage (Chapter VII), and the settling of legal disputes (in homicide, Chapter VI, in wife-taking, Chapter VII) will all be recalled by the reader. In each of these type situations the transfer of goods was largely in the nature of a contractual settlement. Other phases of trading in property will appear throughout the next chapter as levers in informal controls. Services of all sorts, from doctoring to counting coup at the dedication of a new lodge, or the preparation of a new implement—all received their compensation, be it a feast, a tangible good, or even a horse. In good form, no price was set beforehand for services to be rendered, so that the compensation was phrased, and in good part felt, as a gift given in appreciation for a helpful act.

Incorporeal properties, such as supernatural powers, could be contracted for, and no offer of a contract could be refused by the possessor of a power (the sanction was bad luck). This was the novice's one sure way of obtaining medicine power. Again the pipe was used, this time as the symbol of conveyance. Already filled, it was placed on the ground and pushed stem forward toward the doctor of whom the power was being sought. Even when a novice had received his medicine power directly from his own vision, it was still necessary that he obtain instruction from some shaman on ritual and the use of herbs. This instruction was arranged for by "contract." For all his services as tutor the doctor received whatever gifts the novice felt fit to offer. Prestige pressures made the gifts generous. Nor was it unusual for the relatives and friends of a man to come to his support with contributed goods to swell the value of his gift. In so doing, they obtained a definite capital-stock interest in their protégé's medicine powers—an interest which received dividends in occasional shares in the gifts acquired as fees, and a definite pay-off if and when the doctor was given a fee for passing his knowledge on to a newer aspirant to the profession.[8]

In this, as in the instructional rituals for quilling, beadwork, and lodge-making among women, there was "contract" for services in exchange for consideration.[9] Women's activities requiring many buffalo robes could also lead to semi-capitalistic economics, as

[8] Grinnell, *The Cheyenne Indians*, II, 128-43.
[9] *Ibid.*, I, 159-69.

when Kicks The Ball organized a group enterprise in which she engaged thirty-nine girls so that forty robes could be decorated with quill-work embroidery at one time. This involved a sustained production plan. Kicks The Ball, who was a widow, accumulated the robes for the work by lending horses to young men for use in the communal hunts; for each horse "rented out" she received a hide or two in compensation. The whole undertaking was to fulfill a pledge to Maiyun for the recovery of Kicks The Ball's sick son. The whole process had a sacerdotal end and character, and though Kicks The Ball used capitalistic methods to obtain the robes, she gained nothing material herself—forty men were invited into the quilling lodge to have the robes placed on their shoulders as free gifts! The thirty-nine girls received—instruction and free meals and the privilege of choosing a donee.

Property, inheritance, trade, and the rendering of services, though subject to regularized and ritualized usage with much ceremonial coloring, had thus a much blurred "legal" shading in Cheyenne culture, even if one is disposed to accept Malinowski's sanctions of reciprocal obligations as being "legal." Among the Cheyennes there was little dispute or grievance-bearing over property, tangible or intangible, and hence, by present-day canons of "actions in dispute" as final tests of law, the field of property in Cheyenne society reveals only vague outlines of legal institutions. Contracts which are never broken and almost never bargained over are not subjects for *clear* law. Nor is property usage which is smoothly regulated by mere "custom." It is disputes which draw sharp lines and fix them.

Such *in toto* are the facts on Cheyenne property law as they have been gleaned. The harvest may in all likelihood disappoint those whose mental set for law runs largely in terms of property rules. The deficiency, we are confident, rests largely in the nature of Cheyenne culture, wherein property problems were not a matter of great import. Yet to some degree the tenuous quality of the data rests in the nature of the investigation as it was pushed forward.

It is time, therefore, in such a study as this to stop and take stock of things we do not know, and should.

The virtue of inquiry into the trouble-cases has been to turn up, in materially wider range and in materially nicer detail than is otherwise easy, legal material which, when the focus is on the rules or the going practice, rather than on breach or doubt, tends to be lost or blurred. And in Cheyenne, at least, this focus on trouble has brought light on the interplay of the various semi-specialized phases of the culture—religion, government, law, kinship, war, the warrior career, beneficence, and the like—in a way and to a degree which would not have been possible without sustained canvass for the detailed extra-regular case.

Yet when the time for inquiry is limited, all this comes at a price. Those institutions which do *not* happen to have called forth trouble may get lost entirely, or may have their quantitative importance obscured. They may remain, at best, in fogged background. The danger is clear, and it will not be wise to blink it.

We do not, in saying this, wish to be misunderstood as at all backtracking on our fundamental scientific premise, to wit, that that which is shown by test to be legal in character can be objectively known to have that character; and that nothing else can be so known. But that is a premise whose office is exhausted when the discoverable cases of trouble are exhausted. It is a premise not for an exclusive method, but for a preferential one, for one producing a less ambiguous and more reliable, in lieu of a less reliable and more ambiguous, type of evidence on matters legal. It is a premise, finally, which at one stage of an inquiry must of necessity take into partnership other premises which cannot rest directly on the tangible, but rest instead on theory, and on the "feel" of the culture. Mere data, however many, remain meaningless save in a frame of concept and of theory. The concept and theory must indeed be compatible with the data, with all the data, and especially with such disturbing data as the dispute cases with their sharper corners bring. But the data, of themselves, cannot by the nature of the inductive process establish a theory as right. They can show only that the construct could be right, in that it holds all the data;

and they can perhaps make it persuasive as holding the data easily and comfortably.

Hence at that stage of inquiry at which one is searching for constructs to hold the cases, one is among other things framing hypothetical rules of varying range and direction. The cases are to be conceived as examples of these rules, which cover in their terms or implications a vast range of behavior of non-trouble-making character. Here lie the going practices, the living institutions, the working, life-fulfilling patterns, and the normative drives. They are the drives which, whether merely felt or clearly phrased, guide and maintain such institutions. And by the time one has reached this stage of inquiry, his "feel" for the culture has advanced to the point at which his judgment of whether a given way is legal, or semi-legal, or by-legal, or merely social, has become worth expressing as his judgment. Though untested by a case, it is not only the best thing available, it is also a good thing in itself. It is on a par with the constructs and "rules" in terms of which he has, willy-nilly, to frame his cases. Such constructs and "rules" must always stand for their validity on compatibility, first, with the data, and, second, with the culture's "own" nature, and, third, with the particular nature or configuration of the relevant *aspect* of culture in general. What we mean by this last, in regard to law-stuff, is sketched in Chapters III, X, and XI. Illustrations would include such matters as the peculiar speed with which the trouble-case can build into precedent and institution, or the drive of the legal and of action of political authority toward coalescence; the tendency of any practice, as it develops, to companion itself with felt rightness and to roughen the road to deviation; the urge of a claimant to shape his claim under the most favorable variant of basis in fact or "norm" which he can discover or persuasively invent.

What follows is a series of suggestions about Cheyenne ways resting not on sustained inquiry, but on sketchy and haphazard indications in the cases, an expression of our ignorance rather than of our knowledge. It is included here because some background of such operating and untroubled "law"-and-practice, or "near-law"-and-practice, is found in every culture. It is included also because few things more thoroughly indicate the places where a major method needs supplement than a conning over of some of the relevant material which use of that method has failed adequately to develop.

Perhaps the first lacuna lies in the detail of the property system. The most basic fact in that property system, as related to tangibles, may well have been the nomadic nature of the life. There is a limit to things owned which can be lugged around. Horses transport themselves and can be used for transport. Yet it seems probable that the feast-giving, celebration-minded phases of Cheyenne culture are at least in part related to difficulties in effective hoarding. No such relationship is, of course, inevitable. Wealth can move into the form of legal rights, with absentee ownership, hire, and tenancy, or with a debt structure. At least incipient machinery to work such ends is traceable in Cheyenne ways. There is the story of the wealthy woman who used the vision mechanism for organizing the services of thirty-nine girls into a common enterprise of manufacture of buffalo robes. Another, an intrafamilial case, gives account of an ill-advised protest suicide when a girl who had lent her horse to her brother for the hunt took the resulting hides and found them retaken by a sister-in-law (CASE 25). One suspects in this latter case a personal tension below the surface; but one can be almost certain that no agreed or limited return had been explicitly bargained for, even though some return was clearly expected. One sees clearly a recognizable line—absentee use of a woman's good horse by a hunter brought expectancy of economic return.

Such a line is capable of development. It was capable, simply as a legal device, (a) of being carried into long-term arrangements, with pay extending beyond buffalo hides; (b) of explicit agreement for explicit compensation; (c) of extension to men's horses; (d) of extension to other capital. One notes, however, and one feels, as thoroughly characteristic indications, that the lines of force in Cheyenne culture run flatly counter to any such development. And the reasons for such feeling rest on the facts that (a) the enterprise of the forty buffalo robes resulted in reality not in capital acquired by the enterprise, but in a ceremonial investiture of forty young

men by the girls with forty fine, and perhaps supernaturally distinguished, robes; (b) the poor, instead of being driven into the
hands of the capitalist by debt, wage-dependence, or clientage,
seem rather to have sponged somewhat upon the chief, the lucky
hunter, the succession of celebrant givers; (c) there happens not
to be in the cases a single instance of a long-term obligation for a
fixed return; outside of family and marriage relations, *continuing*
obligations running between any parties were most unusual.

A "private-property" system seems to have been, in strict law,
rather clearly established, as a basic aspect of organization. Rights
are clear in respect to killed buffalo, war loot, and horses. This is
true of articles of use, of ornament, of manufacture. Gift was, as
to the article given, certainly largely in the owner's discretion. But
one must speak cautiously. There were certainly family pressures
to give, and not to give; and their extent and meaning are not clear.
Certain "given" articles assuredly had ties which may have been
more than sentimental or good-will preserving, and which required
the gift to be peculiarly cared for. How far a prospective donee
had any power, legal or social, effectively to designate what was to
be given him, remains unclear, though semi-developed machinery
of the sort seems to have been partly available for trading purposes.
But the strict law *seems* to have rested on any owner's full power
of disposal. This was also true of theft—the taking of a good
without implicit consent or intent to return. We read the evidence
to mean that theft was flatly counter to the owner's legal right, if
he claimed his right. But such taking of goods had, to admit, though
not encourage it, only such social pressures as worked against a
chief's recognizing a grievance, or against an ordinary owner's
allowing himself to become unduly exercised in public over a loss,
or the difficulty of using a remedy which caused more rumpus than
the remedy was worth.

We read the evidence to mean also that in those wider and looser
ranges of Cheyenne life which affected people not tied by blood,
marriage, or peculiar friendship, the "reciprocity" aspects of "law"
were rather strikingly other than are to be expected in a society of
economically interdependent specialists. The "customary" obliga-

tion of exchange of taro for fish in the Trobriands gains the legal quality Malinowski[10] properly sees in it, first, because the parties are identified, and second, because reciprocity in performance is vital to both sides. Clarity of interest plus clarity of person means clarity of obligation which can produce clarity of claim and pressure. But the successful Cheyenne had little similar dependence on another. Old Red Robe (CASE 1), bereaved, took measures which cannot well be regarded as legal, measures which urged and induced, rather than exacted, a vengeance expedition. The exact rank of his demand or wish cannot be clear, but one can find no basis for seeing that he was urging a "right" against anyone or all, rather than a desperate desire and hope. And in somewhat similar fashion the demands of "everyone" on anyone, like the responsibilities of wealth, of success, of prestige, rested in what seems rather "custom" than enforceable law. "Custom" dictated prestige to him who put on a feast or a great giving away of goods. How far he called upon family or friends to help, or had claim to their help, and how far they helped without his calling on them, is not clear. It is not enough to rely on inference from the alliance gifts attending marriage arrangements (with their mutuality aspects, and their aspects of recognition of the new marriage). We take it that the successful hunter who piled up meat for public distribution did not thereby hurt his career, but was there other pressure? It may be guessed that too much meat on the racks was not merely a temptation for young rascally Last Bulls, but might tempt guests to come, and might even tempt less fortunate families to put on the appearance of need. Whether gossip distinguished thrift as a virtue, as against hoarding as a non-virtue; whether the ne'er-do-well was sought out particularly as a possible recipient of gifts from the bereaved after the spectacular incidents of bereavement had passed over; whether the burden of aiding the disadvantaged was passed around by hint or informal arrangement; whether the more chronic needers of help were made guests, or made themselves guests, or were sent gifts, is not known. On how far family ties and chief's office limited or expanded *chronic* burdens of the same order—here,

[10] Malinowski, *Crime and Custom in Savage Society*, 23-27, 37-49.

too, detail is absent. One hears, however, nothing of henchmen, and nothing of retainers. Wealth, prestige, and generosity certainly gathered following, but that following would appear to have had a minimum of the political aspect.

Along another line one comes, however, to a possible legal or near-legal phase of this type of "social" obligation. Articulation sharpens obligation (as it does grievance), and identification of obligee does the same. We take it that hospitality was in general not a thing to be denied; there is no recorded denial of food. It is possible that a person asking for food to a certain extent incorporated common custom into his particular person, thus becoming the organ of a semi-right "at law."

The probabilities which emerge from such a canvass come to this: that property rights in tangibles were on their legal side rather increasingly "private" and absolute than otherwise. The explicit new ruling against borrowing without advance permission (CASE 17) marked an extension and rigidification of the law. The public spirited raider who let recaptured horses go back to their original owners is an indication of the non-legal character of the limiting pressures. Our doubts have lain mostly in the intrafamily field, in which semi-communal uses and family variations raise difficulties of description for any culture.

Other doubts lie in the field not of property, but of obligation, to give not particular things, but something, or to give aid and succor. Here one suspects a rather deep-cutting difference. One suspects a general obligation to be beneficent, which is intensified in the tribal chief by his position, in the bereaved by mourning practice, and among the soldier societies by the incidence of flagrant destitution or emergency. Where thus intensified, it is to be suspected that possible gossip and possible prestige-loss might have raised an "obligation" to perform in the specific case to the level of the near-legal. But in the main it is to be surmised that the obligation side of beneficence was somewhat like that known to us on the part of persons who are "expected" to give. Such obligations, although harder to escape when made specific by articulation (which concentrates and directs the latent pressures of the decencies), still

are avoidable when the expected giver decides not to give, though
persistent avoidance of the "obligation" is not socially permissible.
Just as the status—a serious criminal status in many primitive
societies, akin to that of a Public Enemy—the status of "him who
has finally become utterly intolerable," is gained by slow cumulation until either a bale or a straw breaks the back of restraint, so in
lesser measure the status of "unduly stingy" must be seen as capable of achievement in Cheyenne. Short of that status, one inclines
to feel beneficence as an obligation less than legal, and rather of
public than of civil character, in that no private claimant could
readily enforce it. Yet the reader is reminded of the neat integration
of the matter into the legal system, along with the practice of feast
and ceremonial, in the direction of the rehabilitation of the seemingly lost character on whom the ordinary procedures of both
education and the law had proved a failure.

Wholly distinct from obligations to beneficence are possible
limitations, even on property rights, imposed by a bargaining
and trading mechanism which rested in the general machinery of
"gift" exchange. Bargaining was colored with both reticences and
obligations arising from the flavor of more-than-trade, of lasting
friendship-token and association, which "gift" exchange carried
with it. It is hard to refuse to trade, in such circumstances. It is
also hard to ask explicitly for what one wants; certainly without
explicit invitation to do so. When Calf Woman went out after elk
teeth, one sees the story as indicating a little girl going far beyond
what would have been the proprieties for an adult, though bringing
to overt expression what an adult would have worked at by greater
indirection. By the same token, when once the trader who takes
the initiative has managed to convey just what it is he wants, the
gift-exchange machinery has worked in many cultures as a practical
limitation on the other party's property right therein. Almost, the
thing desired has been expropriated from him, and at a price neither
of his seeking nor his choosing. On all of this, in Cheyenne, only
three things seem certain: first, that gift exchange rather than
explicit bargain was the dominant line of trade; second, that there

was no single pattern for it; third, that in many cases much lay in inarticulate intuition.

Cheyenne practice shows relatively little of that side of contract which looks to engaging for the future. Assumption of office or of marriage obligation was felt as change of status rather than as the incurring of modern-type contractual duties. Vows one meets from time to time; and some promises, even partaking half as much of bargain as of beneficence. Two Twists (CASE 1) made one such, as the war party did which refused the elopers (CASE 5). And a reward to a probable thief was paid "because it had been promised." Like the oath for settling disputes of fact, the contract institution was present, but not too much used. The use of the pipe for settlement of grievance, or for concluding peace, one suspects to have been only in minor degree felt as promissory. One suspects it, like marriage, to have been felt much more as accomplishing, by agreement and ceremony, a new status or condition.

There is no point in going further into what is not known. The sketch here has been enough to indicate the manner in which the property system, that of social security, of family, of government, of the personal career, of law administration, weave one into another, and the shading off of personal relation, good taste, public decency, into the near-legal or the legal. The inheritance cases give an indication of the degree to which trouble material, or the remembered single instance, when it can be found, sharpens discrimination. The need for sharpening discrimination, in fields of such nice shading, is also plain. Finally, it has become clear that one must move with some caution in "explaining" the lines institutional growth has taken, among variant possibilities. Explicit bargain, being known, found no important development among the Cheyennes; no highly developed regime of incorporeal property in names, songs, and the like, appeared; coups in this culture of giving were yet not capable of gift to a rising young brave, as among the Comanches.[11] Plainly, reasons "why not" are quite as important as reasons "why," if one is to follow the social processes with understanding.

[11] Hoebel, *Political Organization . . . of the Comanche Indians*, 29.

Meantime, one can do no more than note as inadequately determined the greater niceties of the property system. Like intertribal law, they leave one with some data, many hints, stimulus to speculation, and absence of the crucial cases which give sharp edge to knowledge. In intertribal law, one knows of peace-treaty making on a general pattern which looks much like a cross between private settlement of grievance and the ceremonial pledge of brotherhood (pages 91 ff.). He knows in general of asylum in the lodge of the Medicine Hat (pages 207 ff.), and something of its incidents, but he knows neither its exact limits nor its exact sanctions. One has indications that an alien's personal law followed him to some extent into the Cheyenne, but indications also are that at least the more necessary Cheyenne police regulations controlled the alien (Case 11). Precision is lacking, however, with regard to how this ancient and perennial conflict of principle was resolved; nor do we know whether the vagueness lies in the culture or only in our data. So it is also, despite the greater mass of material, in regard to the delicate interactions between private property, family rights therein, status-obligation, the prestige urge of beneficence, promise and settlement, gift-pressure and return-gift pressure, and trade moving under the careful form of gift.

The nature of the "property" picture makes two points in regard to method. Consistent language *discriminations* can be tremendously revealing. But language-*lumpings* of phenomena, though of high importance, still require testing by the trouble-case, before they are to be trusted. Nor, for the test, is a single case enough; for language can sometimes mislead even one who is native to it. Here the confusions of modern law offer suggestion for study of the primitive.

Chapter IX

INFORMAL PRESSURES AND THE INTEGRATION OF THE INDIVIDUAL

THE success of any legal system depends upon its acceptance by the people to whom it applies. Insofar as the system is an integrated part of the web of social norms developed within a society's culture (with due exception for imposition by some organized minority force) it will be accepted as a parcel of habit-conduct patterns in the social heritage of the people. The eternally primary functions of law in any society (despite the "rule of conduct" thinkers) being to close any breach which has opened between grievance-bearers, and meanwhile to restrain individuals from the breach of certain norms of either initial conduct or adjustment which are deemed of vital importance by the society concerned, it follows in the main that the fewer the demands that are made upon the law, the greater the good for the society. Law-in-action exists only because less stringent methods of control have failed to hold all persons in line, or in harmony, on points of moment. The extension of the sphere and importance of observable law in the more highly developed societies is not in itself an index of social progress. It is merely an index of a greater complexity of the society and hence of the norms or imperatives to be observed, and hence, finally, of an increasing difficulty in obtaining universal adherence to such norms. Conversely, this means that the less call there is for law as law, and upon law as law (relative to the degree of complexity of a society), the more successful is that society in attaining a smooth social functioning.

To what extent harmonious internal integration is a general social goal may be a matter of value judgment. It may be that in some societies the desire for perfect harmony does not exist. It may be also that a reasonable quantity of disharmony is a condition to adequate elasticity of adjustment to new conditions. In societies of Dionysian configuration,[1] this is especially likely to be true. Yet Cheyenne culture, though definitely Dionysian in religious, ceremonial, and (less clearly) in war activities, also aimed at orderliness and restraint in interpersonal relations—an aim definitely non-Dionysian in character, though perhaps imposed upon Dionysian desire. To a harmonizing of such divergent ends the whole system of controls was not only delicately shaped, but shaped with a quality characteristic of Cheyenne, the capacity for successive, even sudden, readjustment.

The Cheyennes began to mould the individual *en gros* to the role he was to play in adult life, from the very early months of childhood. Margaret Mead, in her discussion of the child-world and adult-world of the Manus natives of the South Seas, has set the Cheyennes up as a sterling example of the child-world mirroring the adults'—the extreme contrast to Manus.[2]

Cheyenne babies of both sexes were under the constant attention of the mother, her ever present companions at work or in camp-moving, so the early conditioning for both boy and girl was in the mother's hands. Thus it remained, until the small boy had learned to run free and ride well, when at the ages of four to six the path of the boy was forking from that of the girl. Both boy and girl were then coming under the sway of other influences, such as their imitative playmates, the directing older children, and for boys, the

---

[1] "The basic contrast between the Pueblos and the other cultures of North America is the contrast that is named and described by Nietzche in his studies of Greek tragedy. He discusses two diametrically opposed ways of arriving at the values of existence. The Dionysian pursues them through 'the annihilation of the ordinary bounds and limits of existence'; he seeks to attain in his most valued moments escape from the boundaries imposed upon him by his five senses, to break through into another order of experience. The desire of the Dionysian, in personal experience or in ritual, is to press through it toward a certain psychological state, to achieve excess. The closest analogy to the emotions he seeks is drunkenness, and he values the illuminations of frenzy. . . . The Apollonian distrusts all this, and has often little idea of the nature of such experiences. . . . He keeps to the middle of the road, stays within the known map, does not meddle with disruptive psychological states." Benedict, *Patterns of Culture*, 78 f.

[2] Margaret Mead, *Growing up in New Guinea* (New York, W. Morrow & Co., 1930), 128. Mead stresses the heavy drives of the culture into the brave-warrior pattern, with less attention to the restrained-chief pattern.

attention of their older male relatives. Self-control and self-restraint in deference to the presence of elders was the first lesson learned. When there is respect for the aged, the mores are safe!

"The infant's education," wrote Grinnell, who has a beautiful chapter on this subject,[3] "began at an early age, its mother teaching it first to keep quiet, in order that it should not disturb the older people in the lodge. Crying babies were hushed, or, if they did not cease their noise, were taken out of the lodge and off into the brush, where their screams would not disturb anyone. If older people were talking, and a tiny child entered the lodge and began to talk to its mother, she held up her finger warningly, and it ceased to talk, or else whispered its wants to her. Thus the first lesson that the child learned was one of self-control—self-effacement in the presence of the elders. It remembered this all through life.

"This lesson learned, it was not taught much more until old enough, if a boy, to have given him a bow and arrows, or if a girl, to have a doll, made of deerskin, which she took about with her everywhere. Perhaps her mother or aunt made for her a tiny board or cradle for the doll, and on this she commonly carried it about on her back, after the precise fashion in which the women carried their babies. She treated her doll as all children do theirs, dressing and undressing it, singing lullabies to it, lacing it on its board, and, as time passed, making for it various required articles of feminine clothing. Often as a doll she had one of the tiny puppies so common in Indian camps, taking it when its eyes were scarcely open, and keeping it until the dog had grown too active and too much disposed to wander to be companionable.

"As soon as she was old enough to walk for considerable distances, the little girl followed her mother everywhere, trotting along behind her, or at her side, when she went for water or for wood. In all things she imitated her parent. Even when only three or four years of age, she might be seen marching proudly along, bowed forward under the apparent weight of a backload of slender twigs. which she carried in exact imitation of her mother, who staggered under a heavy burden of stout sticks."[4]

[3] Grinnell, *The Cheyenne Indians*, I, 102-26. [4] *Ibid.*, I, 108 f.

The division of labor and training in mutual responsibilities was ingrained early. Even in play, as our own children do, only how much more so, they projected roles of their future lives. They made of themselves make-believe adults—and it was fun because the interest was there and the responsibility was not. So, Grinnell writes, "little companies of small boys and girls often went off camping. The little girls packed the dogs, and moved a little way from the camp and there put up their little lodges—made and sewed for them by their mothers—arranging them in a circle just as did the old people in the big camp. In all that they did they imitated their elders. The little boys who accompanied them were the men of the mimic camp.

"In the children's play camps the little girls used tiny lodge-poles—often the tall weed-stalks that are used for windbreaks about the lodge—and the boys sometimes acted as horses and dragged the lodge-poles, or hauled travois with the little babies on them. To the sticks they rode as horses, as well as on the dogs, they sometimes fixed travois.

"When the lodges were put up the boys used to stand in line, and the older girls asked them to choose their mothers. Each boy selected the girl who should be his mother, and they played together. The girls played in this way until they were pretty well grown, fourteen or fifteen years of age; but the boys gave it up when they were younger, for they strove to be men early, and usually soon after they had reached their twelfth year they began to try to hunt buffalo, killing calves as soon as they could ride well and were strong enough to bend the bow.

"Sometimes two camps of children, one representing some hostile tribe, were established near each other. The boys of one camp would go on the warpath against those of the other, and they fought like seasoned men, taking captives and counting coups. They tied bunches of buffalo-hair to poles for scalps, and after the fight the successful party held dances of rejoicing. They carried lances made of willow branches, shields made of bent willow shoots with the leafy twigs hanging down like feathers, and little bows and arrows, the latter usually slender, straight weed-stalks, often with a prickly-pear thorn for a point. After the camp had been pitched, another party of boys might attack it, and while its men were fighting and charging the enemy, trying to drive them back, its women, if they thought the battle was going against them, would pull down the lodges, pack up their possessions, and begin to run away. In such a battle the men might often shoot each other, and when the wounded fell, men and women rushed out and dragged them back, so that the enemy should not touch them and count a coup. If the village was captured, all the food its people had was taken from them. This often consisted chiefly of roots gathered by the women, and tender grass-shoots, of which they often gathered a great deal.

"The little boys when playing at going to war rode sticks for horses, and each one also led or dragged another stick, which represented another horse, the boy's war-horse. If an attack was threatened by a pretended war-party, those attacked changed horses, and leaving their common horses and their things together in one place, they rode out to meet the enemy and the battle began. The opposing forces charged and retreated forward and backward, just as in a real battle. Each party knew or suspected where the others had left their things, and if one group drove back the other, it might capture its opponent's horses and other property and thus win a great victory.

"In their pretended buffalo hunts also the boys rode sticks for horses, and lashed them with their quirts to make them run fast. Sometimes, when buffalo were close by and the real hunters of the big camp killed them near at hand, the little boys rode their stick horses out to the killing ground and returned to the play camp with loads of actual meat tied behind them on their horses. Some boys merely picked up pieces of the meat that had been thrown away, but often a good-natured hunter would give the lads pieces of meat to use in their camp.

"If there were no buffalo about, perhaps some children went out from the camp, and returning by a roundabout way, pretended to be buffalo. Others in the camp, discovering them, prepared to go out to surround them. The children representing the buffalo went out on the prairie in a company; they were both boys and girls—

bulls and cows. Some pretended to be eating grass, and some were lying down.

"The boys who were to run buffalo had small bows and arrows. Those who represented the buffalo carried sticks three or four feet long, sharpened at one end. On this sharp end was impaled the flat leaf of a prickly-pear, which still bore its thorns. In the middle of the leaf, on either side, was rubbed a little spot of dirt. This leaf had two meanings: it represented the buffalo's horn or weapon of defense, but, besides this, the little spot of dirt represented the buffalo's heart. If an arrow pierced this, the buffalo fell down and died.

"Some of the boy buffalo runners started out on the hunt far ahead of the others, so as to get beyond the pretended buffalo and cut off their flight. The others formed a wide crescent when making the charge. When the proper time came, the hunters rushed toward the herd, which in turn ran away. The larger boys, who represented the bulls, ran slowly behind the herd, and the hunters avoided them, because, if wounded, they might turn to fight, and chase those who were pursuing them; and if they overtook the pursuers, might strike them with the prickly-pear leaves which they held on the sticks, and fill the hunters' skin with thorns. If this happened, it was told through the camp, 'A bull has hooked and hurt' so-and-so. If the dirt-marked center of the prickly-pear leaf was hit, and the buffalo who carried it dropped to the ground dead, the hunters pretended to butcher it, and to carry the meat home.

"With their dog travois, the little girls followed the hunters out to the killing ground.

"Often some of the buffalo proved too fast for the hunters and ran a long way off, and then stood on the prairie and looked back. The hunters could not overtake them.

"The little girls often had trouble with their pack-dogs, just as did their mothers in real life. Many old and gentle dogs stayed about with them, but others, younger and more playful, were hard to catch when they wished to move camp, or might even run away and go back to the real camp.

"Food must be had for the mimic camp, and the children went

down to the creek to get fish. They thrust straight twigs in the mud
of the bottom, across the stream in a half circle, the concavity being
upstream. The sticks were so close together that the fish could not
pass between them. In the middle of the stream, in what would be
the center of the circle, if it were complete, a taller twig was thrust
into the stream-bed, to the base of which a piece of meat was tied.
Above the half-circle, on one bank, was fastened a flexible fence
or gate of willow twigs closely strung together on sinew, and made
like a mattress or a back-rest. It was long enough to reach from
one bank to the other.

"When all preparations had been made, the boys went a long way
up the stream, and entering it, formed a line across it, and came
down, wading through the water, beating it with sticks, making a
great noise, and so driving the fish before them. If the water was
roily, the girls who remained below near the trap perhaps saw no
fish, but if there were many there, they tugged at the meat and
shook the willow twig which stood alone. Then the girls quickly
entered the stream, and stretched the flexible fence or gate across
it, making it impossible for the fish to pass up the stream. All now
plunged into the water, and with their hands caught and threw out
on the bank the fish that were confined between the half-circle of
twigs and the fence above it. In this way they caught many fish,
and these they cooked and ate.

"The children did not stay out all night, but during the day they
pretended that it was night, and went to bed. During the day they
moved the camp often; even every hour or two.

"These children imitated the regular family life, pretending to
be man and wife, and the tiny babies—who were their brothers and
sisters—served them for children. Little boys courted little girls;
a boy sent to the girl's lodge sticks to represent horses, and if his
offer was accepted received with her other sticks and gifts in return.
Babies able to sit up were taken out into these camps, but not those
that were too young. Sometimes a baby might get hungry and cry,
and its little sister who was caring for it was obliged to carry it home
to her mother, so that the baby might nurse."[5]

[5] *Ibid.*, I, 110-15.

The old Cheyennes of today linger in delightful reminiscence of their childhood participation in such activities. Always such stories are told with smiles and light laughter.

Stump Horn recounts how the ever eager lads in his time held imitation Sun Dances. Imitation of adult endeavors carried right into the field of religious ceremonialism. Nor was this sacrilege to the tolerant adults, who gave only side glances of amused satisfaction.

At adolescence, the hortative power of the old men was turned upon the boys individually by their grandfathers and *en gros* in the speeches of the criers. These moral preachments were effectively backed by pervasive attitudes which marshaled social and supernatural sanctions—both implicit and explicit. The youth who was not respectfully silent in the presence of the elders, who made noises in the lodge, suffered not only direct reproof, but ran the risk of bad luck. The boy who ran or knocked against the lodge of a shaman, or even hit it with a thrown object, was hustled into a purificatory rite in which the offended medicine man subjected the lad to much serious hocus-pocus and prayer to ward off the lightning with which the boy would be smitten unless absolved. Could such beliefs do other than ingrain restrained conduct in the character of the youth?

But positive sanctions were also lavishly used in shaping another and often conflicting phase of character. There were goals of adult glory for the boys who reached the ultimate of Cheyenne good—success in war by reckless individual exploit. Before the growing youth was the self-display ritual of more than two-score ceremonial occasions in which a warrior himself counted his personal coups before an assembled and admiring public. And what modern circus parade can rival the charge into camp of a returning and successful war party?

Not only was the Cheyenne boy able to dream in eager fancy of the time when he would drink the heady delights of such narcissistic self-display (and thus unconsciously order his conduct to gain this social goal), but even as a child his successful acts of individual virtue were greeted with great applause, explicitly formulated as

positive social sanctions. Thus when High Forehead first shot an
eagle with his bow and arrow, his uncle praised him in a lordly
manner. More than this, he stood in the door of his lodge, announcing the deed to all people. That none might escape the fact, he
called for an old man to receive a horse in commemoration of the
event. The behavior of the uncle on this occasion was customary for
fathers at the son's first buffalo kill or war venture. (The maternal
uncle performed the father's Indian functions on this occasion
because High Forehead's father was a white man.) The old man
who received a horse was expected to compose a song to sing in the
camp as he rode about—a song which told how the horse had been
given him and why—a song which praised the skill and virtue of
the boy, the goodness and generosity of his family. Such sanctions
were three times effective; not only were boys conditioned to extend
themselves, but wealth was distributed and parents basked in the
pleasures of largess and altruism, as well as of publicity. Reciprocity balanced the relationships. So, too, when young men followed the advice of their fathers in offering a good buffalo-kill to
an old shaman, the shaman went to the carcass, and in accepting
it performed a short sanctifying ritual in which he blessed the boy
and his family. Returning through the camp, he called aloud that
he had received a buffalo gift and had performed the ceremony.
Here too, the youth received public credit.

The personal history of Calf Woman, as her narrative unfolded,
is rich in the finesse of Cheyenne techniques of reciprocity and
rewards.

«   «   «   I was about seven years old when my mother
was putting porcupine quills on a buffalo robe. She picked out a
nice little calf robe and marked out a design on it for me. My
mother brought this into the lodge and laid it before me. "Now it
is time for you to begin to learn. Do as you see me do."

I did things as she told me until I had finished the robe. My little
nephew—I thought of him. It seemed to me it would be nice to give
my first robe to him. I smoked it over sweet grass, and with its faint
scent I carried it to where my brother's wife had her tipi. I entered

with my robe. I made three motions with it; on the fourth, I laid it over the little baby.

When my brother came home, he asked where the robe had come from. "My husband," said his wife, "your little sister has made it for your son."

"Well," said he with pleasure, "I shall have to give her a present so as to keep her up [i.e., encourage her]. She will learn to expect things for her efforts."

And he gave me a pony.

The next thing, my brother had a baby girl. I made a cradle for it, upon which I put a nice beadwork decoration. I put the baby in it.

When my brother saw it, he spoke to me, "Sister, I will give you your choice." So saying, he put two things before me. One was a mare (because I was a girl). The other was a nice tipi.

I looked at them, and then I made my choice. "Well, I am a single maiden. I have no use for a tipi. My choice is for the mare."

My brother believed in raising mares. My mother had cut the skins for the cradle and outlined the pattern by colors. I finished it in.

My elk-tooth dress. My father when he returned from hunting always brought me the two dog-teeth of the elk. In this way I got my start. I also got them from others. Whenever I heard that a hunter had brought in an elk, I ran to my mother to see if I could go ask for the teeth. She would let me have some little present to offer in exchange—a robe or a pair of moccasins. Moccasins were not so valuable as elk teeth. The men would usually say, "I am not going to trade with a little girl. I give them to you. They are yours." Sometimes one would take my present, though. Or, sometimes, I would give a pair of moccasins to his child. Then I would tell him why I did it, so he would know what I wanted.   »   »   »

Here are three important things: (1) "Trade," in the sense of fair exchange of gifts, of parties dealing (not bargaining) on a substantial equality, was a familiar idea. (2) "Gift," as essentially non-binding (with whatever might result) was also a familiar idea and may have been in process of working out in part into the idea

of "bargain." (3) There was a leeway for persons who knew what
they wanted to abuse the decencies of other persons. Thus was the
little girl aided and abetted by maternal direction and by indulgent
responsiveness of adults in recognition of her ambitious endeavors.
So was social altruism fostered, or individualistic egotism, or both.
The reciprocity of respect and gift exchange, and the way in which
the Cheyennes prepared the normal life for the growing young,
appear further as Calf Woman's story continues.

« « « Many years ago a man who had only one
child—a daughter—came to me. It was Short Sioux, who was sister-
less. He addressed me politely, "I have come to you today to ask
you to become my sister. My little girl needs an aunt; you are the
one we have picked out." [Note "adoption" in the particular relationship felt as needed.]

At his lodge Dog Woman, his wife, greeted me. "Sister-in-law, go
right in and sit down."

At the back of the lodge I found a nice lounge ready for me.
Before going in, I saw a mare and a gelding standing out in front.
I suspected they were for me, but I did not know. Lots of food was
ready. When we sat down, Dog Woman asked after my husband, so
I had to tell her he was out hunting.

Then Short Sioux entered. He spoke, "Sister, my little daughter
has asked for an aunt. I have picked you out for her. This is not
for just now; this is for as long as we live."

The little girl was then called in, and they said to her, "Here is
your aunt."

Just a little one, four or five years old at that time, she came
right over to climb in my lap. She snuggled, and we fondled each
other getting acquainted. » » »

At this point the narrative was broken to ask why the little girl
wanted an aunt, to which Calf Woman replied that she had seen
how nice it was that all her playmates had aunts, and she wanted to
be like others. High Forehead (the interpreter) a second time
added his own opinion in a laconic, "I'd rather have an aunt around

than my mother any time." Aunts were pleasurably indulgent, while mothers had sometimes to be authoritarians. Kinsmen of any degree were also always socially desirable.

«   «   «   When we had put down the food, Short Sioux invited me to follow him out-of-doors. We stood before the horses.

"Now, sister," he said, "here are a mare and a gelding. You may have your choice."

And in reply I answered, "Well, seeing how I am a woman, I will take the mare."

"Good," he ejaculated. "Then this lodge goes with it."

So with Dog Woman's help I took down the lodge and moved it over in place of my own. When my husband came into camp, he could not recognize our lodge. It made him wonder what had happened. "My wife must have done something wrong and had to leave camp." I was waiting behind the door to watch him. Then I ran out and called. I told him what had happened.

"They have done a great thing," was his approving comment.

We went inside our new lodge. "Now," said Sun Road, "it is up to you to get out all those things you have been hoarding. You have been keeping them too long. Dig them up!" [Sun Road was a highly correct man; and here is a highly correct attitude toward over-accumulation.]

When we had collected everything we could muster—an elk-tooth dress for my niece, a beautiful dress for her mother, horses and blankets, we prepared a dinner. Short Sioux's family was invited over to celebrate with us. They came in and sat down. Sun Road greeted his "sister," and Dog Woman wept for joy. After we had cleared the plates, I gave them all the dishes. "These are yours to take when you go," I told her. When they had accepted the dishes, I said, "Now I want to dress you up."

So I went over and combed out Dog Woman's hair and put the new dress on her. I painted her face. Sun Road then leaned back under his bed and pulled out his best leggings and buckskin shirt. "Brother-in-law," he said to Short Sioux, "we don't have much to give, but these things are for you. There is also a Navajo blanket."

After a pause, he added "Now I am going to give you a horse. It is right outside."

When Short Sioux had donned his new trimmings, I then put the elk-tooth dress on my niece and said, "A horse goes with this."

All were now dressed. They stood up to go out. We put the dishes, parfleches, and possible bags in their hands. At this very point Sun Road's mother entered with a parfleche. She spoke to me saying, "Daughter-in-law, you may give these things to them." [Note the maintenance of the proper dignitaries in ceremonial control of the occasion. Compare, on a tribal scale, CASE 9.]

We went outside. There Sun Road pointed out his horse to Short Sioux, and I pointed out the one I was giving to my niece.

This relationship has never died from that day to this. We have kept it up with gift exchanges. Since the first meeting, when I became his sister, Short Sioux and I never addressed each other. But we loved and respected each other; whenever I went to his home, nothing was too good for me. On his deathbed he called for me. "You are an old woman now," he said. "I am dying. I have a few head of cattle. You may use two of them."

When he was gone my niece came to me and said, "Aunt, we are going to include you in the things."

"No," I answered, "I don't want a single piece."

I did not take the cows. I never took anything whatever. I knew they would always take care of me. It was more graceful.

» » »

Here, then, was ceremonial reciprocity shaping the conduct of individuals and smoothing the path of social relationships in the way that Professor Malinowski cherishes. It was an institutional form which pervaded many aspects of Cheyenne life. Its legal significance is indirectly of importance, though the mere fact of its two-way nature, and the fact that Calf Woman's brother thought he had to give her something in return "to keep her up," do not make clear "law" of all of it for the Cheyennes.

These were the ways the Cheyennes relied upon to produce the well-behaved adult. These were the techniques which produced the

Cheyenne gentleman and gentlewoman—the Stump Horns and the Kicks The Balls. But these are the same ways which failed to prevent the production of Last Bulls in their worse aspects, because there were also strains in the Cheyenne ideal which taught impetuosity and impatience when enemies and buffalo were at hand—an impetuosity which in some people carried over into personal relations as well.

George Bird Grinnell knew the Cheyennes well, and he was deeply impressed with the behavior of Cheyenne children; the beauty of his chapter on "The Boy and the Girl" culminates in a pæan of praise. "Children seldom or never quarrelled or fought among themselves, and though, as they grew older, continually engaging in contests of strength such as wrestling and kicking matches, and games somewhat like football, they rarely lost their temper. . . . The Cheyenne boys are naturally good-natured and pleasant, and the importance of living on good terms with their fellows having been drilled into them from earliest childhood, they accepted defeat and success with equal cheerfulness."[6] But—these same Cheyennes are the young men who broke through the lines of the hunt police, who disregarded instructions when out as scouts, who just had to go down to the sighted enemy camp to count a coup or steal a horse, when their duty as scouts forbade it, who by so doing gave ample warning to the enemy of the impending attack by the main body of Cheyennes, who gave the Keeper of their Sacred Arrows a beating when he tried to restrain them, who time and again stole off to the attack before the tribal medicine rituals were completed, even though "all" Cheyennes "believed" such action meant disaster (and disaster did follow).[7] No, Cheyenne education and child-training was not perfection. The informal controls worked on most people most of the time, but they often failed on the young men because the immediate desire for warrior's glory was too strongly instilled. So what has been described up to this point in the chapter is the façade of semi-perfection. The informal controls

---

[6] *Ibid.*, I, 122.

[7] The war histories of the Cheyennes are full of such instances. If the evidence in the cases presented in this book is not enough, more may be found in Grinnell, *The Fighting Cheyennes*, 43, 53, 68 f., 85, 87 f., 151.

have been described as they worked, with emphasis on when they worked well. Nevertheless, there were always the clashes of interest and personality which underlay the legal disputes of later life, and there were the obstreperous antics of the social incorrigibles. Some of these latter, it has been seen, were reformed by successful social action, casting away their asocial behavior to revolutionize their personalities when a ceremonial opportunity was provided. But for all the controls, there were still thick-skinned persons whose hide was proof against the sharpest proddings of a disapproving society. As adults, they remained the "problem children" of Cheyenne society.

Cheyenne women, it will be recalled, had their methods of making husbands behave (CASES 34, 35). Few of them, however, were such furies as the wife of Tall White Man. A female bully, who played havoc with her husband's domestic domain and the peace of the camp at large, she remained intransigent to the end of a long life.

Calf Woman, from whom came the account of this Cheyenne Amazon, knew her well and was present at some of her "scenes." High Forehead, who did the interpreting, was also acquainted with her and her doings. He confirmed—when not interpreting—the story of her character and escapades.

« « « Tall White Man was ambitious and so important as to have three wives. His first wife was so mean and jealous toward the others that Tall White Man could not get his spouses to live together. For a while, it is true, he could hold them under one tipi, but soon they would have to part. He tried living with his wives in rotation, each in her separate establishment, but even this expedient fell short of happiness. For when he was staying with one of his second wives, his shrew would burst into the lodge and seize him by the hair. "That is a hell-of-a-looking thing you are staying with," she would yell. And giving him a yank on his braids, she would pull him out of the lodge.

It got so bad for Tall White Man that he resorted to telling her lies. He told his wife he was going to dance with his soldier society. Then he got out his costume and left the lodge. Later, when his skeptical spouse went to the dance lodge to check up, he was not there. She went straight to the tipi of his favorite wife, and putting in her head, found him braiding her hair. "Is that the way you dance?" she bellowed. Then she withdrew her head and turned to go looking for "man-manure." She found it. Taking a rag full of excrement, she reëntered the lodge and set to rubbing it over the other wife's hair—the hair Tall White Man was braiding so prettily.

"What are you doing now?" he started to demand, when his open mouth received the rag full of filth.

The Terror then gathered his dancing costume and started to drag him home, leaving her co-wife sitting there, smelling. In passing through the door, however, she dropped something. When she turned to retrieve it, the smeared one smote her a blow with a club. While the women set to with fang and claw, Tall White Man fled to wash his face, and to hide. The one pulled excrement from her hair and smeared it on the other. They both scratched and clawed until blood was flowing. Women came running from all the camps. I got there, too, while some of them, not necessarily relatives, pulled them apart.

The first wife went raving through the village, seeking her Tall White Man. "If I find that man of mine," she roared, "I'll beat him nigh unto death." [One wonders how she, a woman, might have managed it, or how she so bullied her husband, until one learns that she was a brawny woman of two hundred and fifty pounds, while her husband of the tall name was a slight man of some one hundred and forty.]

While she was in this state, her son stopped her. "Mother," he scolded, "what is the matter with you? Are you crazy? Everybody is talking about you. Every place I go they throw it up to me. When I talk to the girls they all say, 'I cannot marry you—you have such an awful mother.' I am losing my friends, boys and girls. Now you go home and behave."

This injunction sent her to her tipi, where she sat and brooded, thinking, thinking. The devil in her mind kept plaguing her with the jealous notion that her husband had now gone to the third wife. At last, when she could stand it no longer, she rushed from the lodge.

Her son was on the watch, though, and again he broke in to give her a lecture. Still she was obstinate and set in her purpose. "I am mad," she maintained. "They drew blood on me."

"Whose fault was it?" her son countered. "You brought it on yourself by going over there. Now go back to your lodge."

Again the son's word was strong and she obeyed.

The second wife needed the whole night to get herself clean. When she next saw Tall White Man, she declared herself free of him. "You have a wife you can't control," she announced. "I am not staying with you longer. I am sending for a new husband. Good by." She sent word to Sun Bear that she would marry him. He obliged by coming to take her away as his wife. No pipe was sent to Tall White Man; no damages were ever sought from Sun Bear. [As we read it, none was due. The wife divorced Tall White Man in form and for cause, and only then found herself a husband.]

The next episode came when the brother of the obnoxious woman went to war. Tall White Man gave his costume and war horse to his brother-in-law for the venture. The brother-in-law acknowledged it with reciprocation. He told his mother to give his younger sister to Tall White Man. "She'll get along fine with that sister of mine. The two will make good wives for him, because they are sisters together."

So Tall White Man moved into the tipi of the younger. As may be guessed, however, the Big One was not long in stirring trouble. She came over to pester the new wife. "You were a fool to marry our husband," she counseled. "He has nearly beat me to death. He will certainly do the same to you."

Such talk did not shake the younger sister. "No, I don't think so; I married him on the strength of my brother. I love him." More than that, she had a bolt of her own to shoot. "Yes, I'll get along all right with our husband. But do you know what he was telling me about you the other night? He is going to leave you. Oh, you may stay around here, and he'll see that you are fed. But he is never going to sleep with you again. He is going to bed with me."

Little did she know what lay ahead. The next night, when she triumphantly retired with her husband, the Fury burst into the lodge. She jerked Tall White Man from the bed by his hair, throwing him to the other side of the lodge. "A fine thing! You lying in bed with my sister!" Then the two women started to fight. Their mother hurried over from her lodge to take the part of the younger girl.

Things calmed after a bit; the younger sister escaped from the tipi. Tall White Man went following after a little. When he could not find his wife, he grew apprehensive. He called on all the camp to turn out to help seek her. But she had disappeared completely. No trace was found of her until, after more than forty years, a cowboy riding the range espied a rawhide rope dangling from a tree and beneath it a pile of bones. People believe it was she.

The mother disowned the willful elder daughter, and when a month had passed and the younger sister was yet missing, she mourned her for dead. She gashed herself and announced that she would have nothing more to do with her eldest daughter who had caused this grief. It was many years before they were again reconciled. Every bit of property left by the missing daughter was burned by the mother, so that the other would get none of it.

All this accomplished nothing toward changing the woman's character. [A fact most unusual in Cheyenne.] It only made this one more defiant. In resentment she later rushed her mother's tipi and gashed it to shreds. Leaving this destruction behind her, she rushed over to her brother's lodge where her sister-in-law lay ill, to harass her in a rude loud voice. "What's the matter with you? You are just playing baby. Get up! You are not sick. You just want my brother to take care of you."

She did no damage there, but her brother was tired of her doings, so he went to her lodge with a horsewhip. But she was too fleet of foot for him. He chased her around and around, and when he paused for breath, she yelled, "Go chase a deer! When you catch it, then try yourself on me."

The best he could do to spite her was to start shooting holes into her pots and pans. He was talked out of more drastic action and even shamed out of this by Fat Cow. This woman said to him, "You are doing a woman's job over here, busting up her things."

He tried to explain himself out of it by protesting that he had come to give her a good lashing. But Fat Cow reminded him, "If you don't stop, people will always be throwing it up to you. You are always around joking. They will come back with this."

He was sensitive where his sister was not. He stopped and went away. But from that day, like his mother, he cast his sister off. He nevermore visited her or recognized her existence. At her death he refused to go to look at her. He gave no mourning gifts in her honor, for she was long since dead for him. "She is the cause of scattering our family," he bitterly commented.

Her own daughters and sons had left her too. The girls all ran away with men. Of her eight children [one of whom still lives] not one came to give her a decent burial. Her husband was blind and helpless. Finally Short Sioux called on the people, saying, "She is dead now; you ought to take her away."

In the end she was buried by neighbors without honor from her family, and unmourned.   »   »   »

What a striking example of informal pressures this history is! How dramatically, also, it demonstrates the futility of purely informal sanctions when the object of the pressures is so socially calloused as not to care—especially so, when she has the physical prowess as well as the moral numbness to ignore them. It is like the bee hurling itself against the elephant's back. The women of the community did not taunt her with her misdeeds, says Calf Woman, because they were afraid of her. Her husband could not divorce her, because she refused to leave him. One really good chance to get rid of her, in High Forehead's opinion, was when he was made a tribal chief. Then he could have thrown her off, and she would have had to take it. It is certainly a question, however, if she would have observed the "binding custom" in this case any more than in others. At least, "she would have given her husband one last beating before leaving him." This, says High Forehead, cannily, is why Tall White Man did not divorce her. Could a chief have remained chief, after being beaten by his wife? In law, yes. But in prestige?

That such a henpecked husband could become a member of the

tribal council of chiefs seems startling. Nevertheless Tall White Man was a good person and reliable. Even this terrible wife of his was, for all her truculence, a generous soul, good to all the people except where another woman was conceived to have entered into relationships with her husband. This saving feature may be a fact which caused society to tolerate her to the extent it did. The supposed protest suicide of her sister co-wife missed its effect because the body was not found. Had it been, the stage would seem to have been set for the Terror to share the fate of Red Owl (CASE 26). Perhaps the Cheyennes recognized Big Woman as a psychopath and so made due allowance for her; we failed to follow this clue of mental abnormality in its psychological aspects, and so can give no conclusive statement on this point.

Sometimes hunters came into camp with a surplus of meat. They placed it in a conspicuous pile and left it. It was not for anybody to take, though all who wished could share in it. When a tribal chief saw the pile, he hastened to a soldier chief to tell him to take the distribution of the meat in hand. That soldier chief would gather a dozen or so of his younger men to undertake the work. The women who were wanting meat were already on hand when the soldiers arrived. The meat was set up in equal piles by the soldiers. The distribution was placed in care of two young men chosen by the soldier chief for their reputations in fair dealing. One carried each share of meat to a place in front of the woman designated by the chief to receive it, while the other walked about to check that no one was overlooked.

It is many years since there has been such a hunt distribution, but the pattern is not lost. We glowed with pleasurable remembrance of bygone days when we sat in a little room crowded with Cheyenne men, women, and children, all comfortably ensconced on the floor about the feast goods of dried beef, fried bread, boiled rice, fried apples, and black coffee, waiting while a long, long prayer was finished. Black Wolf, the priest of the Peyote Ceremony of the night before, was the host. He signaled to the young men, several of whom started dishing out the food. Quietly leaning against the

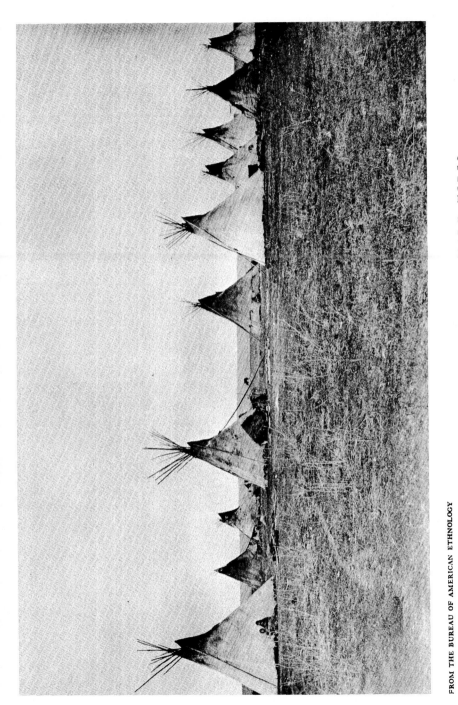

A CHEYENNE CAMP : BUFFALO HIDE TIPIS

wall, Black Wolf's son was watching over all, calling the attention of the servers to the unobtrusive guests whose plates had not been filled—and quietly approving as plates were filled for folk waiting outside, for whom there was no room within.

In the old days, however, not all of the lodge wives were unobtrusive. There were some so ill-mannered as to criticize the distribution; some like Singing Woman hid their share and then demanded more. The soldiers did not refuse her, but Stump Horn says they would take her another piece, observing, "We know you are lying, but here is another piece anyhow." The other women gossiped about it, and eventually the talk got around to the son and daughter, who admonished their mother; but she said nothing. She had her double ration of meat, and a rhinocerous hide.

Other such women even seized what was being offered to those sitting next to them. The issuer is said never to have tussled with such a one about it. The soldiers would not quarrel with women. But then the other women pointed to her as a "fright." When they saw her coming, "they would look at her funny"; nor was she asked to feasts much, and they said of her, "There is a woman with lots of gall." "Men hardly ever talked like that among themselves," says Stump Horn, "or paid any attention to what the women said, but I could not help but overhear the women talking about how this woman did things."

Control pressures were also felt by men on similar occasions; "rascals," as High Forehead calls them, were not invited to help distribute, nor were they allowed to get a share.

Turtle, who was a Shield Soldier, came up to take a hand when the Shields were distributing. Four Sitting Medicine Men, the chief, told him to get out and sit down. "You have no right here; you have been making trouble." (What he had done is not remembered.) Soon after, Turtle left the band and went to the Southern Cheyennes. This was a time when a simple admonition was wholly effective. Turtle said nothing about his feelings, and in accordance with Stump Horn's view, his leaving was not absolutely necessary. "He was not pushed out, but it could be that his feelings were hurt. If I had been talked to like that, I would have felt like going away. I would have felt badly, too, about going South, because I would not have known the people down there." That is where rebuke and ostracism bite.

Ridicule was not overlooked, nor its effectiveness as an informal sanction neglected.

Most boys who presumed to manhood before they had been to war were dangerously open to cutting sarcasms. Courtship, for instance, was full of painful rebuffs for such as they, as when a youth who had not been out to war stepped into the path of the girl he would love. Boldly blocking her way, he would talk to her of the many things swains could think to say. But the words chilled in his throat, his scalp burned with embarrassment, as the maiden archly looked at him and murmured, "Well, and how many times have you stopped the *enemy?*" Had he been even bolder, had he thrown his blanket about her to "grab her for love-talk," she could turn him to flight by innocently asking, "And how many *enemies* have you seized in battle?" Only the brave deserve the fair!

Such a youth did once marry one of the four maidens of a soldier society. The members of the club had great fun calling to each other, "Now we have a baby son-in-law to get clothes for."

The marriage of a single boy to a divorced or widowed woman was scandalous. It had a derisive name—"putting on the old moccasin." Gossip was fed by such marriages, and the girls would say of the boy, "Yes, he was a nice young man before he married that old shoe."

Within the family, ridicule was also a sharp-edged weapon. In Yellow Eyes' experience it forestalled what might later have developed into a legal problem. That it never did so was because it was effectively handled on the sub-legal plane. High Forehead was told the anecdote by one of the boys who played the hoax.

«   «   «   Yellow Eyes was one who did not appreciate the faithfulness of his wife. He was a victim of the annoying obsession that she was generous with others. He was always accusing her of adultery. Every time he left the lodge, he accused her on his return. His game was to creep up on the tipi and spring through the door in hopes of catching an adulterer. This sport annoyed his good wife. In fact, it exasperated her so that she complained to Yellow Eyes' nephews for help. The five boys schemed and plotted, saying they would fix him.

They waited for a night when he was visiting, and in his absence they all stripped to their breechclouts to lie in wait in his lodge. When they spied him coming, one of them crouched within the door. Just as Yellow Eyes' hand fell on the covering—whish! A naked young man scrambled between his legs and was off. Yellow Eyes went chasing after, as soon as he recovered his balance. When his breath failed him, he stopped and yelled an idle threat about knowing who the interloper was. So he turned back to his lodge. Again the same disturbance. And again the same futile search. Five times it happened, as each of the nephews gave him a run.

When finally he was able to enter his tipi without being upset, he accosted his wife. "Were those fellows all lying with you?" he thundered.

"To be sure," she smugly assured him, "All five of them."

Yellow Eyes was so flabbergasted that he was speechless. To have his suspicions so overwhelmingly confirmed took all the power out of him. To finish it off, his five nephews came back the next day to ride him unmercifully. The cure was a complete success. Never again did he annoy his wife with his suspicions. This happened about 1873.   »   »   »

Chastity of unmarried Cheyenne girls was legally sustained by the inviolability of the chastity belt (Chapter VII) and by a rigid social opinion. Among the Cheyennes even intramarital sex abstinence of husband and wife was ideally esteemed. Mention of this is made by Mr. Grinnell, who noted, "It was long the custom that a woman should not have a second child until her first child was about ten years of age." Then the father, with the giving away of a horse at a large dance, publicly announced the expectation of a little brother or sister. "The people talked about it and praised the parents' self-control."[8]

[8] Grinnell, *The Cheyenne Indians*, I, 149.

However, such action was not compulsory, and some families had numerous children. But the ideal was there, and with it a peculiar supernatural tie-up and sanction. The rationalized reason for such severe abstinence was "to give the first child a chance." (How many American families stoutly assert the need to keep the family small so as to give those born every possible opportunity?) Or, as Dog posed it, "If I were to have had too many children, I'd be whipping first one, then the other." Since Cheyennes abhor chastisement, it was, therefore, "better to let the first child grow up before there were others."

To attain this goal contraceptives were definitely not used. The expressed reaction to abortion (CASE 14) has been seen. The Cheyenne technique was rigid sex abstinence fortified by a holy vow. The vow was the crux of the practice. It would not seem that this complex was intended as a population control device, though its effects were recognized as such—"that is what kept the tribe so small in the old days." It is possible, of course, that such was the original cause, but the abstinence took on the character of a great sacrifice to Maiyun, comparable in every respect to fasting in the Sun Dance or staking one's self on the hill top. It gained a general sort of a blessing for the first child, as well as making possible undivided parental attention. This is clearly seen in the dedication of a pony to Maiyun, declared by the Indians to be an analogous practice. Warriors commonly vowed to give a period of rest to their ponies. Each time the number of moons to pass before the vacation ended was stated in the presence of a medicine man. The medicine man rehearsed the well-known obligations. The pony must be brought in every night for grooming, but never ridden. A polished antelope horn in which was inserted an herb was tied about its neck. The thong served as a gauge of the pony's fattening. The pony was incensed, rubbed, and talked to by the medicine man.[9] Then it was turned loose. When the free period was ended, the pony was once again brought before the medicine man. "Now your moons are up," the pony was told. "Wherever he [i.e., the owner] goes in the country, he'll take you."

[9] The application ritual is described in detail by Grinnell, *ibid.*, II, 141.

This dedication and release from all use gave the pony a supernatural potency such as to assure it long wind, speed, and strength. Safety in battle was an additional expected result. The medicine man was given a butchered buffalo for his efforts. Breaking of the vow for any cause meant death to the pony, in proof of which several historical instances were cited by Black Wolf.

An attenuated survival of the practice lingers on. Young Cheyennes of today talk to their horses and turn them loose to fatten, but the ceremony is neglected. Black Wolf counsels his son against promising his horse a specific vacation time. One is too apt to forget, these days, and bad luck is still possible.

Promising a first child a free development for five, six, seven, to ten years, was an identical vow. Though the consequences of parental intercourse during such a period were believed to be the death of the child, no instances of such were obtainable, whether because non-occurrent or unremembered. In strict belief, extramarital intercourse was ruled out as well, and for the same reason. It thus appears (as was the case in fact) that chastity requirements among the Cheyennes did not tend to lead to frequent adultery. Nor does it seem to have been a powerful inducement to polygyny. It is not clearly established whether intercourse with a second *wife* was permissible during the period of the abstinence vow, though there are indications that it was.

The general evidence seems to be that the pattern did not come into serious conflict with sex appetite, except that the survival of "putting a woman on the prairie" points to the existence of an only partially mastered drive on the part of some males. One should know whether men under the vow were free to participate. If they were not, then there is no connection between the two types of behavior. If they were given an indulgence for this custom, then herein might be external evidence of an internal conflict. One cannot determine at this remote date whether or not this is the correct judgment of what would be a deep-lying personality problem. One Cheyenne, in whom we repose the utmost confidence, declares that after the birth of his first child he lived fifteen years in perfect harmony with his wife without any sex relations and without strain.

This man is one who greatly esteemed his position in the tribe. Persons who were lacking in the will to carry through were supposed not to make such vows. The revenge of the supernatural was there for those of that kind who did try it.

One sees, then, among the Cheyennes, the same mixture of pressures and levels of pressure which one expects in any society to shape and reform conduct so as to avoid friction, or to remove it. The basic devices were training, example and spectacle, preachment (which though conscious was relatively unformalized) in how things operate and in the proper conduct of a proper person, with much praise and occasional rebuke. The second type of training was more subtle—how to get what one wanted, within the frame of existing institutions, and without causing a social kickback. As an indication of what the limits of such personal exploitation of social institutions were, put together Stump Horn's stories of himself, and you find a somewhat naïve and unselfish acceptance of the given pattern of the gentleman. Put together Calf Woman's stories about herself, and you see an enterpriser, skillfully using all available social devices to her own ends—which at times included the working out of grudges.

Indeed, no lesson for law from the Cheyenne material is more striking than this: Law smooths the immediate grievance down, but it *can* be used to work out grudges, too. One finds little in Cheyenne of the deliberately unjust accusation—the type of dirty work which led the early Romans to prescribe that he who searched another's house for allegedly stolen goods should approach only in loincloth, and with a platter in his hands. But one finds case after case of the grievance stored and treasured up, while the aggrieved waited to catch the hated person in a vulnerable position. Sometimes this meant later bursting over even into murder. We are unable to tell whether a more adequate system of dealing officially with personal wrongs would have eased these tensions or aggravated them, though we incline to the former view.

It is amazing to see the degree to which informal pressures kept even the more disruptive adults in line. "Public opinion" was indeed opinion among the Cheyennes; but it was a deal more, too. Consider the number of cases in which bystanders seized an attacker's arms, or hid the hunted, or spoke up with quieting counsel duly accepted, or made gifts to pacify or shame the unruly into decency. Consider also the pattern of vicarious release in public: "If he were here, I would do *this!*" Consider the warnings brought anonymously before attack—a function of anticipatory vicarious release plus superficially inconsistent self-goading to action (it is an unstable balance) by the spoken word. Consider the rallying of outspoken opinion in public, and at the very moment, to draw the sting from drumming away a wife, to give praise for noble action, to cry down dirty work. Consider the spontaneous movement of the community into lynching action, when children had been driven by indecent parental abuse to suicide. Last Bull was deposed as soldier chief: "People are talking about us!" The Medicine Hat Keeper was himself deposed, and the whole tribe went out to war to enforce his abdication. "Public opinion," in Cheyenne, had teeth, and showed them; and could bite, and bit. And the record of cures (whose authenticity there is no reason to doubt) is almost startling. It is not, of course, complete, any more than the record of prevention is.

Meanwhile, public opinion simply as opinion was at work by day, hour, and minute. The women chattered. Stump Horn may tell, as he did: "Who listens to the chatter of the women?" But High Forehead knew that "some women were good newspapers"—and Stump Horn's own regard for best form was inescapably based upon what people were saying, have said, will say. Meanwhile the women did more than chatter. They shamed individual members of a soldier society which had put some poor creature on the prairie. They shamed them into skulking; they shamed some into actual denial of participation. And even he who did not listen to the chatter of the women got its square impact from his own wife, or from what his warrior brethren said solemnly in conclave—as their wives had chattered it to them. Not for nothing did a chief feel that not his nominator alone, but the People, whose opinion had made him an honorable nominee, had named him their protector.

The major peculiarities of the Cheyenne combination of child-rearing, prestige models, and informal and formal pressures may perhaps be summed up thus: The games and the instruction by relatives headed directly into training for adulthood, but in education, there was neither the modern type of schooling nor the compulsory and standardized initiation which ethnologists frequently record, though there was a good deal of conscious preaching, partly institutionalized as in coup-recital or the preaching of the chiefs and old men. Neither were there age groups sharply marked, nor age societies. The young warrior normally became a member of a military society when he got around to it; undoubtedly he learned, in that context. One finds little more, except the known religious patterns, to instruct him. The prestige models afforded in life and ideology were of the Plains type; again there is little more to say. There was reasonable variety of type, and so both of stimulus and of outlet. There was, for the sons of the great, a pressure to be worthy of ancestors, but the poorest of male children could become great; Last Bull began as nobody at all. Mobility of class and prestige was, at least during the period of the present cases (and we think, before then) at a social peak.

The informal pressures on adults were not only vocal, but somewhat peculiarly quick to take the form of action—not only in the case of persons interested, but among what one may call the disinterested public. There were few official organs of pressure of the type of a censor, or a Scotch Presbyterian minister or elder. The evidence does not indicate that the semi-official "joking" relative was anything like as important, as, e.g., among the neighboring enemy Crows. One finds instead—apart from the constant pressure of the women—a semi-legal device which almost reminds one of the inherited grievances set forth in a Chagga palaver:[10] a man's past misdeeds, especially those of violence, rose up in every new dispute, to color the level of his opponent's demands and action, even at times to switch the outcome in law. One finds much of that reciprocal relation and consequent pressure to perform civil obligations, which Malinowski[11] has brought into focus; but the relatively

[10] Gutmann, *Das Recht der Dschagga.*
[11] Malinowski, *Crime and Custom in Savage Society.*

exchangeless and unspecialized economic structure of the Cheyennes did not permit of any real flowering of this type of reciprocal
pressure. One finds it present unambiguously in one place only:
in the relation between son-in-law and parent-in-law—a place
peculiarly ill-adapted to public display. And even here, the legal
implications are unclear; one cannot tell when a son-in-law merely
wanted a younger sister to wife and set up a colorable claim, and
when he may have been asserting a real legal right to have her. We
think this was ambiguous in the culture; we suspect that elder
brother's disposal of an eldest sister had not been wholly disentangled from son-in-law's right against parents in regard to a
younger sister of his wife, or, perhaps, from waxing claim to self-
determination.

Elsewhere, reciprocal relations seem clearly present, but vastly
more unschematized. Return-gifts do not seem (save in relation to
a wedding) to have been *definitely* due. They were always welcome;
they arrived, on occasion, after twenty years; they may have been
expected, and often must have been. But one finds no trace of any
dependence on them, and no trace of quarrel because they failed
to materialize. In most cases, we think they were return-*gifts*, not
return-gifts. Their import was good will, good form, and friendship, not the performance of an obligation which was felt as legal.

What must cause amazement to anyone who has studied other
cultures in which law-stuff was plentiful and legal thinking skilled,
is the scantiness in Cheyenne of instances in which the legal and
the minor pressures run one counter to the other, cross-purposing
pressures *among themselves,* with both "right" and "law" in consequent doubt together. Almost uniformly they play in team. So, for
instance, in the claim of a good son-in-law upon the younger sister,
or in the question whether tracker or finder takes the horses, or in
the question of just what does make out good ground for divorce.
Or else the cross-purposing is one within the individual personality,
of differential urges, each of which is furthered by "right" and "law"
and the inviting lines of a career: you must be brave, decisive,
forceful; you must be thoughtful, unselfish, wise. You must love
your wife and cherish her; you must be above dependence on a

woman. You must be a man who can outface any man; you must put self-restraint above all things. It is this type of struggle among patterns, tendencies, ideals, each of which is in itself reasonable and right, all of which are approved. Add, then, the crucial matter: that each of such patterns, urges, ideals, and almost each personality, carries a voltage peculiarly high. Each person within himself, and the "friends" as among themselves, are expected to manage somehow a stable balance among those voltages. The chief machinery the culture offered, to sort out patterns and standards, and help produce a balance, was a career-sequence geared to call forth in succession, first, individual daring, then the responsible leadership of a soldier chief at home and in the field, and finally the grave dignity of a Council member—a sequence which reminds one of the more elaborately structured Roman *cursus honorum.*

But the ways of producing such balance show no sign of having been a focus of conscious and explicit instruction—as, in our own culture, the judge's art of balancing the voltages of his society also shows no sign of being a focus of conscious and explicit instruction. For the Cheyennes there were the living models at hand for any man to study and to model on—forty-four of them marked by office as the men who had worked the full pattern out to satisfaction. The explicit exhortation and more particular stimulations to which a Cheyenne was exposed stirred appreciation of the life values rather quality by quality, or case by case, not all together. And the impact of the more directly organized stimuli, while admirably adapted to the age and interest of the growing youngster or maturing man, could and often did, thrust him too far in the direction of the stimulus of the moment. The over-eagerness of young men to get into battle and the over-exuberance of policing activity belong here. "The way I hit you, that's the way I hit the enemy" generates its own touch of "the way I hit the enemy, that's the way I have to hit you." Indeed, no man will fathom the dynamics of Cheyenne personality-shaping who does not take account of this building of the whole in terms of intensity of living, of living at high potential—to be achieved, if need be, by building one quality after another up to peak, with all the risks that that entailed—the balance to be worked out, after. Consider merely the sex-restraint in courting and after the birth of a first child, coupled with the powerful chastity patterns. Consider then the number of those "who had achieved." There were forty-four tribal chiefs in a population of three thousand—one to every round dozen of males of appropriate age. Consider in this light, first the indulgence shown to fault, to over-ness in any aspect, the effective stress on cure rather than retribution. Consider, finally, the task which faced the juristic machinery when potentials became unbalanced, and threatened discharge.

To keep such a culture going, with dignity, with effectiveness, and with its huge individual vitality in manageable harness, required law-ways of high effectiveness. It required also that the law-ways be reinforced at every point by other ways, and that they coincide in pressure. Merely to work out overt adjustment in so highly charged an atmosphere calls for juristic art. To do it and yet keep the standards of doing it abreast of a culture in movement, and during a period exposed to the severest trials, calls again for art. Such art, if achieved—such juristic method—had of necessity to *keep* the law-ways in close and singing harmony with the rest of the culture, in "harmony" even with what culture-discord there might be.

PART III

The Law-Jobs and Juristic Method

Chapter X

CLAIMS AND LAW-WAYS

THIS chapter and the following set forth the skeleton of a general theory of the nature and function of law-stuff and of the law-jobs with which any group is faced in the process of becoming and remaining a group. The theory applies to groups of any size or complexity. It is here presented with major reference to a primitive society and to any subgroups which may be found within one. Little specific attention is given to the peculiar aspects which develop around the institution of clearly worded rules, gathered in the authoritative books of the modern state. The theory is, however, of general application.[1]

The basic elements which give rise to law-jobs and law-stuff are simple enough and not too numerous. There is first the relevant

[1] This chapter draws at will upon prior publications by Llewellyn which have explored particular areas of the subject matter. Notably, *re* control by use of the criminal law machinery, "Law Observance and Law Enforcement," *Proceedings*, Conference of Social Work, 1928, 127-40; "Introduction" to Jerome Hall, *Theft, Law and Society* (Boston, Little, Brown & Co., 1935), xvi-xxxv; *re* subgroup structurings and their functioning in relation to government, "The Constitution as an Institution," *Columbia Law Review*, XXXIV (1934) 1-40; *re* the role of the individual, of ideologies, and of pattern diversification, "Behind the Law of Divorce," *Columbia Law Review*, XXXIII (1932-33), 249-94, 1281-1308; on the behavior phases of law-stuff in general as they occur in modern society and their relations to the social disciplines, "A Realistic Jurisprudence," *Columbia Law Review*, XXX (1930), 431-65; "Legal Tradition and Social Science Method," *Brookings Essays on Research in the Social Sciences* (Philadelphia, 1931), 89-120; *Präjudizienrecht und Rechtssprechung* (Leipsig, 1933); "On Reading and Using the New Jurisprudence," *Columbia Law Review*, XL (1940), 581-614—also *American Bar Association Journal*, XXVI, Nos. 4, 5 (1940), 300-07, 418-25; on the influence of particular men in key positions as compared with the general economic sweep and ideological configurations, "Horse Trade and Merchant's Market in Sales," *Harvard Law Review*, LII (1939), 725-46, 873-904; "On Warranty of Quality, and Society," *Columbia Law Review*, XXXVI (1936), 699-744; and, *ibid.*, XXXVII (1937), 341-409, especially 341-73.

More directly underlying Chapters X and XI is the general presentation, "The Normative, the Legal, and the Law-Jobs: The Problem of Juristic Method," *Yale Law Journal*, XLIX (1940), 1355-1400. In that particular paper the application of these concepts to modern law-stuff is given more attention.

entirety, or group, or Whole. By this is meant two or more persons who are engaged in some kind of observably joint and continuing activity, and who recognize themselves in some fashion as being parts of a Whole. Given in the same concept is some type and degree of actual patterning of behavior-in-the-group, a patterning which affords an interlocking of the behavior of individuals, a back-and-forth, a building of this one's behavior together with that one's into a working whole. And given in that is, in turn, some degree of predictability of behavior, some quantum of those advance adjustments by one person to the anticipated behavior of another which we call expectations.

The second element or set of elements is the occurrence of *divergent* urges or desires among members of the group; these tend into friction and disunity. And this is quite as fundamental a constituent of law life as is the group order which it may disturb.

The third basic element or set of elements is found in the claims made by some member or members upon or against others, and the relation of those claims to the order of the Whole; for, presupposing such an Order, they are sought to be "justified" under that Order. Either expectation or wish can generate claim. Claim, moreover, for reasons which we do not attempt to fathom, shows an inveterate drive to take the form of being a right and *rightful* claim. It takes the form of an alleged right or rightfulness which tends inevitably, in the context of any particular group or Whole, to get itself set up as being properly a part of the way that Whole is going round, or of the way it ought to and is about to go round, if the claimant be successful.

These are the basic elements. The members of the group, working within its order, then either manage so to handle divergent claims as to keep the group still "the group," or else the law-jobs fail to get done, and the group explodes or dribbles apart or dies. The way of the handling, the machinery for the handling, the precision and wisdom or fumbling and folly of the handling, are the crux of the law life of the group, and they cut to the heart of the conditions for its continuance. Thus it seems worth-while to go into a rough sketch of how these elements play upon one another, because the lines of such a sketch bring out the lines of fruitful comparison between the law-stuffs of different groups or different civilizations.

But it is very hard to develop the matter with either clarity or sound result, if one uses as his basic tools such still commonly enlisted broader concepts as "custom" or "mores." Such concepts are slippery under the hand in three ways.

First, they are ambiguous. They *fuse* and *confuse* the notion of "practice" (say, a moderately discernible line of actual behavior) with the notion of "standard" (say, an actually held ideal of what the proper line of actual behavior should be). Whereas it is vital to keep such existing standards describable in terms which make easy and almost inescapable the measuring against them of the behavior which does occur. Such ideas as conformity, or breach, take meaning only when set against a known or felt standard for behavior.

Second, such terms as "custom" and "mores" lack edges. They *diffuse* their reference gently and indiscriminately over the whole of the relevant society. Whereas one key to getting at the ways of law-stuff is to keep in mind *which* of the various possible entireties is the one whose order is concerned in any matter of adjustment: Is it Crooked Elbow's immediate family? Is it his band? The Elk Soldiers? The tribe? This is exactly what such a concept as "custom" or "mores" makes it seemingly unnecessary to inquire into. In the same way, these concepts obscure that great range of trouble in which practices (statistical "norms" of behavior: the normal) plus their appropriate standards ("norms" in the sense of the ethicists and legal philosophers: the normative) can conflict within a society at all complex. It is as a result of such conflicts between various sets of ways-and-standards that there arise some of the most significant conflicts between men, each urging an extension of his own patterns as proper to prevail in the context of the larger Whole which embraces both conflicting subgroups.

Third, such terms as "custom" and "mores" have come to lend a seeming solidity to any supposed lines of behavior to which they are applied, and a seeming uniformity to phenomena which range in fact from the barely emergent hit-or-miss, wobbly groping which *may* some day find following enough to become a practice, on through to an established and nearly undeviating manner in which all but idiots behave. The terms obscure also the very important range of unnoticed or unrebuked scatter of behavior around the "line" concerned. Even on the "normative" side, that of the accepted standard, they obscure the question of how many hold the standard to be proper, and how uniformly they hold it so, and who may be feeling differently—though "mores," of course, does take account of the matter of intensity of the feeling.

Finally, such terms as "custom" or "mores" lead emphasis and attention away from the fact that the firmest and clearest practice or standard operates only upon and through the minds and activities of persons. Nowhere is the fact more basic to understanding than in regard to law-stuff. And in what follows the effort will be never to let that fact or its importance slip from attention.

The dynamic tensions which lead to law-stuff, feed it, and give it material to work on, show up peculiarly in *claims*—claims repudiated or resisted or merely unfulfilled; claims asserted as "right" or "rightful" in the context of the going order of some particular group or Entirety. For a claim never exists *in vacuo*. The particular group order which it presupposes is as much a part of it as is the claimant. We shall examine first something of the mechanics of the growth of such claims, and of their assertion and acceptance. We shall then examine something of the nature of the law-stuff which they tend to generate. We shall then come to a sketch of certain of the major law-jobs which the group faces in using law-stuff to keep claims from disrupting the group, culminating in the problem of juristic method (the art of keeping claims and the order in balance). For juristic method is the heart of the law-work of any group and of any culture.

Claims, Claimants, and Group Order

Perhaps the first point about claims is that they are always in one sense divisive, although they need not be disruptive. Always, a claim in some manner sets one person or portion of the Entirety concerned against some other person or portion; else there would be no claim. But both purpose and effect of the claim may work toward the interest of the Whole, as when the claimant (be he individual or official) moves to penalize a clear infraction of the known order of the group. There does exist, indeed, as part of the structure of any group, an area of leeway within which even patently divisive and potentially disruptive claims are tolerated; but there always exist limits to such leeway. This means that the Order is called on to control claims. The backing of the Order, moreover, is a strength always worth a claimant's effort to enlist. This means that the Order is called on to support claims. Finally, such enlistment of support is rarely possible without the production of at least "colorable" ground for holding the claim either to rest in the order already, or to further it. This means that claims get made and urged in terms of the Order. From these facts there flow, whether in petty groups or whole societies, the following:

First, there is a frame of feeling, thought, discourse, and action in regard to claims, in which they tend powerfully to be set up as serving the welfare of the relevant Entirety, and so as deserving of recognition or acceptance as part of the order thereof. Or, and more simply, they can be set up as already a part of that order, and so as needing no further justification. In either case, judgment of bystanders and officials, and to a real degree the self-judgment of the participants in a trouble-case, moves in similar terms.

Second, and by the same token, there recurs the problem of whether recognition or acceptance of a claim furthers the commonweal of the group either directly or indirectly; and if not, whether tolerance of it passes the limits of the endurable. And there inescapably recur in the picture, feeling and thinking and acting by some in terms of self or subgroup, in terms of interest or need or passion, directed against others of the Entirety; and, on the other hand, feeling and thinking by some in terms of the welfare of the Whole.

Third, if it be a group into which children are born, there will, along with variant inheritance, be an almost inevitable material range of conditioning stimuli afforded, with particular reference to what claims will appeal to them when made, or will appeal to them for making.

The dynamics which generate a *legal* order, which keep one going, and which produce change in one, have two main aspects: drift and drive. Drift is the relatively impersonal and unnoticed lumping of behavior into belts around semi-lines which come to interlock, together with the further relatively impersonal and unnoticed shifting of the "centers" of such belts. Drive, on the other hand, is individuated and personal. Moreover, it takes on of necessity a *conscious* aspect in things legal, if and whenever it meets with *challenge*.

It is important to get clear the manner and degree in which the dynamics of legal institutions are in this matter peculiar. Other institutions can grow by mere drift, and the entrance of drive into them from time to time can go almost unnoticed, because challenge is not a necessary part of the processes. But with the legal, the recurrent impact of conscious thought and action is inescapable, though the range of the conscious thinking may remain narrow, step by step. For in any conflict situation—and conflict situations present the legal problem, par excellence—drive elicits challenge. And challenge forces conscious shaping of issues, conscious moves to persuade or to prevail by other means. Indeed the conscious character of legal dynamics affects also the phenomena of drift in legal institutions. For first, the results of drive and challenge in a conflict situation tend powerfully toward conscious incorporation into the order of the group concerned. A trouble-case is dramatic, it is memorable; it costs brain-sweat, it may cost blood; its solution, once achieved, presses for repetition as few phenomena of life can press. Further drift in the institution is urged thus into a channel with a wall, and conscious challenge and new drive are in the likely offing to block any least departure. You can see this as between husband and wife, when some thorny situation has once been talked out and a "basis" settled. You can see it in Cheyenne life, when horse "borrowing" gets faced and "ruled on."

The importance of looking into the mechanics of the processes appears when one compares legal with religious institutions in the matter of unchanging continuance. The general urges toward persistence of form, ritual, and substance which are common to all institutions appear of course in both of these. But the additional factors which are present differ. The peculiar additional force in religious institutions is a fear of slipping away from known efficacious procedures. This operates by observation, imitation, instruction, and if there be organization, by authoritative supervision of all these. In legal institutions each of these elements is present, but with a further addition—the check, in most instances, of conscious interest-challenge to any departure. The resultant conserving mechanism in legal institutions is therefore in itself more powerful than that in the religious. Yet the latter tend to persist without change over longer periods than do the legal. Obviously, there should be in legal institutions some counterfactor or factors at work to force remodeling. There is. It is the continuance in the general life of the group of the processes which first led to the emergence of legal institutions, at all.

Against this background, and for the moment without reference to the presence or absence of legal institutions of any kind in the group or culture, let us turn for a moment to the raw material which either serves as grist for such institutions or may serve to generate them—claimants and their claims and the effect of the group order on them and of them on it.

It is, we believe, psychologically impossible to see any act or any claim as "right" or "rightful" without setting up implicitly or explicitly a *general* standard of right acts or claims to which the one in hand conforms. In any event, it is impossible to urge an act or claim as right, save against such a standard. Even to see and urge a thing as right "because you want it so," presupposes a general proposition that what *you* want has particular reason to be considered. And the standard is, we believe again inescapably, a standard assumed as a right portion of the whole order controlling the relevant group.[2] This lends to every claim of any group member upon any other a potential legal aspect in the relation of the claim

[2] In odd cases, this can be: the order proper to control the group.

to the total order of the Entirety in the context of which the claim occurs.

While claims thus refer to an order and take color and flavor from it, their possibilities are neither limited to, nor dictated by, the order as it is. Claims derive not only from experience but from desire, not only from observation but from urge and dream. A single fairy story can touch off expectation and demand about the right behavior of pumpkins, mice, and princes-to-appear. The building of claims, spoken or unspoken, and the building of frames, implicit or explicit, to set them in is creative action. It is creative above all in selecting some portion of the relevant group order and expanding it or twisting it to the submergence or dwarfing or even negation of other portions. One recalls that in this process the drives of "better for me," "better for my outfit," and "better for everybody," can all be present, in overlap or in conflict. One recalls that in any conflict situation there commonly are some who urge unchanging continuance of some portion of the order, others who urge some change in precisely that portion. One recalls, finally, that in any area of actual flux or leeway, individuals can visualize mere tendencies as already fully realized, or as the case may be, can urge them as a dangerous waning or disturbance of the good ways.

Amid this tremendous range of potential claims, ranging from the work of psychopath or revolutionary prophet through to the unthinking acceptance of any prevailing pattern, there are two lines which are of peculiar import to things legal, along which particular standards move into position to affect the order of the group. Again one can sloganize them as drift and drive; but the reference is this time not to legal institutions directly, but to the general course of the institutions of the group.

What comes to be in the way of practice produces in due course its flavor of felt rightness among its practitioners. This takes no planning, no preaching, no thinking; it just happens. Changes of practice change the base line of standard. If there be conflict or uncertainty of practice, there thus ensues conflict or uncertainty of standard. We shall speak of this type of felt rightness as direct, primitive sense of justice under the order of the relevant group. It is primitive in that it needs no organ to build or create it; the primitivity is one which continues into, and continues to affect, the most elaborate and sophisticated culture. This line of normation has peculiar interest to matters legal, because it operates so generally, so inescapably, so similarly in most persons concerned as to be fairly regarded as *quantitatively* important. But we must keep in mind that the drift involved is not directly or immediately a drift in *legal* institutions. It is a drift in whatever other aspect of the group's ways may come in question, a drift in non-legal institutions which then gives off the raw material of expectation and felt rightness out of which a claim can emerge into a conflict-situation, and can emerge with excellent chance of recognition. But that only takes the matter *into* the legal field. The way of disposing of it there, once it has made its entry, is not by simple drift.

It takes some person or persons to incorporate and voice a claim. And the manner of the voicing shapes the claim. No matter how sharp the basis in practice, the *articulation* of the relevant claim or standard is a process of shaping and of lending direction, bias, and extent, not merely a process of mirroring. The claim can be staked wide or narrow, its front can be angled in one direction or another, one or another fact or set of facts can be stressed as vital or disregarded as "immaterial." Consider the Cheyenne difficulties over the "right" of a proper son-in-law to receive his wife's junior sister as an additional wife. The voicer, the articulator, the proponent, enters here as a creator. He continues as a creator while the matter draws to an issue, and while whatever phase of strength or support he can muster is being drawn upon, with further effects of coloring, deflecting, reshaping the issue. In a word, a claimant's way of advocacy is as creative a process as is his first rough-hewing of his claim. A good cause can be lost, and a bad cause won, by the handling; personality, prestige, and accident of the claimant play here to shape a culture. Last Bull's whole history serves as illustration.

If this be true of the claimant whose claim is drawn from the common well of going practice, how much truer is it of him whose

claim is in a larger sense creative—one who voices an emergent
tendency, or leads against an established abuse, or stakes out new
markings within the area theretofore left open for free play. Claims
which involve wild or even wide deviations have, however, in general smaller likelihood of success. The crucial ones are much more
commonly those in which conflicting practices or lines of growth
come into first or full articulation and so into dim or full consciousness. Often enough a trouble-case can have an effect like that of a
stone flung into an over-chilled fiord, and set off sudden crystallization over an area vastly wider than was aimed at or thought about
beforehand.

Whether the area of crystallization set off be wide or narrower,
the second major germ of law-stuff in any group or culture is forthwith obvious. It consists in what in net result, instance by instance,
gets done about cases of trouble. Such cases can run off without
setting up precedents or inducing action along the lines of the norms
or standards which have come to prevail in their solution. But their
crisis-character and their memorability give them a likelihood of
setting up lines, patterns, and structures of behavior, of setting up
known "rightnesses" of behavior, and *of setting up anticipable
consequences of deviation,* which is, we believe, unrivaled in other
phases of culture. Hence, beside the quantitatively important
pressure of direct, primitive sense of justice, there stands the
qualitatively important pressure of what has happened in prior
trouble-cases, to provide ground for claims that have peculiar likelihood of winning their way into acceptance, and so of affecting and
altering the order of the relevant group.

What has been said sets up a picture of any group or any society
being subject occasionally or insistently to the annoyance or even
disruption of members at odds or outs with one another over
expectations and demands disappointed or resisted. It sets up no
less a picture of the very voicing of an expectation or demand as
involving willy-nilly an appeal in some manner to that group order
which represents the Whole of which the members are but parts.
It sets up, too, a picture of the necessity of some kind of settlement,
on pain of ultimate dissolution of the group, whether the settlement

be by club, by bargain, or by love feast. In the picture, therefore, lies a continuing and powerful (although escapable) pressure for instances of settlement and of settlement procedure to find imitation and to become institutional. The raw material *for* law-stuff is thus given by the claims; and with the settlements the raw material *of* law-stuff is produced. What then of the legal institutions which result?

The Forming and Form of the Legal: Authority

The legal in the order of a group or culture is more than mere norm, more than mere normative standard. The legal has teeth. What it protects is *protected;* if its prohibitions be disregarded, somebody can *do* something about it. Legal philosophers call this the presence of "sanction"—not sanction in the sense of approval, but sanction in the sense that something will happen to make disregard uncomfortable. The heart of the legal lies in this character of being *imperative* rather than merely normative. Its formula is: "You *must*," or "You *must* not—*Or else* ..." Or on the other side: "You may—and be safe from 'or elses.' " This does not mean that the legal has no normative aspect. Of course it has normative aspects. Things legal exist not merely to clean up trouble, but also in order to get somebody to do or not to do something, or to make doing easier by lending it efficacious aid and comfort—as by offering enforcement to properly made wills or contracts. There is thus always a more or less direct normative *"purpose"* in any legal phenomena, and that purpose is important. But it is not the sole characteristic aspect of the legal; indeed, the more elaborately structured legal institutions become, the more their normative aspect tends to slip into the background. Which causes problems, as will appear.

Meantime, one observes another attribute of the legal when one contrasts legal imperatives and the norms or standards which they serve with any other norms or standards which are found in the group or culture: manners and etiquette (which in some cultures can be close to top rank in the hierarchy of norms); the norms of "justice"; the norms of morality and decency; the norms of good taste. In the event of any conflict between the legal and any of these, you will know the legal by the fact that if appealed to, it *prevails*. It may be often disregarded: decent people often forego their strictly legal rights. But if appealed to, the legal prevails.

Yet what prevails, and what has teeth, need not be legal. For the legal is not successful force alone. Fang and claw are law in a group or culture only if fang and claw are the going way of that group or culture. The legal is *part of the going order* of the relevant Entirety, and violences which are outside the going way, outside the going order, are extra-legal or contra-legal, even when successful. Because, moreover, one essence of the legal lies thus in being part of an order, it is the *order* which must have teeth and the character of prevailing in the pinch which were discussed above. Occasional successful gangsterism may partially disrupt, but does not displace, the legal in the relevant community, unless and until it turns into "the" regime.

Because the legal is part of the order of the group, again, there is about it a certain extra flavor, easier to sense than to describe —a flavor that anything done or commanded or set is so done or commanded as if for, and on behalf of, the Whole of the relevant entirety. The legal has an aspect of recognized *officialdom* about it, which mere claims (for instance) lack until they have been *recognized,* and which "manners" or "morals" lack until they acquire "legal" backing.

If one now looks back over these four characteristics of the legal in a group or culture, he will find that they cluster together to make up the phenomenon which is summed up as Authority in the group or culture. There is the "must" element, with its "or else" attached —the enforceability of an imperative. There is the supremacy element in the event of challenge. There is the system element, which holds each part of the legal into a legal whole to which it belongs. And there is the element of officialdom, that quality which holds the legal whole and all its parts into the whole order of the group, which it is recognized as representing.

Now authority of this sort, in settling conflict, or in prescribing imperatives, tends strikingly to center in any person (or subgroup) who acquires military or governmental power. But it can also center in other types of specialist. It has been acquired by shamans or priests or prophets. It has been acquired by wise men who became peacemakers or judges or known mediators. It has been acquired by "law-men" who specialized in advocacy or in the lore of precedents. The first thing to note is that its emergence may be very gradual, may be interrupted and never come to full growth, may set up within a single group or culture in seven different places at once, in harmony or in rivalry. The second thing to note is that any authority, containing as it does a claim for supremacy, tends to expand through the whole order, and to integrate itself both within its own sphere and with the whole order of the Entirety concerned.

The third thing to note is that there is expressed in nothing which has as yet been described any necessary aspect of either *regularity or justice*. Justice we shall, for the moment, disregard. Regularity, we cannot.

Legal philosophers who describe regimes which they call "despotism" or "tyranny" tend to forget or understress that to continue as a group at all, the people of the group require some regularity of conduct. And they tend to understress especially that a despot, with the worst will in the world, can still be despotic and arbitrary only while he can stay awake. Any control or supervision which he exercises beyond his personal commanding, instance by instance, simply has to be put into some type of form and frame which is regular, and so, general. In a word, the operational necessities of continuing despotism force on the veriest Caligula, despite all devastation he can wreak, an important degree of regularity in the lines of control. Arbitrary particular changes, departures, exceptions, and wholesale cruelties he can compass, but not in any meaningful sense a whole regime of arbitrariness. This means, in terms of sociological process, that the inevitable regularities drive constantly to creep up on him; continuously, they exude the direct, primitive sense of justice which has been spoken of. To check the encroachments on despotism which derive therefrom requires a vision, an agility to strike, and an unrelenting energy which few despotic regimes have been able to maintain.

There is yet another aspect in which regularity requires discussion under the general heading of authority. For in many groups and cultures it has happened that authority has become attached less to persons than to patterns of action ("procedures") or to norms for action. There can be known "ancient law" (e.g., tabu) with no standing officials to enforce it. There can be recognized procedures for settling grievance, say, by treaty and composition, or by oath, or by ritual combat, with no official even to mediate or preside. "Law" in its earliest buddings knows procedures quite as rude as, say, dumb barter. The matter can be summed up thus: As soon as the course of behavior shows, recognizably, authority in procedures or persons for cleaning up trouble-cases, or authority in standards whose infraction is met not only by action, but by action carrying the flavor of the *pro tanto* official, at that point the peculiar institutions called "legal" have become perceptible in the group or culture. They have budded.

Regularity

But as has been indicated, the authority aspect of the legal cannot be sufficient unto itself. Even when the legal does not derive from the regular, the regular makes its way into the legal. It is vital to an understanding of the processes to remember that they begin in non-sophistication, in the operation of direct, primitive sense of justice out of life practice. As they then pass through the crucible of conflict into recognized result, they move into a process of more conscious drive toward a regularity which rests not on *life*-practice but on *legal* practice. In consequence, the regularity drives strike things of law in two phases, which can indeed (with luck and skill) be made to harmonize, but which much more frequently move partially at odds each with the other. The one continues to rest directly on the general course of life; the other rests on continued regularity of the specialized course of the legal. And it should be noted that whenever a legal philosopher mistakes this latter of the two as offering in and of itself that kind of regularity and predictability which it is "law's office in society" to provide, he is in error. That ideal type of regularity and predictability which it is "law's office" to provide is one in which laymen's reasonable expectations are not upset by over-crystallized law-stuff, and in which "law" and "justice" do not get sufficiently out of touch to come into sustained and conscious opposition. But since juristic method rarely achieves that ideal, the regularity drives more commonly strike things of law, as stated, in two aspects which tend in different ways.

Another thing to be remembered is that just as "authority" does not commonly appear full-blown and complete, but is capable of accumulation in a man or in an office, so also "regularity" begins as some single instance of behavior, moves into the stage of better than a coin-flip chance of recurrence, can branch into four equally probable alternative variants of which it can be predicated only that a fifth variant is extremely unlikely.

Still another thing to be remembered as one approaches the matter of regularity is that the standard for behavior must here as in other institutions be distinguished from the relevant, actually recurrent behavior—but with a double difference. For in the first place, this being a legal matter, the standard for behavior is likely to be also and chiefly an imperative with teeth. In the second place, the fact that the result in a trouble-case drives so strongly toward becoming precedent gives the imperative or standard repeatedly a chance to leap ahead of the actual behavior pattern—not to flow from a behavior pattern, but perhaps to create a pattern on the model of even a single instance. And the possibility of the standards being created before the pattern of actual behavior holds, of course, also in regard to any new regulation set by persons in authority.

With these things in mind, three major aspects or phases of regularity become easy enough to see and to handle—each of them companioned by its appropriate "corresponding" standard of obligation. First, law serves to control behavior, and in one major phase, to control the behavior of the layman, the law-consumer. Second, law has teeth for the case of breach or trouble, and the manner of showing those teeth tends into regularity. Third, law tends into self-limitation, and that is a matter of the impact of regularity.

When the regularity elements in a legal system not only gain the upper hand, but get out of hand, there results the wooden, externalized, graceless, and cumbersome maladaptation which is summed up as legalism.

In order that the "legal" may yield effectiveness, it is well-nigh indispensable for a culture to develop some type of personnel for the purpose. But that it may yield bearable legality instead of legalism, or what will be felt as acceptable rather than as arbitrary, requires that to the elements of pure form thus far discussed there be added certain minimum matters of substance:

(a) The content and substance of the norms and activities of the imperative system, as a whole, must be felt by the social Entirety concerned to serve that Entirety reasonably well—a quantum of general satisfaction. The tolerances here are huge, but they have limits.

(b) The manner and substance of working out particular matters must remain somewhat understandable (as a proper part of a reasonably proper system) to most of the persons interested directly, in sympathy, and as observers.

Legality thus seems to us marked by one type of result of the working of things legal when those things contain some quantum of the elements of regularity; that type of result is the result which gives moderate satisfaction. Legalism is marked by unsatisfactory results, by wooden arbitrariness, as compared to the tyrant's arbitrariness of whimsy or temper. A primitive with much time, much patience, much fatalism, and no comparative study of alternative possibilities may find results satisfactory, while an observer rooted in a legally more artistic culture may grow impatient with them. But however subjective the judgment of what distinguishes legalism from legality, three objective phenomena remain which make the terms worth saving. One is that when men feel the imperative system to be too much and too persistently out of gear with what they want from it, they hold back, and they even kick over. Another is that, in all cultures, judgment frequently diverges widely about the system as a whole, which may be taken as blessed with proper legality, and about particular details, which may, despite approval of the system, be seen as "technical," "legalistic," as, briefly, "outrage." The third phenomenon, as the curious and lovely Cheyenne material makes clear, is that when juristic art and method happen to be abreast of their function, there is no need for legalism, in anybody's definition of that term, to raise its head.

The reader will note that the forms of legal institutions thus set forth have been presented with little note of justice. That is as it should be. Philosophers dealing with a particular society at a particular time may well hesitate to call anything "law" which does not meet their own standard of the just, lest by giving it a fair name they give it standing. But sociological analysis must see legal institutions as they are: a result of the eternal interplay of interest and justice; a structured machinery, then, upon which interest and justice continue to play; a machinery which, however, at any given moment, is whatever it is, smoothly designed and lovely or a creaking semi-wreck. The test of its value lies in the work it accomplishes upon the law-jobs; but the test of its reality is what it is. And its work upon the law-jobs is not its work alone, but the work of *men* who use it. This means that always there is give in it, and remodeling at work within it; it is remade by the work which men use it to do, remade by such traditions as they develop for the use of it—serving interest or serving justice, or serving one now, and now the other.

Chapter XI

THE ·LAW-JOBS

THE law-stuff and the law-ways, as has been said, travel paths of their own, once they specialize out into recognizability. Upon them, play human interests and the normative generalizations thrown into the ring by men. The whole takes meaning, before one's eyes, if it be set against those law-jobs whose sufficient doing is necessary if the social group is to continue as a group.

The law-jobs are in their bare bones fundamental; they are eternal. Perhaps you can sum them all up in a single formulation: The law-jobs entail such arrangement and adjustment of people's behavior that the society (or the group) remains a society (or a group) and gets enough energy unleashed and coördinated to keep on functioning as a society (or as a group). But if the matter is put in that inclusive way, it sounds like mere tautology, almost as if one were saying that to be a group, you just must be a group. Whereas what is being said is that to *stay* a group, you must manage to deal with centrifugal tendencies when they break out, and that you must preventively manage to keep them from breaking out. And that you must *effect* organization, and that you must *keep* it effective. And that you must do all this by means which do not choke off, but elicit, your necessary flow of human energy.

There is another preliminary matter. It is to make unmistakable that the law-jobs hold as basic functions for every human group, from a group of two persons on up. They are implicit in the concept of "groupness." In any community or society which may be taken as a larger unit, the law-jobs therefore appear at least doubly: once for the big unit, and again for every subunit within the big one; and again, of course, for every sub-subunit. This requires to to be made explicit, because modern thought about "law" takes as its frame only that great unit called the state, or some other recognized political whole. But in a functional view a newly wedded couple, a newly formed partnership, a two-child casual play group have each, qua group, the problems to deal with which are here of concern; and the peculiar aspects which those problems take on in the modern state are clarified and not obscured by observing the problems at work, also, within such simpler groupings. It is of course vital to clarity that the level of discourse be kept clear. We shall therefore attempt, when a complex great-group (a "society," "the Cheyennes") is in question, to distinguish the specific Law and Law-stuff of the larger Whole from the specific bylaw and bylaw-stuff of any designated subgrouping within the Whole. Around the functional similarity, the institutional differences and even conflicts gain precision of focus. The uncapitalized "legal" and "law-job" and "law-way" are reserved for general applicability to the functional aspects common to groups of all kinds.

It is to be remembered, moreover, that those matters of claim and of the legal which have been under consideration above, hold in full measure for the smallest sub-subgrouping within a larger one, if only that small grouping be taken as, for the moment, a unit, or the unit, of observation. To put simple examples: with the arrival of the first child at talking age, certain portions of family bylaw are simply forced into verbal form; and the consequent juristic problems of "construction," "distinction," "true meaning," and "underlying principle" come promptly into being; nor can any arbitrary telling of the child to hold his tongue take them out of being: Father said he was going to take me to the circus, and you mustn't lie, and you must keep your promises. Or again, in any modern family in which graver matters are put up to father, or "told" to him, a three-person group suffices to produce problems of harmonizing a formal Legal system of the Entirety of the Three and the "by-legal" system, of lesser and local jurisdiction, belonging to the mother-child subunit. Father's precedents on the occasional matters put up to him stand out as the basis for a distinctive set of imperatives—to control, or to be evaded. Thus law-jobs and law-ways, we repeat, go to the essence of any group; and the presence of a larger and more inclusive one does not at all displace their functioning within subunits. It may importantly condition problems within subunits; for example, "under" the law of our modern state, wife-beating is no longer privileged, and wife-desertion may have consequences visited upon it. But such alteration of conditions no more does away with the family's own fundamental bylaw problems than the condition of embarrassing war between neighbors does away with the internal problems of a neutral "sovereign" state. Indeed, it is when one marks out sharply what group unit one is dealing with as being the Entirety concerned, that such a concept as "social control" loses its amorphousness and takes on sharp edges in the query: "control of whom, by whom, for what, and within the order-configuration of what Entirety?"

Thus each law-job, and all of them together, presents first of all an aspect of pure survival, a bare-bones. The job must get done *enough* to keep the group going. This is brute struggle for continued existence. It is the problem of attaining order in the pinch at whatever cost to justice. But beyond this, each job has a wholly distinct double aspect which we may call the *questing-aspect*. This is a betterment aspect, a question so to speak of surplus and its employment. On the one side, this questing aspect looks to more adequate doing of the job, just as a doing: economy, efficiency, smoothness, leading at the peak to aesthetically satisfying grace in the doing of it. On the other side, the questing aspect looks to the ideal values: justice, finer justice, such organization and such ideals of justice as tend toward fuller, richer life. It no more does to forget the bare bones in favor of these things than it does to forget these things in favor of the bare bones. And in Cheyenne, in particular, the great cultural configurations which drove toward fuller life came at times into conflict even with the very bare-bones aspects of the law-jobs.

For purposes of study, it is wiser to break down "The Law-Job" into lesser phases—doubly so, because to a very considerable extent the major lines of institutional machinery which men have hit upon for getting "the" job done have proved to focus interestingly around certain of the particular phases.

Of these there are five around which matters legal group themselves to advantage:

I. The disposition of trouble-cases.

II. The preventive channeling and reorientation of conduct and expectations.

III. The allocation of authority and the arrangement of procedures which legitimatize action as being authoritative.

IV. The net organization of the group or society *as a whole* so as to provide cohesion, direction, and incentive.

V. The job of juristic method, which has been indicated roughly above as that of keeping claims and the order in balance, but which may here be defined more fully as that of keeping both law-stuff and law-personnel up to the demands of *all* the law-jobs.

We shall be concerned here chiefly with the first two of these foci, and with the last.

The Trouble-Case

The phase of the law-jobs which repays study first and fastest is the adjustment of the trouble-case—offense, grievance, dispute. Roughly described, this is garage-repair work on the general order of the group when that general order misses fire, or, in the extreme instance, threatens total breakdown. Typically, the trouble is minor trouble, "individual" trouble which in itself is bearable trouble. Typically, it would disrupt continuance of group life only if sufficiently multiplied and sufficiently cumulative. This holds true even of most homicide. The tighter the group, the more there is in its order of the traditionally accepted or of emotional closeness or of geared and structured interdependence, the tougher is its resistance to disruption from this quarter. Yet picking up one's marbles and going home remains a symbol of factional strife which may mean bolt or civil war. Thus the adjustment of the trouble-case has a surface appearance not of life-saving so much as of life-easing. Nevertheless, the elimination of conflict and grievance remains a significant basic line of need and of activity, whether the individual instance corresponds to bruised finger or to emergency operation.

Enough unhealed breaches between members break the group, and tensions, left alone, can build up potential toward explosion.

The bare-bones aspect of this law-job is plain enough: get enough of it done to leave the group still in being as a group. One or another member or faction can be cut down or cut off, and the group be still "the" group; bitterness can seethe; the line of adjustment may prove to be merely that what Big Fist wants, he gets. But if the group stays a group, and neither explodes nor dribbles away into disintegration, the bare-bones survival-need is met. The questing aspects of the matter, on the other hand, run into reaches which few societies have penetrated in their High Official Law save in the person of some occasional transcendent judge (Mansfield) or law-giving mediator (Solon). To adjust trouble-cases with speed, smoothness, deep permanency, minimum outlay of effort and disruption of other activities—and, on points of fact, with accuracy —this is still a quest. Nor is it less a quest, still, to reach felt justice in the settlement, or to uncover and lay down in settlement the line of greater social health, or to combine either of these achievements with a modicum of speed and economy.

Preventive Channeling and Shift of Orientation

The second phase centers on the effective channeling, preventively and in advance, of people's conduct—and attitudes—toward one another. Its importance lies peculiarly in areas of patent or of latent conflict of interest—in arrangement of division of the scarce and desirable, from physical things on through to power and prestige. And this has been easy to see. But no less important is the avoidance of hitches in the coördination of life and work. In any organized action, slips of expected performance, or break of rhythmed timing, can produce conflict by mere disruptive disturbance. The main Cheyenne instances are found in war; no plan for ambush is certain of success, when unruly young warriors have been worked up like race horses.

In general, then, the job is that of producing and maintaining a going order, instead of a disordered series of collisions. It is this order on which the first job does its garage-repair work. The function includes not only the channeling of overt behavior but the channeling of claims. It includes, too, provision of some degree of clarity as to what free play and leeway are permitted, and even protected.

One meets here a matter which is curiously easy to feel accurately in the particular, but which taxes the ingenuity to state accurately in the general. The problem is how to get clear the aspect of the legal that lies in phases of Culture which seem to the observer to have no legal content—so long as they present no hitch or trouble. The legal aspect may well be conceived as largely confined to *so much* of the patterning of behavior as *prevents grievance and conflict:* that is, not in ways of making shoes or bottles or books, but in the ways of keeping some of the makers off others' toes and necks and tempers while the things are being made. Plainly, this means that the legal fairly infests the culture. But, as has been suggested, any other basic aspect of culture will be found to have a similar infesting quality. So does the economic, for example. The same piece of concrete behavior belongs to a number of the "intellectual" realms at once, according to the context chosen by the observer. Behavior in a factory is not "economic" and *not* "technological," technological and not social, social and not legal. It is any or all, according to the chosen context. Familiar as this is to the social scientist, the philosopher of law can yet do with the reminder.

The next difficulty is even more perplexing. Side by side with preventive channeling of behavior in men's life and work together goes creative, organizatory *re*channeling of such behavior. The child grows up. A man and a woman marry. A new recruit joins a work or war group. Someone is promoted, or elected to an office. A command is given. A contract is made, or there is death and succession. So long as such rechanneling is relatively rare in incidence upon a life, so long as the new patterns entered on are themselves clear, largely understood, and relatively permanent—so long, this rechanneling amounts to little more than what is thought of as channeling *ab initio.* The new may indeed be a bit more likely to meet challenge, expectant heirs may readily conflict, and the like; conduct that is not yet habit is more likely to produce knocks and bumps. But neither is education (which is a foundation-part of what is conceived as initial channeling) a process wholly automatic, or one free from the problems of reorientation and reconditioning. ("You are a big boy now.")

Yet a real difficulty in grouping together channeling and rechanneling is likely to come when one is dealing with a culture both complex and mobile of relations. If the possible lines of reorientation are highly diversified, there is call for the specialist, to advise. If, in addition, the possible lines are not severely limited and fixed in content—are not lines of known "status" such as Cheyenne chieftainship or soldiership—but are capable of intricate custom-tailoring to particular desire (like modern contract or association devices), then the problems flood upon the specialist: there are techniques; there are also limits on their use; there are contingencies of which only the specialists' lore accumulates accessible knowledge. In such a culture, the interest, the attention, and the building of working tools by the legal specialists will concentrate upon the side of shift of reorientation of relations, rather than upon any "normalities" of relation. The absence of such legal specialists in Cheyenne thus goes hand in hand not only with relative absence of the rigidly legal, but also with a relative absence of reorientations fixed in advance in individualized lasting detail. Laymen can readily fix a new basis of working relation, clear in "principle" and tacit outlook, if no legalistic niceties are in the offing. "Let's get together on this." Laymen can also move easily into a new, well-understood relation, as by adoption or marriage. These relatively primitive forms of rechanneling fit the initial channeling picture; they contrast with the modern corporate indenture, or twenty-five page statute: with deliberate, detailed, *guarded* "shift" of channeling.

We sum up this second law-job, then (or, for developed and mobile law systems, these two "second" law-jobs), as that of preventive channeling and of shift of orientation of behavior and expectation. Be it noted that the emphasis here is primarily upon channeling and shift of the smaller units—the individual, or the subgroup, seen in their relations to other individuals or other subgroups; the emphasis is on the life-career of person or enterprise or transaction, seen from its own end, not on the net organizatory efforts of a complex society taken as a whole. The distinction is artificial enough, but still worth making; enterprises or individuals can learn to keep off one another's toes and still leave, for instance, a continuing or cyclical business depression which raises problems of a different order or level of organization. To use J. M. Clark's neat illustration:[1] An enterprise can meet certain problems of labor overhead by simple layoff; not so, a nation.

Meantime, the bare-bones and the questing aspects speak here largely for themselves, save in this: that high efficiency in preventive channeling ("discipline," if you like it; "regimentation," if you do not) competes as an ideal with large leeways ("license"; "liberty") and creative use thereof ("captain of industry"; "industrial pirate").

Juristic Method

The lines of law-job which have been picked out as major foci of emphasis are not related like logical subdivisions. They overlap. They play one into another. Thus, for instance, Grasshopper's Case (CASE 13) was a "case of trouble," adjusted; it plainly also resulted in making more effective the "channeling" of behavior in relation to the buffalo hunt; third, it plainly involved and strengthened the allocation of authority to the military society on duty, to prosecute offenses against the hunt, and under our interpretation it contributed to defining the proper manner of exercising that authority in regard to suspected secret offenses. Such definition was itself in turn a "channeling" of behavior—that of the police; and was also a neater articulation of machinery for handling future cases of one kind of trouble. Finally, the case partook also of the fourth law-job, in that it moved toward more effective integration of the political, the economic, and the more strictly legal phases of tribal life. Indeed, even the social aspects of Cheyenne life moved into that integration, for the free-moving independence of the individual Cheyenne received its due recognition and encouragement against even a Last Bull on official duty.

[1] John Maurice Clark, *Studies in the Economics of Overhead Costs* (Chicago, The University of Chicago Press, 1923), Chapter XVIII.

Despite overlapping of contexts, the authors hold that a grouping and regrouping of the phenomena around these different foci sheds material light on the law-ways of any culture and on their relations with the culture at large. The focus on allocation of authority, for instance, displays the law-ways in their eternal interplay with the political. Again, the focus on "net drive" brings out, as no centering on the "first" three law-jobs can, the directive forces of society at work on that positive and constructive side so well stressed by Lowie,[2] and so much in peril of neglect by those whose interest is primarily the formal phases of law. Such "allocation of authority" aspects, among the Cheyennes, have been dealt with throughout Part II, and especially in Chapters IV, V, and VI. The "net drive" aspects have been treated less explicitly; but reference is made to the latter portions of Chapters VIII and IX.

In much the same way, what has been spoken of as "juristic method" spreads itself over the whole of law-stuff. It is not a something separate, but rather an *aspect* present everywhere. It is that set of law-ways which goes to the *how* of handling law-stuff in order to get the law-jobs done. For it is plain that in any field a sufficiently skilled and ingenious man can often tinker out a good job with what seem offhand to be institutional tools of desperate inadequacy. It is equally clear that a heavy-fisted fool can botch a job, no matter how delicate and well devised are the tools to his hand. It is clear, finally, that what is thus true of the one man can be true of a whole tradition of work which shapes successive generations of the workmen. To this only one important qualification is needed, to wit, that if there is a sustained tradition of work, then the tools offered the craftsman by the law-stuff will shortly take on something of the character of that tradition; for the devices undergo remodeling as they are put to use, and sustained use of law-stuff in any given "style" shows necessary cumulative effect upon the law-stuff itself.

The point that juristic method spreads over the whole of law-stuff must be made carefully explicit, because the tendency of the modern man of law is to think of such a concept as confined peculiarly to the work of the modern judge, and especially of the judge

[2] Lowie, *The Origin of the State.*

in an appellate court.[3] But the concept as it is here used includes, to pick further scattered instances out of modern society, such other matters as reform legislation; the handling of administrative trouble-cases; the speedy and accurate disposition of disputes of fact; the "treatment" phases of criminal-law administration; the legal scholar's job of reformulating concepts adequate to make a moving body of doctrine effectively manipulable; the job, where party-advocacy is the way of the law, of getting advocates' skill on the two sides reasonably balanced. Specialization of legal institutions, in a word, may concentrate some phases of the problem of juristic method, but it diffuses other phases. No phase of legal activity is free of it.

We pick up, therefore, especially in the area of the trouble-case and of channeling, certain outstanding problems of juristic method, with an eye to canvassing the nature of the problems by examining some of the happier roads to solution. The easiest lines of partial solution to discuss are those which involve invention or growth of well-adjusted *devices;* but one must try not to allow attention to slip away from the old truth that part of any device-in-a-culture consists in the technique and manner of its employment—in other words, that method continues as a problem, even after the most skilled invention.

In order that inventions (or lines of growth) may take on perspective, one recalls that the earliest emergence of law-stuff may have a character which can on a different level become proverbial as contra-legal. So "club-law," conquest and ruthlessness, outfacing and submission; so, in general, the establishment of what social psychologists call the pecking-order of the flock. One recalls also that the brute violence or fraud which at any moment yields present outrage can generate not only future legal imperative but even future "right." The course runs from power into recognition, repetition, expectation, and tradition, until authority finds itself backed by going morality. It takes, for instance, no great flight of imagination to see in a succession of overbearing *but successful* Cheyenne

---

[3] Cf. Benjamin N. Cordozo, *The Nature of the Judicial Process* (New Haven, Yale University Press, 1921).

military chiefs the genesis of their legally "absolute" control over their soldiers. Juristic method must thus wrestle with whatever has come successfully to be the going law-stuff. More, to be part of a culture, rather than the mere dream and socially ineffective art of an individual or subgroup, juristic method must itself be successful in putting over the results of its wrestling. Take one admirable corrective to abuse of the Cheyenne soldier chief's "absolute" control—deposition. To have deposition invented is not enough; it must be put over, as well; it must, in addition, be so put over as to become recognized, even by the deposed. There is a long road to travel from Stuart deposition and Stuart return through new Stuart deposition and two generations of Pretender rebellion, to the quiet case of Edward VIII. Last Bull's deposition is not recorded as involving any backfire; one therefore cannot help bringing it into relation with that much smoother device for social and govern-mental stability, the institution of changing the status and social impact of a military chief by electing him to the Council of Forty-Four. Here are two lines of politico-legal institution working in harmony, a sustained chord upon which Grasshopper's case (CASE 13) sounds then like the stirring, half-disturbing development of an augmented seventh.

In the story of Last Bull's deposition no precedent was cited. The Buffalo Chief Case (page 102 f.), which rested seemingly on mur-der done and consequent exile, remained of necessity ambiguous on the point of a soldier chief who was still present and available for duty. But if no precedent existed, one was set by Last Bull's case (CASE 15). The drive for merger of the results of adjustment—any adjustment—into the order and so into the expectation and sense of right of the relevant culture, is unceasing. An adjustment which has both general import and general notability drives direct for *general* recognition. Buffalo Chief's case need not have *controlled* Last Bull's (as a modern precedent "controls" a later case), but as soon as Last Bull's happens, its results color Buffalo Chief's and, in turn, take body from the action in his case. Indeed either case alone, as a precedent, would be improbable of confinement to the particular soldier society concerned. This turns on the texture of the culture, seen in terms of the case. The matter "feels" like "military chief," not like "chief," not like "Elks" or "Dogs," or "Last Bull." One may contrast an adjustment of some son-in-law's claim to a younger sister, which would be unlikely, in the normal course, thus to focus and channel later cases over the whole tribe. Its effect on other families would move by initiative in pattern-setting, and then by possible imitation—by drift rather than by the decisive impact of drive. It is the "range" of the order which is directly concerned, and the "range" of the *authority* which is directly concerned, which condition or even determine such more decisive strokes of precedent. Yet if the manner of disposing of even a minor matter fits with the flavor of surrounding groups and persons, then not only the substance but the method of the disposition has its chance to enter into a general tradition. The petty crisis and the great can weave together. And the dramatic invites imitation.

One vital matter of method which was touched on in Chapter III concerns the building of specialized personnel to handle legal matters. For one thing, a close-knit culture is commonly also a culture which places restraints upon easy voicing of a grievance. Subtle relations can be shattered by noise about them; and face is likely to be precious. A grievance which does break out is likely therefore to be breaking *through,* with violence, which means that if redress is left to the aggrieved it is likely to go beyond measure, and so to become itself a countergrievance. On the other hand, the weak may in such circumstances lack redress at all; and minor matters may rankle the more because suppressed. And finally, there are abuses, which may grow flagrant, but which hit no particular person with force enough to "warrant" his assuming the difficult initiative. Long Jaw, in CASE 33, presents an instance of rather inadequate method in dealing with such a situation: known incest went without direct penalty upon the guilty father because the only mechanism for articulating the offense was lynching (for which the case was not flagrant enough), or else use of the lurking spite of an ancient grudge to unleash initiative against the scandal. Hence to develop a specialist with the *office* of articulating grievances—be he joking relative, censor, Presbyterian deacon, or political head—is a notable advance in cutting through the social inertia involved. At the same time it offers a mechanism for *admeasuring* the style and severity of the rebuke more adequately to the offense. As mentioned above, rebuke which must, without mechanism, break through inertia is likely to burst out in hot blood. But to launch public indignation may mean to wind up with a lynching; and such overpunishment can, after reflection, turn back upon the person who set it off. Malinowski gives a case in point: a young man who called public attention to breach of a formal "incest" tabu by a girl he loved, with penalties not to be winked at, once the thing got into the spoken open; the guilty boy, by protest suicide, then threw the onus of outrage back upon the informer.[4]

If there be no official voicer of rebuke, much that deserves rebuke goes thus unrebuked; and some device for graduation of pressures to fit the case in hand has patent social value. It is in terms largely of the absence of such machinery that one must understand the extreme of tolerance often displayed by primitive communities to the horny-hided nuisance. On the other hand, one is reminded of how long a job the development of such machinery can be, when he finds classic Greeks assuming as a matter of course that if you lay your complaint for ten drachmas and prove only nine, you get nothing. It is interesting that such should be the fact of Athenian law in the golden century; vastly more interesting is the uncritical attitude toward that fact of highly critical thinkers in a highly sophisticated age.

But machinery for graduation of rebuke or redress, though a gain, leaves further problems of juristic method open. If the graduation is stereotyped, as in the familiar tariffs of the early Germanic laws, it becomes wooden. If the graduation is by act of persons in authority (the King's "mercy," or a Solomon's judgment), it hinges on continuing wisdom, courage, honesty, and strength of the particular official. If these qualities fail, the official either goes arbitrary, inept, or corrupt: or, as the case may be, shelters himself

---

[4] Malinowski, *Crime and Custom in Savage Society*, 84 f., 95, 97. It must be a slip that this is followed by the suggestion that "suicide is certainly not a means of administering justice." See also suicide among the Comanches, Hoebel, *Political Organization . . . of the Comanche Indians*, 112-17.

behind a frame of precedent and practice of which he "is the mere voice." In both modern criminal law and modern administrative practice, as in the handling of business management or labor leadership, both phenomena remain uncomfortably live and familiar.

Hence, although to use graduated "rules" effectively, one needs specialized personnel with some leeway of action, yet the introduction of such personnel, with such leeway, simply sets a new problem. We have referred before to traditions in and of the *office* as one road into handling this; an apprenticeship type of training has often proved a help; the modern American system has sometimes also sought gain from substituting a bench of judges for one judge, a commission for a commissioner ; and from not only substituting many heads for one, on individual matters, but building up practices of the office and machinery for breaking new men in. But on the one hand no externalized device wholly covers the ground; on the other, reliance on the happenstance of particular individual ability and effort is tricky. From this it follows at once that training of prospective personnel, to be effective training, must be training not only in the stuff of the Law, but equally or more in the *ways of handling* that stuff, to serve the law-jobs. Which provides an interesting point of view from which to look over modern American schooling "for the law."

The balance to be achieved is not a simple thing, nor is it a matter of working with two simple factors—such as "law" and "the justice of the case" might lightly be conceived to be. On the particular matter of handling grievance and redress, for instance, one may call attention again to the fact that not only an offense is involved, but also an offender who is a whole person with a history and a future. This is one portion of the familiar problem of "crime," lapping over, of course, into the handling of any type of "wrong." But there is much more involved than merely the possible cross-purposing between the existing applicable "rule" and the needs of the individual offender or case as an individual case or offender. There is at issue also the question of stiffening the behavior patterns of other members of the community. There is the question of whether the rule itself is a wise one, in long-range policy. There is the question of how the official "rule," in this case and others, and the lines of official "treatment," in this case and others, interlock or interact with the other institutions of the community, and of *which* of the other institutions the handling first of this case and this man, and second of this type of situation, ought most wisely to be geared into. In modern America we have partly subdivided the work of coping with these matters, say as among legislature, sentencing judge, parole officer, warden, preacher, teacher, psychiatrist, pardoning authority, and the spirit of business enterprise. In a culture of less striking institutional specialization more of the aspects come to bear at once. Where the aspects are subdivided among various personnel, the problem of method is that of intelligent integration; where the aspects are lumped in one set of hands, the problem of method becomes that of intelligent analysis, weighting, and choice. If the Cheyenne cases of clear offense and its handling are looked over with this seeming tangle of multiple social and juristic objectives in mind, then matters which are *fused* in the tale will prove on analysis to have been curiously *uncon*fused in the handling of them. The readiest comparison one thinks of lies in some of Kipling's tales about right leaders dealing with cases of trouble.

What thus holds of the central trouble problem of the primitive culture, that of known and clear grievance or offense, holds no less of the two other types of basic problem which take on larger quantitative significance as a culture grows more complex. The one type is trouble over what is right, for the legal decision; in modern parlance, "the question of law." The other is trouble over what is so; in modern parlance, "the question of fact."

It has been seen how the making of claims and their resistance generates "the question of law," and how settlement of such a question drives toward building into "binding" precedent. It has been seen also that the living practices of the group can shift into new lines which exude primitive justice at odds with the officially recognized imperatives. It has been seen that new tendencies in the group institutions generate new desires, new needs, new claims, and that sub-specialization of practice around conflicting subobjectives will generate conflicting emergent claims. It has been seen that individual or group power drives can enter the picture, on the part of either "lay" or "legal" personnel. And it is obvious, once governmental personnel appear at all in a culture, how the legal needs which their office equips them to fill drive with peculiar power toward bringing law-matters into their hands. This is true of rebuke or redress of grievance, which affords, along with the general service to articulation and admeasurement, certain special incentives to governing personnel; of profit from lending help; and of repetitive excuse for lopping dangerous rivals. But it is true no less on the side of "questions of law," because they come up so frequently on matters of crucial underlying policy and of somewhat balanced strengths that they present peculiar opportunity to him who can ride the seesaw.

What concerns us is to get clear where in this scene the problems of juristic method make themselves peculiarly felt. They do this first of all in regard to the leeway open for proper decision under any system of law-stuff. For by the nature of men, groups, and claims an authoritative answer can be given in any one of several ways on the same case.

Thus, inherent in the nature of direct and primitive justice is the "rightness" of a claim which rests on going practice. It needs no lawyer, no professional, to make this claim or to make it appeal. But inherent also in any specialized law-stuff which is known, is the essential "legal" justice of a claim which rests on demand for repetition in a new case of what was done officially before. And it needs no lawyer, no professional, to make that claim or to make it sit solid and appeal. The lay mind generates legalism as fiercely as, on the other side, it generates the claim for primitive justice. Finally, the lay mind, especially when not involved in partisan emotion, has quick appreciation of effective compromise, and huge appreciation of the middle course which saves face on all hands. If such appreciation be not native to the human race, all observation of little children is at fault.

There is, in a word, never any single answer forced by a legal system to a case which bears on flux in the Society. Even when the traditions of using the legal system have so hardened as to bar out listening to the claims of primitive justice, and juristic method has thus for the time being slipped out of balance, corrective action finds backing. To be sure, the paths of resiliency may become tortuous, the monopoly of the curiously skillful; trouble for all is then commonly not too far ahead. Where, however, such hardening of the juristic arteries has not set in, the easy leeways which are open include not only choice between conflicting claims, but also the statesmanlike discovery of an alternative sounder than that urged by either litigant. That is one point. The other is that use of that leeway means the incursion into the settlement of "questions of law" of what is either statesmanship for the whole or politics for person or faction. Both the incursion and its manner and substance are matters of method. This can be typified moderately well by contrasting the results in the Cheyenne deliberative cases with the results when an out-facing contest failed to find its by-stander at hand with the solution at the proper moment. Plainly, the deliberative machinery, though more cumbersome, and, save when the messengers were circulating in a tense camp, less exciting, was the more skillful device. Plainly, also, the device is not the crux of the matter. Muddled heads can deliberate to no purpose; and some of the neatest solutions one meets emerged from a pleading-by-action and outfacing. The problem of sound method lies deeper.

How deeply some feeling for sound method was indeed ingrained in the Cheyenne culture comes out perhaps more particularly when one turns to that other problem-type which so baffles most primitive cultures: the dispute of fact. A close-knit community comes readily to depend on general knowledge and report. True dispute of fact, secrecy of the relevant truth, tries ingenuity. Consider then the extraordinary number of devices recorded in the Cheyenne cases which were invented from occasion to occasion to deal with some doubtful point of fact—and this although the culture showed no sign of working toward a single general pattern for the purpose. A horse had been borrowed and was long overdue; what are the borrower's intentions (CASE 17)? An aborted fetus was aborted by whom (CASE 14)? Was there truth in jealous suspicion of a wife

BEAR WINGS

(CASES 22, 53)? Had a suspected warrior actually been aiding the enemy whites? Had there been an adequate degree of intention in a drunken, "accidental" killing (page 137)? Who was the attempting rapist (page 177)? Was the accusation of bootleg hunting true (page 117)? Which was the real horn of the Sacred Hat (this time a question half "of law"—CASE 24)? Was the claimed coup actually struck (CASE 23)? Who stole the bowstring (CASE 15)? Who stole the buckskin suit (page 226)? This, without more, is a fairish range of fact-questions faced by the Cheyennes. All but two got answered to satisfaction; and in almost as many different ways as there were questions. And quite typical of sound juristic technique is the case in which detection by way of the supernatural was distinguished from actual search for the stolen article in an attempt to establish the fact (page 227).

The range of the Cheyenne procedures, not only in the doubt of fact but in redress of plain grievance and in getting settled a disputed point of right, is enough to warn how slow one must be to assume any easy crystallization or single patterning of the legal. But by the same token, even when what can be seen clearly as the legal does become "legally" exclusive, the Cheyenne range should be enough to remind one that beside it—and sometimes in conflict with it—he must expect to find persisting, or growing up, *or both,* other ways, other personnel, and other standards for doing the same job. Today, for instance, strike, negotiation, conciliation, mediation, arbitration, business adjustment, commercial arbitration— all these are procedures which do the law-job in the very process of keeping men from "going to law."

Juristic method sums up at once man's achievement and man's quest in matters legal. It is the search for serviceable forms and devices. But it is also the quest for their skillful use. It is also the seeking to keep vital and vigorous under any form, any formula, any "rule," its living reason, its principle. We have sought to give enough illustrations of the multiple problems involved to avoid any possible inference that it can be regarded as simple phenomenon. "Judgment" or "sense of balance" or "statesmanlike intuition" do not become simple by being given simple-seeming names. Nonetheless the aspects of work with law-stuff which are summed up by the term are usefully viewed as a single cluster. Through them run common factors of importance, a few of which the writers have sought to put into words. But the matter is one for long and concerted study. For as in any other phase of the partially explored, there hide under a single label things quite different, and alike only in being known to be there, but unknown as to their nature. There are the series of knowable, analyzable factors which have thus far not been seized upon and isolated for study and communication. There is also what one suspects to be a rather different something—the on-going quality of a working whole, which factor-analysis is a poor tool to reach. Juristic method is not dissimilar in nature from style in art—an extremely complex and subtle set of somethings which affect in varying degree a whole range of craftsmen at once, yet which allow huge divergencies, and seemingly vary from style to style around lines of essence more basic than any style alone. And even as style in art begins to yield somewhat to hard-headed study, and yet retains much of its mystery, so may it be here.

In any event, it is clear that the strain on "juristic method" is not constant. That strain grows greater, the more elaborate the other phases of law-stuff become. It takes better method adequately to handle structured forms and law-stuff frozen within the bounds of articulated words, unless those words are themselves built in terms of adequate juristic method. It takes better method to handle older law-stuff adequately as the culture grows more rapidly mobile, pressing upon those older forms whose office is always to frame, but never to crush or hamper, the society. Wooden legalism is urged on the one side, primitive justice on the other. The legalism may be the tool of conscious and planned greed, hate, or oppression—not blind only, but vicious. The primitive "justice" aspect may be devoid of justice; it may blur down into mushy sentimentality. Form holds down passion and ambition, but form can bar out wisdom, too. The wise answer may be anywhere between that legality which sees virtue in a legal system (though it must sacrifice the occasional individual for the commonwealth) and that longer-range view of even personalized justice which sees the man in terms of what he needs (be it mercy, favor, or discipline) rather than in terms of what he thinks he needs or what in an even scale he has deserved. There are, finally, the long-range wisdoms for the polity which leap ahead of all legality, and which the primitively just is more likely to obscure than not—and which must look also to the fact that only men, with whatever skills and schooling there may be, can be used in future doing of the work.

Emphatically, juristic method is not mere legal method. Legal method is the lawyer's tool—that with which Njal of Iceland could bring to naught (in the saga) each last suit in a whole term of court.[5] Legal method may be skillful, it may be ingenious, splendid of technique, and varied; but where its purpose is to serve a litigant or client only, and not Justice, it is only legal. Juristic method is the problem and the technique of *solution, for the Entirety,* and the problem of keeping the machinery of the law abreast of the needs of the Entirety. Most cultures which develop high legal skill have found it not only a help, but a hindrance as well. Skill in *juristic* method, by man's good fortune, can be not only a personal attribute, but a tradition; and that the next chapter will seek to demonstrate. By man's bad fortune, skill in juristic method has not as yet been reduced to readily communicable form. But even on that, it may be that the Cheyenne way can offer some suggestion.

[5] George U. Dasant, *The Story of Burnt Njal* (A translation from the Icelandic Njal Sagen, New York, 1911).

Chapter XII

THE CHEYENNE WAY

IT might bear a surface appearance of romanticizing for us to attribute legal genius to a people of those aboriginal American Plains which have long been thought to be so relatively barren of legal culture, if the data had not been laid before the reader. The data have their own direct persuasiveness, but more may be added, for when thrown into comparative relief against the modern juristic techniques the Cheyenne way is cross-lighted.

It is familiar fact that the legal sides of two cultures can vary hugely, within what are for ethnological purposes very similar economic conditions, and in spite of easy commercial intercourse between the peoples under consideration.

Take American legal institutions and more particularly our ways of legal work and thinking, as contrasted with the German ways during two decades on either side of the completion in 1897 of their Civil Code. In the forefront of American legal thinking is the judge, the judge of a highest appellate court, the judge working with and on case law, on rules and concepts developed out of successive wrestlings with problems of concrete adjudication, the known judge who signs opinions and whose individual labors leave a cogent record. Here, advocates and counselors sink slowly into anonymity, and legislators tend to; not so that judge whose mark is stamped upon the law. Reinforcing this judge-centered legal thinking is the American doctrine and practice of judicial review of legislative and administrative action. Reinforcing the importance of adjudication as the essential crucible of law, despite the wealth and welter of the statutes, is the absence of the systematic-theoretical in our general culture, with its muddle-through, "Is it practical?" get-down-to-cases flavor. There is the looseness and vagueness of our theorizing, our unwillingness to be precise of phrase and definition, and our greater unwillingness to follow the logic of an "accepted" premise through boldly to an unacceptable conclusion. All of this means a way of juristic thought and concept which, despite written records, despite conscious building of traditional wisdom and technique across the centuries, still works well-nigh as much by intuition as by rational construct and rational development thereof. "The wisest jurist and the most skilful," wrote Holmes, "can still feel the ground of a decision as he cannot state it." And perhaps because the complexities of whirlwind industrial changes have outrun the capacities of such intuitive operation in the hands of any but the great, the resulting legal institutions are somewhat muddled and cross-purposed, and the intuitional judgments which they in part condition often turn out to be groping judgments, or lagging judgments, and often to need legislative correction.

Now in contrast to this, the German attitude strained constantly and consciously toward rigorous articulation and intellectualization of juristic thought. Concepts were labored over, to be got into the broadest terms men's minds might reach, for system's sake. The edges of definitions were stated and taped with the explicit precision of a tennis court. Such definitions were marked sharply as to denotation where possible and as to connotation always, staked down with fixed, unyielding words, so that "application" might become a matter not of feeling but of reading. The center of German juristic method was for decades not the judge, but the systematic scholar, and after him "the legislator," who had cast authoritative law into words of rigid command and limitation— both abstract thinkers of abstract thoughts. And from the surrounding culture came reinforcement from the curious German urge to follow through the logic of a premise the more tenaciously, the more outrageous the conclusion might appear to be. Against this rock-structure of German juristic thought beat the waves of Germanistic mysticism, of Jhering's gibes, of the "free-law" movement, of "fact"-research, of "interest"-interpretation; but it took a lost war (1914–1918) and an inflation to even begin to shake it. As a *way* of juristic operation, it was conscious, intellectual, systematically organized, and articulate, to a degree almost outside the American legal imagination. Its error lay in attempting too definite and too rationalized a control upon a life that was not a single piece and would not stay so if it had been.

It was indeed known to those German thinkers who, on and out of the Roman materials, were building so coherent and articulate a legal structure—it was known to them with a touch of bewilderment that the Roman jurists themselves had operated along wholly different lines. For the great Romans had worked case by case, as have the Anglo-American judges. The great Romans defined little, and they seem to have done little in the way of explicit system-making on the grander scale. System they had. Indeed, they had a queerly clear perception of where one concept or principle left off and another came properly to bear; but the system in terms of which they worked was implicit far more than explicit. It was felt far more than it was articulated. In this they differed from their German admirers. They differed from American judges of today in that what they felt and acted on was notably coherent, and showed notable net order and consistency.

Perhaps this last judgment is fallacious. Perhaps the legal life of Rome was in fact as full of third-raters who were as frequently muddled and many-minded in their legal intuitions as any double-hundred of American judges whom you can pick at random out of this year's *Who's Who*. Perhaps if some Justinian's Commission should arrange for us a selected Digest of Opinions, with Mansfield and Marshall, Cardozo and Holmes, Cowen and Scrutton, featured as were Ulpian and Papinian in the *Corpus,* the jurists of another age would admire the unbelievable "instinct" of the English and American judges for implicit, coherent system, for "instinctively" sure and admirable application to any ticklish case of undefined but sharp-edged underlying concepts, principles, and distinctions. That we do not know. What concerns us is that when, with these other legal systems in mind, we turn to the Cheyenne materials, we meet a curious phenomenon. It is not merely that we find neat juristic work. It is that the *generality* of the Cheyennes, not alone the "lawyers" or the "great lawyers" among them (whom they show no signs of having recognized as such) worked out their nice cases with an intuitive juristic precision which among us marks a judge as good; that the *generality* among them produced indeed a large percentage of work on a level of which our rarer and greater jurists could be proud. This is the more notable because explicit law—i.e., law clothed in rules—was exceedingly rare among them. It is the more notable because they did not have many fixed rituals of procedure to guide them, around whose application or whose ceremonial formulae and behavior, concepts of legal correctness so readily come to cluster.

It is not wise to overpress an analogy, but one finds no ready parallel to this legal genius of the Cheyennes among primitives. Many Africans, for instance, are litigious; they possess developed and formed procedures; they have articulate legal precepts cast in proverb form; instances enough are recorded of judgments wise and neat. But one gets from Spieth on the Ewe,[1] Gutmann on the Chagga,[2] Rattray on the Ashanti,[3] no such cumulative impression as the Cheyennes give of utterly clean juristic intuition, individualized yet moving with singular consistency whither tribal welfare demands that it shall move. And, indeed, the phase of Roman law itself, with whose effective spirit we find the Cheyenne comparable, is not the early form-bound Roman law, nor the archaic semi-certainty of the late Republic, but the sweet flowering of the classical jurisconsult. We are not speaking of the explicit intellectual structure of the Pandectists.[4] We are speaking of what we hold to be equally rare, and quite as admirable, and to have application to a simpler culture as it does to a complex: we are referring to the classical Roman jurist's *ways of work,* the deftness and boldness of line with which the apt solution is marked in swift, sure strokes that fit at once justice, policy, and the given body of legal and social institutions—those ways of work which are the modern Romanist's delight and his despair.

[1] Jacob Spieth, *The Ewe-Speaking Peoples* (Oxford, 1911).
[2] Gutmann, *Das Recht der Dschagga.*
[3] Rattray, *Ashanti Law and Constitution.*
[4] The course of development is suggested in the article by A. Arthur Schiller on "Roman Law," *Encyclopedia of the Social Sciences,* XIII (1934), 419-25.

Evidence is in order. Let us turn back to a series of Cheyenne cases of invention and clarification which met emergent needs, and to an outstanding case of notable institutional adaptation on a large scale. One may call attention in each to the Cheyenne ability to deal at once with the problems of social policy presented and with the most delicate features of the particular case in hand, letting neither obscure the other. The histories are already familiar to the reader.

There is first the announcement by Sticks Everything Under His Belt of his intent to disregard the law in the hunting of buffalo (CASE 3). It will be recalled at once that there is no trace of anything like this in prior Cheyenne experience. If the suggestions available from disowner of a child, or throwing away of a wife, or banishment for murder, had been considered cogent, it is unthinkable that the case would have been considered by the supra-supreme extraordinary tribunal which was convoked—nay, seemingly invented for the emergency.[5] The results are not merely juristic poetry. They have two other qualities: neither Cheyenne nor American, layman or lawman, can help but understand each part of the results; and, once stated, they are utterly inevitable.

The next instance is Walking Rabbit's effort to turn a war party into an elopement instrument (CASE 5). One recalls first that the finding of the delicately faceted solution there did not call for any extraordinary council; an ordinary war party plus the unarranged team-play of Walking Rabbit's father was adequate. One recalls, second, that a new precedent that war parties should not meddle with divorce-and-remarriage was set even while this one war party did so meddle. An ability to get the essential social issue de-confused from the accidental issues and needs of the individual case, and so to make possible machinery to handle both at once, *and differently,* is no small juristic achievement. Only in 1932 did the way open clearly for an American appellate court to do so constitutionally.[6]

[5] The case of Cries Yia Eya presents no such extraordinary tribunal. The Council of Forty-Four there summoned the soldier chiefs not to consult, but to delegate the consultation.

[6] Great Northern Railway v. SunBurst Oil & Refining Company (U. S. Supreme Court, 1932), 287 U. S. Reports 358 (Cardozo).

The third instance again shows an individual at work. This was Chief Eagle's father, in CASE 4. The ban he placed upon the possible killer-bully ("Let him never raise his voice against another man!") is sure diagnosis of a serious social ill and is sound remedy. This time the device failed to become institutional. It was not dramatized, and it did not stand out for imitation. The skillful refinement on what was, as has been seen, an already admirable machinery may have slipped from notice precisely because the machinery was already so relatively satisfactory. As an invention, the device—an aggrieved individual's invention—is superb; but even Cheyenne law failed to cumulate all of its best.

The last case of this series is directly Roman. It is the case of Two Twists (CASE 1). By dramatic action, dramatic intervention, grandiose, but also grand, manipulation of the nobler sentiments, and the shrewd handling of the legal device of carrying the pipe, civil government was temporarily abolished, and Two Twists made dictator in what by acquiescence was agreed to be a tribal emergency. The tribe resolved itself into a war party and put itself under "one-man" government for the event. If one then wants further light on juristic "instinct," let him observe the interpretation placed on Two Twist's promise to Red Robe. He had promised glorious death; he had come back alive. Yet all men saw that the essence of the promise had lain not in its wording, but in uninterrupted glorious exposure, which had been performed. And he was released.

The next body of evidence clusters around a single core—that of homicide. What is to be reviewed is a series of knotty problems on the substantive law; namely, what "constitutes" homicide, within the meaning of the law? These cases are borderline puzzlers; they are theory-testers, if one has theories; they are probers of intuition, if intuition is the basis of one's work. For such a body of cases to come out in some confusion would be pardonable, in any legal system; and for some of them to come out wrong would be normal, even in a developed, schooled, skilled legal culture. The cases are complicated, moreover, by the fact that each reaches into that troublesome field in which government was overriding what we take to have been an older self-right of the family.

A girl hanged herself (CASE 25). This tests the fundamental definition of the law. Was it "killing of a Cheyenne by a Cheyenne," or "killing of a Cheyenne by *another* Cheyenne?" Even with regard to the religious sanction, suicide proved to be not homicide. In a society troubled by turbulence, but not by plague of suicides, this marked a course of thought. But the girl's suicide was a protest suicide. Still of no moment. There was nothing important to protest against; the girl "was silly to hang herself for that."

Another girl hanged herself, again in protest (CASE 26, 27). Her mother had outrageously beaten her. The protest was this time for grave and proper cause; it was justifiable and appropriate in tribal morals; there was also no known legal remedy for the wrong. But the law—at least the soldiers' administrative "law"—took cognizance of the justification and of the cause: her mother *caused* her death. The Arrows were renewed for the girl; her mother was banished *for the homicide*. The prior lynching of the mother almost to death bears witness to the soundness of the soldier authorities' feeling for community reaction.

A girl disemboweled her father in warding off attempted incestuous attack (CASE 32). This fits the letter of a rule against killing which was so well understood that it can almost be said to have a letter. But rape in Cheyenne was heinous. Incest was disgusting and eternally disgraceful. Chastity was a tribal pride. For a Cheyenne to attempt rape on his daughter could without difficulty be construed as "un-Cheyenning" himself, by his action, into "wolf's head," out-of-law status. To disregard this defensive killing, moreover, did not violate the purpose or policy of the law of homicide; this killing was not vengeance, it was not even chance affray. The precedent set by disregarding it was not dangerous; rather the contrary. Such is the available background. The girl was in fact acquitted. Here is the most clearly formed, the most developed, the most articulate large branch of Cheyenne law; it is one which the prior case shows to have been capable of immediate expansion. But what could the most enlightened articulate jurist do but write a painstaking opinion to escape the hard letter and achieve the same result. Limit the precedent? It was automatically limited, in Cheyenne feeling. This was not "justification by self-defense." Self-defense, in Cheyenne circumstances, was no sound legal concept; it would invite an early breaking over in an outfacing contest. No, what this was, if you want it modernized, was a carefully limited "justification by self-defense against incestuous rape." But the Arrows were renewed.

The process of feeling the way through to solution of a very nicely balanced problem comes out strongly in the fourth homicide case. White Bear accidentally killed his mother while drunk (page 137). If these were the facts, the case fell outside the utilitarian purpose of the law. Yet the facts were bothersome, and the supernatural penalty of homicide was dangerous to gamble with. "Accident" during drunkenness had also its strong initial touch of unclarity of fact; and drunkenness alone, as other cases show, was no excuse. Intuition wavered. Temporary quarantine was imposed pending reference to competent authority. Competent authority adjudicated in terms not of blind superstition, but of social and religious dominant sense, declaring, "It *was* accident." Had the matter not been intrafamilial, one hazards that the state of mind of the afflicted family might have entered heavily, for banishment had also a peace-keeping function.

On the secular side the treatment is thus clear and deft. On the religious side it is not up to the Cheyenne best. For it is not good to leave a man in a half-status of uncertainty on such a matter as a murder curse. The appropriate machinery for procuring an answer was known; namely, the seance. In the more greatly public matter of the mutilated Holy Hat (CASE 24) that machinery was used. Failure to use it here indicates what appears repeatedly: to wit, that resort to the supernatural to supplement the secular side of law-work was by no means so clearly developed as the secular side itself. Cheyenne religion lay deep in the culture, and touched all things. At the same time, it had an other-worldly character which kept it from full coalescence with the work-a-day cultural machinery. This can be seen most clearly in the phenomena of war, where religion now supplemented or implemented, now came into twisted tension with the secular impulses. In the field of law, there was no tension which we have observed, but there was notable lack of full integration. The available religious devices outside of the field of killing, and excepting the pipe of accord, remained relatively unexploited.

Though not fully exploited by secular law, religion was yet neatly hedged against being exploited by the individual to escape the law. Dying Elk was under compulsion from Maiyun to kill his wife (CASE 19). Now as a case from Stump Horn shows, a vision could be basis enough for the whole tribe to go under a temporary dictator for a great, supernaturally guided (and, incidentally, unsuccessful) hunt. Public attention to visions was thus not only understood, but was understood on a scale which, save for innate balance, could carry political dynamite. Nor were visions on matters of lesser and more personal moment rare. And some grudges rooted deep and hardy among Cheyennes. And visions were not infrequently of the type the vision-seeker hoped for. One notes with interest, for instance, that Dying Elk had been "mean to his wife." One can thus feel the legal dynamite stored in the situation. The man was sincere and the vision was real; he could not escape the supernatural command. Thus there was no moral guilt attaching to his act. Still, to disregard the killing, to deal with it as socially innocuous because it was morally blameless, would be to lose the Cheyenne feel for homicide policy, amid the particular tensions of the culture. The vision could be either a revelation or a curse to Dying Elk. There was no hesitation about which way to resolve that choice. Not retribution in terms of moral responsibility, but social security, was the underlying policy achieved; although, as indicated in Chapter VII, no man can say what the Cheyennes felt or stated as the rationale.

We repeat that we are not attempting in the above to reproduce Cheyenne legal thinking, nor are we attempting to attribute to the Cheyennes such modern criminalistic concepts as justification, responsibility, "legal" causation, and their modern refinements. We are attempting so to canvass the relevant phases of the culture and the relevant possible lines and bearings of decision as to make clear an active, living, highly predictable consistency in their actual handlings of a whole sequence of tough, knotty cases. Theirs was a living consistency which we submit to be on the juristic level of the most advanced modern criminalistics, and to be too accurate in cumulative bull's-eye work to be attributable to chance. What we do attribute to the Cheyenne, in this, is the ability to solve the next tough case with equal consistency and precision, without the "advantage" of the more sophisticated processes of legal thought: for instance, the abortion problem.

Let a number of other scattered materials now pass in review which touch on what a modern jurist would call Cheyenne juristic method.

One weakness of Cheyenne law anent religion has been mentioned; let us again regard its strength. First, and without undertaking to pass on the relation which sorcery may have held to religion in Cheyenne ideology, we recall that sorcery of high power was familiar to them, but that we find no trace of its use in legal matters, unless the "white magic" of detection by way of dreams, to guide the finding of evidence, be such a trace. Otherwise, this make-shift "resource of the weak" which can so easily become a scourge to all or any, was absent; as in a sound juristic scheme it should be.

Secondly, in a number of points, especially where law touches religion, the Cheyennes were faced with the need for (legal) fiction, or else with pressure to use fiction for mere, but unnecessary, expedition. Legal fictions consist in the taking of a form, typically a ritual or a formula—at all events some externally plain pattern to which a known effect is attached—and pretending that it applies to what it does not in fact fit. This is to achieve the known effect where that effect is needed, although the originally appropriate facts are absent. Fictions are legalisms, in insisting on the precise form; they are juristic adaptations, in not being blocked by the form. The most striking legal fiction in our own civilization, for example, is the turning back of the clock on the last evening of a legislative session, in order that four hours' business may be done after mid-

night, before midnight is allowed "officially" to have arrived. Now
ritual and ceremonial have an important part to play in life and
law; and light-hearted disregard of them jeopardizes real values,
notably those which go with taking institutions as serious and
conscience-binding controllers of behavior and desire. On the other
hand, too rigid an attention to ritual and ceremonial leads under
any change of conditions to defeat of felt right and thwarting of
needed result simply because rituals will not remodel fast enough
to meet emergency. Light use of legal fiction thus destroys respect
for the form which is manipulated; but failure to employ fiction,
while retaining the sacred form, can throttle justice. It is a rare
folk who can work through consistently to the answer, which lies
in this: to reverence the form, always; but to remember that its
function is more precious than itself; and never to be deceived,
later, into taking as real what is in fact mere fiction, or to be
limited, as against a new and real need, by the fact that the form
has been preserved.

With this in mind, consider the Cheyenne use of fictions. An oath
is needed, on the Sacred Arrows or the Sacred Pipe; the Sacred
Arrows or the Sacred Pipe are not at hand. Then any arrow or any
pipe will do. It does so effectively. The dispute is sworn off and the
false oath bites back (CASE 23).

On the other hand—the chiefs are to be renewed, and the ritual
opener of the high ceremony will not come. But he is not dead and
truly unavailable—for which event we may be sure a remedy,
fictional or other, would be at hand. Because he simply deems himself to have become unworthy, he is ruled necessary, he is waited
on, he is waited for, and he is brought. The constitutional ceremony
proceeds in proper constitutional form *without* fiction (CASE 8).

The material shows repeated cases in which fiction comes
in question, or that extended "interpretation" which verges into
fiction. For instance, did the mother "kill" the daughter who committed suicide? The material shows no single instance in which
need fails of fulfillment because of empty form, no instance in
which sound form is not respected. Not least in importance was
deliberate insistence on ritual, to avoid an otherwise embarrassing

dilemma. When the "bitter-ender" husband (Case 42A) had finally run the eloper down as a companion on a war party, the circumstances forbade a private settlement; yet could a man refuse a request to carry the pipe of reconciliation? Ritual offered the answer: "The pipe is full"—for a known and different purpose. But persuasion *without* the pipe was both available, and was just what the husband needed.

In the chapter on military societies (V), there has been developed at length the net legal tact with which a needed constant expansion of control and law was again and again knit into the existing governmental frame, with which sprouting arbitrary action was pruned off, and the new branch made, largely, to take clear form as a branch of *controlled* government. Here we point to a single instance. In the matter of illicit buffalo meat sneaked into camp, there are three cases. In one (see page 117), on the first accusation-move of the soldiers, the accused came out, hands up in non-resistance, invited search, and was acquitted. In one (Case 12), on the accusation-move, the accused sat in tacit confession inside his lodge as it was cut to bits around his head. We find a common element in the two, an element of *legality* in the policing —a chance to deny guilt and be heard, after notice of accusation. General theory leads one to believe that the "hearing" idea, in any culture in which it has made itself known and felt, becomes a precious idea; that it can be precious even to the guilty; and that man in a culture in which rights are fought for will fight for due procedure almost as hard as for essential justice.

With this in view, one approaches the third case of this series, that of Grasshopper (Case 13). Last Bull, a soldier chief on duty, had found a horse outside Grasshopper's lodge, bloody as if from carrying buffalo meat. He forthwith killed that horse. Grasshopper does not appear further in the picture; we take him to have been guilty, and to have wisely kept out of the policing soldiers' sight. Grasshopper's mother, however, was indignant. What at? She gashed Last Bull's lodge. Why? This is on its face outrageous and hopeless resistance to due authority engaged on authority's due business. But her husband backed her in her action with a gun.

And Last Bull, the arbitrary, while he rallied his soldiers to enforce authority, was curiously slow to force issue. Why? We see the case as a just protest, skillfully taken into other hands than the culprit's, against the outrage of a punishment even of the guilty man, without a chance at hearing, when not caught red-handed in his transgression. We see Last Bull himself, his anger spent in action, appreciating the soundness of the rebuke. We see the later withdrawal of Grasshopper's family from the camp as a declaration that they were not and did not want to be disturbers, or to be placed where they might have to defend their son's wrongdoing. We see the effective intervention of "one" of the soldiers before the thunder was loosed against the protesters as an articulation of the fact that every point in the case had now been made, and it was time to stop before new, ugly points of killing people might come in. Of course, then, "nobody bothered" Grasshopper's family as they moved out of camp. Again, we are not urging that the participants thought in the terms we use, or in remotely equivalent Cheyenne concepts. The lines of intellectualization which one can turn up in Cheyenne material are more frequently directed to the instance and the concrete answer than to the general, or to a pattern for answer; and intellectualization shows on the surface, disappears, reappears in different context and as if independently, like a thread in an ancient carpet. What we are urging is that the behavior in this case comports with the lines of juristic *feeling* described. We are urging, moreover, that such behavior is almost impossible to reconcile with any other lines. And we are suggesting that the promptness, vigor, and effectiveness of the representation by Grasshopper's family of a real public interest in a valuable check on arbitrary police procedure, the success with which the issues were disentangled instead of tangled further, and the reliance on some anonymity to *feel* the time and manner for resolving the tensions of the pleading-and-litigation-by-action, are not only the Cheyenne way, but are a way open only to the juristically gifted.

Cheyenne law thus lived into application, into sure application, a whole range of implicit institutions. How intricate an apparatus is needed to intellectualize their complex law of homicide appears in the summary on page 165 ff. Nor would a similar summary capable of holding the interplay of the different levels of normation discussed under inheritance be much less complex. There are institutions of importance in which patterns are less clear in the culture. This holds, during the period from which the materials come, for much of government. Here the flux was so great, the creative drive so dominant, that what stands out is less the detail of result than the adequacy of the machinery and the men for achieving a result, and one which is essentially healthy in its whole growth. Some particular lines can be grasped for an observer's intellectual systematization. The recognition of a hearing, just discussed, is an example. But in the main a rationale would have to run in terms of semi-open points or areas, of which one could predicate only interdependence in the precise lines which growth might take, so that however one detail might shape, some other details would provide much of whatever corrective might be needed. And throughout, all patterns retained around their normative or imperative cores a joyous range of flexible adaptability, called on repeatedly —a regime of implicit principle and case work, both attuned to the net dynamic need of the people. This the Cheyennes had, rather than a regime of letter or of rule or of form. And, throughout, the net dynamic need of the people can be felt as a living order in which the individual life was urged into expansion and fulfillment, and thereby furthering the social good, rather than being thwarted in the interest of the social good, or repressed thereby.

We feel the presence of this even in places where we have not had skill to grasp it for communication. An example is the substantive law of divorce—that body of law which tells *when* a divorce is had, and can be had, and can be properly had, rather than *how* one happens. In concern over the procedure of divorce-and-remarriage we feel with some certainty that there has been left unrevealed a delicately faceted institution which was being lived-on when divorce was proper. Divorce-and-remarriage has the flavor almost of a different institution from divorce-declared. In each case of the latter there was a ground, and a good ground, and in no case is there report of any compensation. We cannot help wondering whether if we had full report on the divorce-and-remarriage cases, the presence or absence of such a good ground for the wife's severance of the tie would not shed clearer light on the hugely varied range of what was done. There were checks on simply leaving husbands; one finds a brother looking into whether his sister was justified, and into whether, if so, there had been due repentance and reform. One finds a limit on the number of times a woman could "be divorced" (ambiguous term) without losing status. One suspects drum-divorce to have a possible arbitrariness other divorce may lack—doubly so, since a man did not lose his wife, as a woman did her husband, by remarriage.

One feels certain that upon any rules of strict law about grounds for divorce there must have played the lights and pressures of other levels of norms, some of them perhaps as clearly patterned as the legal. There would be good taste and social correctness, as in cases of inheritance; perhaps also semi-legal rather than legal claims of the wife's family in the marriage relationship, akin again to what one finds in inheritance. All of this we derive not by mere deduction from the nature of the Cheyenne law-way, though our discomfort in the matter is greatly increased by the persuasion that the Cheyennes being what they were, this intimate matter of conflict must have run off in terms of their law-way. We derive it rather from the direct impact of the cases, which is the impact of sure variation around a sure core; there is a sureness of "feel" about the action taken in most of the individual cases. The trouble is that both core and variation were lived too subtly for us to give form to them. We felt their presence too late to reach their substance. But the confusion in the picture of Cheyenne divorce law may well be our confusion, not that of the Cheyennes.

The course of the most unmistakable legal genius is not uniform. Of our own heroes, Blackburn was known to falter and fumble, and Holmes and Brandeis have written on two sides of the same case. Ulpian and Papinian, as the famed Law of Citations reminds us, could also be found at odds. Neither is the Cheyenne legal picture perfect. There were abuses. There were the greedy, the arbitrary, the exploiters of the decencies. There were "naturally mean" persons. There were some who turned legal devices deliberately to low ends. Of the dispute-settling oaths of which there is record, three were false. Brady's has the appearance of a headstrong whim, perhaps provoked by the manner of his accuser, certainly persisted in partly because his face had been engaged by his denial of guilt; and that error in action could at times have the same directive effect that sound solution drove toward, in breaking and then channeling the tensions of a situation, is evidenced by Chief Eagle's following Brady into false swearing. There is no means of knowing whether admission of guilt by the two together would have made out that twofold adultery which gave a husband the right to put a wife upon the prairie; nor whether, such action being in the picture, Brady was following an urge of other than egotistic nature. What is recorded is the double, knowingly false, oath.

Again, the heating of the law crucible by stoking with threat of violence proved repeatedly in the cases to produce not the more normal pure gold, but an explosion. This holds with regard to certain of the homicide cases. It is inexcusably present when in a dispute over finder's right versus tracker's right to five horses, the horses were killed instead of adjudicated (CASE 49)—inexcusably, because other persons were present to mediate, or to suggest the "proper" settlement. For one notes with interest how rare such explosion was when other persons were around who could intervene. The general Cheyenne pattern of moving toward definition of issues, heaping up of tensions, and testing of strength in law and in prestige by overt moves as if on a chessboard—what one may call pleading-by-action—that pattern seems built to presuppose these intervention possibilities; and the soldiers' penalization of brawling reinforces the idea that the matter was so felt. The common use of chiefs as intermediaries, or the sending of messengers to give notice of prospective action about a grievance, has the same implication. So does the incident of willing compensation's being given for a cut inflicted by misadventure when the imaginative Long Jaw went after a scalplock as retaliation for flirting with his wife (CASE 37).

That Cheyenne pleading-by-action was built to look toward an intervening sound resolution before violence occurred, underlies that whole body of phenomena in which a new angle or even an explosion resulted when the controversy became injected with a departure by one side from the understood procedures. We have instanced Last Bull's infliction of penalty without notice. But consider the superficially unununderstandable attack by Sleeping Rabbit upon Bird Face (CASE 16). Sleeping Rabbit had, and to appearance quite indecently, left his wife to struggle alone through the deep snow. Bird Face had, in the right tradition, taken her on his horse. Being her uncle, he was also thereby administering a direct and personal rebuke to her husband. Sleeping Rabbit, when they caught up with him, could not but be shamed and baffled-angry with himself and the world. He was not only a husband, but a chief, and a chief publicly put to scorn. But when Bird Face proceeded now further to stinging words, he was un-Cheyenne-like in his action, he was wrong. This is the only case in the record of open rebuke, in words and in earnest, to a tribal chief by any man. The harshness hit Sleeping Rabbit at the worst moment, and in the worst way; the unparalleled was too much. So he shot. Had he missed, a Cheyenne-balance would in our view have been established, on a level of reinforcing moderately well all things that were proper. But he not only shot true, he shot with terrible effect. This changed the whole aspect of the case, and the results give fair indication of the lines an explosion would have taken in Grasshopper's case, had an explosion there occurred. Protest against improper procedure is good; but protest, carried too far by a grievance-doer, finds its virtue overwhelmed in public need for order. The desirable balance having thus been missed, first by Bird Face, then, and cumulatively, by Sleeping Rabbit, the camp went into turmoil and confusion. But consultation and time were now available, and a peak of Cheyenne legal ingenuity resulted.

The case is of peculiar interest because it is sufficiently sustained in the report to show what is a necessary characteristic of any really fine juristic machinery; that is, a wherewithal from within itself to catch up and work out its own slips and mistakes into reasonable net satisfaction. For instance, if penalization to the point of near-destruction be viewed as an overswing of Cheyenne criminal law, the beneficence and rehabilitation machinery in Pawnee's case is in point here (CASE 2). So, also, and more immediately, is the case of the Dakota boys caught bootlegging buffalo; and more particularly in regard to the soldiers who then failed to do their duty (CASE 11). Directly in point is of course Grasshopper's case (CASE 13) and, to our mind, that of Winnebago (CASE 20) when the normal homicide machinery had failed to work regeneration upon a particular man. Protest suicide can accomplish this for social balance, when used well; but it sacrifices the individual case. It is thus never on as high a juristic level as the Cheyenne best.

Once more, let us be sure not to exaggerate the smoothness of the Cheyenne juristic method by letting its quality be taken to suggest infallibility of incidence. What was accomplished superbly when accomplished at all, what was so geared as to be accomplished normally, did yet sometimes fail to be achieved. And it could fail at a moment when the stake was ruinous. The drives and tensions which it is law-stuff's business to hold in balance were no poor and weak things in Cheyenne culture, nor did the incessant bombardment of the white incursion ease the problem. Two instances from Grinnell's account of the destruction of Dull Knife's village drive home that the normal does not mean the certain, that deviation could and did occur. One instance is petty; another is big with consequence tragic to the people. During the fight, a warrior who had lost his son came upon a Cheyenne who had been with the enemy. He sought to kill him, but was held back by friends.[7] Issue joined on what seems to have been an implicit assumption that if the refugee had been active for the whites he could properly be killed even though he was now returning in peace (but under possible suspicion of further hostile purpose). The issue that joined was thus one of fact: should the refugee's story that he had been

---

[7] Grinnell, *The Fighting Cheyennes*, 365. The implicit assumptions are not clear in their outlines. Is the grievance that the accused was supposed to have been active for the whites at all? or against the Cheyennes? or in this campaign? or in this attack? Is the supposed privilege to kill limited to the battle? to one with a personal grievance to avenge? Would the killing have been justified?

captured and helped to escape by friendly scouts be taken at face? The normal procedure of general acquiescence by disputants and all others in the first suggestion toward solution made by any bystander is strikingly absent; argument, efforts to kill, and forcible restraint go on and on. And it may be noted that the whole matter rested in the secular; the refugee made no suggestion of swearing innocence.

The second matter concerns an occasion of complete disruption of command, and an instance of the utter breakdown, under arrogance, of the normal flow of action into the sound solution, when sound solution had been offered. Dull Knife's camp had been apprised that the whites were moving against them. It was badly located for defense. Removal and the building of breastworks was counseled, commanded, and begun under the orderly leadership of a soldier society. Into this burst Last Bull and his soldiers. Under his command, they forcibly stopped the movement and succeeded in insisting that an all-night dance begin. Why, we do not know. How, is not clear; the lack of wisdom is so obvious as to leave the reader baffled. What does appear is abnormality in both proceedings and result. Dawn brought destruction to the camp.[8]

We have been running over some of the evidence as to whether the Cheyenne juristic method shows peculiar sureness in the application of felt, living institutional norms, and peculiar adjustment of the felt "rules" and the treatment of the particular cases to something bigger and more vital than any "rule" of an individual case —whether it served to reach positive, pervading purposes which infused the whole law machinery with health. Attempt has been made to show off-center shots along with the bull's eyes, and not to let the occasional total missing of the target slide out of attention. The raw evidence is not selective on the issue. Certainly it was not, by our choice, selected favorably. For the focus of inquiry was "Where was there a hitch?—Where was there trouble?—Then what happened?" The resultant selection of reports, viewed in

[8] Grinnell, *The Fighting Cheyennes*, 355, 360 ff. As a speculation, Last Bull's action could be fitted into a combination of desperate bravado and the type of flight from reality which keeps many impending bankrupts from facing their accounts.

terms of the life of the people, ought to have turned up a weighting of the sampling in favor of such cases as failed of sure settlement.

The question recurs now on the matter of the generality or normality of juristic skill among the Cheyennes. One piece of the evidence is that neither Grinnell nor we had any word of persons famous for their wisdom in handling trouble-cases. If skill therein were not known, indeed familiar in the culture, this would mean nothing. But when skill is familiar in use, and recognized in its result, then absence of reputation for skill is a matter for remark. A second piece of the evidence, not to be slighted, is the normality, to the informants (and its fitness in the texture of the tales) of juristic work which in another culture would make the reputation of a Solomon or a Marshall or a Njal. Nor will it do to wave this aside because there was no profession of law-man among the Cheyennes whose trade tradition would readily call attention to professional distinction. For governors there were, and moderately busy ones, handling important cases; and law-stuff there was a-plenty, interesting, and important; and neat solutions, when offered, were, as has been noted, appreciated and acted on. But law-stuff needs no gathering by a skilled profession when the general run of the culture and chance-grouping after chance-grouping of its people can bring forth results to rouse a jurist's envy. We find only one persuasive conclusion: When an important skill exists and is practiced with high frequency, but goes unremarked on by those among whom it is practiced, the simplest and most likely explanation is that the skill is too general to deserve explicit mention.

But if the Cheyenne law-way has, among recorded law-ways, the unique quality we find in it, there opens the question of what general bearing Cheyenne law-material has. Is it eccentric to the point of non-comparability? Is it atypical freak stuff, and of scant meaning to law in general, as the ten thousand "wives" attributed to the King of Dahomey are unique and of slight meaning to marriage, as distinct from military organization?[9] Our answer is

---

[9] The more fruitful comparison runs, e. g., to Chaka's army organization, not to his marital establishment.

that its general meaning lies precisely in its unusual character. It is not typical in that it is one characteristic example out of many; it is typical in a deeper sense, as a living example of an ideal type, in whose case histories vital processes which elsewhere lie half or wholly hidden stand out to be seen, and against which the case histories and legal institutions of other cultures take on meaning.

Let us illustrate. Among the Kiowas, as Richardson's[10] extremely interesting cases show, loud announcement by a disputant of "What-I-Am-Going-to-Do-to-Him" is a clear pattern, in finest little-boy fashion. One sees the emotional release and the channeling of turbulent action into words, and also, where the other party is at hand, the build-up of outfacing tensions. One sees more; one sees the expectation of being restrained; when the Kiowa Ten Medicine Bundles which can be fetched to "force" peace are within call, the noise is great, but only then. And the prolongation of the bring-me-my-horse proceedings, into tacit request for intervention and "compulsion" to desist, is unmistakable. But in Kiowa, when you have seen that, you find the development swirling into successful outfacing as a quick career-making device. You find those legal phases of a situation which relate to justice becoming obscured by the political and personal phases which relate to power and prestige. The threatening talk when the grievance-giver is not present looms chiefly as release; the intervention of bystanders chiefly as a peace-preserver.

Read this now against the Cheyenne cases (which show one with base lines almost on the Kiowa level—CASE 42A), and you see in it a germ, undeveloped though latent in Kiowa, of achieving and of enforcing legal norms. The conflict situation, thus under restraint, thus built toward anticipated intervention, can become the drama which sweats issues into clarity, not as between two contestants merely, but for types of contestant and for the tribe. Thus is created or crystallized general law for other persons in a similar situation. Move from this to that famed scene on the shield of Achilles which has given so much trouble to legal historians: the drama of dispute, looking this time expressly toward bystanders'

[10] Jane Richardson, *Law and Status Among the Kiowa Indians.*

judgment, the general public standing round, the old men sitting, and a reward there awaiting the old man "who speaks the straightest judgment." "We do not know," says Vinogradoff mournfully, "how and by whom the merits of the different judgments were estimated."[11] Read the Cheyenne material, and you do not need to know. You are persuaded of the obvious: that there did not need to be a fixed procedure for determining the straightest judgment. A judgment straight *enough,* though hard to speak, is yet unmistakable when spoken. Add now a third situation, this time from the Comanches, where a husband can and does call on a powerful warrior to go with him after his eloping wife. Here the outfacing bluster-talk is eliminated in advance. The eloper is outfaced by the champion's mere presence. But the intervention of this outsider, as a semi-public functionary, has effect. It has removed the deflecting influence of power-struggle from a situation which can thereby be felt more clearly as drama over rights. To invoke, by way of the decencies, the aid of a warrior-champion is to incur the pressure, also, of the decencies. Levels of proper limit on the husband's action proceed to make themselves felt, and to transgress them in pique, meanness, or the headiness of sudden power, may be to incur the repercussion of the adversary's "glorious death" in protest. The Kiowa pattern, the Comanche, the Ancient Greek, thus take unity of context among themselves, and take richer color, each one within itself, when seen against Cheyenne.

Let us illustrate again. If there be one central problem of legal philosophy, it is that of the relation between law and justice. Or, if one divides that problem (as one should), it is the relation between law, the specialized control device, and the general health of society, on the one hand; and, on the other hand, the relation between law, the general regulation, and the individuated need of the particular case. The problems are familiar enough in the general sociology and theory of institutions and of thought. Various aspects are dealt with under such heads as form and function,

---

[11] Vinogradoff, *Outlines of Historical Jurisprudence,* I, 348. The passage continues half in insight, half in woodenness: ". . . possibly the standard was simply the number of votes cast in favor of each sentence; or the 'persuasiveness' of the judicial dicta may have been measured by the effect on the popular audience."

structure and purpose, or the price paid in rigidity and abuse of any specialized institution for the values it may offer of continuity, control, and accumulation of wisdom and technique. But in the law field, the problems have ever taken on peculiar importance. This is because law tends, as few other institutions do, into fixity and consciousness of procedures and even into their explicit verbalization; and also, because in the law field, as has been seen, institutions take on a peculiar flavor of purporting to speak for the health of the whole (which is the social aspect of "Justice"). Further, they claim observance and control not only as imperatives, but also because of some inherent rightness (which reaches into parts of the more individual aspect of "Justice").

Now it so happens that most of the cultures whose legal aspects we know in any detail have obscured this law-and-justice problem almost as much as they have clarified it; and for a reason. The reason is that it is extremely rare for the law-stuff and the justice-stuff of a culture to be found in such reasonable balance that the true art of adjustment between them can come in for sustained effective study. On the one hand are those cultures in which the regularization aspect of things legal is too undeveloped to be clearly grasped. Their need, the emphasis of any development within them, the attention of their observers, runs to growth of the *law* side of the law-justice relation. Such is the situation among the Eskimos, the Chukchi, the Barama River Carib, and even, in many respects, the Kiowas. Such is readily, too, the situation if juristic work is entrusted to "personal" hands, and administrative personnel operates without control by explicit rule or ingrained tradition. On the other hand, cultures which have developed the regularity side of law and procedure have rarely managed to avoid having the major emphasis of their technique and theory turned to the development and manipulation of these tough, slow-yielding regularities. In such a situation (which has been that of Western Europe and of these United States) machinery to give any leeway has been so hard to manage that getting a measure of justice into the individual case has tended to swamp effort to handle justice's broader aspects. And "law" not only comes into an artificial opposition to justice, but the "opposing" factors also become skewed, both in their content and in their relation to each other.

Now opposition or contrast of "law" and "justice" is unhealthy. Even if you wish to avoid subjective valuational judgments, you must concede, as was said earlier in regard to "legalism," that such opposition produces a strain in the culture which is bothersome. "Law" is, in function, a means to reach much the same ends which the feeling of "justice" also reaches for. When the two grow distinct, the tool "law" has ceased to be clean-shaped to its reason. And what the Cheyenne law-way shows here, for any man to see, is that a significantly high development of certainty and clarity of prospective outcome, felt even by most litigants in the heat of controversy, can be achieved on a not unelaborate scale, without the growth of such "law" and "legal procedure" as rigidifies upon itself, and comes so into opposition with the felt justice of a newer generation. The Cheyenne law-way shows more. It shows that developed ritual, together with some quantum of very clear rule and imperative procedure, can be handled in favorable circumstances with flexibility, in terms of need, yet with no sacrifice at all of feeling for certainty and form.

It cannot of course be asserted that the Cheyennes could have maintained their juristic sureness and malleability in the teeth of a regime of accumulating written records, or in the teeth of the development of a class of specialized law-men whose trade skills might tend to drown out the common sensitivity, or in the teeth of complex economic development. One does note, however, that the presence of highly developed and appreciated ritual in other matters, rivaling in complexity and exactitude the legal rituals, say, of Iceland, neither infected law with formalism nor lost touch with function even in religion. Indeed it has seemed to us that in the American legal tradition, notably in the appellate courts, the specialization of law-men and the written record have at times for considerable periods failed to break in too seriously upon a law-way rather akin to the Cheyenne. At least it is easy to see that the more complex and specialized the underlying institutions come to be, and the less clearly they are integrated to respond bell-like to the tongue of justice-in-controversy and of wisdom, the greater and more unique the calibre of man required to do Cheyenne-like work under the cross-thrust of the case, the given "law" materials, and the future.

The need for individuation and for reshaping in official hands continues. Let "law" become relatively fixed, however, and such individuation and reshaping appear as an attribute not of "law," but of power. When approved, they are spoken of as the wise introduction of "equity" into the administration of "the law." When disapproved, they are spoken of as arbitrary or corrupt discarding or disregarding of "law." The more primitive cultures give such pictures as the situation of Iceland, where law fails to do half of law's work, or as the Bantu scene, where much law is clear, and much justice, too; but where either or both are subject to sudden deflection by a well conceived favor-present ("bribe"), or a king's impulse, or his views on policy in his own interest or that of the state. The phenomenon is not, then, merely one of the homogeneous community versus complexity, though complexity does call for a higher, surer skill. The problem is one, no less, of an aptitude which may be in a culture—or even, perhaps, in a people —quite as much as in a man.

If this be so, the suspicion must be that written form of law and specialists are no absolute block to a law-way of "Cheyenne quality." The suspicion must be, no less, that neither ritualization of procedure nor fixed wording of legal rules is needed to produce much of predictability. It may well be that a very large degree of the regularity and predictability which we ourselves now enjoy in things of law is actually due not to the rules of law to which we have long been ascribing it, but to underlying legal institutions of our own which are as inarticulate, but which in their own way are as effective as those which one can observe at work in the Cheyenne cases. For two decades now the American legal world has been troubled by the inescapable demonstration that the rules of law as they stand are simply incapable of producing the results in terms of certainty and predictability of case-outcome which used to be ascribed to them. The demonstration has made for uncomfortable thoughts. It is good, then, to have a culture—such as Cheyenne —open a line of inquiry which offers hope of discovering a clearer understanding of the true working of such certainty as exists in our own law system.[12]

Still another, and a rather amusing angle turns up for modern law out of the Cheyenne juristic method. For centuries now Anglo-Americans have left the settlement of delicate law-points to the judge, putting it up to him, tacitly, to serve good policy; officially and explicitly putting it up to him to serve law, and unofficially or semi-officially putting it up to him to serve justice in the immediate cases before him. Of late years, men have begun to discover that other persons, called administrators, are no less important in this matter. When one comes then to explain to administrators how they are to go about it, one discovers that the articulate jurisprudence of an articulate legal system has, thus far, just this to tell them: that in essence they are to act like a judge, except, again, that they are not. And if the administrator asks when yes and when no? and what *is* acting like a judge? and when he is not acting like a judge, how is he to act?—there has been no clear answer. For the work of the judge's office, for reasons some bad and some good, has been wrapped in mystery, even in mysticism. The reports of those few judges who have tried to describe that work have made it clear that both the common factors and the variant ones are still very largely intuitional in character. What the Cheyenne law-way does for Americans here, by its presence in such high degree among so heavy a percentage of the Cheyenne population[13] is to make clear that in ideal conditions the art and the job of combining long-range justice, existing law, and the justice of the individual case, in ways reasonably free of the deflecting pressures of politics and personal desire, *need* not be confined to the judging office. It can be learned elsewhere and learned rather generally. It shows that the *ways* of accomplishing such a combination are capable of study, even on

---

[12] Llewellyn, "On Reading and Using the Newer Jurisprudence." See also Karl N. Llewellyn's forthcoming book, *The Common Law Tradition*.

[13] If the authors were guessing an estimate, they should feel that at least one out of ten Cheyenne men was apt at it; and another two out of the ten, not awkward; and seven of the ten, sensitive to a good job when it got done.

a rather narrow body of Cheyenne cases. They ought to be capable of more revealing study, and perhaps even communication, in our own society, whose law-way has on the case-law side been so significantly similar, and whose resources of case material are boundless.

But the juristic method of the Cheyennes is not limited in its bearings to such problems of legal philosophy, however central they may be. Let us instance a single matter of sociology, political theory, and social psychology which takes depth and color against the Cheyenne material. It is the matter, the manner, and the meaning of arrival at unanimous consent, and of requiring such consent. In the first place, the range of behavior to which the term is both applied and applicable runs from the most grudging tacit acquiescence under pressure through to overt enthusiasm, a fact of importance not only in the less articulate cultures, but also in those which formalize the spoken or written word. Contrast a girl pressed into marriage by her brother, with the "Thank you, thank you, Soldiers" which greeted the great decision to make the Kiowa peace (CASE 9). In the second place, and of particular interest in the law field, active and approving consent may be sought when it has no touch of legal necessity. Pawnee's rehabilitation is a fine instance (CASE 2). No one could stop a chief from beneficence; but rehabilitation of an ego and a character calls for group backing. One admires the new chief's skill. "I will not ask this man how he came to be in this condition"—and the soldier guests are barred from accusatory explanation. "This is my first good deed since I became a chief"—and how can any person refuse to go along? When moving a person into "consent" against his will, the essence lies in capitalizing the decencies on the side of the action proposed. In the third place—and Pawnee's case is again an instance—the procurement of consent is a process, or hides under one label a set of processes, of huge variety. "A chief is not refused." "Father, I am set on this thing. Do not ask me not to." These anticipate difficulty. "Any one who doesn't hit hard must give a Contrary Dance," anticipated as little difficulty as does a boy running for the swimming hole yelling, "Last one in gets paddled." The decision on the Kiowa peace proposal runs the gamut of cautious, conscious feeling of the way. The decision against letting an eloper go out with a war party (CASE 5) shows two successive proposals made, one by the boy's action and one by a warrior's words, and both rejected. The rejection is, however, a carefully thought through and worded "opinion of the court," from that leader who constitutionally had absolute command. On the other hand, the remark which saves from near civil war in Grasshopper's case gives in the report almost nothing of either its reason or its result; and no occasion offers for believing that in life it went further: the situation had grown too clear, without words, to need words.

Against such a body of material, the reading takes depth and life when one reads of a primitive assembly that agreement can be found and felt without a vote, without even a murmur of approval. Or, when one reads that the ancient Polish Diet showed the regime of required unanimity to be politically unworkable, one sees that the writer is presupposing a non-face-to-face group, whose members are affected by modern individualistic drives, and do not root in a sure-felt common body of institutions. Or when one reads or thinks of *consent*, or of *authority*, in any culture, he finds each word posing not a fact, but a field for inquiry.

For one major part of the Cheyenne law-way throughout, (which we perhaps have not duly underscored in words) is the *persuasiveness* to its people of its results. Where the people needed persuasion to find the results persuasive, then there turned up the skill and labor which were needed for such persuasion and procurement of effective agreement, in advance. Always, and everywhere, this means sense for a sound issue, and skill in drawing and in urging it. In the field of direct government, it appears in such matters as selection of tribal chiefs, in movement of the camp, in the notable case of the Kiowa peace. In the field of "private charity" it appears in Pawnee's case, in which it was neither private, nor charity, but performance, in the particular instance by a chief, of a vital portion of administration of the criminal law. Wherever pleading was by action and straining of tension, this persuasiveness appears in the deliberately incurred suspense, the dragged-out moments focusing toward resolution. Abruptness or secrecy of movement are the marks of the weak case, the unrighteous cause. One wonders, as one reads the Cheyenne cases, whether publicity, or public relations, or propaganda, if you will, or whatever leads law's people to "agree" actively with law's results, has not along with justice a function among us as in Cheyenne.

It would, however, give a sadly inaccurate picture of the Cheyenne law-way if one were to stress the flexibility of its machinery alone. For this might lead to the conclusion that the law-way was flexible only because the law machinery was flexible, that it waited only for that hardening process which legal historians are fond of observing, as it settled first upon the early Kings' courts, then upon the Chancery, then and again upon the American courts of the nineteenth century. We have no intention of denying that such calcification of the juristic arteries might have crept upon the Cheyenne; but it is important to point out at least that the machinery capable of hardening into legalism, and the wherewithal to harden it, were present, throughout the period studied. It was present and it was used. The way in which it was used, is a crucial test of their law-way.

False oath apart—which had at least the social virtue of cleaning up the grievance or dispute—here are the outstanding cases of Cheyenne legalism:

Black Horse, in CASE 3, wanted, for reasons which seemed inadequate, a personal dispensation; and when he did not get it, he undertook in petulance to announce what was most definitely an arbitrary rule for the coming Sun Dance. Black Horse was met by what may look like purest legalism: the chiefs "had nothing to say to that," without the pledger's consent. But the pledger could agree to nothing that had not been "mentioned in the meeting" with the chiefs. No formalist could more effectively use procedural technicality to block a case from hearing on its merits. But Black Horse's case had no merits.

In CASE 42A, the absconder, finally caught up with, was in fear of his life. The aggrieved husband, for all his rigor, had put his case magnificently when he made it a challenge to uttermost bravery before the enemy, pledging himself if need be to death. He was entitled at least to a fair opportunity to shame his rival by outdoing him. Was it legalistic to refuse to carry the pipe to the husband merely because the pipe "was full"? Nothing could have been more legalistic—if it had not produced the right result.

Finally, if one considers that last renewal of the chiefs, and the insistence on Little Wolf's attendance, one can see it as pure formalism, if one will. But one can also see, in the nature of the insistence on utterly legalistic correctness in the procedure, an effort to break up the ingrowing seclusion of a great old man.

In sum: Cheyenne law-ways did not lack form, formalism, or legalism, because of any lack of understanding of these things or of their uses. It is hard, then, to escape the conclusion that what was lacking was sustained appreciation by the general community of the values which accrue to individual litigants from the abuse of form. For legalism creeps upon a legal system. It must be permitted to prevail repetitively, if it is to gain shaping power. If detected and parried by a sure juristic method whenever it would lead to *wrong* answers, then it gets no foothold to obscure the fundamental juristic task, that of getting the right answer with the tools at hand.

Nonetheless, the Cheyenne legal system, as such, suffered under its absence of legal form. For all the prodigality of juristic ingenuity, not enough of its results were cumulated into easily accessible patterns to draw minor trouble-festers to a head, and so to get them settled. This shows again and again in smouldering irritations over points of fact. It shows in the hanging-on of minor grievances. It shows in protest suicides which had too little reason. It shows in the non-development of pipe-settlement into all the cases where pipe-settlement with its power of true appeasement would have been good to have. Had the chiefs of their own initiative, for instance, picked up pipe-carrying as a usual matter, the efficacy of the whole legal system would have been stepped up immeasurably.

What such a relatively minor institutional shift—merely, that is, the assumption of slightly more active initiative in a field and by way of a mechanism already thoroughly recognized—what such a shift would have meant in affecting the tone and color of Cheyenne life, no man can say. But it is hard to believe that if a vastly more serene scene had been really wanted, the chiefs would have left this easy avenue untraveled. For if "skill's a joy to any man," so is the appearance of opportunities to exercise the skill. But if life is to be lived intensely, by each, then young rascally Pawnees, overbearing Last Bulls, howling Terrors, will have also to be lived with. And pleading-by-action, with a spectator waiting tensely for the apt moment to step in, can make the law-ways part of common life, indeed. All in full flux—while the buffalo vanish, and the white man moves inexorably in.

Cheyenne law leaped to glory as it set.

CASE-FINDER

*An Index and Abstract of the longer or more frequently
discussed histories appearing in the text*

THIS CASE-FINDER includes only those histories which are presented in full form in this book, locating their position in the text as whole histories. The richer histories touch each one of them so many points of law so varied that full exploration of them becomes burdensome. Thus, CASE 1, in addition to vital material on the position of tribal chiefs, war-party organization, homicide, the supernatural, the family, inheritance, other property matters, and contract has also important material on the military societies; but in essence it merely buttresses the material presented in Chapter V ("The Military Societies") and is not there mentioned.

The quantitative basis of the study can be roughly gauged by considering the basis of that single chapter. Apart from general observations from the literature and from the authors' field notes, it presents seven histories indexed in this finder (CASES 11–17), six more from Grinnell, four more from the authors' notes (which are given in the text in too brief a form to deserve inclusion here); it also draws explicitly on CASES 2, 3, 7, 8, and 9, all of which are presented in other chapters. The chapter is further buttressed by an approximately equal body of case material in other portions of the book—material which is not explicitly drawn upon in the discussion in Chapter V.

The reader should also realize the large background body of data and paralleling cases which are not included in the text of this book for obvious reasons of economy of space and reader's patience.

CASE	ABSTRACT	PAGES
1.	Red Robe mourns the death of his sons; Two Twists organizes a revenge expedition of the Cheyenne tribe against the Crows.	3–6
2.	Pawnee, the incorrigible, is punished by the Bowstring Soldiers and rehabilitated by High Backed Wolf.	6–9
3.	Sticks Everything Under His Belt is ostracized by the tribal council and rehabilitated through the giving of a Sun Dance.	9–12
4.	Cries Yia Eya is banished for the murder of Chief Eagle and later readmitted by tribal and private action.	12–13

17. Wolf Lies Down places the matter of the failure of his friend to return a borrowed horse before the Elk Soldiers; they send a messenger who effects the return of the horse and elicits an explanation from the borrower. The Elk Soldiers formulate an ordinance making it a public offense to borrow another person's horse without explicit permission. 127–128

18. Bull Hump and Starving Elk are dissuaded from taking revenge on the murderer of their friend, Sharp Nose.   135–136

19. Dying Elk murders his wife, is banished and reinstated in the tribe after five years of exile.   138–139

20. Walking Coyote kills White Horse for taking his wife. Winnebago later takes this woman in the absence of Walking Coyote; the latter retaliates by taking the wife of Winnebago, whereupon Winnebago slays Walking Coyote. Later Kutenim quarrels with Winnebago and is slain by him. Still later, when living with the Arapahoes, Winnebago is led into an ambush by two Cheyenne Dog Soldiers and is shot dead by Rising Fire.   140–143

21. Grey Thunder, the Arrow Keeper, would delay the Arrow Renewal ceremony, but is beaten by the Bowstring Society, whose members are eager to go to war. Under duress he performs the ceremony, but predicts misfortune for the war party. The entire party is annihilated by the Kiowas. Porcupine Bear undertakes to organize a tribal revenge expedition against the Kiowas, but participates in the murder of Little Creek while drunk. He and his associates are exiled. Little Wolf takes up the responsibility of organizing the great war party. In the next summer, the attack on the Kiowas and Comanches is successfully carried out. Porcupine Bear's band of exiles strikes first coup and annihilates a large band of Kiowas, but they receive no formal recognition for their act because of the civil disabilities of exiles. 146–148

22. Chief Eagle and Brady take a false oath on the Buffalo Hat; Brady is wounded and Chief Eagle is killed in the next battle with the Crows.   151–152

23. Lone Wolf swears an oath on a pipe with regard to the validity of his claim to a coup. The next day he dies of his wound.   153

24. Broken Dishes is deposed as Keeper of the Buffalo Hat. It is discovered that the Hat has been disfigured by the

removal of a horn; a new horn is substituted. When Ho'ko, wife of Broken Dishes, dies, the old horn is discovered on her person, but is destroyed because Maiyun pronounces it a mere husk. 154–156

36. Round Stone quarrels with his three wives and throws away two on the drum at a dance. He is put out of countenance by the jibes and jeers of the women. 186

37. Brave Wolf is accused of adultery by Long Jaw, who thinks his wife is involved. He attacks Brave Wolf and removes his scalplock. Because he accidentally cuts Brave Wolf's back, he offers a horse in compensation, since he wants no more than the scalplock. He also releases the wife. 188–189

38. The wife of Shoots Left-Handed becomes pregnant while the latter is away on a prolonged war journey. She reveals that the lover is his good friend, Sharp Eyes. Shoots Left-Handed lays the matter before his society, the Elk Soldiers, to see what should be done. Sharp Eyes' father sends a chief with horses. Sharp Eyes agrees to assist in the care of the child, so Shoots Left-Handed is advised to keep his wife and accepts the proffered settlement. 190

39. Stump Horn's wife deserts him for another. The absconder sends a chief with a horse in settlement. Stump Horn accepts, thus closing the matter. 193

40. Two Moon absconds with the wife of Black Coyote. Two Moon fails to send a chief with a gift, whereupon Black Coyote confiscates three horses from among the herds of Two Moon's relatives. 194–195

41. A brother of High Forehead absconds with the wife of Two Moons. No attempt at settlement is made by the absconder, so Two Moons' family announce they are going to take three good horses from the young man. High Forehead threatens to kill the horses if the attempt is carried out. 195

42. Coyote, who has adulterous relations with Red Eagle's wife, is beaten by Red Eagle, who on a later occasion attempts to shoot him. The Fox Soldiers protect Coyote until he has a chance to flee from the camp. 197–198

42A. An aggrieved warrior-husband prevents the wife-taker from making a settlement and forces him into competitive military exploit. 199–201

43. Big Laughing Woman is "put on the prairie" by her husband. 203

44. One Eye "puts" his unfaithful wife, Buffalo Woman, "on the prairie" as punishment. She is saved by her brother, who comes armed to kill. Buffalo Woman divorces One Eye and destroys his lodge.   203–204

45. Carries The Arrows believes he has a claim on his wife's younger sister, who refuses to marry him. He engages Last Bull to abduct the girl and "put her on the prairie" for the Bowstring Society. Blue Wing and his wife, Tassel Woman, save the girl by a ruse. The brother-in-law and father-in-law of Carries The Arrows attack the Bowstrings, divorce Carries The Arrows of his wife, and destroy his lodge.   204–206

46. Buffalo Hump attempted to "put" Little Sea Shell "on the prairie." She is saved by taking asylum with the Holy Hat Woman. Little Sea Shell's father kills his own horse to demonstrate his anger.   206–208

47. Crane goes to meet his death by lightning. His body is disposed of by the members of his soldier society, for which service Crane's brother gives them most of the deceased's horses.   216–217

48. Last Bull quarrels with Point over the possession of the horses belonging to Point's deceased wife, Last Bull's sister.   220–222

49. Bull Kills Him and another warrior dispute over the priority of claims on stray horses, the tracks of which are discovered by one; but the horses are discovered by the other before the tracker reaches them. Bull Kills Him settles it by slaying the horses.   224

50. Calf Woman makes a robe and a cradle for her nephew.   247–248

51. Short Sioux adopts Calf Woman as his sister in order to provide his child with an aunt.   249–251

52. Tall White Man is bullied by his jealous wife, who causes one of her co-wives to divorce Tall White Man and another to commit suicide. She is proof against all social pressures which are applied.   253–257

53. Yellow Eyes plagues his wife with his suspicions of her unfaithfulness and is cured by a prank arranged by his five nephews.   260–261

INDEX

Abortion, Cheyenne crime: 119

Absconding, Cheyenne: with married woman, 14, 178, 190 ff., 193, 195 f., 199, 228, 321, 337, 338 f.; composition of, 192, 201; with unmarried girl, 178; *see* Marital relations, desertion; Divorce

Abstinence, sexual: Cheyenne vow of, 261 ff.

Acculturation, Cheyenne: 79; effect on government, 115 f., 127; effect on tribal council, 88; *see* Social change

Achilles, shield of: 330 f.

Adolescents, Cheyenne training of: 246; *see* Child-training, Education

Adoption, Cheyenne: 6, 249

Adultery, Cheyenne: 58, 187 ff., 190, 325; composition of, 190; free woman penalty, 202 ff.; infrequency of, 263; *see* Chastity

Africa: fetishism, 156; *see* Ashanti, Bantu, Chagga, Shaka, Ewe

Age-grades: Cheyenne absence of, 266

Agency Indian: nature of, 154; Tongue River, 197

Agency, special: in Anglo-American law, 105

Aggression, Cheyenne: 210; relation to law, 48; *see* Personality

Aginsky, B. W.: on Pomo Indians, 56

Algonkian, Central: political organization, 110; lodge-shaking séance, 91

Alien: represented in Cheyenne Council, 76; status in Cheyenne, 149 f., 166, 238

Alienation of affection: 185

Altruism, Cheyenne: 247, 249; of chiefs, 79; *see* Gift-giving

Amalgamated Clothing Workers: 54

Amitate, Cheyenne: 247, 249

Amputation: Cheyenne attitudes toward, 123

Animus: *see* Intent

Apache: Cheyenne raid on, 91

Appolonian, cultural configuration: 240

Arapaho: acceptance of Cheyenne exiles, 133, 142; relations with neighboring tribes, 90; Sun Dance, 147; United States treaty with, 9

Arbitration: relation to law, 307

Arikara: United States treaty with, 9

Arnold, Thurman: on capitalism, 68

Arrows, Medicine (Cheyenne): capture by Pawnees, 146; Dance, 209; effect of homicide on, 87, 132 ff., 146, 166; in oath, 152, 320; keeper, 79, 97, 147, 252; murderer barred from, 82; origin, 84 f.; on war party, 209; renewal of, 9, 110 f., 133 ff., 137, 142, 143, 146 f., 149, 161, 167 f., 179, 316; renewal, policing of, 126 f., 134

Articulation of rules: in growth of law, 235 f.

Art style: 308

Ashanti law: 60, 313

Assassination: Cheyenne case, 146

Assiniboine: in Cheyenne mythology, 68; United States treaty with, 9

Asylum, right of: Hebrew, 133; Cheyenne Medicine Hat, 207 f., 238

Atonement, 17

Attainder of Blood: 50

Attitudes, Cheyenne: 125, 144, 146; on punishment, 262; toward amputation, 123; toward child play, 246; toward marriage of single man to widow, 260; toward tribal chief, 172; *see* Behavior patterns; Values, social

Authority: abuse of, 121 f.; as element in law, 21, 42, 231, 279, 283 ff., 293, 298; Cheyenne, brother over sister, 170, 173, 176, 181, 183, 206; limitations of, 104 f., 140, 322; male, 209; of executor, 214; of husband, 170; parental, 181, 250, 301; peacemaking, 92, 105; tribal council, 98, 124; in social functionaries, 203 f., 284 f.; *see* Chief, tribal; Chief, war; Military societies

Avoidance, Cheyenne: mother-in-law, 24, 182 f.; *see* Kinship relations

Trustee: Cheyenne, 162; tribal, 74
Turtle: 259
Twin Woman: 172
Two Forks: 111 f.
Two Moon: 195 f.
Two Twists: 3, 33, 158, 162 f., 209, 237, 315
Two Twists: the younger, 120 f.
Tyranny: 285

Ulpian: 312, 324
Unanimity: as social process, 90, 337
United States: army, 165; Indian agency, 154; Indian policy, 82 f.; treaty with Arapaho, Arikara, Assiniboine, Crow, Gros Ventre, Shoshone, Sioux, 9

Values, social: 240; Cheyenne, 246
Vinogradoff, Sir Paul: litigious custom, 26; shield of Achilles, 331
Visions: Cheyenne, 138, 232, 318; for thief detection, 127

Wagner Act: 53
Wagon Box Fight: 165
Walking Buffalo: marriage of, 171
Walking Coyote: case of, 140 ff., 178, 193, 198
Walking Rabbit: case of, 13 ff., 191, 314
Walks Last: 86, 94, 96, 103, 164, 165, 188, 212, 216
War Bonnet (personal name): 141
Warfare, Cheyenne: ambush, 148; breastworks, 4, 199, 328; control of warriors, 294 f.; imitated in child play, 242; Cheyenne v. Crow, 3 ff., 153, 163 f.; v. Kiowa, 146 f.; v. Pawnee, 115, 199, 209; v. United States, 165
War party, Cheyenne: division of booty by, 223; formation of, 147, 163; leadership of, 13, 147, 163; Medicine Arrows on, 209; wife-absconding with, 191

Wars, Indian: Custer Battle, 12, 198; Nez Percé outbreak, 82; Wagon Box Fight, 165; see Dull Knife outbreak, Warfare
Wealth: in law, 232; Cheyenne, 235; see Altruism, Bargain, Economics, Giftgiving, Property, Trade
Wergild: 140; Germanic, 302; see Composition
Wessels, Captain: 105
White Antelope: 92 f., 101
White Bear: case of, 137, 316
White Bull: 95 f., 103
White Dirt: 171
White Horse: 140 ff., 198
White River: 155
Wilkes, John: case of, 37
Windbreak, Cheyenne: 242
Winnebago (personal name): 141 ff., 145, 178, 327
Wissler, Clark: Plains Indian police, 109
Witnesses: 223
Wolf Creek: 146
Wolf Lies Down: 6, 227; case of, 127
Wolf Mule: 115
Woman, position of: Cheyenne, 78, 176, 181 ff., 185 ff., 189, 265; putting on the prairie, 202 ff.
Woodlands, North Central: political organization of tribes, 110
Woodlands, Southeastern: political organization of tribes, 110
Workmen's Compensation Acts: 53
Wounded Eye: 156
Wrapped (personal name): 117
Writing: effect on law, 333 f.

Yellow Eyes: case of, 260 f.
Yellow Nose: 150
Yellow Tangle Hair: 187
Yellow Wolf: 140
Young Two Moon: 194 f.